POLAR CASTAWAYS

Polar Castaways

THE ROSS SEA PARTY
(1914–17)
OF SIR ERNEST SHACKLETON

Richard McElrea
and
David Harrowfield

McGILL-QUEEN'S UNIVERSITY PRESS
Montreal & Kingston • London • Ithaca

Copyright © 2004 Richard McElrea and David Harrowfield
Copyright © 2004 Canterbury University Press

ISBN 0-7735-2825-3

Legal deposit fourth quarter 2004
Bibliothèque nationale du Québec

Published simultaneously in New Zealand and Australia
by Canterbury University Press, Christchurch, New Zealand

National Library of Canada Cataloguing in Publication

McElrea, Richard
    Polar castaways : the Ross Sea Party (1914–17) of Sir Ernest Shackleton /
Richard McElrea and David Harrowfield.

Includes bibliographical references and index.
ISBN 0-7735-2825-3

    1. Imperial Trans-Antarctic Expedition (1914–1917) Ross Sea Party.
2. Aurora Relief Expedition (1915-1917). 3. Antarctica—Discovery and
exploration. I. Harrowfield, David L., 1940- II. Title.
G850.1914.R68M33 2004   919.8'904   C2004-901438-2

Designed by Richard King at Canterbury University Press
Printed by SRM Production Services Sdn. Bhd., Malaysia

A catalogue record for this book is available from
the National Library of New Zealand

Front cover: *Aurora* in the pack ice of the Ross Sea.
(Middleton collection, Canterbury Museum)
Back cover and half-title: Æneas Mackinstosh shortly before his death.
(Richards collection, Canterbury Museum)
Endpapers: Six of the seven survivors of the Ross Sea party about to board *Aurora*.
(Joyce collection, Canterbury Museum)

CONTENTS

FOREWORD

by the late R. W. Richards, GC

It gives me singular pleasure to contribute this foreword to *Polar Castaways*. It is a token of gratitude written by the last survivor from the party of marooned men who arrived back in Wellington in February 1917 and were overwhelmed with the kind reception given us by the New Zealanders. This was during the darkest days of the First World War and most critical stage of that great conflict, but despite the fact that there must have been great tragedy and sadness in many New Zealand homes at that time, their welcome was kindness itself. I have never forgotten this.

Sir Ernest Shackleton's *South* tells the full story of an ambitious failure but also records a remarkable episode in polar adventure. Many, no doubt, at the time wondered how such an ambitious project as the Imperial Trans-Antarctic Expedition could be undertaken during the war. As explained in *South*, the expedition was organised well in advance and was just setting out from England in August 1914 when war was declared. Shackleton immediately offered the expedition's resources to the Admiralty but was given the laconic instruction 'Proceed', so, with also the blessing of the King, the expedition set out.

No fears were entertained at that time as to the outcome of the conflict. The press were agog with stories of the 'Russian Steamroller' that was rolling west to overwhelm Germany and many thought the war would be over by Christmas. In fact, while we were away the war was very seldom a topic of conversation.

How mistaken we were! I well remember that day in January 1917 when *Aurora* had just arrived in McMurdo Sound to effect our rescue and had tied up to sea ice some miles off shore at Cape Evans. When we survivors had reached two or three miles from the ship, three small black figures detached themselves from *Aurora* and we slowly came together. To our surprise, the three men (Sir Ernest Shackleton, Commander Moyes and Dr Middleton) lay down on the ice. They later explained that this was the signal arranged with Captain Davis on the ship to indicate the number, if any, who had perished.

One of the first questions asked of the rescuers was when the war had ended. The reply staggered us, for the situation was described as 'worse than ever'. We had left in 1914 with the somewhat naive outlook of that time. What we learned from the relief party and the newspapers they had on board was a devastating shock to us. Since December 1914 we had heard absolutely nothing of what was going on during those momentous years and were completely ignorant of that fact that the world had changed and could never be the same as when we left.

However, all that is in the very distant past. In an effort to make known the struggles of ten men marooned in McMurdo Sound from early 1915 to 1917, some time ago I gave the Canterbury Museum some medals presented to me. I am indeed grateful for this opportunity, even at this late stage, to have the chance to publicly express my lifelong feeling of gratitude for the way New Zealanders received us during those trying days of the First World War.

The work now being written by Richard McElrea and David Harrowfield will, for the first time, give a complete and definitive account of the Ross Sea side of the Imperial Trans-Antarctic Expedition. I think the job they are doing is first class. As one of the marooned men, I am particularly satisfied that this story is being told at long last.

R. W. Richards

Point Lonsdale
Australia

This foreword was written for the authors in the early 1980s by Richard Walter Richards, GC. Known at the time of the expedition as 'Wally' or 'Richie', but more latterly as 'Dick', Richards was the last of the Shackleton men and died at the age of 91, on 8 May 1985.

Richard McElrea, who had the honour of giving a eulogy at his funeral, corresponded with him from the early 1970s and interviewed him in 1980. David Harrowfield also enjoyed several years of correspondence with Richards and interviewed him. Dick Richards gave generously of his time and views, which were forthright and vigorous, witty but never unkind. The authors sent him early draft manuscripts of sections of this book, and he encouraged and supported their objectives of writing this definitive account of the Ross Sea party, including the drift of the ship and the relief expedition.

PREFACE

The genesis for this work was a challenge made by Shackleton's 1957 biographers, Margery and James Fisher, who noted that the scope of their book did not allow of an adequate treatment of the Ross Sea party side of the Imperial Trans-Antarctic Expedition:

> The whole of the Ross Sea adventure, its inception, the mixture of personalities, the endless battle to contrive something out of nothing, the politics and complexities of the relief arrangements – all these are material for an interesting addition to the literature of Antarctic exploration.

Polar Castaways is a response to this challenge. It covers the entire account of the Ross Sea party, including the drift of the expedition ship *Aurora* and the relief expedition.

The drama of this episode in Antarctic history has long been recognised. H. R. Mill wrote in 1929 of 'life on the very verge of existence . . . of men . . . who have struggled on for weeks half mad and utterly exhausted with cold and hunger and exertion . . .'

It has taken many decades for some of the details of the extreme difficulties of life under these kind of conditions, where men survived as 'derelicts', to emerge, as some diaries and personal material have been under strict embargo. After the expedition was over, most participants simply wanted to get on with life, to make up for time lost and apparently wasted. Inevitably, in the telling of their story, some old wounds will be reopened, but the authors hope that readers will consider this a sympathetic account.

The 'politics' of the relief of the sledging party resulted in the overlapping of two expeditions. The Imperial Trans-Antarctic Expedition terminated after the survivors of the Ross Sea party returned to New Zealand in February 1917. The requisitioning of the expedition ship in 1916, arguably without legal authority, by the three governments footing the bill for the relief of the party, was the precursor to what those governments termed the *Aurora* relief expedition, whose leader was Captain J. K. Davis.

Richard McElrea started gathering material for the book in the 1970s following work as a volunteer at the historic sites at Cape Evans, Hut Point and Cape

Royds in 1971. At Cape Evans, he and fellow New Zealand Antarctic Society volunteer Harry Burson retrieved the unique man-and-dog harness used by the Ross Sea party from outside the hut, and had it identified by Dick Richards, a veteran of the expedition. Richard McElrea visited archival institutions in England, Australia and New Zealand, and established contact with survivors and families of many of the expedition members. Some years later, he wrote an extensive manuscript – the precursor of this book – in conjunction with David Harrowfield, who joined the project in 1981. Copies of early sections were sent to Richards, who was a great supporter of the authors' work.

David Harrowfield, who has made numerous trips to Antarctica, retrieved on behalf of the Canterbury Museum, a key Spencer-Smith diary and correspondence from a garden shed in Winton, New Zealand, in 1981, and Ernest Joyce's lantern slides and glass negatives from Hastings Boys' High School.

The authors interviewed and corresponded with three of the survivors of the expedition: Richards and Irvine Gaze, both members of the shore party; and Commander M. H. Moyes, who was part of the relief party and had shared the same cabin as Shackleton on *Aurora*. The authors also had the pleasure of generous communication and contact with immediate members of families of expedition members.

The three decades of research that has informed *Polar Castaways* brought together a great deal of material, much of it original and some not used before. The book has been extensively annotated to provide the reader with indicia of source material. Distances and measurements are as in the original sources, which have been edited only where necessary to convey sense.

In a 1956 BBC interview, one of the then-survivors, Professor Alexander Stevens, said of their plight in the south: '. . . we found ourselves marooned, on an island, a desert island for these two years, with nothing but what we stood up in . . .' They were castaways not only in the literal sense, but also in the metaphorical sense in that their story has only in recent times become better known.

Following the account in Shackleton's *South* (1919) and Joyce's *The South Polar Trail* (1929) – historically inaccurate in some key respects and to an extent self-serving – the next book about the Ross Sea party was Richards' *The Ross Sea Shore Party 1914–17* (1956), an important and accurate work by one of the key members of the party. The eminent New Zealand polar historian L. B. Quartermain wrote significant historical accounts in the 1960s as part of his wider works. Biographers and other authors, including Mill (1923), Hayes (1932), Bickel (1982) and Huntford (1985), have also related or referred to the story of the Ross Sea party. In an attempt to rectify the situation highlighted by the Fishers, and in an endeavour to avoid perpetuating inaccuracies (particularly those arising from Joyce's 1929 account), the authors of *Polar Castaways* have chosen to tell the tale as much as possible from the accounts of the participants and from other original source materials.

The project was put aside for a decade until the manuscript was reshaped with considerable assistance from Richard King at Canterbury University Press. Richard McElrea has been primarily responsible for the writing, and David Harrowfield for the maps and illustrations, as well as research assistance.

A recently published account by Jennifer Niven of an abortive Arctic expedition that set out in 1913 and in which 16 people died, including two who had been with Shackleton on the *Nimrod* expedition, suggests betrayal and dishonour among some of the personnel in the dire circumstances that party found itself in. Although there were many parallels with the Ross Sea party (and even more strikingly, the Weddell Sea party) of the ITAE, nothing in the authors' research for *Polar Castaways* suggests that the men of the Ross Sea party acted other than honourably in the often tedious and sometimes urgent circumstances they found themselves in, although they were a disparate group and at times there were petty arguments and differences.

The expedition in which the Ross Sea party played such a tragic role was the last in the heroic age of Antarctic exploration. Rarely again would humans venture into inhospitable regions without a means of communication with the outside world. The Ross Sea story is surely worthy of greater recognition than it has received, and the authors hope that *Polar Castaways* will contribute to a richer understanding of this enterprise.

Richard McElrea
David Harrowfield

Christchurch, New Zealand
January 2004

ACKNOWLEDGEMENTS

The authors wish to thank all those people and institutions that contributed to the production of *Polar Castaways*. Besides those listed below, they acknowledge the many others who provided valuable information.

The authors feel honoured that Canterbury University Press is publishing this book and thank Richard King, editor, Kaye Godfrey, office manager, and Jeff Field, director, for their professional input and support. Rachel Scott also provided valuable editorial and proofreading assistance. Former managing editor Mike Bradstock gave early and important recognition to the work.

David Yelverton of Hitchin, England, catalogued the Stenhouse papers and has provided ongoing assistance, support, encouragement and advice particularly concerning medals. Stephen McElrea of Auckland and the late Roger Perachie, formerly of London, also provided valued research assistance and support. Stanley Newman of Christchurch helped with early editing of the manuscript and offered encouragement. Bruce Alexander, Colin Monteath and Nigel Watson, all of Christchurch, also lent support, as did John Claydon (Christchurch) and Murray Ellis (Dunedin), veterans of the Commonwealth Trans-Antarctic expedition.

Messrs Richards, Gaze and Moyes, since deceased, all survivors of the events recounted in these pages, became generous supporters of the authors in the provision of personal information.

The authors thank the families of expedition members who have given much original and personal material. Patricia Lathlean of Adelaide supplied information concerning her father, Dick Richards, and Peter Lathlean allowed use of his valuable taped interview with Richards. Tony Gaze of Nagambie, Victoria, provided a tape of an interview and some biographical details about his father, Irvine Gaze. Dr John Middleton of Yarra Valley, Victoria, offered access to the relief expedition diary, medical report, correspondence and a transcript of taped reminiscences of his father, Dr F. G. Middleton, of the relief party. Malcolm Thomson of Gladesville, New South Wales, gave copies of the extensive diaries of his father, Leslie Thomson, a key man on the drift of *Aurora*. John Hooke of Killara, New South Wales, provided a copy of the diary of his father, Sir Lionel Hooke, wireless operator on *Aurora*.

Patricia Mantell of Bedford, England, gave access to the extensive papers and diaries of her father, Joseph Stenhouse, master of *Aurora* during the drift, as did Elizabeth Dowler of Teddington, England, the daughter of the expedition leader, Æneas Mackintosh. Dr John Stevens of Sheffield, England, gave a copy of a taped interview of his father, Professor Alexander Stevens, and provided biographical and other information.

John Mauger, of Napier, New Zealand, provided a copy of the diary and unpublished manuscript of his father, Clarence Mauger, ship's carpenter and a vital man in outfitting the jury rudder on the drift of the ship. John Curlett of Auckland supplied a copy of Joyce's sledging diary, a key document that differed from two rewritten versions of Joyce's diary and other papers. Dorothy Frazer, formerly of Winton, New Zealand, gave permission to access the Spencer-Smith diary and papers now with the Canterbury Museum. Margaret Grayson of Auckland gave biographical details of her father, Alf Larkman, engineer on *Aurora*.

The authors acknowledge with thanks permission to quote from the extensive archival sources listed in the bibliography, held variously at Alexander Turnbull Library, Wellington (Joyce, Mauger and Wild diaries and other archives); Department of Defence, Canberra (Australian Archives); Canterbury Museum, Christchurch (Spencer-Smith papers and other archives); Hocken Library, Dunedin (Ninnis papers and other archives); La Trobe Library, Melbourne (Davis papers); Museum of Victoria, Melbourne (Jack diary); Mitchell Library, Sydney (Moyes diary); Otago Regional Council (Otago Harbour Board archives); Public Record Office, London (Mackintosh archives); Royal Geographical Society (Ninnis and Paton diaries and other archives) and Scott Polar Research Institute, Cambridge (Fisher papers and other archives). Thomas Darragh of the Museum of Victoria, Melbourne, Robert Headland and Caroline Gunn of Scott Polar Research Institute, and Baden Norris and Kerry McCarthy of Canterbury Museum are only some who have kindly assisted.

Selena Lynch of London alerted Richard McElrea to Jennifer Niven's apposite account of the doomed 1913 *Karluk* expedition.

The Trans-Antarctic Association, Wellington, contributed valued financial assistance in recognition of the historical significance of the subject matter.

The authors also thank cartographer Tim Nolan for production of maps, and Monika Gerdes for meticulously typing much of the draft.

David Harrowfield thanks his parents, Joan and the late Laurie Harrowfield, for their support and interest in this venture.

Richard McElrea thanks his wife, Rosemary, and sons, Paul, Edward and Jeremy, for their support and encouragement in seeing this work to fruition.

Polar Castaways is dedicated to the spirit of the men who sailed south from Hobart, Australia, in December 1914 on the polar ship SY *Aurora* and who fulfilled a promise to lay depots to Mt Hope, Antarctica, despite enduring conditions that tested their will and their sanity. A tribute to three members of the party who had died in the enterprise is perhaps a fitting epitaph to all of the party and those who sailed as part of the relief expedition.

Things done for gain are nought
But great things done, endure.

– A. C. Swinburne

Wind Vane Hill, Cape Evans, Antarctica with a memorial to three men who died as part of the Imperial Trans-Antarctic Expedition 1914–17.

Richard McElrea

CHAPTER ONE

An expedition to cross Antarctica

I N THE EARLY YEARS of the twentieth century, an expedition to cross the continent of Antarctica was, by its very nature, an extremely hazardous enterprise. Those embarking on such a venture would be cut off from civilisation, and any hope of rescue or assistance, if needed, could be thought of only in terms of months, if not years. Communication by wireless, although successfully pioneered by the Australian explorer Douglas Mawson during his expedition of 1911–14, was fickle at best. Navigating through ice-filled waters in sailing ships augmented by steam engines of limited capacity was an arduous prospect, and sledging parties would have to cross unknown ice-covered terrain in a hostile climate with inadequate food supplies and using equipment that was primitive by today's standards. This era has become known as the 'heroic age' of Antarctic exploration and would draw to a close when the survivors of Shackleton's Ross Sea party stepped ashore in Wellington, New Zealand, on 9 February 1917.

British explorer Ernest Shackleton,[1] born in County Kildare, Ireland, in 1874, had been twice disappointed in his polar endeavours. As a member of the National Antarctic Expedition (the *Discovery* expedition), he was sent home in March 1903 after the first season on account of ill health.[2] As leader of the 1907–09 British Antarctic Expedition (BAE), also known as the *Nimrod* expedition and surely one of the most unheralded ventures of the era, he failed in his attempt to reach the South Pole, turning back at 88° 23' S on 10 January 1909.[3] Two years later he wrote to Wellington solicitor Leonard Tripp: 'I do not feel settled down myself at all. I long for the unbeaten trail again.' Shackleton's solution to this wanderlust was an ambitious plan to cross the continent of Antarctica, an enterprise he named the Imperial Trans-Antarctic Expedition (ITAE).

Despite James Cook's crossing of the Antarctic Circle in January 1773, it would be almost 50 years before the first sightings of, and landings on, Antarctica were made. Contention about who was first to sight the continent has been well documented, with the names Thaddeus Bellingshausen, Edward Bransfield and Nathaniel Palmer featuring prominently.[4] From November

1840 to April 1841, James Clark Ross voyaged into the sea to be named after him and discovered what he termed the Great Icy Barrier.[5] (By the early twentieth century, this was known variously as the Great Ross Barrier, the Great Ice Barrier or simply the Barrier. It is now the Ross Ice Shelf.) Over 30 years later, HMS *Challenger* became the first steamship to cross the Antarctic Circle.[6] British expeditions led by Robert Scott and Ernest Shackleton reached inland from the Ross Sea in the first years of the twentieth century, but just how little was then known of the regions south of the Weddell Sea is illustrated by the Scottish explorer William Bruce, who noted as late as 1911:

> There are two theories regarding the Antarctic continent: one, that it is one continuous land mass; the other, that it is divided by a channel from the Weddell Sea to the Ross Sea.[7]

The idea of a transcontinental crossing to prove which of these theories was correct was not new. Bruce himself had issued a prospectus for such a journey,[8] and had outlined his plan in greater detail to the Royal Scottish Geographical Society on 17 March 1910. He estimated the expedition would cost £50,000, and hoped it could sail by the following year.[9] In the event, he could not raise the necessary funds.

Bruce had earlier led the Scottish National Antarctic Expedition, which achieved significant exploration in the Weddell Sea, reaching 74°1' S, 22° W in March 1904 and naming Coats Land after two brothers who had funded the expedition.[10] During the ITAE in *Endurance*, Shackleton would put great reliance on Bruce's excellent work and live to regret passing up an opportunity to make landfall at a place he would name Glacier Bay, south of Bruce's farthest south position.[11]

Wilhelm Filchner and his German South Polar Expedition in January 1912 reached 77° 45' S, 34° 34' W in the Weddell Sea, proximate to what would be named the Filchner Ice Shelf. The expedition ship became beset in the ice and drifted north for nine months. Filchner's original plan, also thwarted through lack of funds, followed that of William Bruce, as did Shackleton's. There would be two ships in wireless communication with each other; the main party would sail as far south as possible into the Weddell Sea, and from there set out on a southern sledge journey while a support party would approach over known territory from the Ross Sea side.[12]

Late in 1913, Shackleton published a 30-page prospectus setting out his plans for an expedition that would leave England in the summer of 1914 with the objective of crossing the Antarctic continent from sea to sea, thereby 'securing for the British flag the honour of being the first carried across the South Polar Continent'.

His proposal met a mixed reaction. Bruce's response ('one explorer should not stand in the way of another, in such matters')[13] contrasted with that of Felix König, who claimed priority for Austro-Hungary in the Weddell Sea and protested strongly to Shackleton.[14] Lord Curzon, president of the Royal Geographical Society (RGS), showed some enthusiasm for the proposal.

> It was a task that was worthy to be undertaken by an Englishman . . . crossing the Polar zone from sea to sea, and discovering what lies in that great white blank . . . [is] one of the few great achievements in exploration that are still open to the human race.[15]

However, Sir Clements Markham, the 84-year-old former president of the RGS, dismissed it as a 'useless journey . . . geographically of no value, and entailing a great waste of money . . .' He opined that a journey without laying depots would be 'simple when in the hands of a capable leader. It is no more than Amundsen did.' Markham predicted, accurately as it transpired, that 'the task of laying a line of depots of provisions . . . seriously complicates the work of the Ross Sea Party, and increases the difficulty . . .'[16]

In March 1914, Shackleton put his proposals to a committee of the RGS,[17] although he had little wish to meet with the society and anticipated the grudging response he would get from what he considered a 'hide-bound and narrow' institution.[18]

Addressing the committee, he said the crossing of the continent, a distance he estimated of some 1,800 miles,[19] would be undertaken by six men (he would later propose a larger party) and 120 dogs. He planned to travel from the Weddell Sea over unexplored territory to the South Pole, first reached (from the opposite direction) by Roald Amundsen's Norwegian party in December 1911.[20] The expedition would then travel westwards by reference to the Queen Maud Range, discovered by the Norwegians, and link up with depots to be laid by a second party, travelling overland from the Ross Sea to the Beardmore Glacier. Shackleton knew much of this latter route well, having pioneered the ascent of the glacier in 1908.

The sledging dogs would be half-breed huskies (husky-collie, husky-St Bernard or husky-wolf crosses)[21] and, following Amundsen's example, would be progressively killed to provide food for the remaining dogs, estimated to number 25 by the end of the crossing.

Shackleton claimed that his crossing party would be self-sufficient and that the support party, intended only as a safety factor, would be travelling over a known route and carrying out a relatively straightforward task. The auxiliary barquentine *Aurora*, from Mawson's 1911–14 expedition and procured at a bargain price, would service the Ross Sea party, which would leave from

Australia in November 1914. The depots they would lay would be sufficient, in Shackleton's words, 'to help us along and give us a little addition to our supplies'. His ploy in understating the importance of the support party is in contrast to his approaches to the Admiralty a few months later. The RGS committee, which was openly sceptical, made the token gesture of contributing £1,000 'on Lord Curzon's personal initiative rather than because the Society as a whole is strongly supporting the scheme'.[22]

It was proposed by Sir Ernest that funds for the expedition would be raised by appealing to wealthy individuals and not by public subscription, which 'causes endless book-keeping worries', he told the committee. Even if funds did permit, he said it was unlikely that wireless communication between the expedition ships and bases could be established because of the distances involved and conditions expected.

Shackleton did have a promise, given in December 1913 by the Chancellor of the Exchequer, David Lloyd George, of a government grant of £10,000, half to be paid in 1915 and the balance in 1916. The offer was conditional on Shackleton's obtaining elsewhere the 'full balance of the funds required for the expedition'.[23] In making this approach to the government, however, Shackleton had not first consulted with the Admiralty, apparently thus 'indicating that [the ITAE] was not considered as being connected in any way with naval requirement'.[24] He then spent some time over the next few months combating the cantankerous First Lord of the Admiralty, Winston Churchill.

Shackleton eventually asked the Admiralty to lend naval personnel for the Ross Sea ship. The Merchant Service, he said, would man the Weddell Sea ship:

> The Ross Sea ship will have the onerous work of landing a party to proceed south to establish communication with the trans-continental party, and after that will hold a roving commission to chart, sound and survey as much as possible of the Ross Sea quadrant of the Antarctic and the navigable seas between that continent and New Zealand and Australia. For this purpose I would ask for the loan of three executive officers and fifteen to twenty men. The ship will not be wintering in the Antarctic and therefore in the event of war, these men would not be away from touch with civilisation for more than three months and could immediately return to their duties if necessary.[25]

In another memorandum, Shackleton assured the Admiralty that he proposed to pay these men from the funds of the expedition.[26] He asked if he could have 'one of the ships fitted out in a [sic] Admiralty dockyard', but failing this, perhaps he could be lent 'the necessary chronometers, surveying instruments and sounding gear'. Neither of these requests, he pointed out, would create a precedent.

Shackleton continued to press Churchill:

Let me assure you that I will return the men safe and undamaged from the Expedition, as far as God wills it . . . I really want to have a naval wing to the expedition on the Ross Sea side for navigational purposes . . . Regent Street holds out more dangers on a busy day than the five million square miles that constitute the Antarctic Continent.[27]

Churchill appeared to partially acquiesce 'now that [Shackleton] only wants one officer'. Sir Ernest was pressing for the appointment of Colonel Thomas Orde-Lees, whom he described as 'a first-class motor and all-round man'.[28] In the event, Orde-Lees travelled on *Endurance* and proved a difficult personality. However, a fortnight later the Admiralty, perhaps mindful of some unsatisfactory matters following Shackleton's first expedition in 1909, stated that no officers would be available but instruments could be lent.[29]

In July 1914, Sir Ernest approached the Australian authorities requesting personnel for *Aurora* from the Royal Australian Navy for five months from December 1914. He proposed that the crew would return to other naval duties from May or June 1915, and be required in December 1915 for a further voyage only if the transcontinental party had not crossed from the Weddell Sea in the first season.[30]

There was some enthusiasm in Australia for the idea, which would also have the merit of saving the cost of a relief ship being sent to the government meteorological station at Macquarie Island. The Commonwealth Naval Board recommended acceptance subject to 'a Captain or Chief Officer with polar experience [being] appointed, as the Royal Australian Navy cannot supply this officer'. They had in mind Captain John King Davis, who had served as first officer with Shackleton on *Nimrod* and captain of *Aurora* with Mawson.

Shackleton's success in raising approximately £60,000 with the help of private supporters, some of whose names (such as Dame Janet Stancomb-Wills, Mr Dudley Docker and Sir James Caird) are consequently part of polar history and geography, is well recorded elsewhere. The gift of £24,000 from Caird, a Dundee jute magnate and millionaire, made 'the expedition financially safe', wrote Sir Ernest to a supporter.[31] Contributions 'ranging from 2s 6d upwards' came from all classes of people – 'omnibus drivers, miners, and metropolitan policemen'.[32] However, his fundraising fell well short of his target, perhaps by as much as £40,000.

The outbreak of war on 4 August 1914 almost stopped the Imperial Trans-Antarctic Expedition in its tracks. 'The present war has altered matters,' the Naval Secretary cabled Shackleton on 27 August 1914.[33] However, most observers thought it would be a short war, likely to be over in a matter of weeks or months,[34] and the party left with Churchill's brusque blessing. There would be many critics who would question why it embarked at all, and Shackleton was to go to some lengths to explain and justify the decision.[35]

The Ross Sea party was to receive considerable government and public support in Australia, but that would be negated somewhat after the ship sailed for Antarctica because of what Davis described as the 'haphazard and badly organised state of this section of the expedition'.[36] That the Imperial Trans-Antarctic Expedition embarked at all was attributable entirely to Shackleton, and the responsibility for inadequate financial support of the Ross Sea party must inevitably rest with him.

Sir Ernest Shackleton originally intended to appoint Æneas Mackintosh as one of the party of five men that would cross the Antarctic continent from the Weddell Sea coast under his command.[37] By the time he met the committee of the RGS on 14 March 1914, however, the expedition leader had changed his mind. When asked who was to be the commander of the Ross Sea party, Sir Ernest announced that it would be Mackintosh.[38]

Shackleton needed a reliable and experienced man to lead the support party, and Æneas Lionel Acton Mackintosh seemed to have most of the attributes that would be required. Born in India on 1 July 1879 of British parents,[39] he attended school in England, then, from the age of fifteen, trained on the skysail-yard ships *Cromdale* and *Mount Stewart* before moving to the P&O Company as a junior officer on RMS *Victoria*. Importantly, he was a Shackleton protégé, having served as second officer on the *Nimrod* in 1907–09.[40] There he gained some sledging experience as a member of a party of four men with eight dogs, under the leadership of Ernest Joyce, that laid a depot at Minna Bluff from 16 January to 19 February 1909.[41]

Mackintosh had lost his right eye when struck by a cargo hook while unloading stores at Cape Royds a year earlier. Although the damaged eye (later to be replaced with a glass version) was removed by the ship's surgeon,[42] Mackintosh then went to New Zealand instead of wintering over, before returning the next season.

After the *Nimrod* expedition, Mackintosh and Davis, under the direction of Sir Ernest, travelled to Hungary to assist Douglas Mawson, who was investigating for Shackleton an allegedly rich but undeveloped reef of gold-mining ore at a village called Nagybanya in the Carpathian Mountains.[43] Mackintosh then spent three months at the Cocos Islands in the Indian Ocean, unsuccessfully searching for Spanish treasure. He received his commission as sub-lieutenant in the Royal Naval Reserve in July 1908, during his time on the BAE. He later resumed a more orthodox lifestyle, married in 1912, and was assistant secretary to the Imperial Merchant Service Guild in Liverpool when appointed to the ITAE in 1914.[44]

Shackleton's appointment of Mackintosh to lead the support party in 1914 was made in the knowledge of an incident that had almost cost him and another man, Thomas McGillon, their lives near Cape Royds in early January 1909.[45] Mackintosh and three 'volunteers', at the direction of the master of *Nimrod*, Captain Frederick Evans, had set off with the mailbag and other supplies to cross the pack ice to Cape Royds, a distance of some 32 miles. Two of the men soon returned to the ship because of exhaustion, but 'Mr Mackintosh decided to push on which was a very risky undertaking', wrote one of the seamen on *Nimrod*.[46] Some nineteen hours after setting out (and an overnight camp), the pair had found themselves adrift on the sea ice, eventually reaching the safety of land near Cape Bird through desperate efforts. In Mackintosh's own words, the 'business had been very near ending my life, and what is worse I am responsible for my good mate'.

After four days of recuperation, Mackintosh and his companion set out for Cape Royds over high terrain on the slopes of Mt Bird, leaving behind the tent and mailbag. Searchers from *Nimrod* found these four days later, a discovery that raised hopes because it had been feared that the missing men might have been carried away on an ice floe. '[Mackintosh and McGillon] started off for Cape Royds, armed with two days provisions, and a Primus lamp, nothing more – madness!' an incredulous member of the search team wrote.[47]

The two men survived the ensuing alpine journey to Cape Royds without any crampons or other basic equipment. Near the summit of Mt Bird, at an altitude of some 5,800 feet, McGillon slipped down a 'yawning chasm' and was rescued from a fragile ice ledge by Mackintosh's improvising a rope using pack straps and a waist belt. Their stove and most of their provisions could not be retrieved. On an impassable 'hotbed of crevasses' the hapless pair had to climb higher in an effort to find a route, and they resorted to crossing a crevasse by a narrow ice bridge. 'The idea of Hell was not comforting . . . one slip, or the breaking of the bridge, would have precipitated us into the black depths below', wrote Mackintosh. Unable to descend or ascend, at McGillon's suggestion they put themselves 'in the hands of the Providence that guided us throughout'.[48] Mackintosh recalled:

> . . . if we had to die, it was better to go in this way than die of starvation at the bottom of a crevasse, so we took our lives in our hands; dug our knives deep in the snow to act as brakes; stuck our heels well in, and let go. Down we went, the knives

were soon torn from our grasp, but we managed to keep our heels in the snow, and the packs on our backs acted as brakes . . . when we brought up at the bottom in safety we could scarcely believe it.

The two men were soon overtaken by a blizzard but were later found by chance near the Cape Royds hut. Shackleton had noted that the pair 'had a narrow escape from death, and probably would have never reached the hut had not [Bernard] Day happened to be outside watching for the return of the ship'.[49]

By 1914, Shackleton was presumably prepared to overlook this reckless journey in 1909 and regard it as a valuable learning experience. In fact, Mackintosh's appointment as leader of the Ross Sea men may have been a consolation prize for a man whose eye injury probably ruled him out of contention for the polar party.

Shackleton needed a spot on the ITAE to reward Ernest Edward Mills Joyce, another loyal supporter from earlier days. 'On this expedition he will have charge of the dogs at one of the bases,' he stated in the 1914 prospectus.[50] By the time he named Mackintosh as leader of the support party, Shackleton had decided that Joyce should also be part of that group.

On the *Discovery* expedition, Joyce had been a member of a six-man party, led by Lieutenant Michael Barne, that laid a depot south-east of White Island over eight days in September 1903. Spring temperatures went as low as −67° F and Joyce suffered severe frostbite to his face and foot. He also went with Barne on another sledging trip in November 1903.[51] On the *Nimrod* expedition, he led the four-man party, including Mackintosh, that laid a depot at Minna Bluff on 26 January 1909. The dogs hauled over a hundred pounds of supplies per animal on this journey, and at times three men rode on the sledge, which averaged over 30 miles per day. The party then trekked southwards of the Bluff to search for Shackleton's overdue polar party before returning to base. Although not a major venture, this was an impressive and efficient exercise.

Prior to his Antarctic experiences, Joyce's career had followed something of a family tradition: his grandfather and father had both served in the Royal Navy, and Ernest himself joined up in 1890 at the age of fifteen. He received a thorough training on sailing ships, his first trip being to Iceland. When the *Discovery* called at Simons Bay, South Africa, in October 1901, Joyce was chosen to join that expedition from among 400 Royal Navy volunteers who, with the Boer War over, were eager for action of a different kind.[52]

After the *Discovery* expedition, Lieutenant Michael Barne gave Joyce a glowing testimonial:

> I have served with Ernest Joyce in two ships – first HMS *Cordelia*, 1895–6, second in the Antarctic ship *Discovery* 1901–4, and can say with perfect confidence that

I have never come across a more trustworthy, honest, sober and hardworking man . . .[53]

Joyce was promoted to petty officer first class but left the navy in 1907 when, along with fellow *Discovery* member Frank Wild, he joined the British Antarctic Expedition. According to an often-told story, Shackleton was looking out of his office window in Lower Regent Street, London, when he recognised Joyce 'on the top of a passing omnibus' and sent his secretary in pursuit.[54] Thus Joyce's acquaintance with the ice was renewed and he travelled south on *Nimrod*. However, his hopes of being in the polar party were dashed when Dr Eric Marshall advised Shackleton that Joyce was not fit enough for the journey.[55] He also suffered his share of frostbite, being afflicted again in October 1908.[56]

Following the *Nimrod* expedition, Joyce delivered 38 dogs from Copenhagen to Australia for Mawson and anticipated appointment to that leader's expedition.[57] On 12 October 1911, *The Times* reported that

> The King conveyed to Mr Ernest Joyce who is leaving England today to join the Australian Antarctic Expedition as zoologist his 'best wishes for the success, good health and safe return' of the explorers . . . The expedition will leave Australia on 27 November . . .[58]

The royal announcement proved to be premature, as Mawson did not appoint Joyce to his expedition.[59]

Joyce stayed on in Australia for the next four years, working as wharf master at Bowen, North Queensland, and then managing a hostel for seamen on behalf of the Sydney Harbour Trust.[60] It was there that he received a letter from his old leader, written on 22 February 1914 and published in the *Sydney Morning Herald* on 29 June:

> Sir Ernest's letter to Mr Joyce reads:
>
> 'Following my cablegram, I will take you on the expedition subject to certain conditions. I propose to have the expedition divided into two sections – the Weddell Sea section and the Ross Sea section. The party for the Weddell Sea will include the transcontinental party. The Ross Sea section will consist of a party of six men, who will lay a depot at the foot of the Beardmore Glacier for the transcontinental party, and will possibly winter in either our old hut or the Cape Evans hut. This programme can be adopted if the full amount of money necessary for the expedition is forthcoming. In the event of that not being so there will be but one ship, and that will be the Weddell Sea ship, and one small party for the transcontinental journey. I do not anticipate the latter alternative, but if that occurs – and I will know shortly – I cannot promise you a position in that party unless there is a wintering party as well.'
>
> Then followed the conditions to be observed. Among them, Sir Ernest stated

that Mr Joyce would be attached to the Ross Sea party, in charge of stores, sledges and dogs.

'If necessary', the letter continues, 'I might send you to the north-west coast of America to pick up the dogs. The shore party for the Ross Sea would be in command of an officer, to whom you would be responsible. The Ross Sea section would leave an Australian port about November 1, and land a shore party as early as possible. This party would proceed to lay out a depot at the foot of the Beardmore Glacier, returning then to the hut, and would either be part of the complement of the ship, if sea exploration was done, or, if too late for the ship, would remain at winter quarters until the following year, supplementing this work by again proceeding to the Beardmore Glacier, and perhaps ascending the same on the lookout for the southern party.'

Mr Joyce welcomes the opportunity. He knows perhaps more of the transport and stores side of a polar expedition than anybody else . . .

Mr Joyce has written to Sir Ernest Shackleton accepting his offer, and is daily expecting further details as to when he would leave, and where he is to join the party.[61]

Both Mackintosh and Joyce were *Nimrod* men but from completely different backgrounds. In the published letter of appointment, Shackleton clearly spelt out who was to be in charge of the support party. Mackintosh was that person and was known as 'the Skipper' or 'the Captain' by his men on the expedition. In later years, Joyce was to seriously misrepresent this chain of command.

CHAPTER TWO

The Ionic *contingent: Australian preparations*

O N 18 SEPTEMBER 1914, Sir Ernest Shackleton bade farewell to eleven members of the Ross Sea party as they left St Pancras Station, London, for Tilbury to board the *Ionic.* Later that evening the White Star liner sailed from Dover under naval escort and Mackintosh's men began the first leg of their journey south.[1] Shackleton was to have sailed with the *Endurance* party the next day for Buenos Aires, but delayed his departure for a week, citing 'family affairs' as the reason.[2]

The composition of the Ross Sea party was far from clear right until its departure. When Mackintosh, travelling separately from the main party, arrived in Australia in early October, he suggested that two Cambridge University scientists – James Wordie and Reginald James – would be in his party.[3] In fact, this pair was destined for the *Endurance* group, and the final support contingent included two other Cambridge men.

Arnold Patrick Spencer-Smith, the Ross Sea party's photographer and padre, was born on 17 March 1883 in Streatham, Surrey, and attended Woodbridge Grammar School before studying English and theology at Queen's College, Cambridge. He taught French and mathematics at Merchiston Castle Preparatory School, Edinburgh, from 1907 until he joined Shackleton's expedition seven years later.[4] Ordained as a deacon in the Church of Scotland in Edinburgh Cathedral in 1910, he served as curate of Christ Church, Morningside, Edinburgh, until 1912, and then as assistant curate at All Saints', Edinburgh, where he was ordained as a priest just five days before embarking on *Ionic.*[5] The rector of All Saints' stated that Spencer-Smith (who was called 'the Padre' or 'A.P.' by those on the expedition) 'would exercise his priesthood in circumstances unique in the history of the Anglican Ministry'.[6]

John Lachlan Cope, a 21-year-old student at Christ's College, Cambridge, joined the party as a biologist on the recommendation of Sir Arthur Shipley, master of the college and a noted authority on scurvy.[7] The young man had earlier attended Tunbridge School Manor House.[8]

The party's geologist, Alexander Stevens, was born in Kilmarnock, Ayrshire, on 11 January 1886. He was educated at Kilmarnock Academy and Glasgow University, from which he graduated with distinction in geology in 1913.[9] Before his appointment to the Ross Sea party, he taught at the Nicholson Institution, at Stornaway on Lewis in the Outer Hebrides.

Significantly, none of these three men had any experience that prepared them for sledging duties, which was the main purpose of the expedition, and the appointments of Stevens and Cope were to ill-defined scientific positions.

A more conventional appointment was that of Joseph Russell Stenhouse, aged 27, a lieutenant in the Royal Naval Reserve, first officer designate for *Aurora* and in charge of the *Ionic* party. Born in Dumbarton, Scotland, in 1887, he came from a family associated with the firm of Birrell, Stenhouse & Co., famous as builders of clipper ships. After attending Barrow Grammar School, Lancashire, he spent a year as a clerk with Lloyd's Register of Shipping before going to sea in 1903 as an apprentice aboard the sailing ship *Springbank*. After gaining his master's certificate, he went into steamships before his appointment as chief officer of *Aurora*.[10]

Shackleton made three other appointments in England for the Ross Sea shore party.

Recognising the need for a first-class dog driver, he chose Victor Hayward, a 25-year-old Londoner who had gained experience with dogs on cattle ranches in Canada.[11]

Henry Ernest Wild, a younger brother of Frank Wild (veteran of three Antarctic expeditions and appointed to the *Endurance* party), was put in charge of stores. Born at Nettleton, Lincolnshire, in 1879, he went to sea at the age of fifteen and spent the next twenty years in the Royal Navy, including three years in South African waters at the time of the Boer War. He assisted Italian authorities in 1908 at the earthquake in Messina, Sicily, and was a petty officer before he joined Shackleton in 1914.[12]

The role of 'motor expert' was assigned to Aubrey Howard Ninnis, a distant relative, according to Davis, of Lieutenant Belgrave Ninnis, who had died on Mawson's expedition.[13] Born in England in 1883, Howard Ninnis had seven years on Admiralty service before joining the second Scott expedition in 1910, but left that party when injured in Cape Town.[14] He then spent time in western Canada, where he had suffered frostbite.[15] For the next four years, until joining the Ross Sea party, he worked with motors, aeroplanes and wireless.

Ninnis's main responsibility was to operate the Girling motor sledge, one of several purchased for the ITAE.[16] This machine had been tested in Russia, Switzerland and on the Hardanger Glacier, Finse, Norway. The *Daily Graphic* had reported in May that Shackleton considered the results of these trials had been 'quite beyond his expectations' but highlighted various structural weaknesses 'due to the vibration of the engine over constantly varying surfaces'.[17] He had told his critics: '100 dogs will be the mainstay of the expedition, but . . . if I can go 200 miles on 500 lb. weight of petrol, which is what it will weigh, [the sledge] will be a tremendous asset to me.'[18] *The Motor* magazine predicted: 'From the Ross Sea side, towards which the expedition is making, motor sledges will make depots for 300 miles right up to the foot of the Beardmore Glacier.'

The appointment of the youngest member of *Aurora*'s crew, 22-year-old Clarence Charles Mauger, perhaps best shows Shackleton's selection style. Hailing from Connemara, County Galway, this young man served his apprenticeship as a shipwright in Wales, later boarding at Greenwich Naval Hospital, a school for the sons of serving naval men (his father being in the Coastguard Service).[19] Mauger applied for the shipwright's position on *Aurora* after poor eyesight had prevented him from gaining his mate's ticket in the Merchant Service and from joining the Royal Navy. Shackleton evidently took an instant liking to him. Mauger wrote:

> Some time ago in July 1914, I had paid off from the three-masted barque *Inverramsay*. I had completed a round voyage out from Cape of Good Hope and home around Cape Horn. They paid off seamen in gold coins in those days and I collected quite a handful . . . Owing to my father's death while [I was] at sea, I found myself without a home to return to . . . the Germans declared war, and the shipyard I was working at switched to a war-time footing . . . I got a letter of introduction to Lieutenant Mackintosh in Sir Ernest Shackleton's office in New Burlington Street . . . I was not dressed in my best to go ashore clothes, but clean and tidy in a semi working rig. I had lost neither my rolling gait or my deep tan, and with my well worn blue suit and blue cotton shirt, I must have looked a proper deep water man.
>
> Sir Ernest did not waste any time, but gave me a hard look, and his face lit up with a smile, as he said: 'Been in sail?' 'Yes, sir,' 'Been in steam?' 'Yes, sir'; 'Joiner or shipwright?' 'Shipwright, sir'; 'Married or single?' 'Single, sir'. He then asked me one or two questions about my background and education, had a hurried glance through my discharge book, and said: 'Royal Navy Reserve, I see?' 'Yes, sir'. 'What salary would you require?' 'Well, sir, the wages of the port of London are £7.10.0 a month, but I think it is worth something more to do down there'. 'Good for you,' said the boss. 'How would £120 a year do you?' 'That would be wonderful,' said I. 'I must have someone reliable,' said Sir Ernest, 'so you have the job.'[20]

Prior to joining the *Ionic* party, Mauger had taken a temporary job on a hospital ship transporting war casualties across the Channel from France. 'London was already crawling with troops, a lot of them already wounded. We brought back wounded from the Battle of Mons,' he wrote. The timing of the departure of the ITAE prevented others from playing any part in early war action, and Mauger was the only member of the expedition to do so.

Ionic, painted wartime grey, steamed by night unlit. Early in the voyage, half a dozen troopships and a four-funnelled cruiser were sighted, and the liner kept in wireless contact with 'the fleet'[21] before putting into Cape Town on 10 October 1914 to recoal and resupply.

Ashore doing a spot of photography, *Aurora*'s engineer designate Alfred Herbert Larkman was arrested as a suspected German spy and taken under escort to a Major Bidwell of the Cape Town Highlanders. On learning Larkman's true identity, the major treated him 'most courteously' and introduced him to his two daughters.[22] Larkman had been appointed from the Radcliffe Line as second engineer. Trained in mechanical engineering, he had skills in navigating and surveying, no doubt honed by his father, who ran an academy for ships' officers in Southampton.[23]

From Cape Town, *Ionic*'s master, Captain C. E. Starck, took the liner on a more southerly course than usual as a result of receiving reports of a German cruiser in the Indian Ocean. In the Roaring Forties, with snow on the liner's decks, Stenhouse lamented the absence of 'foresail and topsails' to take advantage of the fair winds.

The Ross Sea men gave lectures and two concerts featuring songs such as 'Mister Noah's Ark', 'Jolly Old Sports' and 'John Brown's Body'. Not all the passengers were impressed by the Antarctic expedition: one 82-year-old lady told members of the party that they should all be fighting for their country and 'not playing the fool out in the snow'.[24]

Stenhouse attempted to establish a routine through 'orders of the day'.[25] All hands turned out at 4.45 a.m. They tended the dogs, held in 26 crates on the boat deck, and later exercised them. Cope acted as factotum veterinarian. Attempts were made to train the dogs in teams of nine, including giving commands such as 'Mush!', 'Get-e-up!', 'See!' – a command to turn right – and 'Haw' – turn left.

Wild conducted seamanship and signalling classes. Games of tug-of-war, deck tennis and wheelbarrow races provided some recreation during the warmer parts of the voyage. On Sundays, Spencer-Smith conducted divine service in the saloon.

Most of the Ross Sea party travelled first class, but engineer-designate Larkman was in the saloon class. The men had plenty of time on their hands. Hayward and others took an interest in the art of stoking the liner's eight double furnaces, which consumed vast quantities of coal.[26]

At a farewell dinner on 29 October, disembarking passengers wished Stenhouse and his men 'God speed and success'. The next day the liner docked in Sydney Harbour, though the Ross Sea party was to carry on to Hobart, Tasmania.

On Mackintosh's arrival in Sydney on RMS *Osterley* on 8 October 1914, Captain J. K. Davis offered his old friend from the *Nimrod* expedition 'every assistance'.[27] At the age of 30, Davis had already established a formidable reputation as a polar mariner. During the Australasian Antarctic Expedition, *Aurora* had logged, under his command, approximately 23,000 nautical miles in three summer voyages to the continent and two winter subantarctic cruises. Earlier in 1914 he had turned down an approach from Shackleton, his former leader from the *Nimrod* days, who wanted him to captain *Endurance*:

> I ... absolutely decline to be associated with any enterprise with which people of the Joyce type are connected ... If you expect to land in the Weddell Sea in time to begin your trans Antarctic journey the same year, I am quite unwilling to accept the responsibility.[28]

Davis's response was also echoed in a letter he wrote to Joseph Kinsey in Christchurch: 'You know Shackleton, he is so full of promises which so seldom come to anything.'[29] By October 1914, in command of an impounded German vessel,[30] Davis was arranging the embarkation of troops from Australia but found time to dine with Mackintosh, Stenhouse and others of the Ross Sea party.[31]

In his final instructions to Mackintosh, Shackleton wrote that he was remitting £1,000, which he trusted 'will be sufficient for you to get the ship out of dry dock with the minimum of repairs compatible with safety'.[32] He instructed Mackintosh to seek the services of Professors Edgeworth David and Orme Masson 'and ask them to do everything they can to assist the expedition, explaining to them the need for economy'.

Professor David, then professor of geology at the University of Sydney and president of the Australasian Association for the Advancement of Science, immediately took up Mackintosh's cause with the Australian Prime Minister, Andrew Fisher. Referring to his 'esteemed former colleague on the first Shackleton expedition, Lieutenant Mackintosh', David wrote:

> ... the *Aurora*, now at Hobart, is sadly in need of dry docking and overhauling ...

Sir Ernest Shackleton is not asking the Commonwealth, or any of the States, for financial aid to his present expedition, which is nevertheless so short of funds that the most rigid economy is needed; but if you could see your way to authorise this docking and overhauling being done at the Cockatoo Island Naval Dockyard [in Sydney Harbour] either free of charge or at the lowest cost price, it would be a great boon to the expedition. The total cost of the docking and overhauling would probably, in the opinion of Lt. Mackintosh, not exceed £500 . . . There can be no doubt, in my opinion, that if Sir Ernest is able to carry out his present scheme he will again accomplish work of permanent benefit to Science . . .[33]

When Mackintosh met Fisher, the latter acquiesced to David's suggestion, although 'not very keen at first on agreeing to even the £500'.[34] A second application for assistance was refused: 'We have made a handsome contribution and regret no further financial help can be given,' the Prime Minister noted.

Mackintosh hurried to Hobart, where he found *Aurora*, idle for eight months since Mawson had finished with her, far from shipshape.[35] He quickly employed a crew of thirteen for the short voyage from Hobart to Sydney. Forty-five-year-old James Paton, born in Kirkudbright, Scotland, and a veteran of seven trips to the Antarctic, cabled Mackintosh from Sydney and was taken on as boatswain.[36] Other seamen employed included Sydney Atkin from Sydney, Charles Glidden of Hobart, and S. Grady, a Glaswegian who was taken on as fireman.[37] All four would also sail to Antarctica.

Mackintosh struggled to find a suitable ship's engineer for the trip to Sydney but eventually appointed Albert Thompson, who hastily assembled the dismantled engines. Fifty tons of coal were taken on, partly as ballast. Soon steam was raised, the sails were aired and once again *Aurora* beat into the wind. The four-day voyage gave Mackintosh 'an anxious time'[38] and a valuable opportunity to assess the ship under seagoing conditions. On 1 November, *Aurora* reached Sydney, where Mackintosh received a telegram from Stenhouse advising of *Ionic*'s arrival in Hobart.[39]

The Australian papers reported on 29 October the news of Shackleton's having sailed from Buenos Aires to South Georgia en route to the Weddell Sea. Mackintosh was now under pressure to head southwards at the earliest date so that the depots could be laid.

Stenhouse and his men disembarked at Hobart from *Ionic* on 30 October to find a letter from Mackintosh reporting *Aurora*'s recent departure for Sydney.[40]

One of the first tasks the *Ionic* party had to attend to was the transfer of the dogs to a quarantine station at Taroona, some seven miles from the Hobart wharf. Wearing muzzles, they were taken down the steep ladders from *Ionic* to a waiting boat, towed by a motor launch. 'We took all day on the job and had a rare time getting them ashore through the surf,' noted Larkman.[41] With Wild and Ninnis in charge, the dogs were taken to kennels near the beach at the quarantine station.

The accommodation for the two men at Taroona comprised a ten-foot room in a shed at the end of three horse stalls: '. . . four biscuit cases suggested a bed, two others give a dining table, other improvised affairs give a wash stand, a table and cases make good seats. Made two mattresses of four sacks and straw.'[42] Spencer-Smith visited them a day or two later and wrote to his mother about the experience: 'It was a lovely drive, all along the long inlet at the head of which Hobart stands.' On the Sunday, the Padre assisted in the service at Holy Trinity Church: 'I sang Matins and helped at the celebration . . . and had lunch with the Rector afterwards.'[43]

Before sailing for Sydney on SS *Moeraki* (the first twin-screw vessel of the Union Steam Ship Company) to join up with Mackintosh and *Aurora*, Stenhouse and those of the party 'who could resist the attractions of the shore' (as Stevens later recorded) tallied and checked the stores offloaded from *Ionic* to a nearby warehouse. Labour union laws prevented the men from retrieving cargo from the wharf, and although no such restrictions applied inside the warehouse, the Sabbath was strictly observed.[44] There they separated 43 cases of sledging rations, which would be held in cold storage until *Aurora* returned from Sydney, from 38 cases of skis, sledges and equipment to be taken to Sydney for public exhibition.

To guard against theft or other loss of stores, Stenhouse asked Wild or Ninnis, who were remaining with the dogs in Tasmania, to come from Taroona to Hobart to 'overlook the transferring of stores from the wharf shed to Hammond's Bonded warehouse and also to search the wharf shed afterwards for stray cases'.[45]

From the quarantine station, Wild wrote on 3 November: 'Saw the others go past on the *Moeraki* bound for Sydney.'[46] He and Ninnis would spend until late December training and exercising the dogs over the hills and gullies of Taroona. They constructed a 200-pound sledge to which they attached a twenty-foot trace spliced with eight sets of dog harness. At times they would add timber for extra weight. The dogs were divided into three teams.

> We have made a heavy brigade led by Nigger, the saucy black dog, and running Oscar and Dasher, Hector and Buller, Duke and Gunboat. A middleweight led by Jacky, another impossible dog, but in my opinion a possible leader. It runs Pinkey and Shacks, Briton and Tiger, Pat and Beechey, Scotty and Tug (two fat dogs who will be good leadership when 'trained down'). The light weights led by Major, Canuk

and Bobs, Jock and KayKay, Towser and Pompey, Nell and either Minus or Captain . . .[47]

Nell and Minus were seen as 'two useless hounds who took all the whip before they agreed to pull at all'; Shacks was 'hopeless'; Duke 'nearly right'; and Dasher 'quite satisfactory'.

In his diary, Ninnis painted a picture of a training session:

I have my camera in the pocket of my breeches, a hide whip stuck in one top boot and part of the trace end in my left hand. Then we just dash off. I am standing on the old sledge and we jump big rocks too on it . . . On the return journey its quite usual for the dogs to make a dive for the duck pond and oust the ducks . . . The light team did splendidly and we tore around like a cloud of steam and dirt for nearly an hour. They earned their rest after an extra biscuit . . .[48]

There seemed little chance for the dog minders to relax. 'By the time we return and hitch up all the dogs in the paddocks and water them it is tea time, and after that writing, photographs to do, or the three logs to keep up to date . . .' noted Ninnis.[49] However, he and Wild did manage to bathe in the sea and go fishing. They found little to interest them in Hobart but enjoyed the company of Mr Vickery, the station manager, and his daughters.

The pair learned some veterinary skills, including giving Oscar five stitches after he sustained a bite to the foot. They requested further medical supplies and wired Mackintosh and Cope, 'as delay will result in weak skin and render susceptible to frostbite on [the] slightest temperature drop'.[50] One dog, Captain, would not work and was thin and in bad shape, so was shot and skinned. After an autopsy of sorts was performed, 'Minus ate him'.[51]

Moeraki reached Sydney on 5 November, the same day that *Aurora* went into dry dock at the government naval dockyard at Cockatoo Island.[52] Mackintosh arrived by launch from the island to greet his men. The Padre seemed impressed:

He's an absolute 'dear', such a neat wee chap, with a gold eyeglass on his remaining eye, and an 'Oxford' voice: a glutton for work and very cheery. We are all, staff and men, absolutely in love with him![53]

At lunch at the Wentworth Hotel, the Sydney base for the party, Mackintosh gave a speech of welcome, ('a few words to spur us on', noted Hayward). The next day they all went by ferry to view *Aurora*.[54] To Spencer-Smith, it was 'a joyous errand . . . We gave a cheer as soon as we saw the tub on the mainmast sticking out above the sheds.'[55] It was a scene of great activity. 'Caulkers are at work on the hull and the decks are a busy scene with fitters and other artisans at work overhauling winches, steering gear, pumps and the hundred and one things which require attention after a ship's spell of idleness,' recorded Stenhouse.[56] After ten days, with all work beneath the waterline completed, *Aurora* vacated the dry dock. Refitting and repairs continued at the nearby dockyard wharf for a further three and a half weeks, prolonged by a week-long strike of shipwrights and plumbers, a delay Mackintosh could ill afford.[57]

The ship's engineers, Donald Mason (until he left on 3 December) and Alfred Larkman, carried out a general overhaul of 'sea-cocks, tail shaft and stern tube, [and] propeller leading edges'.[58] They also supervised the stripping and overhaul of the aged engines and the examination and cleaning of the single boiler. The compound two-cylinder engines had a capacity of 98 horsepower and drove a four-bladed propeller at 60 to 70 revolutions per minute. The boilers, cylinders and steam piping were relagged with asbestos to minimise condensation.

Larkman introduced steam and electrical heating and installed a low-voltage lighting system using a 30-cell Pritchett and Goulds battery hired from the Sydney City Train and Trams Department. The German Telefunken wireless plant used by Mawson was purchased from the proceeds of a public subscription, publicised through the *Sydney Morning Herald*, and the ship's tiny pantry was adapted as a wireless room.[59]

Mackintosh appointed eighteen-year-old Lionel George Alfred Hooke as wireless operator. He had attended Brighton Grammar School, Victoria, and served an apprenticeship with the Melbourne Tramway Board before joining the Marconi Company in 1913.[60] He boarded *Aurora* a few days before the party left Sydney.

Bosun Paton (straight out of *Treasure Island*, according to the Padre) led a team of eight hands sorting old stores left over from the Mawson expedition and then working aloft. Decks were caulked and repaired, the saloon, captain's cabin and galley were stripped out and refitted, the laboratory was overhauled and the bridge strengthened. A fourteen-foot launch was constructed, as was a portable hut (for 'the Cape Crozier party') from material donated by the Fibro-Concrete Company. Cabins and decks were painted, a 90-fathom port cable was repaired, and blacksmiths made fish traps and small dredges. A complete set of sails, hatch tarpaulins, covers for ventilators and winches, and a three-year supply of paints, small tools and similar stores were taken aboard, along with a canvas awning to give winter cover over the ship.[61] By any estimation, *Aurora* was given an extensive overhaul in the time available.

Spencer-Smith wrote to his mother:

We broke off at 12 yesterday and I went with the Captain and Stenhouse to lunch with the officers and men of the *Medina*, the ship which took King George round the world – the most luxuriously appointed 'hotel' you can imagine. We had a jolly time. In the evening a party of us went to 'Iolanthe' – quite a good company – and so to bed at midnight.

On Sunday 8th, I went to Matins with the Captain at the Cathedral – a fine building – and heard an excellent war-sermon from the Archbishop, who is quite an orator. The music was good and the National Anthem at the end quite overwhelming.[62]

The same evening, Spencer-Smith, Stevens, Cope and Stenhouse attended the Roman Catholic cathedral for benediction, and a fortnight later Stenhouse wrote in his diary: 'Went to vespers and benediction with the Padre and Stevens.'[63]

Spare time was agreeably spent with such activities as Saturday nights at two Gilbert and Sullivan operas, surfing at Manly, dining with friends and sight-seeing around Sydney.[64] Stenhouse, Spencer-Smith and Cope motored to the Sea Breeze Hotel at 'Tom Ugly's Point' and saw a cockatoo 'reputed to be 118 years old'. It had one or two quills left, but no feathers: one of its sayings, wrote Stenhouse, was, 'My God, if I had a feather I'd fly.'[65]

On 16 November there was a special dinner at the Australia Hotel, attended by Captain Davis, John Hunter (a biologist on Mawson's expedition) and senior members of the Ross Sea party.[66]

Mackintosh was faced with two key vacancies. Second Officer H. G. Leonard left on 30 November after falling out with Stenhouse. Mauger, who recalled Leonard as a 'perfectly decent unassuming likeable sort of chap' suggested that Stenhouse had taken exception to Leonard's friendliness with the passengers on *Ionic*.[67] Leonard, who had been trained on one of the 'poor boy' ships on the Thames River, had commanded his own ship. Stenhouse told Mackintosh that if his second officer remained in the party, he would resign. Leonard felt he had no choice and departed. There was particular poignancy in Leonard's leaving the party, as his old training ship had presented him with an engraved sextant to take south.

First Engineer Mason, who had also travelled out on *Ionic*, 'got cold feet on seeing the *Aurora* set-up' (according to Larkman) and staged a 'drink act on purpose to get sacked'.[68] Mackintosh then promoted Larkman to chief engineer. 'Many engineers came on board with a view to sailing as second [engineer], they took a look at the engines and promptly went ashore,' Larkman later wrote. Finally, on 12 December, Adrian Donnelly, a 21-year-old 'fresh out of his time in a loco shop in Sydney', accepted the position. Although he had no marine experience, Donnelly soon proved 'a real right hand man' to Larkman.[69]

Mackintosh filled other crew vacancies in Sydney from applicants who were employed as casual labourers during the ship's refit. A. ('Shortie') Warren, aged 34, from Minster, Isle of Sheppey; W. ('Ginger') Kavanagh (30), from Windsor, England; and Arthur ('Jack') Downing (21) from Buffalo, New York, were signed as able-bodied seamen at £6 per month.[70] Downing had served three years in Cornwall, England, as an apprentice to shipmasters James Boyd and Son, and then on the four-masted barque *Madagascar* and SS *Dalhanna*. He had worked briefly on the coastal trade in Australia before joining *Aurora*.[71]

E. Wise (aged 38), from Sussex, was signed on as cook, and W. Mugridge (27), from Devonport, as a second fireman. Stenhouse recorded a few days later:

> On Sunday December 16 a party of ladies visited the ship on which account I told the cook to stay on board for the day . . . he told me I had done him a great injury as 'he had intended that afternoon to get tied up to a nice bit of stuff, only 38 with six houses etc.' Well the cook being a philosopher decided to put it off until our return from the South but the opportunity offered . . . he got spliced. He came down aboard looking extremely happy and smoking a vile cigar.[72]

CHAPTER THREE

'God-speed and a safe return . . .'

WHILE *AURORA* was being provisioned, Stevens and Cope endeavoured to assemble scientific instruments, equipment and books, helped by Professor David, who introduced Cope to biologists at Sydney University. Stevens was able to check meteorological instruments at the Sydney Observatory. Spencer-Smith put up some of his own money to purchase photographic equipment, while the firm of Burrows-Welcome donated chemicals. The Colonial Sugar Company gave spirit for scientific use, and Hasdale, an optical-instrument firm, offered a solar-radiation thermometer. Medicines and 'medical comforts' were purchased from a sum of money presented for this purpose.[1]

An earlier report that Dr Alexander Macklin would be the surgeon to the Ross Sea party came to nothing, as he sailed on *Endurance*.[2] Shackleton wanted Mackintosh to engage a surgeon and a physicist in Australia but, despite enquiries though university medical faculties and professional bodies in Melbourne and Sydney, the demands of war meant there were no doctors available. A salary of £150 per annum was offered and, in addition to ordinary medical duties, 'naturally everyone is expected to help as required in the working of the ship to the ice, and when the sledge-journeys commence, the doctor will be expected take a share in them'.[3] A promising applicant, Dr H. A. Andrews, of Melbourne, withdrew a fortnight before the projected sailing date.

By default, Cope, who had no clinical training and was not qualified to practise medicine, is shown on the crew list as surgeon.[4] The *Sydney Morning Herald* inaccurately reported that he had the degree of Bachelor of Medicine, so the Ross Sea party appeared to be leaving with a competent medical person.[5] Cope declined any increase in salary over what had already been agreed for him.[6]

Richard Walter Richards, attracted by an advertisement calling for a physicist, wrote to Mackintosh explaining that he had completed two years' 'work' at the Melbourne University in natural philosophy and mathematics. A 22-year-old, he was currently 'on the instructional staff' of the Junior Technical School, Ballarat. Responding to a request for more information, Richards was as sparing in detail as he had been in his first letter. To the best of his belief his health was excellent and he had 'always been athletically inclined'. As for testimonials, he 'could arrange better if [he] knew what particular specialisation in science work was required'.[7] He accepted the position after an interview on the ship at Cockatoo Island.[8] Mackintosh had expected to sail from Sydney on 6 December, then from Hobart four days later. However, last-minute delays that held up the ship for a fortnight enabled Richards to meet a tight timetable and join the ship in Hobart.[9]

A 'considerate father' encouraged Irvine Owen Gaze, in business in Melbourne, to visit his cousin Spencer-Smith in Sydney.[10] There he learned of a vacancy on the ITAE and volunteered, 'willing to do any work allotted to me . . . I am well acquainted with electric motors . . . and as far as I know I can stand the cold.'[11] Born in 1889 and educated at Scotch College in Perth, Gaze was a keen sportsman, active in cricket, football, tennis and yachting circles. He was appointed to the Ross Sea party as a 'lamp and oil man' and to assist as required with meteorological observations, but was immediately put in charge of stores while *Aurora* was in Sydney.[12]

The third of the 'Australian volunteers' was Andrew Keith Jack, aged 29. He had attended Brighton Grammar School and the University of Melbourne, where he graduated Master of Science with honours in chemistry, and had taught science at Dookie Agriculture College from 1911. Irvine Gaze spoke 'warmly in his interest', and Professor Masson provided an excellent reference.[13] Mackintosh initially declined Jack's application after Stevens advised that 'there was no provision or apparatus for physical work' and it was 'likely that all scientific work would require to be relegated to spare time'. Jack then offered his services in 'any capacity, assistant, anything if you could find a post . . .'[14] He was taken on, 'but in what capacity seems to be a matter of obscurity', Stevens was to note in his post-expedition report.

In addition to appointing staff, Mackintosh needed more money than was available to meet the party's requirements. He was expecting £2,000 and a further £1,000, if required, from expedition headquarters in London. Instead, he received £1,000 with an authority to 'mortgage ship to £3,000'. Mackintosh consulted with his senior personnel, Stenhouse, Spencer-Smith, Cope and Stevens, and it was agreed that unless the promised money was forthcoming, 'it would not be possible for the *Aurora* to proceed to the relief of the Trans Continental Party, in which case [Mackintosh] would require to communicate with Lady Shackleton'.[15] Mackintosh thereupon telegraphed headquarters and advised 'it is now impossible to have mortgage on vessel'. The ITAE secretary, F. W. White, responded: 'Follow instructions. You must endeavour mortgage ship . . .'

Mackintosh could see little chance of obtaining 'money here by mortgage or otherwise', and insisted he 'must have £1,500 before ship can start'.[16]

Even if Mackintosh could find a financier, there was no one in Australia with power of attorney from Shackleton to sign legal documents on his behalf. Nor had the sale of the ship to Shackleton been registered at Liverpool. 'The Sydney committee', headed by Professor David, partially retrieved the position by providing £700 on the security of a ship's mortgage signed by Shackleton's attorneys in London. Sir Douglas Mawson (he had been knighted in May 1914) was able to confirm that he had been paid £3,000 for the vessel by Shackleton and that it was free of mortgage.[17] In the meantime, £500 had been sent from England, but on 10 December Mackintosh cabled 'cannot sail without £200', which resulted in this further sum also being sent.[18]

On 14 December, Wellington solicitor Leonard Tripp sent a cable to Mackintosh suggesting profligacy:

> Cannot understand extra expenditure. You received one thousand, then requested further one thousand, increased five hundred without explanation, then requested seven hundred – five hundred sent; you then requested two hundred enable you to sail we sent two hundred. You have received in all two thousand four hundred . . . Awaiting fullest particulars and confirmation that you have sailed.[19]

Shackleton wanted Mackintosh to solicit gifts, including coal, but eventually he purchased 470 tons of 'very poor quality' coal and 25 tons of coke at a cost of £260.[20] He did have some success in getting other donations: the Nestlé company sent chocolate products (which were to be inadvertently left on the wharf at Sydney); Wills donated some Capstan tobacco; the Sydney Dairymen's Association gave some butter; and private gifts included jams, books and a dozen eggs.[21]

Gaze carried out a vital assessment of provisions and found shortages of flour, sugar, tea, chocolate, milk products, butter and pemmican – a standard fare for polar parties, being 'best beef with 60% of fat added'. Enquiries to Brisbane for pemmican 'similar to what Mr Bancraft used to make' brought the response that this was no longer manufactured.[22] Purchases were made of tinned meats from the Sydney Meat and Preserving Company, powdered milk from Glaxo, and five cases of Johnnie Walker Red Label whisky were added to the seventeen sent from England.

Reindeer-fur boots (finnesko) sent from England were found to be damaged by rats and moths, and could not be replaced in Australia. With the shore party now expected to number eleven, more equipment was needed to add to the existing six pairs of skis and four sledges. Supplies purchased in Sydney included soap, matches, lampwick, straw mattresses, hurricane lamps, blankets and oilskins.[23]

Stevens would later criticise Mackintosh for being 'careless in dealing with the press and keeping appointments', and for 'ungraciously' declining the suggestion of a civic reception in Sydney.[24] Mackintosh, however, did invite guests to the ship before it left Cockatoo Island, and publicly thanked the people of Sydney for their donation of a wireless for *Aurora*.[25]

On 10 December, *Aurora*, with tug in attendance, steamed ('with difficulty' owing to condenser troubles) to Pyrmont Wharf, where stores were shipped.[26] The crew was signed on for a voyage from

> Sydney to any parts or places between the limits of 90° North and 90° South latitude sailing to and fro for any period not exceeding three years or until the first arrival at Sydney after the expiry of that term . . . [The crew sails] entirely at their own risk . . . and the Expedition will not be liable for injury or death . . .[27]

The shore-party members joined the expedition at a nominal salary of one shilling per week.[28] However, an undated and unsigned agreement with Ernest Joyce indicates a salary of £250 per annum.[29] Their duties while on board *Aurora* were described as those of 'purser' or 'assistant purser', with the exception of Cope, who signed on as surgeon. In fact, the so-called 'afterguard' were in effect passengers with minor duties, such as painting, disposal of ashes and taking a turn on watch, as required.

Before sailing from Sydney, Stenhouse sighted members of the crew, on 24 hours' leave, 'in a taxi and all bound for the land of non-remembrance'. Three of the seamen were to prove him right, being absent without leave for an extra twelve hours.

The Cockatoo Island shipwrights were called in by Stenhouse to deal with some troublesome leaks near the stern of *Aurora* and cemented and tarred the rudderpost. Engineers installed the wireless system assisted by riggers, who fixed the aerials aloft. *Aurora* was then towed by tug to Circular Quay and took on supplies of coke, petrol ('benzine'), flour and other stores. 'The scientists have put in splendid work in the stores, the Padre especially distinguishing himself,' noted Stenhouse. The ship was measured for a winter awning and 'for topsails, foresail and head sails'[30] before steaming, with a tug in attendance, across the harbour to anchor in Neutral Bay, where 200 bags of coke and a quantity of benzine were taken on board.

There was an embarrassing incident when Stenhouse, accompanied by Cope and Gaze, set out across the harbour in a newly constructed motorboat, known to make sea 'like a Dreadnought'. The wind was 'blowing hard from the south and making a nasty sea' and the engine was swamped. As the launch drifted towards a rocky shore, the men's hurricane lamp extinguished and they were almost run down in the darkness by a passing ferry. A Swedish steamer came to the rescue, and Stenhouse and several of the afterguard recovered the boat at dawn in Neutral Bay.[31]

Aurora left Sydney Harbour in the early afternoon of 15 December, with passing ferries and steamers sounding their whistles. After a delay at the heads for military clearance, she then proceeded to the open sea.[32] Mackintosh sent a wireless message: 'To all kind friends, adieux. We won't forget Sydney.'[33] Stenhouse noted in his diary: 'Thank heaven, we are started on the Lone Trail.'

Several of the afterguard suffered as the ship rolled prodigiously, frequently 30 degrees in either direction, in a headwind and a long swell that lasted most of the voyage to Hobart.[34] There was an anxious time as a dozen cans of kerosene and some sheets of iron came adrift from their lashings on the deck. 'This isn't a ship, she's a jolly pendulum,' Larkman remarked to Stenhouse. The first officer, however, formed a favourable impression. 'The old packet rolls like a log … but [is] a splendid sea vessel.'[35]

The men took time to relax on Saturday evening, raising a toast to 'sweethearts and wives' and enjoying a singsong after supper.[36] As the ship approached Hobart, Stenhouse noted that 'thick weather, heavy swell and two searchlights in the neighbourhood of the Iron Pot at the entrance to Storm Bay made navigation difficult and the night an anxious one'.[37] *Aurora* passed through the harbour heads in the early hours of Sunday, 20 December, and dropped anchor at Hobart at 7.10 a.m. Later, three troopships arrived with New Zealand soldiers bound for active service, some of whom greeted *Aurora* with a haka.[38]

By good fortune, the vacant position of second officer was filled just before the Ross Sea party sailed for Antarctica. Leslie James Felix Thomson, aged 28, from Sydney, was in port on the Union Steamship Company vessel *Kakapo* and signed *Aurora*'s articles on 23 December, barely an hour before she departed.[39] He was well qualified for the job, having served in square-riggers before becoming an officer in the Merchant Marine.[40] Thomson's appointment avoided further delay, as another applicant was due to arrive in Hobart four days later.[41]

There were other last-minute additions at Hobart to *Aurora*'s complement. The cook at Hadley's Hotel, one E. D'Anglade, was 'engaged in such a manner that gave not unreasonable offence to Hadley', Stevens would later write. D'Anglade had recently served as cook on the French ship *La Curieuse* under Captain Rallier du Baty to Îles Kerguélen.[42] He was appointed as ship's steward on 23 December, the day before *Aurora* sailed, and 31-year-old Englishman and former policeman Harold Shaw was taken on as third fireman and trimmer. Stevens said that 'Mackintosh told me (and others) on several occasions that he had no authority to engage him [Shaw] or such a numerous crew'.[43]

After Sunday lunch, a large party went ashore and drove to the Taroona

Quarantine Station, where Ninnis, Wild and the dogs were found to be in fine heart. Ninnis noted: 'Aurora is refitted throughout. I hear made comfortable. Lit by electric light too!'[44] Welcome mail from home greeted Hayward when he returned to the ship late that evening.[45]

While the ship was docked in Hobart, carpenters were engaged to erect dog kennels, upgrade the wardroom and help prepare her for sea. Local engineers installed new bilge pumps, as the stokehold plates had been awash by the time the ship reached Tasmania. Some 80 tons of stores, offloaded from Ionic and held in a warehouse and cold store, were taken on board, as were about 50 sheep, half of which were destined for the recently established Australian meteorological station at Macquarie Island.[46] Joyce put in a 48-hour unbroken effort assisting Stenhouse as final preparations for sailing were made.[47] The crew was given a night's leave, causing Stenhouse to ruminate: 'Drink is a curse . . . but I suppose they will be better after a blow-out . . . can't blame them – they have worked well and proved their mettle.' The night watchman was found intoxicated and unfit for duty.[48]

When Aurora had been in Hobart early in November, the Governor of Tasmania, Sir William Macartney, and his wife had expressed a wish to meet the ship's officers on their return.[49] Thus, on 22 December, Lady Macartney and her children came on board and presented the expedition with a framed portrait of her brother the late Captain Robert Falcon Scott, who had died in Antarctica two years earlier.[50]

On the evening of 23 December, the ship left the wharf and anchored in the bay for the night. 'Had rather an exciting few minutes getting her head turned round and nearly took a piece off the end of the new wharf,' noted Thomson in the first entry in his diary. The following morning Aurora took on board Ninnis and Wild and their 26 charges at the quarantine station. The muzzled dogs 'looked in excellent trim and as keen as mustard', noted Stenhouse. They joined a Greenland samoyed ('a pukka Esquimau', according to Stenhouse) named Conrad, from a litter born on Amundsen's ship Fram on her return to Hobart two years earlier. It had been purchased only a day or so earlier by Joyce, and, such were the parlous finances of the party, the purchase price of £5 was met by a deposit of £2, with the balance payable after the expedition. The dog could be returned if found to be unsatisfactory.[51]

Late on Christmas Eve, the ship passed the Iron Pot and by 9.15 p.m. the Tasman Island lighthouse was astern.

The other ITAE ship, *Endurance,* had sailed from the whaling port of Grytviken, South Georgia, bound for the Weddell Sea, almost three weeks earlier, on 5 December. Whalers had reported very bad ice conditions in the Weddell Sea, and Shackleton realised that the proposed trans-continental land journey could not happen during the first summer. He wrote: 'It seemed to me hopeless now to think of making the journey across the continent . . . as the summer was far advanced and the ice conditions were likely to prove unfavourable.'[52] H. R. Mill, in his 1923 biography of Shackleton, maintained that 'the decision was sent home in time to reach the *Aurora* before she sailed for the Ross Sea.'[53] However likely it may be that Shackleton would try to send such crucial information to Mackintosh, there is no evidence that he received it and Shackleton does not mention it in his 1919 book. Rather, he wrote:

> I had told Captain Mackintosh that it was possible the trans-continental journey would be attempted in the 1914–15 season in the event of the landing on the Weddell Sea coast proving unexpectedly easy, and it would be his duty, therefore, to lay out depots to the south immediately after his arrival at his base. I had directed him to place a depot of food and fuel-oil at lat. 80° S. in 1914–15, with cairns and flags as guides to a sledging party approaching from the direction of the Pole. He would place depots farther south in the 1915–16 season.[54]

As *Aurora* set sail from Hobart, *Endurance* was negotiating the ice of the Weddell Sea, and her carpenter, Harry Macnish, recorded in his diary: '. . . tomorrow Christmas. I think we are drawing near the end of the pack as it is fine and open. Now we are doing 7 knots all afternoon . . .'[55]

In anticipation of *Aurora*'s sailing, the Royal Society of New South Wales had a few weeks earlier resolved that

> Captain Mackintosh and his brave comrades may be able to join forces with those of the leader and share in this great journey for the honour of the Flag and for the Advancement of Science. Most heartily do we wish God-speed and a safe return to every member of the expedition.[56]

Despite these sentiments, on the day of the ship's departure, the Ross Sea party, in their old whaler and with their farmyard of animals on deck, seemed to have been forgotten. Stenhouse had been moved to write the previous night: 'No one cares a "hang" about this Expedition . . . a few loafers and others were the only people on the wharf when we left.'[57]

CHAPTER FOUR

Voyage to the ice

O N CHRISTMAS DAY 1914, the first day of the voyage for the 28 men of *Aurora*, the weather was fine and by noon the ship had made 111 miles southwards.[1] The Padre held a communion service, wireless messages of greetings were sent and the cook prepared 'a grand Christmas dinner'.[2] In the evening a hearty session of music and song in the wardroom, decorated with ship and sledge flags, concluded with the singing of the national anthem. Bosun Paton considered it the happiest Christmas of his life.

In favourable winds, *Aurora* reached Macquarie Island four days later.[3] When the weather allowed, lunch was taken on deck. Larkman and Donnelly worked twelve-hour shifts in the engine room 'on those rare days when nothing went wrong'. The five seamen responsible for working the ship – Warren, Atkin, Downing, Kavanagh and Glidden – shared three four-hour watches each night from 8 p.m.

The non-sailors on board took up various tasks. Richards volunteered as a greaser and was fascinated to see the piston guides move against the rolling of the ship. Helping to trim coal to the bunkers, he observed water coming through the ship's seams.[4] Ninnis, working on an erratic lighting system, noted: 'Frequently we ship considerable quantities of water but there is no question about the seaworthiness of the old *Aurora* . . . very little leaks, rides well . . . but she does throw things and us about a bit!'[5] The afterguard also helped with meteorological readings and had the four-hourly task of hoisting ashes from the stokehold, suffering blistered hands and strained tempers in the process. 'Even [the Padre] assists to convey an eloquent stream of exhortations down the ash hoist when things go wrong . . .'[6]

Jack enjoyed 'hauling on the halyards', and Stevens assisted the steward in 'peggy duty', serving meals and cleaning up afterwards. Ninnis felt it was 'not cricket' for some of the shore party (himself exempted, 'being in the engine room') to 'systematically shirk duty aloft and sail drill generally'.[7]

Wireless communication was possible during hours of darkness, but all war news was suppressed because of censorship.[8] Stevens put a tow net over the side for marine samples and took some deep-sea soundings.

A westerly storm brewed as the ship hove to off Macquarie Island at night-fall on 29 December. Because there was no light on the island to guide *Aurora* to anchorage, engines were stopped and the ship's head was held to the wind 'under lower topsail'. Despite anxious times as she drifted in heavy seas, by 2 a.m. there was sufficient daylight to sight the Judge and Clerk Islands, which stood 'like grim sentinels . . . a bleak, treacherous place . . . seas were dashing and spraying to a tremendous height'.[9] The ship rode out heavy squalls in full gale conditions and by 5.40 a.m. she was in the comparative calm of North East Bay, at the northern tip of the island. By evening the storm had abated sufficiently to allow the ship's boat, with stores aboard, to reach the beach through heavy kelp beds.

Three 'Crusoes' (as described by Stenhouse) greeted the seafarers when they reached shore. These men were in charge of the Macquarie meteorological station that had been established by Mawson three years earlier, and taken over by the Australian government in November 1913.[10] Two of them, J. Ferguson and F. J. Henderson, had been due to leave two months earlier but remained on the island owing to a last-minute change of plan and did not return on the Commonwealth Fisheries Investigation ship *Endeavour*, which subsequently disappeared with the loss of 21 lives.[11] Ferguson, a black-bearded Scot, and *Aurora*'s Alexander Stevens, kinsmen on this windswept, craggy seascape, struck up an immediate rapport.[12] Three hands from the ship went ashore to kill fur seals and elephant seals on nearby beaches to supplement food supplies.

Mackintosh, in a letter home from this outpost, expressed an awful realisation: 'We have no ski boots which have been paid for . . . £65 spent, hindrance now caused.'[13] A Sydney manufacturer was to supply 50 pairs of boots and, according to Stevens, Mackintosh had been told they were on board, but the day after the party had reached Hobart, Robson, the supplier, had cabled Mackintosh: 'Wireless if pleased with footwear. Sending 20 pairs to Hobart.'[14] However, the Ross Sea party departed the day before this consignment was due.

The offloading of stores and sheep at the meteorological station was completed by midmorning on New Year's Eve. Paton wrote: 'We steamed away from the island, dipping our ensign and tooting our whistle by way of farewell to the lonely inhabitants of the island.'[15]

The New Year was 'let in in good old Scotch fashion in the ward room, having had some kind of gentlemen's concert and a wee drop of something hot to keep the chill out of our hearts',[16] noted Thomson. The seamen in their fore-castle quarters did not fare so well, as the bosun lamented:

The first time in my life that I have seen New Year's Day pass without being recognised which to me coming from the land of the thistle, was not far short of a crime. Not even a drink, not even a plum pudding . . . 'tis true we were not asked to work, but we could only lie in our bunks and think how happy other people were.[17]

The first few days of 1915 saw *Aurora* make good progress in strong winds and heavy seas. 'The ship is bowling along with 9 knots with the help of her engines which race unmercifully as she lifts her stern to the gigantic rollers.'[18] Albatrosses, mollymawks and petrels, the sentinels of these southern waters, were seen in abundance.[19] Seas occasionally broke over the ship, so oil was spread in an attempt to calm the water, but to little avail. The remaining sheep were at first sheltered below the decks to lessen their misery from constant soaking, but were then slaughtered some weeks ahead of schedule. Their carcasses were placed in a refrigerated 'ice house' and their pelts retained to make into footwear to substitute for the missing boots.[20]

Chained to their kennels on the forward deck, the dogs had a miserable time of it. Minus was strangled on his collar, and another broke a leg. Oscar, already recognised as one of the party's 'best dogs', suffered a violent fit. Cope diagnosed a difficulty with the dog's scrotum and, despite a gloomy prognosis, carried out a successful procedure. Convalescence would render this dog out of action for the first season's sledging.

With the ship making approximately 160 miles a day southwards, hours of darkness rapidly reduced.[21] Ninnis and Hooke fixed a faulty wireless generator in time, before the ship got beyond range, for Mackintosh to send the last messages as *Aurora* crossed latitude 60° South. Heavy seas and the rolling ship caused Thomson to note: 'There is not much comfort to be found anywhere, even in our bunks. We could hardly keep from pitching out on to the floor and some of our gentlemen passengers looked very displeased.'[22] Heavy seas occasionally flooded Mackintosh's cabin, near the bridge, and the galley and caused great difficulties for the steward ferrying food to the wardroom, situated aft. Wise, the ship's cook, proved temperamental, at times reporting sick, though Cope examined him and could find nothing wrong. D'Anglade substituted to good effect, with Stevens then acting as steward.[23]

Mackintosh devised a competition to 'invent a patent ski boot, to serve in place of the ones left behind'. This was an extraordinary and desperate prelude to a major polar trek. 'We are trying rope soles and canvas uppers lined with skins of sheep,' recorded Ninnis. Larkman proposed a sheet-metal sole. The sewing machine was located under some butter cases, and while Joyce and Wild cut and sewed, others made the rope material, or sennit.[24]

The officers issued woollen Jaeger clothing as temperatures dropped, the first iceberg being sighted on the evening of 3 January. *Aurora* passed through loose pack ice, with the scientists keeping lookout on the forecastle head in driving sleet, then proceeded under sail only, in a belt of brash ice some 'half a mile wide'.[25] She negotiated an extensive ice field for a day or so, with the winds rising to the force of a moderate gale, and by noon on 5 January was south of the Antarctic Circle, at 66° 33' S. Mackintosh described a startling change in conditions that followed: '. . . light westerly air, smooth sea, clear horizon – no ice in sight. In fact we might be doing a yachting cruise in the Mediterranean in summer time.'[26] The midnight sun was a novelty for most of *Aurora*'s complement, and men and dogs revelled in its warmth and the steadiness of the ship.

The first glimpse of Antarctica showed up to starboard in the form of the snow-covered Admiralty Range, with Mt Sabine '10,000 feet high standing out in prominence like an immense sentinel to the south'.[27] As *Aurora* sailed southwest towards the Victoria Land coastline, Mackintosh recorded: 'Numerous whales have been spouting about us. On the skyline, jets of vapour showed in mirage, appearing like fountains in the distance.' The stunning scene continued as Coulman Island, some 80 miles way, stood out against the skyline in the early hours of 8 January. The rich tones of Italian tenor Enrico Caruso wafting from a gramophone that had been positioned on deck added a surreal touch.

The rapid progress of the ship offset time lost in Australia. On 8 January, Mackintosh announced the composition of four teams, each of three men, and a food ration of 35 ounces per man per day. The first objective was to lay a depot at Minna Bluff (usually called simply 'the Bluff') about a hundred miles from base. Joyce with the two Australians Gaze and Jack would be first away, and Stevens, Hayward and Cope would make up the second party. Ninnis, Hooke and Richards would have the task of operating the Girling motor sledge. The fourth party would comprise Mackintosh, Spencer-Smith and Wild.[28]

Ninnis had doubts that they would have time to lay depots to the Beardmore Glacier in the first year. He considered the dogs would take 'three weeks at least' to recover from the voyage, including the effects of 'sore feet from salt water',[29] though now the ship was in calmer waters there was a chance for the kennels to dry out. As *Aurora* made good progress through the Ross Sea, Thomson wrote:

> The sea is smooth as oil with just a slight head swell, which makes the vessel pitch as gracefully as a dancing-girl. The weather is so mild that it is almost impossible to believe a person is really in the Antarctic. I have felt as cold in Sydney on a winter's morning as I do this morning.[30]

During working hours all efforts were directed towards sledging preparations and making canvas boots. 'Our decks are more like a midshipman's chest,' noted Paton. Mackintosh, with assistance from Ninnis, gave an evening lecture on navigation.[31]

As the ship made for Cape Crozier, where the fibro-concrete hut was to be offloaded, first Franklin Island and then Beaufort Island were sighted in the early hours of 9 January off the starboard bow. Later in the day, Mt Erebus and Mt Terror were visible to the south at 80 miles distance. After steaming through numerous small bergs for most of the afternoon, *Aurora* passed close to a large Adélie penguin rookery near the cape, 'which hitherto had not been recorded'.[32] The ship stopped at 5.30 p.m. near the 'Great Ice Barrier' and a six-man landing party led by Stenhouse set out in a boat loaded 'with the hut in sections and a few stores'.[33]

This party had a fortunate escape before they even attempted a landing. 'Scarcely had we gone 200 yards when a huge part of the Barrier, under which we had just pulled, collapsed into the sea. Stenhouse, our Chief Officer, estimated it at almost 3,000 tons weight.'[34]

The party initially endeavoured to scale a steep ice foot under the cliffs, but Joyce and Stenhouse then succeeded in cutting steps onto a ledge between the cliffs and the ice, and followed this around for some distance until it became impassable. On retracing their steps, Stenhouse fell into a small crevasse but was not injured. In the meantime, the rest of the party had returned to the ship, which had been manoeuvred closer to shore but soon became engulfed in a thick fog.

> We knew we were heading towards the Barrier, but we did not think we were so close until the ice cliffs showed up right ahead. The engines were put astern but refused to answer and the ship crashed up against the ice cliffs and broke the jib boom off short but did not do anything serious and after an hour's work we had the broken spar and gear aboard.[35]

Aurora's bow had ridden up on the ice before the boom snapped, making 'a crack like a rifle shot'. As the vessel slid back into the water, 'a great mass of ice weighing many tons came crashing down missing the bow of the vessel by a hair's breadth'.[36] Richards would later recall that the dogs at their chains set up 'a tremendous howl'.[37]

After Joyce and Stenhouse came back on board, Mackintosh abandoned the attempt to offload the hut and sailed westwards. When heavy pack ice was encountered, anchors were put out, a good quantity of ice was taken on board for drinking and refrigeration purposes, and some ski practice was undertaken. The Padre held a well-attended Sunday service. 'It was in the nature of a Thanksgiving for our safe passage and good weather. Sincerely appreciated by all,' noted Ninnis. Mackintosh described the scene from the deck:

... masses of ice as far as the eye can see, Erebus and Terror on our port side, white and majestic with a veil of light cirrus cumulus cloud shielding them wholly from view. Beaufort Island is on our starboard side – black and a contrast to the white surroundings. From the shadow of Erebus a white sheet is showing like glass, over the water, from the dizzy whiteness.[38]

Some of the men passed their spare time shooting at the prolific wildlife. 'We have been amusing ourselves by killing penguins and gulls and there are some very good shots amongst the chaps on board.'[39] These birds provided welcome variety to the crew's menu.

After several days the pack ice loosened somewhat and *Aurora* pushed her way up McMurdo Sound. 'She took everything, either shoving it out of her way, or plumping down on top of it with a thud, which sent everything shimmering throughout the ship.'[40] Thomson sought to coax one of the seamen to resume his work when he refused to go aloft because it was 'too cold'. He changed his mind when brought before Mackintosh, 'his only excuse being that he could not do himself justice as a sailorman in such weather'.[41] There was a minor hitch when the engine-room telegraph broke down and messages had to be relayed down from the bridge.

By 14 January, the ship was within six miles of Cape Royds, with ice blocking further progress. After being carried some ten miles northwards, by early morning on 16 January *Aurora* was near Cape Bernacchi, on the western side of McMurdo Sound. She was worked into clear water and, by 5.45 a.m., was at the ice foot off Cape Evans. *Aurora* had arrived at Ross Island after a record-breaking southward voyage.[42]

Meanwhile, in the Weddell Sea, Shackleton had reached the coastline of Antarctica near the Dawson-Lambton Glacier and would later regret not setting up base there rather than pressing southwards to his preferred destination of Vahsel Bay.[43] This decision would also render the work of his support party in the Ross Sea unnecessary, as it meant that the transcontinental journey would be abandoned and, eventually, the survival of the *Endurance* men would become Shackleton's desperate objective.

Mackintosh, Joyce, Spencer-Smith and Stevens set off on ski to investigate the hut left at Cape Evans by Scott's party two years earlier. Outside were stacks of stores and equipment, including sledges. The pony stables, smelling 'like any old farm stable', were partially filled with ice, and the windows of the hut were shuttered. Aided by candlelight, the party found numerous items of discarded clothing and, importantly, a quantity of ski boots. Mackintosh took possession of official accounts of the Scott expedition left by the men who had embarked on *Terra Nova*, and his party returned to the ship with a sledge loaded with clothing, boots and 'quite a number of other curiosities'.[44] After the usual Saturday night toast to 'sweethearts and wives', the Skipper proposed a toast to the Ross Sea party's 'first landing'.

The wind freshened overnight and by morning a large quantity of ice had broken away, enabling the ship to approach close to the shore. Measurements by Thomson, at the stern using a sounding machine, and Paton, on the bow using a hand lead, indicated a rapid reduction in water depth, and *Aurora* was suddenly stuck on a shoal. However, fourteen hours later she floated free, undamaged, on a rising tide.[45] *Terra Nova* had also run aground on a shoal in the same vicinity four years earlier.[46]

Mackintosh took advantage of *Aurora*'s stranding to offload stores at Cape Evans. The crew worked one of the ship's 'whale boats', and 'the scientists' another, in friendly rivalry. The working parties bagged what Paton described as '5 tons' of coal but, as recorded by Thomson, was likely to have been a third less than this, and stacked it on the beach to the west of the hut 'well above the high water mark'.[47] The men struggled with the heavy load over loose volcanic stone to place it high on the beach. They also landed a quantity of kerosene and benzine.

Later the men were allowed to visit the Cape Evans hut, Larkman taking 'as a keepsake' a leather belt off the bunk formerly occupied by Captain Lawrence Oates of Scott's southern party.[48]

Mackintosh planned to depot sufficient stores to last twelve men for six months southwards of the cape, preferably at Hut Point, the base established during the *Discovery* expedition and used as an essential shelter and staging post on the *Nimrod* and *Terra Nova* expeditions.

Aurora left Cape Evans on 18 January but was soon held up in the ice near Tent Island. Apparently overlooking his flirtation with disaster at Cape Bird in January 1909, Mackintosh decided he should send a sledging party to Hut Point, a distance of eleven miles over sea ice. Chosen from many volunteers, the final party comprised Stenhouse, Joyce, Stevens, Hayward, Wild and Gaze, all except Joyce sledging novices.

Taking a sledge, tent, Primus and what Larkman described as 'one day's grub', the party set off from the ship on ski, but without dogs, their departure at 9.50 p.m. being recorded on 'the cinematograph' by Spencer-Smith.[49] The ice conditions proved difficult and Joyce and Stenhouse, in the lead, soon went through a crack in the sea ice up to their knees. After this pair had partially thawed out in the tent over a brew of tea, the party pushed on. Many hours later they had still not reached their destination. Stenhouse wrote: '5.30 a.m. Ice becoming broken; encountered much sastrugi and bare patches of ice; hard going; took skis off.' To the men's dismay, there was open water for 'about 100 yards', blocking access to Hut Point Peninsula. They skirted around this until they found an ice crack, which they just managed to bridge with the sledge. Gaze fell into the water up to his neck and, when rescued, started shivering uncontrollably. He would later recall this as the worst moment of his time in Antarctica.[50] Fortunately, the travellers were not far from the hut, but on arrival found the entrance blocked by an accumulation of snow and ice. They smashed a window on the western side to gain entry. Stalactites of ice hung from the ceiling and there was a thick coating of ice on the floor. The stench of seal blubber permeated the bleak structure, in which Scott's men had contrived an inner hut made of packing cases and had constructed a rough stove from a kerosene tin and firebricks. Gaze found sufficient discarded clothes to change his sodden and frozen gear. They lit the stove, but smoke filled the hut and temporarily drove all but Stenhouse and Stevens outside. As a storm detained them, the men took turns to rest in two sleeping bags found at the hut. A stores tally revealed a useful quantity of food and supplies, including cocoa, coffee, dried mixed vegetables, sledging biscuits and pemmican, as well as cigars.[51]

The party also found a stores tally book belonging to Henry ('Birdie') Bowers of the *Terra Nova* expedition, and a Wolsey jersey bearing Oates's name, which Hayward took back to the ship as a gift for Spencer-Smith.[52] Hayward walked to the top of nearby Observation Hill and was thus the first visitor to view the jarrah cross erected to the memory of the Scott party by their fellow expedition members.[53]

The weather and ice conditions improved markedly on 21 January. The men nailed up the hut after writing their names on a wall near the blubber stove,[54] and returned to the ship across rough ice without further mishap. The blizzard conditions during the previous two days, together with the lack of a good anchorage, had forced Mackintosh and Thomson to rely on the ship's engines, at the cost of valuable coal supplies. Supplies of water had run out and the Hut Point party had to wait for some hours until more ice was taken on board before they could enjoy the luxury of hot water.[55] Hayward noted: 'A good sleep and a good meal put us on terms with ourselves and the prospect of our long journey to the Bluff Depot appears not so formidable.'[56]

Mackintosh was anxious to start the sledging immediately, having been directed by Shackleton 'to place a depot of food and fuel-oil at 80° S. in 1914–15, with cairns and flags as guides to a sledging party approaching from the direction of the Pole.'[57] The confusion about Shackleton's intentions was apparent. Although Joyce suggests in an account written, it would seem, contemporaneously that Shackleton's 'plan of campaign' was not to cross in the first season,[58] Ninnis noted: 'His last words, in letter, were that he could probably do so and it has been so fine he may be coming already. If so it is a bad lookout, as our delay has altogether stopped the chance we had of meeting him.'[59]

As something of a bad omen, the dog Jackie, dubbed the 'leader of the middleweights' by Ninnis and Wild in Tasmania, was accidentally strangled, reducing the pack's number to 24. Some of the dogs were sick, so Mackintosh regrouped the remaining animals into two teams under his and Joyce's control.[60]

Members of the sledging parties were issued Burberry and Jaeger clothing,[61] and provisions for the depot-laying trek were weighed and placed in linen and canvas bags. Mackintosh had carefully calculated a scheme of weights and distances to depot supplies for the transcontinental party at the Bluff and then at 80° South.[62] His plan required 880 pounds to be transported by four teams to the Bluff depot. Allowing an average trip of ten miles a day, the 200-mile journey 'out and home' to the Bluff would take twenty days, with one party then taking a similar length of time to travel the extra distance to and from 80° South. After allowing for supplies consumed by the depot-laying parties, this would result in 350 pounds (160 man-days) at the Bluff and 220 pounds (100 man-days) at 80° South. As further back-up, the first party, under Joyce's command, would have time for a second return trip to the Bluff, and the motor party would perhaps prove to be effective but was an unknown factor.

Mackintosh assumed that a man could pull 100 pounds, and a dog, 80. Thus, a party of three men and nine dogs had a theoretical capacity of 1,000 pounds. Although he allowed a small margin in calculating a sledge weight of 900 pounds, the total included only a pound of rations (comprising 'Spratts dog cakes' and 'dog pemmican') per animal per day. This would prove to be a disastrously meagre formula.

The dogs had enjoyed two pounds of meat per day at Tasmania, and some seal meat had supplemented their shipboard diet of biscuits and pemmican.[63] Scott had found a ration of one and a half pounds of dog biscuits to be quite inadequate.[64] For Mackintosh to have increased his dogs' rations to even that level would have required a further 360 pounds of loaded weight, equivalent to the total supplies his plan envisaged being left at the Bluff for Shackleton's party.

On the eve of departure of the first sledging party, Mackintosh decided he needed more supplies from Scott's reserve of stores, so *Aurora* steamed back to Cape Evans through scattered ice floes. Thomson attempted a further tally of stores in the environs of the hut, concluding that to do the job properly would take 'at least a week'. Pemmican, chocolate and bamboo poles were retrieved before the ship edged southwards to drop off the sledging party.

Spencer-Smith found time for reflection as the various parties made their preparations. On 23 January, he wrote: 'Turned out at 4.45 for watch – glad of the opportunity to say M[orning] P[rayer] which I have been neglecting lately in the general bustle and confusion . . . A bright cold morning; killer whales cruising round and waking the penguins . . .'[65] On the voyage south, he had conscientiously worked in his tiny darkroom for up to fifteen hours a day, developing black-and-white photographic plates and films and cinematic films, and experimenting in colour photography. Larkman had made him a 'very neat sky shade' for his Kodak lens, and Atkin had kept him supplied with fresh water. The Padre packed his Kodak camera, along with 72 films and 'also Sten[house]'s little camera and 64 films', and, before leaving the ship, enjoyed 'a splendid bath' in the darkroom[66] – his first since leaving Sydney and the last he would have for two months.

The customary Saturday night gathering in the wardroom was a time to pause and wish the sledging parties well. Mackintosh wrote: 'We toasted Joyce's health at dinner this evening. Every one is keen to start sledging, and I am most anxious to make a start in order to do something towards our part in the Expedition.'[67]

CHAPTER FIVE

Laying the Bluff depot

ERNEST JOYCE'S sledging party, comprising himself, Jack and Gaze, left
Aurora on the afternoon of 24 January 1915. It was the dogs' first run after
being on board the ship for a month. Joyce and Wild (for Mackintosh) had
selected the teams by lot, Joyce's team being considered the better, although the
Skipper had reservations: 'Most of his dogs are fighters.' Anticipating difficulty
with the animals, he detailed Spencer-Smith, Richards, Larkman and Hooke to
accompany Joyce's party for the first five miles of the journey across the sea ice.[1]
As he watched the party leave the ship, Mackintosh reported that

> Nigger made a splendid leader and as soon as he was traced on to the sledge, was
> all ready, legs spread out in the orthodox fashion . . . when once the order was
> given to start they made a wild dash, ran into each other and furiously bit their
> partners which brought the sledge to a standstill. Another try was then made after
> adjusting the tangle they had put themselves into. The method was tried then of
> each man leading a dog, which went well at first: but again, a bundle of dogs fight-
> ing in their keenness to be off again occurred. A third and fourth try and then at
> last with three men sitting on the sledge they went off fairly respectfully. A parting
> shout and three cheers, and then they gradually were specks in the distance.[2]

After travelling about four miles, the men stopped for a brew of tea and a
rest before the support party returned to *Aurora*. 'We mutually took photos and
we cheered them farewell,'[3] wrote Larkman.

The dogs had too much pulling power for the load of less than 550 pounds,
but it was intended to pick up additional stores at Hut Point. Gaze, somewhat
prophetically, wrote: 'This weight will steady the dogs down and knock any
fight out of them'.[4]

The sledgers reached Hut Point at 11 p.m. in a state of exhaustion and
camped in the *Discovery* hut. The dogs were pegged out in their harnesses, and
some were muzzled. Gaze recorded the day's work with evident satisfaction:
'After some cocoa and sardines we all turned in feeling jolly happy and prepared to do full justice to an A1 sleep.'[5] When he went to feed the dogs in the

morning, however, he found Dasher 'quite dead and stiff', Scotty maimed and Hector with a badly bitten ear.[6]

Despite this setback for the first sledging party, Joyce impressed his novice companions. Jack marvelled at his great capacity as a leader 'not only on account of his genial personality and unselfishness but on account of the care and thought exercised in everything pertaining to our party'.[7]

The ice was too dangerous and the weather too threatening for the men to move from the hut on the following day, but they enjoyed a plentiful supply of food, tobacco and magazines from earlier expeditions. During a lull in the storm they walked to the Gap, a low saddle south of the hut on the spur of Observation Hill, and saw 'hundreds of seals' near a large ice crack: a likely sign, according to Joyce, that the ice was unsafe.

After two days the weather cleared and the party set out from Hut Point. As planned, they took on more provisions, which resulted in their sledge load increasing beyond the limit of 900 pounds contemplated by Mackintosh. The additional 200 pounds of dog biscuits, 170 of general stores and 70 of kerosene, combined with the existing load, tallied about 1,000 pounds.[8] Gaze wrote:

> Got off at 9 a.m., and had a ripping start down the slope from the hut. All went beautifully for about a mile and we were congratulating ourselves at getting through so easily . . . then we struck it properly; slush up to our knees. The dogs refused to pull . . . It really broke our hearts, for we'll pull and pull, then look round and find the dogs calmly looking on – how we cursed the swines . . .[9]

The soft ice conditions forced the men to unpack the sledge several times and relay the load forward. Joyce, in harness leading the team of eight dogs in place of the dead dog, fell through the ice but was quickly rescued by his companions. The sledge at first could not be moved and the men were in a dangerous position on the sea ice abreast of Cape Armitage. They prospected on ski and, in Gaze's words, found a 'sort of a pathway'. When the party paused for lunch and pitched the tent, Joyce changed from his wet clothes. 'The tent was pretty high,' he confessed.[10]

After a day's march, estimated by Jack as 'about three miles at the outside', the men were forced to chance their luck and camp on the sea ice, something Joyce said he had never done before because the ice could break up and drift out to sea. When Hector was again the victim of an attack, the men rushed to separate the dogs and thrashed the culprits 'with the Greenhide, until we couldn't lift our arms'.[11]

In the meantime, the second sledging party, of Mackintosh, Wild and Spencer-Smith, with nine dogs and a support team, had set out from the ship to travel to Hut Point on 25 January.

At 7 p.m. all was ready and shortly we started off. All hands came on to the ice to see us away, and lend a hand at the last lashings on the sledge, adjust the dogs' harness and keep them also from fighting . . . When all was prepared a parting handshake all round, a shout and we were off.[12]

This would be Mackintosh's last contact with *Aurora*.

After about two miles the weather deteriorated and Cope, Richards and Donnelly turned back to the ship. Stenhouse, now in charge of *Aurora* in Mackintosh's absence, was glad to see their safe return at 8.45 p.m. Light snow was falling in a moderate southerly wind and he had been anxious that the escorting party might lose their way or be caught out on dangerous ice without shelter.[13]

Mackintosh proceeded as hard as he could, anxious to get to the safety of the hut, but after a further five miles and with visibility reduced to zero, he reluctantly decided to camp. 'It was against my wish to do this as I did not like the idea of a "pitch" in sea ice, especially at this season when there is a danger of the ice breaking out.' On board the ship Stenhouse was also concerned: 'By midnight the wind had increased to [force] 4 with heavy snow and I feel apprehensive about the Captain's party as the ice is beginning to break up.'[14] He rated the prospects of getting *Aurora* to Hut Point over the following few days as 'good'.[15]

Setting out again, Mackintosh's men soon became disorientated. Their compass was of no assistance to them 'owing to dip',[16] and Mackintosh's Arrowsmith chronometer had stopped.[17] In a season of perpetual daylight, it was easy to lose track of time.

Another camp was established and domestic activities brought some comfort to the wayward party. The new tent was proving a success, Wild noting that it was 'easier to put up than the pole tents'.[18] The Padre recorded the scene:

The dogs at once snuggled into the snow and slept, while we unpacked the sledge, pitched the tent, with snow shovelled all around, got the Primus working and the hoosh water on the go. The hoosh was very thin, but quite acceptable as we have had no food since lunch at 1 p.m. Also had tea and several smokes and are now in sleeping bags about to fall off for eight hours. Everything is very cosy: temperatures 28°F and snow falling.[19]

On 26 January, Mackintosh's party 'plugged on', with two or three halts, in an almost continuous blizzard. Hut Point was still obscured, and when their sledge-meter showed thirteen miles 50 yards, four miles in excess of the estimated distance from ship to hut, they camped again, still lost. The surface had changed considerably, causing Spencer-Smith to wonder if they had 'got onto the Barrier'.[20] When the weather cleared on the following day, he observed: 'We found we had been steering a course diametrically opposite to the true one: we had been heading for White and Black Island and Hut Point lay four or five miles to our left. Had we not needed stores, we were on a good line for the Bluff!'

The weary dog team, on a restricted diet because Mackintosh planned to pick up more food at Hut Point, had eaten only 'two biscuits for 48 hours'. When Jock fell down and let himself be dragged along on his side, he was given a ride to the hut on the sledge. The Padre regarded the dog's antics as a mischievous 'dirty trick',[21] but he and Wild put on the man-harnesses and started hauling with the team.[22]

When the Skipper's men eventually reached Hut Point at 4 p.m. on 27 January, they had travelled over seventeen miles on their wayward course to achieve a trip from the ship of only half that distance in a straight line. However, they had inadvertently stumbled on a better and safer route than that taken by Joyce, towards the edge of the Barrier and thence the Bluff.

A fastidious man, Makintosh found the hut in a foul state and wrote to Stenhouse: 'Instruct other parties keep hut clean and clear up when sheltering here, expect Cope's party ... to get it in order, clean and habitable – it's anything but that now – like pigsty. Parties not to open new cases; but first to eat what's out as we have done . . .'[23] Spencer-Smith echoed this concern: 'The hut is not nearly as nice as the one at Cape Evans and is in a horrible condition of dirt and untidiness.'

The party members' duties were divided up: Spencer-Smith to be cook, Wild to look after the dogs, and Mackintosh to be navigator and handyman. The Padre noted in his diary that he had no difficulty in concocting a satisfying meal: 'Fried bacon, frozen sardines, biscuits, strawberry jam and tea – all from Scott's stores.'

While at Hut Point, Mackintosh made an important decision: 'The weather is so fine and the days so warm, we have decided to travel at night.' In this way he hoped for a better travelling surface.

Joyce returned to the hut on ski late the following morning[24] to warn Mackintosh of dangerous ice conditions ahead and to seek advice on 'the best way out of our difficulties'.[25] The Skipper told him of the better surface out towards Black Island and advised him to steer in that direction. Joyce returned to his party full of the tale of Mackintosh's wayward journey and 'simply bursting himself with laughter'.[26] His men had previously seen the others approaching Hut Point from the west, an unexpected quarter, so they knew something had not gone to plan.

Joyce, Gaze and Jack were unable to travel southwards on the 'rotting ice' and retraced their route to Hut Point Peninsula, where they experimented successfully with a lighter load and a man travelling some distance ahead instead of merely leading the dog team. Gaze wrote: 'Halted on a nice hard place for lunch at 2 p.m. Dressed Joyce's foot with vaseline and Boric Acid (bandaged). His boot had rubbed all the skin off the top of his big toe. Intend to stay on this patch until we have done some exploring and found a safe passage.' The party was now in a safer position but could not find any satisfactory route towards the Barrier despite skiing 'for miles' in all directions, radiating out from Cape Armitage.

The second party set out from Hut Point on 28 January with a load of 1,200 pounds. 'Mac says that the load is in excess of that ever drawn by a dog team,'[27] Spencer-Smith recorded. Added from supplies left at the *Discovery* hut were 250 pounds of dog biscuits, 160 pounds of sledging biscuits, five tins of kerosene, 15 pounds of crushed biscuit and a broom (an item 'overlooked when leaving the ship').[28] The Skipper considered the extra load practicable 'taking into consideration the way the dogs were pulling'. By comparison, in February 1911 Amundsen had loaded each of his sledges with 550 pounds of provisions, a total load of 717 pounds including the weight of the sledge and gear.[29]

Of the first day's travel from the hut, Wild wrote: 'We left Hut Point in grand form for about 40 yards and then it took us about 8 hours to go 400 yards. We stopped then and had tea and then started again and have come about five miles. We got here at 3 a.m. . . . .'[30]

Spencer-Smith was sent ahead to make lead tracks for the dogs, but instead went towards Joyce's camp to rendezvous with Irvine Gaze, who advanced to meet his cousin: 'I ski'd over to A.P., he came back to our camp and had pemmican. Said he'd never tasted its equal. After staying for about an hour he started back, Keith [Jack] accompanying him for a mile or so.' In an apparent reference to Mackintosh's account of the wayward trip from *Aurora* to Hut Point, Gaze added: 'A.P.'s story is rather different to the Skipper's, so I think [Mackintosh] must have been dreaming.'[31]

Mackintosh's party, resorting again to 'beating the poor beasts', at last rounded Cape Armitage, a short distance from Hut Point, past Joyce's camp. Wild and Spencer-Smith put on the man-harness to help the dogs, which, in the Padre's estimation, had 'worked excellently at the excessively heavy load'. Towser, a collie among huskies, was the exception, proving to be very lazy, though the Padre hoped he would improve 'as he is rather an attractive beastie'. Early in the morning Spencer-Smith recorded in his diary:

> We now know what utter exhaustion is! We could only do short spells, halting at hard spots – and hard spots seemed very few and far between; I was too done to pray for them! We had only about four miles, though it seemed like twenty. At last the sledge nearly capsized and stuck in a deep place, and Mac, very disappointed, decided to camp. It was 3 a.m. and felt like it![32]

Bad weather kept both parties tent-bound for the day. 'It's a curious sensation remaining silently in the bags, with just the sound of gentle snow pattering on the tent,'[33] wrote Mackintosh.

When the Skipper's party made a delayed start at 11 p.m., the extra six inches of snow that had fallen added to their difficulties:

> After the first 100 yards we, dogs and men, found it absolutely impossible to move the sledge. We tried again and again. 'Team. Come along then! What about it today? Getty-up!!!' – and she hasn't moved an inch! We used the boot, the whip, words and blandishment, but it was all in vain, and Mac had to give in to Fate, and order a relay.[34]

Mackintosh had some menacing sores on his right hand, which the Padre lanced 'and freed pus'. He then applied Boric wool and 'Borofax' and bandages. 'Gave Tonic,' he noted.[35] Before setting out from the ship, Spencer-Smith had checked the medicine chest and Cope had instructed him in the use of a hypodermic syringe.[36]

The party's progress was negligible – a little over a mile in four hours – and, like a Chinese proverb writer, Wild declared: 'Relay work no good makes you swear.'[37]

Having made little progress over six days, Joyce and his companions were also feeling frustrated. Before leaving their camp near Cape Armitage, Joyce and Jack returned to the *Discovery* hut for some further grocery pickings, taking six pounds of pemmican and five of sugar to replenish their stores. Despite the Padre's visit to their camp a couple of days earlier, they thought the other party might still be at the hut. A perplexed Jack wrote: 'They must have passed quite close to our camp as their tracks trended in our direction and it seems most strange . . . they did not let us know of their movements.'[38]

Like Mackintosh, Joyce had to relay his team's load in two lots. He now steered a westerly course direct for Black Island and, after two miles, cut across eastwards direct for the Barrier. 'Dogs pulled well, but going was awfully heavy and it took us from 1 p.m. until 6 p.m. to reach that blessed Barrier,' recorded Gaze. This was a milestone of sorts.

Returning to pick up the balance of the load, the party decided to 'take a shortcut' to visit the Skipper's camp. Jack wrote: '[We] found the Captain and Wild just starting with their first relay load to the Barrier, 1½–2 miles distant. Spencer-Smith was at the camp washing up. It seemed strange to the three of us that we were not invited to have a cup of tea . . .'[39]

Gaze does not refer to visiting the Skipper's camp. Both Spencer-Smith and Mackintosh recorded only that they heard Joyce's dogs when they both were 'turned in', and Mackintosh put on his skis and went out to see the visitors.

In taking the route they did, Joyce's men cut across ice they knew to be mushy but considered that an empty sledge would allow them to get through without difficulty. In so doing, however, they returned to the dangerous area from which they had spent the previous days trying to extract themselves. Gaze wrote:

> It very nearly proved fatal for Joyce. These blasted dogs as usual jibbed when we were in danger. Joyce threw caution to the winds, got off his skis to lead them and promptly went through up to his neck. If I hadn't been near him to lend a hand he would have gone down for keeps. The tide was extremely swift. Keith [Jack] and self had some awfully narrow shaves also, at times we were well over our boots even with our skis on. After a nerve racking hour however we managed to pull through and reached our tent at 10 p.m.; all of us pretty well fagged and jolly thankful for our luck in getting through![40]

Jack confirmed that

> but for the fact that Gaze happened to be close to [Joyce] and held out a ski stick for him to grasp, he would without the slightest doubt have gone, because as he told us later a strong current running beneath the ice simply swept his legs from under . . .

Perhaps not surprisingly, Joyce in his diary ignored the near-drowning incident. He was severely chilled and laid up for a day in adverse weather. His party was only a mile or two from the point reached seven days earlier but on a better surface and in a position to advance.

The Skipper also struggled, with minimal reward: in twelve and a half hours his men advanced only two and a half miles, although Wild recorded it as five. The dogs had been worked to exhaustion moving forward the heavy load in two trips. Mackintosh wrote: 'Our throats are hoarse – as soon as one dog appears to slacken his name is yelled out, they are doing their best, poor brutes – Jock the leader dropped out, refusing to pull. Towser, a great fat hulking animal is a fool and is a great nuisance . . .'[41] As a punishment, Jock was denied a share of a baby seal killed by Wild, and, cut adrift ('hunger may bring him to his senses'), made his way to the Joyce camp. Mackintosh's overladen party could take only limited stock from a colony of some 150 seals. The men tried seal meat but found it 'indigestible', and Spencer-Smith administered dyspepsia tablets. 'Had to deal out two Gingamint Tabs to Mac and myself tonight!'[42]

The route to the Barrier was up a gentle fifteen-foot slope from the sea ice. However, it was not without risk, as Wild discovered when he 'fell down a small crevasse with one leg only. It was about a foot wide but went down a long way.'[43]

Mackintosh's men battled on for fourteen hours to advance just two miles. 'Surface just too dreadful for words; we sink into snow, at times up to our knees, the dogs struggling out of it panting and making a real struggle!' wrote the Skipper. They ate at Scott's 'Safety Camp', which was almost buried under 57 inches of snow, and dug out a bag of oats, two cases of dog biscuits, some pemmican, seal meat, 'and last of all a Motor Car',[44] wrote the laconic Wild. An experimental Wolseley motor sledge, one of three from the *Terra Nova* expedition, had been abandoned there on 30 October 1911.[45] Mackintosh recorded in his diary that he had left a note advising the following parties that 'the provisions here were to be left intact, and if Ninnis could see any practical use in getting the motor sledge up he was to do so'.

Before turning in, the Padre read some Robert Browning poetry and from St John's Gospel. 'All the old questionings seem to come up for answer in this quiet place: but one is able to think more quietly than in civilisation.'

Joyce's party, having returned to Cape Armitage from the Barrier where they had placed a depot of stores four days earlier, could see Mackintosh's tent on the Barrier with the aid of binoculars. Jack doubled back to the *Discovery* hut to warn the following teams of the dangerous sea-ice conditions. There he found the motor party: 'Cope was in charge but I had difficulty in rousing him and giving him Joyce's message. Six of them had been man-hauling one sledge. They included Cope, Stevens, Ninnis, Hooke, Hayward, Richards. They told me the motor had shaken itself to bits just below Hut Point, where it had been abandoned.'[46]

Jack passed on news of the first two parties' progress. A day or two later, when his report filtered back to the ship by way of one of Cope's party, the death of one dog had somehow magnified into the loss of seven. Paton recorded: 'Out of the two teams of dogs seven were dead and two they had sent back to Hut Point and gone on with one dog team only.'[47]

Joyce's dogs performed 'beautifully' with a reasonable load as the party finally had an encouraging journey. They reached the Barrier by lunchtime on 1 February and 'felt very elated', wrote Gaze. Finding the abandoned Jock, they could not believe their luck: he was considered a welcome addition to their dog team in place of Dasher, killed a week earlier. Gaze wrote: 'Ski'd over and got the dog; turned out to be Jock – we hitched him up with our team and he pulled like the best. Skipper hasn't any damned idea of managing dogs, any more than he has of managing anything else.'[48] Gaze, by nature a careful and accurate man, noted that Jock had been 'tied up to a flag pole set in ice mound'. Apparently unaware of the tethering, Wild was anxiously awaiting the dog's return to the other party. 'Jock hasn't come on yet, we can see him where we left the seal. I expect he has pulled it out and is eating it.'[49] On the following day, he added, 'Jock the dog hasn't joined up yet. I expect he will join up with Joyce.'

While at Safety Camp, just a mile or two away from the Skipper, Gaze wrote:

'Found plenty of seal meat for dogs there and a note from Mac saying it wasn't to be touched – what b . . . y rot, didn't take any notice of it and gave the dogs a real good feed; they deserved it too.'[50] Joyce's men took the opportunity to raid the motor sledge from the Scott expedition, from which Jack took 'a priming can, a wrench and a sparking plug', and Gaze, some tools and a blow-lamp, 'which will come in very handy for the motor boat'.[51] They had succeeded in travelling two miles to the camp from the edge of the Barrier with a full load of 1,100 pounds, and the dogs had responded well to following the other party's trail.

With the surface hardening in the colder night, Mackintosh's team also tried hauling a full load. The Padre described what happened:

> It was cruelly hard work. Wild went in front. Mac and I harnessed up, but of course could not have our ski on as we both had to be pulling. The heartbreaking part is the preliminary 'hoicking'. Mac and I swing the sledge to get a smooth starting place and to break the frozen runners: then I heave back the team with one hand ('Jeam'), keeping up the swinging with the other: then 'Getty-up' and a mighty heave from both of us to get a slight move on (it usually takes about three repetitions of the above) and then we get a strain on our own trace – starting breathless, of course – and plug on through the yielding snow, until our combined energies, dogs and men's, give out . . . We took about three hours this afternoon to go ¾ mile!!![52]

In Mackintosh's words, the dogs were 'entirely done up, poor brutes: we want another dozen of them at least'.

On the first evening of the new month, Joyce's party set up camp alongside Mackintosh's as they were preparing to leave, and Joyce accepted his leader's challenge to race him to the Bluff. Already there had been some friendly interplay with messages in the snow, such as Wild's 'Pub ahead!'.[53]

The Padre was anticipating 'the touf-touf of Ninnis' motor' in the hope that the Girling would improve their prospects. 'If things go well with Ninnis, the motor sledge should catch us up in a day or two and alter the complexion of affairs altogether,' he wrote just a week out from base.[54]

Each party made a determined effort to pass the other as they alternated, Joyce travelling by 'day' and Mackintosh by 'night'. The better surface of the Barrier meant they could advance without having to relay. The Padre wrote:

> Joyce and co. came by at 4.15 p.m. The barking of our team woke us; and we found that our Jock had joined them, and that they had their full load and were proceeding merrily . . . We passed Joyce a little before lunchtime, amidst a tremendous howling of the combined teams. Our lot made a great spurt as we drew near and were much disappointed when we turned aside to go on. They don't like passing a depot. Almost at once we got stuck in deep snow and finally had to camp for lunch about 100 yards beyond Joyce's camp. After lunch the dogs were fractious and

Major especially – but when at last they go on the move we made splendid progress. There was quite a good crust on top of the snow, and the dogs went well: also Mac and I were able to get into our harness and do useful work on the ski. The surface was undulating and we soon found it necessary to haul like demons up the slopes, with plenty of 'getty-up' at the critical moment: the snow was inclined to be soft, on the slope. Three or four times we were stuck in these drifts and had to dig to get the sledge on an even keel for starting. We had three good sprints – 2 miles, 1 mile, 1 mile and are fairly satisfied with the work done. Given such a surface, we ought soon to be doing our daily 12 miles, or perhaps more . . . Apart from the 'hoicking' and the sprint to catch up after it, this pulling on a good surface is great fun, though the continual shouting rather takes one's breath – compare a *very* long football match at Merchiston![55]

From the other camp, Gaze noted: 'Skipper passed us about 12 p.m. last night with his full load (following our example). His dogs must have been labouring, because he was knocking hell out of them with a big stock whip. It's a pity he doesn't leave the management of them to Wild – he does know something about dogs.'[56]

Wild had to splice broken ski 'sticks' that 'had come to grief on the poor dogs', commented Mackintosh. Spencer-Smith found himself in a dilemma having to use the whip, and explained to the Skipper: 'I do feel sorry, but we have to get on and as persuasion has no effect, this is the last resort.'[57] The Padre expressed his misgivings: 'The whip should be used as sparingly as possible, at least on this team.'

On 3 February, Mackintosh's team struggled for two and a half hours to gain 150 yards with only five of their eight dogs pulling. Bobs' shoulders had worn through in patches two inches square. Spencer-Smith was sent as an envoy to Joyce's 'shack' and reclaimed Jock, although finding him in a pitiful condition and 'useless at present with sore shoulders'.[58] Gaze, however, lamented the return of the dog: 'We miss old Jock.'

By contrast, Joyce's party seemed to be having some success. Jack wrote on 4 February: 'Our dogs have pulled our load without any assistance from us, except when starting after a rest.' There was no sign of Scott's 'Corner Camp', despite a determined search by Joyce's party. 'We wish to reach there before Mackintosh's party, because of his rather shabby treatment of our party,'[59] noted Jack.

Eventually, Joyce had to abandon the injured Hector, one of his best dogs. 'Found it absolutely necessary to depot poor old Hector who can scarcely move . . . left him with a supply of biscuits for eight days,'[60] recorded Jack.

Following twelve hours behind, Mackintosh's party saw the abandoned dog, and the Padre noted: 'They have left poor Hector behind at their last camp, with a supply of food of course: but it's doubtful if he will pull through, poor chap.'[61] It was the last time Hector would be seen.

Mackintosh blamed the dogs for his party's poor progress, but Spencer-Smith disagreed. 'I am convinced that this dog team, even when at full strength, is not powerful enough for the load we are dragging unless the surface is perfect. Even when three men are hauling, it's a rare struggle to get the sledge through some of the hollows. I can't agree with Mac that the dogs are slack . . .'[62]

Canuk, a lightweight dog, 'revoked' for the first time after lunch on 4 February. 'He seemed hungry and weak. We tied him behind the sledge at first, but found that he let himself be dragged by the neck, so we put him on top of the sledge. The dogs had a well-earned extra feed tonight: they are a gallant little pack . . .'[63]

The men suspected that Canuk had been poisoned by eating faeces, or 'unconsidered trifles', to use the Padre's term. Wild also described the sorry scene. 'Canuk having a ride on the sledge again, expect we will have to kill him. Bob going along without harness, so we've only got seven dogs pulling.'[64] On the following day: 'We had to carry KK as well as Canuk today and Jock nearly done in, Bob without harness and Towser not pulling so that left four dogs pulling.'[65] Rather than kill Canuk outright, they set him free. That this 'game little dog' had lasted just eight days on the trail was the result of inadequate food.

Mistakes of the past were being repeated. Scott had lost his team of nineteen dogs, on a similar diet of biscuits, during the southern journey twelve years earlier.[66] In contrast, two members of his second expedition, Cecil Meares and Dimitri Gerof, had concocted a dog diet of melted-down seal blubber mixed with lumps of seal meat and meat from slaughtered ponies, and used it with success on a 450-mile journey.[67]

'I intend to increase their biscuits – we ought to have double the number really,' Mackintosh declared on 4 February. He called at Joyce's tent the next day and suggested that extra dog biscuits, sufficient for 26 days instead of ten, be left at the Bluff for the use of the party that was due to sledge to 80° South. This raised the ire of Joyce, who responded that this was out of the question because it would leave his own team short. He also advised the Skipper to 'use the lash as little as possible'.[68] 'This man is mad,' wrote Gaze, echoing Joyce's sentiments.[69] While Mackintosh was at Joyce's camp he inspected their load, 'which seemed less than ours by one tin of biscuits and one bag of dog-biscuits',[70] noted the Padre.

While at the tent Mackintosh took the opportunity to ask for Joyce's map because he had lost his own.[71] He advised that he would turn south towards the Bluff after lunch, and left directions for the other party to follow. In case

Joyce had not understood, the Skipper wrote messages in the snow to indicate the course he was to steer. These instructions were ignored. 'Joyce is steering NNE which is outside the course I have told him,' noted Mackintosh the following day. In fact, Joyce had spotted some big crevasses and was keeping to the east of White Island to avoid these. With his men roped together, he marked the route with a small cairn every two miles and set up some black flags.

The Skipper's party did not take such precautions. Spencer-Smith wrote: 'We are in the vicinity of the crevasses now, but are not worrying about them: the ski are long and the snowfall has been heavy.'[72]

Although Joyce did not mention it to Mackintosh, he had been feeling stiff and unwell for a few days. On 2 February, Gaze wrote: 'Joyce is not feeling too well tonight, his dip off Cape Armitage on Saturday last has given him a chill. Gave him a couple of tabloids of Eastern Syrup to buck him up.' On the following morning he added: 'Joyce feeling rotten so we slept in a bit. Gave him two Tabloids of Xaxa as he was feeling feverish.'[73] Another two days passed. 'This morning Joyce again complained of pains in back and thighs and a sore throat . . . Joyce . . . wondered if it could possibly be scurvy but symptoms of this – swollen gums and legs – are wanting in his case, thankful to say,' wrote Jack. The two Australians kept a close eye on their leader, but the party was able to advance on a 'glorious day for travelling' with the sun so warm that Jack stripped down to his singlet. Joyce showed signs of recovery, and that night Gaze administered '4 tabs of Trional to put him off'.[74]

Despite Joyce's condition, there was something to feel cheerful about. Gaze wrote on 5 February:

> Getting well up along White Island, but have so far come across no crevasses. This is absolutely a most perfect day, sun shining beautifully and you can feel that crispness in the air that makes you feel as if you could just jump out of your skin. In fact, I've never before experienced such a day, and feel it very good indeed to be alive and up and doing . . . The surface we came over this afternoon was very 'troubled' and hard; for all the world like an 'angry sea'. Dogs went A1 – Jolly good fun. By the way we easily did our longest tramp today, quite 18 miles.

The party claimed to be making good progress, but doubts were raised about the estimated distances. On 2 February, Gaze had written: 'Our B . . . sledge meter is no good, so we're dumping it.' Mackintosh was sceptical about the other party's claims:

> Joyce tells [Wild] his sledgemeter does not register sufficiently so he does not rely on it! We are amused at Joyce's miles – his 5 miles equals 1 by our sledgemeter. Consequently he reckons he does 15 miles daily, but at end of march we find it to be under 9 usually. They are more fortunate than us having a good team of dogs,

also a lighter load; we have to pull our sledge whereas his companions follow in his wake.[75]

Spencer-Smith also observed Joyce's progress with some envy: 'Joyce goes on ahead, while Irvine and Jack follow behind at some distance: no hauling, no hoicking, lucky men!'[76]

Mackintosh had promised a tot of rum to Wild and a bar of chocolate to the Padre if his party achieved twelve miles in a day. Wild wrote on 2 February: 'Seven miles today. We're bucking up. When we do 12 miles in one day we are going to splice the main brace with brandy . . .'[77]

When Wild called on Joyce's camp four days later to have 'a good yarn', he was offered a tot of rum to 'buck him up', but his anticipation was cruelly dashed when the neck of the precious bottle broke. Gaze wrote: 'Joyce was awfully cut up about this, remarking all the time that he wished he had what we had lost inside him.'[78]

Jack noted on 6 February that the lowest temperature met so far was −10°F, 'and this was when the instrument was level and fixed'. Wild reported that the Skipper's party had recently recorded −22°, though Jack found this questionable, 'for upon enquiry I found he had been carrying the instrument on the sledge when this happened'.[79] Mackintosh disregarded the thermometer four days later when he found it had obviously malfunctioned.[80] Ironically, the low temperatures did bring some relief for the travellers:

> The tops of the waves are smooth and slippery and one has to be careful on the ski. Wild had a spill today, but managed to get up without stopping the team. The general surface is well nigh perfect, and the dogs travelled well: the slippery places made it rather harder for us, but not bad. The old days of hoick and struggle are like a bad dream . . . We did not notice the cold until the wind set in, when our beards etc. (which are always thick with frost) stiffened into ice in a moment. It was quite painful once when I opened my mouth rather wide to shout and every hair on my face seemed to be tearing out at the roots![81]

As the steam from the cooker froze on the inside of their tent, it showered down like snow.

Observation Hill, sentinel of their starting point, at last was almost below the horizon. Wild wrote: 'Obs. Hill has nearly sunk out of sight. I shall be glad when it does. It's a bit painful seeing that sticking up behind us every day.'[82] Cape Crozier was clearly visible to the east. Southwards, the Bluff lay dead ahead, 'wonderfully miraged. It looks as if a huge calm lake lay in front of it.'[83]

Joyce's party, somewhat incensed to learn from Wild that the Skipper intended to take the best of their dogs from the Bluff in order to lay the depot 60 miles further south at 80°, gradually pulled ahead of the other team. 'Joyce's encampment is barely visible, about 3 miles ahead,' wrote Spencer-Smith on 7 February. This was despite Mackintosh's men making good distances over previous days: ten miles on 4 February, almost eight and a half on 5 February, eleven on 6 February, and '100 yards under 10 miles' on 7 February.[84]

'We intend today to set him a hard nut to crack,' noted Jack on 7 February. Joyce's party set out at 11 a.m. and marched for fifteen hours. From the other camp, Wild wrote: 'Haven't seen Joyce today. We've passed two of their camps so they must be doing a forced march to reach Bluff depot.' Joyce's course was not a straight line, but he 'laid the trail as a huge S', observed Spencer-Smith. Joyce now realised that night travel offered a firmer snow surface, and next day his party set out at 2 p.m. and travelled until 2 a.m.

Just as it looked as though Joyce would win the race to the Bluff, the weather turned. 'Joyce after consideration thought it best to wait and see if it would stop drifting. This drift would have got [in the eyes of] the dogs properly and they would have refused to pull.'[85]

A few miles northwards, Mackintosh tried to catch up. On 9 February, he wrote: 'Shortly after getting away the whole team began to waver, it's the drift getting in their eyes, they can't stand it, but we must shove on. First faithful KK dropped, then Bobs; we carried them on sledge but only proceeded a short distance when the drift increasing. A halt was called and camp pitched.'[86] Although they were only a mile short of Joyce's camp, the advance was not achieved without cost: that day Mackintosh found Jock dead in the snow. The Padre marked the spot with a cairn and photographed it.

Mackintosh realised that his dogs were starving. '[Jock] has been a good puller but the food has been too little for him; in fact they are all getting thin on it.' Bobs was in moribund condition and died two days later, the sentimental Padre building another makeshift headstone.[87] Both dogs, plus Canuk,[88] abandoned on 7 February, were lightweights from the Tasmanian teams. Mackintosh had noted three days earlier:

> Jock and Bobs, a breed different to the rest, having a light coat, black coloured, have not turned out as well as expected, may be alright for fast journeys of short distances with light loads, but here [are] absolutely useless, these two with Canook always keep to themselves; they are regular scavengers, eat anything, including their harness that is attached to them. They are good leaders but after short distance are knocked out; they never will rest either when they have an opportunity but walk about, yet when sledging they scrape a hole in the snow to sit down in which is most annoying.[89]

Laid up during the blizzard, with the wind cutting through their old tent, Joyce's men dozed in their sleeping bags, which in Gaze's case was 'at least six inches too short'. Gaze finished his last book and the men yarned about the war, weather, sledging, music, cards and food. Gaze could not get his feet warm, while Jack suffered frostbite to the three middle toes of his right foot after a moment of carelessness when he checked the thermometer outside. 'Joyce had to light the primus for about ¼ hour before I got them around again,' wrote Jack on 10 February.

In the other tent, the Padre noticed something more sinister: he and Mackintosh were almost certainly exhibiting the early signs of scurvy:

> No travelling today: in its place rather a hard and chilly sojourn in the sleeping bags. Dressed Mac's finger: his right ear seems affected in a similar way and the gland beneath it is also swollen. We must start the lime juice tonight. I feel sure that my toes and his hands are missing vegetables.[90]

Spencer-Smith himself had for some days nursed 'two sore heels and one sore toe'. Leather boots, remnants from the Scott expedition, were partly the problem. 'It was a struggle to get into them before the daily march.' He tried the finnesko boots, 'but I'm not sure it was worth it, as the foot-slogging was a tremendous strain'.[91] Mackintosh echoed this observation: 'Then the struggle: the boots, hard as iron, this operation takes the longest . . .'[92]

The Skipper decided that the struggling Padre should take Joyce's place in the party returning north from the Bluff. 'It's horribly disappointing, especially from my own selfish point of view as I shall not reach Scott's tent after all . . . Still, fiat voluntas Dei: no doubt it's all for the best,'[93] recorded Spencer-Smith.

Joyce's party laid a depot on 11 February. Jack, a careful recorder of fact, wrote:

> We got up this morning very early – the weather had moderated slightly. After our usual breakfast of pemmican and biscuit we continued on our way, in approximately a southerly direction in search for Scott's Bluff Depot where we were to establish the one of our own. After proceeding a couple of miles however, Joyce concluded it would still take several days searching before we could get Mt Discovery and the Bluff in transit and decided to double almost on our tracks and establish our depot at another point off the Bluff. We did this and built there a large snow cairn upon which was mounted and stayed a long bamboo pole comprising 4 flags, 1 red and 3 black.[94]

Gaze wrote: 'Up at 6 a.m. Still blowing and drifting . . . Started off at 10 a.m. weather having cleared a bit – after going for 2 hours we laid the Bluff Depot . . .'[95] Poor visibility and the lack of a sledge-meter hampered them. It did not help that they had to guess the time because the party's two watches had stopped.

Meanwhile, Mackintosh's party had breakfasted at 2 a.m. 'Left camp at 5 a.m. After an hour's march sighted a depot ahead which turned out to be

Joyce's camp. After a hard pull came up to it about 11a.m. when we pitched our tent and had lunch . . .'[96]

The Padre's record of their start was an hour earlier:

[at] about 4 a.m. . . . We soon sighted a gorgeous depot rather to the left of the course and naturally thought it was either the Discovery or the Shackleton Bluff depot . . . It took us over three hours to do the three miles, only to find that it was not the depot at all, but merely Joyce's encampment. He had to depot his stores there, having only four days food left, and was on the point of starting homeward.[97]

In accordance with instructions given by Mackintosh on the ship, the intended position of the depot was twenty statute miles from Bluff Peak with the 'little Peak on the end of Bluff in transit with Mt Discovery, (bisecting) Mt Erebus in transit with Mt Bird (if seen)'.[98] Mackintosh had stated that a good bearing for the depot was ten statute miles further out from the Bluff. This would accord with the traditional position as placed on previous expeditions. According to Wild and Jack, each from different parties, they were aiming for the position 30 miles from the Bluff.

The Skipper's party arrived on 11 February, while the others were building a depot. Joyce had laid this prematurely and, as he recognised, not in the intended position, because his supply of food for the return trip was already inadequate. He had won the race, which had not run its full course, by a few hours. [99]

CHAPTER SIX

Farthest south – 1915

M ACKINTOSH'S PLAN was to have two support parties depot 440 pounds
of supplies at Minna Bluff. Cope was to lead one party, with fellow
Britons Stevens and Hayward; and Ninnis the other, with the Australians
Richards and Hooke. However, at about the time Mackintosh left the ship on
24 January, it was decided to combine the two parties.[1]

The first team was to have been supported by eight dogs, after the two nine-
dog teams had left with Joyce and Mackintosh, but was then reduced to five
when Jacky became the third death on *Aurora*, hung by her leash. Oscar and
Buller, both 'heavyweights', were on the sick list,[2] so this left only two 'middleweights', Tiger and Bitchie (also called Beechee, possibly an Australian variant),
and the 'lightweight' bitch Nell. It was something of an irony that these five
dogs were finally left on the ship, given Hayward's status as the expedition's
official dog-driver.

The second team, 'the motor party', was in charge of a Girling motor sledge.
Built by the Dispatch Motor Co. Ltd, it was powered by a two-cylinder nine-
horsepower Coventry-Simplex engine that drove 'a large toothed wheel, 36 inches
in diameter, built up with bicycle spokes. The wheel itself [being] 20 inches
wide . . . with grooves of semi-circular section to obtain a grip on the snow.' It
was designed to tow three sledges, with a ton of equipment, at an average speed
of five miles an hour, consuming a gallon of petrol every ten miles. The sledge
had several novel features. The enclosed engine was primed by a Primus paraffin stove, and a water tank above the engine had small 'manholes' for cooking
food and melting ice for drinking water. Another tank, mounted on the side of
the water tank, kept oil liquid. A drum mounted on the front of the sledge
carried wire cable to enable the machine to negotiate steep slopes by warping.
The runners were heated by exhaust gases to form a film of water between
the sledge and the snow, thus reducing friction 'to a negligible quantity'.[3] The
Endurance party had a similar model.

Only Stevens and Hayward of the six men in the combined team had any claim to sledging experience, having made the return journey from the ship to Hut Point a week or so earlier. Thomson, now acting first mate on *Aurora*, was an interested observer of the party's preparations.

> There is great excitement among the rest of the scientific staff as they are to make up a party of six with the motor tractor if possible to land it and three sledges with provisions which are intended for the Bluff depot and also provisions for themselves and fuel for the tractor. If we get this tractor ashore safely this should be a very interesting party as they are all young men and like the rest of us except the Captain, Joyce and our Boatswain Paten [*sic*] down here for the first time. This party will be in charge of Dr Cope [*sic*] with Professor Stephens [*sic*] second in command. They are all working like demons to get ready for an early start.[4]

Stenhouse and Thomson attempted to manoeuvre the ship as close as they could to Hut Point because they could see that the ice was in bad condition. Stenhouse wrote on 28 January:

> I hope the ice goes away very soon in order that we may put the party with their motor sledge as near to the Barrier as possible. I shall certainly not risk lives by sending the party away over this thin cracking ice, if these conditions continue I shall send them away without the motor as I feel sure it would never negotiate the cracks and thin places in the sea ice.[5]

Before leaving the ship, Mackintosh had appointed his first officer leader of the expedition in case of his death.

> Dear Stenhouse,
>
> This will serve – in the event of anything happening to myself and not returning – to give you complete command and authority of this section of the expedition.
>
> I have verbally told you other particulars relative to the relief of partys [*sic*] and our programme to run thru until March 1916. All my personal property, diaries, books, notes, photos, is, in the event of my not returning, the property of my wife to be disposed of by her as she wishes.
>
> Æneas A. Mackintosh
> 24/1/15
>
> To J. Stenhouse,
> Mate,
> S.Y. Aurora
> McMurdo Sound 24.1.15.[6]

Almost a fortnight earlier, Mackintosh had written in his diary: 'I have left Stenhouse in charge – he is doing excellently, he is a good fellow, always ready in any contingency keen and an enthusiast of the highest order – it's such a comfort to have him.'[7]

Stenhouse was anxious to conserve coal but had to keep *Aurora*'s fires banked in order to raise steam at short notice. 'What a relief it will be when we are snugly fast in our Winters Quarters . . . will be glad to get to a place where we can say "Finished with engines".'[8] Thomson was equally concerned: 'This ship is not very handy to sail as she has only convenience on the foremast, the other masts are not seriously intended to be used for sailing a ship.'[9]

Stenhouse ordered the cook to burn wood on the galley fire, which resulted in a near-calamity when the deck around the galley funnel started to smoulder. Thomson recorded the incident:

> By 10 a.m. there was a moderate blizzard blowing. I was talking to the cook about stores and what we should have for dinner tonight when I happened to notice the deck of the galley was on fire, so we immediately proceeded to put it out. The fire had started behind an asbestos sheet and under a sheet of tin and it was very hard to get at, but when I thought it was out I went along and reported the occurrence to the Chief Officer Mr Stenhouse and he came forward and had a look at it. Just shortly afterwards the fire began again so I told the Chief Officer that it was dangerous, especially as there were a number of benzine and methylated spirits cases stowed on top of the house which the galley formed part. The Chief Officer immediately called the watch below and proceeded to put out the fire and shift inflammable cargo off the top of the house and stow at a safe distance away on deck. The carpenter was then put on to get the deck around the stove pipe thoroughly safe from fire by means of packing asbestos around the pipe and between it and the wood and we hope to hear no more of this trouble.[10]

Sighting two sea leopards on the sea ice, Paton, Atkin and Glidden set off and clubbed them to death after the animals had 'given a grand fight for their lives'. Stenhouse ordered the bosun to preserve the skins as specimens and told the crew to stop the indiscriminate shooting of wildlife: 'Numbers of skuas, petrels etc. are wounded and left in pain. To kill for his use is surely man's prerogative but to kill for sport is wanton cruelty.'[11]

Cope's party finally set out on 31 January, when the weather and ice conditions appeared to be much safer for travelling. Thomson recorded:

> The third depot-laying party is to be landed . . . I will be very glad to see them landed safely and on their way, as the ship will begin to look like a ship and less like a pleasure yacht out of hand. Everything was as usual until about 11 a.m. when all hands including myself were called to help to get the party away, which I found out afterwards meant to do everything for the party excepting to go away in their steads, while they looked on with a certain amount of awed respect. But this trip should be a great breaking in for the party as they must learn to rely on themselves instead of waiting until everything has been done for them.[12]

At first the motor sledge performed well without any load, managing speeds of up to seven or eight miles an hour, before being tethered to two sledges, one of 600 pounds and the other, 500. Ninnis, accompanied by Hooke, drove off as the crew cheered. They soon overtook the man-hauling groups but the Girling soon broke down. In the most detailed of the accounts of this event, Ninnis wrote:

> A mile out I had ignition trouble, wet plugs, snow falling on them from hopper of tank, big job to restart so much water about. The water leak increased and I traced it to the bottom seam of water tank against which a rope sling had been bearing when lowering. I stopped and examined it, then decided to proceed scooping snow into tank each 100 yards to replace water. Then clutch got wet and slipped and tank opened out badly and I stopped once more. Decided to make a dash for Hut Point and make a fresh tank. Left the sledges with a black flag over them and caught up the manhauled sledge, which had passed me again and reported trouble. Borrowed Hooke who stood on the rear side runners and scooped snow continuously and off we went at high speed, crack opened badly and snow came out as quickly as it went in. Had to run in low gear and increased vibration, renewed trouble, engine shook loose. Secured all and off again. Clutch slipped owing to engine shifting and oil feed pipe broke and throttle control altered its rotation. Adjusted and off again holding engine in place, driving and steering also, standing on offside runners and we rushed off the next five miles filling with snow as fast as Hooke could scoop it up. Jumped three big cracks in the ice safely at top speed and got quite happy over it, both ready to jump clear if sinking. Then pulled up at 3 feet from a 5 foot wide sea crack, a dead stop for us and we had to run round to the beach by Hut Point. Left motor and climbed up to hut, to find nothing to repair tank with.[13]

Hayward's diary entry was terse: 'On getting approx. 1500 yards from ship, sledge failed to cope with the load and broke down.'[14] Thus ended the only motor-sledge journey of the whole expedition. Richards, in his contemporary diary, noted: 'Went well alone but seems to have little power when harnessed. Front crawl [wheel] dug out of snow. Design defects.'[15]

Ninnis's decision to drive the damaged motor sledge to Hut Point after trouble struck only a mile from the ship, rather than return for repairs, spelt the end of the motor party as such. He could have learned from Stevens or Hayward, who had visited the *Discovery* hut a week or so earlier, that it had no workshop or tools. Before he set out from the ship, Ninnis had written: 'I wanted 2 days more and have not had them . . . to run the motor successfully means all to me and to have it fail means a dead loss.'[16]

In addition to problems caused by the leaking water tank and slipping clutch, Ninnis suspected the engine may have been damaged through overheating 'due to running on low water supply'. He attributed its failure to 'the entire lack of opportunity to test it and adjust it for running in actual conditions on the ice and being sent straight away to make a non-stop [journey with] hauling power unascertained in fact, untried entirely save an engine test, and also suffering damage in the actual lowering to which method I lodged a protest ineffectually'.[17]

The sledge remained in a precarious position on the melting sea ice for the next week. Sent to investigate with Larkman, Thomson reported that Ninnis's party had left

> all their ski and ski-sticks, their bundle of flags and tent poles and two cases of stores at one place and about 60 yards away they had left part of the tractor which was portable and spare tools, four tins of Antarctic biscuits which was about 160 lbs., 2 bags of dog biscuits, 2 ice picks, 2 shovels, a couple of tins of kerosene and one of methylated spirits belonging to primus stove . . .[18]

They 'morsed by flag' the news to Stenhouse, who meanwhile was having trouble as the ice started to break and bear down on the ship. 'I then signalled to the two on the ice, to "hold on" as I had enough to do without trying to read their signals (difficult owing to glare of snow). They immediately returned to ship and arrived 10.30 p.m. . . .'[19]

For the men on *Aurora*, the mystery of the abandoned gear deepened further when, twelve hours later, there was still no sign of the Hut Point party. Again Thomson and Larkman, this time with Atkin, were sent off to investigate. Stenhouse gave Thomson orders to proceed to Hut Point and take charge of the party in the event of anything having happened to the designated leaders, Cope and Stevens. He was to send Larkman, Atkin and 'the ones who were incapacitated, in the event of accident' back to the ship and proceed on south with the Bluff depot party.

Stenhouse could ill afford to lose the services of his only officer, who had somewhat reluctantly also taken over the role of storeman. Thomson wrote: 'After breakfast I wound chronometers, watches and clocks, served cook out with dinner stores and then got into my Burbery suit and ski boot [*sic*] preparatory to starting.'[20]

Just as the party was about to leave, Stenhouse reported that he could see the Hut Point party but told Thomson to proceed regardless. His men, all novices, abandoned their skis at the sledge depot because of difficult ice conditions and a fresh wind that caused them to 'slip about'. Almost an hour later they met up with the Hut Point party walking six abreast. Thomson was impressed: 'They looked like soldiers in their Burberry and sledge harness.'[21]

The second officer was given an account of the events of the past two days. He was told that as the motor-sledge party had set out on their escapade, Cope, Stevens, Hayward and Richards struggled to man-haul a load of 1200 pounds. At 2 a.m., with a moderate blizzard blowing, they were met by Ninnis and Hooke, who had returned from the *Discovery* hut after a snack of cocoa, biscuits and jam, followed by a cigar, all left over from the 1903 stores. The pair had struggled on the seven-mile journey back to the man-hauling team. All six then set off for the hut. Ninnis wrote: 'We could only do 500 yards and then lay in snow for 5 minutes each spell, and after a terrible time of it reached hut at 6.30 a.m. dead tired 16 hours on the march.'[22]

After a meal of pancakes and sardines from stores found in the hut, the men were asleep when visited by Jack, who had come from Joyce's camp. 'Unfortunately we were far too done to take the interest in it all that we might have done . . . when we meet him again the exchange of explanations will be quite entertaining,'[23] wrote Hayward. It was perhaps not surprising that Jack returned to his companions somewhat incredulous as to his apparently indifferent reception at the *Discovery* hut.

Ninnis, nearly delirious through fatigue, had vomited his evening meal and, while he slept, his arm had become stuck between two boxes on which he was lying. His cries for help were unheard.[24] Unable to extricate himself, he had fallen asleep again but was eventually lifted out, his left arm feeling quite dead, after ten hours in this position. In all, the party had rested for some seventeen hours, finally waking at 2 a.m.

> After an impromptu meal, we sallied forth at 3 o'clock to inspect the tractor, then loading an old 'Discovery' sledge with tent, cooker and biscuits, we set out on our return to pick up depot left Sunday afternoon. Even with this in light load we found things tough, and were greatly relieved to find a party setting out from the ship to our assistance.[25]

Stevens and Ninnis were much more exhausted than the rest, observed Thomson after the two groups had met up. 'Stephens [*sic*] dropped off to sleep every time they halted for a spell and took quite a lot of rousing. It was funny to see everybody lay down in the snow whenever they stopped.'[26]

Rather than turn for Hut Point with the two sledges, Cope and his men made a dash for the ship, where they promptly retired to their bunks for another lengthy sleep. Stenhouse wrote: 'They came on board at 12.45 p.m. – without welcome. Most of them seemed to be exhausted . . . They must have been cooked or they would not have returned to the ship.'[27] They did, however, bring Stenhouse a letter from Mackintosh, left by him at the hut, in which he said (referring to the wayward journey from the ship during 24–27 January) that he had 'experienced hard-going, had camped three times during a blizzard and when clear at noon on the day following [the party's] departure found they were on the Barrier 4 miles from Hut Point.'

Meanwhile, *Aurora*'s crew kept a sharp lookout over the abandoned sledging equipment, Paton realising that 'the ice may break away at any time and the loss of the sledges and the depot stores would be a great loss to us'.[28]

By the morning of 3 February, the ice began to break away as the wind freshened from the south-east, causing the ship to drift. The sledges and gear abandoned on the ice in two lots drifted northwards, 'but fortunately both depots were left on different ice floes and drifted about half a mile apart'.[29] The ship's logbook records the midafternoon position: 'Unable to steam thro' to pick up, ice unfit for travelling. Ship standing off in readiness to pick up sledge if possible.'[30] Stenhouse doubted that the risk to *Aurora* warranted recovery of the provisions. 'I do not think that I was justified in taking the ship into the pack to recover two sledges although their loss would have meant much to depot laying parties.'[31] Despite his misgivings, in the evening he manoeuvred into the pack ice and forced a passage to each sledge. 'The floe on which the food sledge rested had split along the side of the sledge . . . wonderful luck,' he wrote. The sledging party eagerly scrambled onto the floes and, with plenty of helpers on the ship, loaded every item safely on board, 'which of course cheered us no end',[32] noted Hayward.

An admiring chief engineer wrote: 'It was good work on Stenhouse's part to get the ship through the heavy floe ice up to them. My word, he gave that telegraph Hell! Under steam all afternoon and evening.'[33]

Because of the ice conditions, the sledging party obtained a reprieve for two further days, during which time Larkman made a new tank for the Girling. 'Why the snow tank was not brought to [the] ship for a new bottom instead of asking for a new tank I don't know. 'Twould have been simpler and quicker.'[34] In fact there was a general feeling that Ninnis should have brought the entire sledge back to the ship, and Thomson suggested that it had acted 'as a convenience for keeping Ninnis's feet dry'.[35]

Early in the afternoon on 5 February, the ship's officers decided the ice conditions were safe for sledging, so Cope and his five companions, the 'No. 3 party', again departed, assisted considerably by the crew 'in the landing of the stores and the lashing up of the sledges'. *Aurora* was adjacent to Castle Rock, only three and a half miles from the *Discovery* hut, but in order to reach it the party had to head westwards over difficult ice, an actual distance of about seven miles.[36] It was agreed that Cope would signal to the ship by mirror or smoke signals that all was well once they had reached the hut, but no signal was received.

The six men pulling two sledges took almost twelve hours to cover the distance, including a two-hour camp for tea. They safely crossed the many cracks in the sea ice and arrived at the hut at 1.30 a.m. on 6 February. This was a determined effort given the desultory events of the previous week.

Cope's party lacked elementary cooking utensils and was forced to improvise:

'... porridge and snow water the only food, but it took long time to prepare ... Shortage of spoons and I ate my share out of a 2 lb syrup tin with the help of a strip cut down from the lid of a wooden box.'[37] Ninnis spent six hours trying to repair the motor sledge but then gave up. It was hauled onto the shore and abandoned.

Stevens reported to Stenhouse by way of a letter written on 7 February 1915:

Discovery Hut
7 Feb., 1914 [*sic*]

My dear Stenhouse,

We are about to clear, and I am sorry to see your masts still in the offing – you will be still chafing at delay & Cope 'has no time' to make a certain signal.

First I wanted to tell you that if the twelve men sledging have to stay here till May they will be starved on the stores left here. Second, if by any chance you do come up with the ship, and can reasonably and conveniently do so, will you land for me one of the dredges in the lab. – not the one with the net on it which you and I used, but another together with twine, canvas and needle & palm to make a net and bag; and also a length of line to pull the dredge with; the more the merrier, 30–40 fathoms or more if you can conveniently spare it? I don't mean the request to be an annoyance to grant, but only to be granted if it doesn't trouble you or stint you.

We have done fairly so far. Cope & I prospected ahead yesterday; the ice is vile; it is dangerous and difficult at least for two–three miles offshore, and difficult everywhere. I think we shall be 3 days in reaching the barrier, and we must steer much astride of Joyce & the Skipper.

Au revoir bientôt, old man. I wish you good luck, and a busy & profitable time to your heart's content – The minimum of anxiety.

Ever yours sincerely,
A. Stevens.

P.S. I am glad to say Cope still continues to belie the Skipper's distrust. He is doing A1 and I hope & think he will continue to do so.

A.S.[38]

Cope and his men set out from the hut on 8 February, man-hauling two heavy sledges, each weighing over a thousand pounds. They had to relay the load from the outset and travelled by night to take advantage of firmer surfaces. The load was at least 500 pounds too heavy, even for a fit party.

On the first day they advanced only four miles over soft and dangerous sea ice in fourteen hours; the following day only two miles, and then another four miles. There were lengthy delays on the march and at campsites (they had to learn how to erect a tent), much to the frustration of Ninnis. 'It's just gross mismanagement and incompetence.' He told Cope to 'cut out all the spells etc. and slog on'. Cope had the only reliable compass and the only watch, yet he often reported times that Ninnis suspected, from the position of the sun, were inaccurate. Richards made no mention in his brief 1915 diary of such problems, indicating a more sympathetic attitude to Cope.

It was arduous work, as recorded by Ninnis: 'Ski back and have another rest, relay 2nd sledge painfully (as 3 cannot pull much on ski due principally to unsuitable footgear.) . . . two of the others "died" in the snow, one even went fast asleep a mile from base, dead beat.' Richards was starting to feel the effects of a rupture he had sustained at football the previous season[39] and was later to comment when typing out his 1915 diary:

> . . . under medical advice at the time I wore a truss. I cannot now imagine how incredibly foolish I was to conceal this disability which could have had disastrous results had things gone badly with me the following year. In the upshot I threw the truss away when discarding everything possible in our retreat from Mt Hope the following year.[40]

Cope, Stevens and Hooke shared one tent, and Hayward, Ninnis and Richards, self-named 'the Bandsmen', the other.[41] This gave rise to some good-natured rivalry, as recorded by Ninnis: 'Getting cheerful the 3 Bandsmen alone hauled one of the sledges . . .'[42]

Despite Ninnis's complaints, within four days of leaving the hut they were on the Barrier with their heavy load, a better performance than the two parties that had preceded them, and on 10 February, they passed Scott's Safety Camp.

As competition developed between the two teams, 'the Bandsmen' settled on their own routine: 'Call 6 p.m., breakfast, March 8 p.m. slog on hard till 12.30. Lunch till 2 a.m. and slog on till 6 a.m. Camp . . .'[43] With a sense of satisfaction, Richards wrote on 12 February: 'Ninnis, Hayward and self are the three strongest pullers in the party . . . We get on well together. Sledging is monotonous. Very often too short of wind to talk and travel for hours without a word spoken . . . the bunk at night on the hard snow is relished as much as any feather bed.'[44]

In the other team, however, Stevens, who had a month earlier celebrated his twenty-ninth birthday, was struggling with the arduous physical demands. 'Personally I fear seriously that Stevens may not stand it. He "drops" a lot of time and seems very fagged so perhaps we must try and meet this contingency,'[45] Ninnis noted on 11 February.

The party's momentum, such as it was, continued fitfully for a few more days and was recorded in the brief diary of the journey kept by Richards:

Sunday Feb 14th. Lying to in a blizzard. It is very uncomfortable. Sleeping bags are wet and we are all stiff and cold. I think we should have moved before this.

Monday Feb 15th. Probably about 6 a.m. We had a hard march yesterday and covered about 3 miles. This was a 14 hour march and the direct distance gained would not have been more than 2 miles. (Relaying and maybe dodging crevasses in this particular area.) It turned very cool towards evening and when I came to take my boots off socks were frozen hard to the boots and were with difficulty removed without damage. The sleeping bag was frozen. On running my hand inside I could feel ice all over the bottom. However notwithstanding I managed to get through a fairly comfortable night. I am changing my footgear for today's march. In place of boots which freeze as hard as boards and are very cold I shall wear a pair of fur finneskoe. We are now off the end of White Island.

Tuesday Feb 16th. 10 a.m. Marched 12 to 13 hours yesterday. Covered 4 miles – part over rising ice. Very cold night everything frozen. Temp 0 on turning in. Minimum for night –15. Cooking breakfast of oatmeal and biscuit. Some beautiful atmospheric colours visible in sky last night around Cape Crozier – deep purples and red.

Wednesday Feb 17th. 5 p.m. started at about 10 p.m. yesterday and marched till 7 a.m. without a stop for meals. Covered 3 miles. Temperature fairly low –7 being recorded. Not unpleasant cold however. We are in transit with Minna Bluff and Cape Crozier and I think 6 miles from Corner Camp. Expect to reach tomorrow.[46]

Meanwhile, to the south, Mackintosh, Wild and Joyce, with nine dogs, parted company with the north-bound trio of Spencer-Smith, Jack and Gaze on 11 February at the Bluff depot. The Padre's party retreated with the four weakest dogs.

The Skipper gave Spencer-Smith detailed instructions as well as an encouraging tribute, some consolation for his not being in the 80° South party:

> It is with deep regret that I have to part with your company as a sledging companion, for it has been through your ready aid and shoulders that we have been enabled to reach so far on our journey. I now depute you the charge of the Bluff depot laying party, as I consider by your tact, discretion and character you are a fit person to take over this responsible position . . .

The Padre was to proceed 'with all speed' to Hut Point and attempt to 'junction with the Motor party which will be leaving or have left ere this'. Mackintosh left matters largely to his friend's own judgement, 'but ever bear in mind the necessity of assisting in every way possible the carrying out of stores as far as possible . . .'[47]

Gunboat and Duke, both heavyweight dogs, had been sent back with Spencer-Smith in return for the middleweights Shacks, Pinkey and Major, and Pompey, the only survivor of the lightweight team. Mackintosh now had a team of nine dogs, led by Nigger, the sole heavyweight, and including Pat and Briton, Tug and Scotty.

As his party set out from their depot at the Bluff, Mackintosh noted: 'With this new team we find no pulling is required of us, the dogs fairly hopping along. This to us, who hitherto have done nothing but man-haul is a great pleasure.'[48] He may well have been underestimating the assistance his originally lightweight dog team had given his party to date, and overestimating the assistance the heavyweight team had given Joyce in reaching Minna Bluff.

Aware that the Bluff depot was not in its correct place, Mackintosh was anxious to fix the true position with the summit of Mt Discovery in line with the Bluff. A cairn could then be erected as a marker. After lying up for a frustrating 36 hours in a blizzard, the party set out on 14 February. Ernest Wild described the day's activities:

> Sunday 14th. Nearly 8 miles. Turned out at 6.30 a.m. After breakfast Captain found out he had looked at his watch upside down and it was 4.30 proper time, dead loss. Couldn't get any bearings till lunch and then we found out that we had passed Bluff depot so we are going on to One Ton Camp. Briton chucked his hand in we had to carry him on the sledge. Port lug and starboard big toe slightly frost bitten . . .[49]

Although they were south of the intended position of the Bluff depot, the Skipper's men built a cairn and left a note for following parties telling them of their movements.[50]

Mackintosh appreciated his sterling sledging companion: 'Wild slept like a top; he is a remarkable little fellow, always merry and bright, as soon as he lays down he starts snoring; he has been reading a book in which there are three murders, and he expects several more . . .' But he fretted over the delay:

> Shacks relief getting worrisome, food going! What can we do though? Only wait for the weather. I lie in the bag reading and sleeping and when not doing either wondering how we are to prosper. Plans are easy to make, but quite a different matter to carrying them out.[51]

As Mackintosh, Wild and Joyce passed 79° South, their daily distances increased. They had a single purpose: to push as hard and quickly as they could to 80° and then turn for base. It was no longer necessary to travel at night, because lower air and snow temperatures allowed satisfactory sledging surfaces by day. With the season rapidly advancing and temperatures plummeting, day travel also protected them from the worst of the cold. Even in the tent Wild had to resort to attempting to write up his log with his 'mit' on.[52] Nor was the refuge of sleeping bags enough to keep out the insidious chill and draughts. Temperatures at the evening camps were now regularly between −10° and −15° F and dropped further as the night progressed.

Monday, 15 February, marked a special occasion for the Skipper:

> Was half an hour late in waking up. A real beautiful morning. Anniversary of my wedding day – thoughts turn to 4 years back and what a change! What on earth am I doing here? That's what I ask myself and such thoughts wish me back at home to the dear ones, waiting so patiently.[53]

By now the Skipper's ears and fingers were continually festering, Joyce's fingers were 'going' frequently, and Wild's nose was affected, as well as his toes and ears.[54]

Despite the weeks of marching, the 'tot of rum' (or, more precisely, 'a peg of brandy out of the medical comforts'[55]) as a reward for a day's march of twelve miles had not yet been won. This prospect loomed large in Wild's thoughts as they approached their goal: 'Friday 19th. Hooray nearly 11 miles. That tot of rum is looming up . . . Saturday 20th. Hooray 12 miles today. Just had that tot . . . Joyce set fire to his brandy when he was trying to warm it. Excitement reigned supreme (I don't think) . . .'[56] In fact, Wild overestimated the distance for 19 February, which was a little less than nine miles.

The Skipper had plenty of opportunity to assess his two subordinates in arduous circumstances:

> Wild, ever a jolly cheerful, an optimist, keen and ever ready to take up anything, very humorous with a large vocabulary of naval expressions, fairly tough, and plucky as any Britisher. Joyce, a different character – quite alright while humoured, when he is willing and would do anything for any one, but he has no stability; alright while all goes well, not very hard, feels the cold very easily; but he always sticks it out.[57]

Apart from Briton, who ceased pulling at the Bluff and thereafter tagged along or was a passenger on the sledge, the dogs pulled like Trojans. They ravenously tried to eat everything within range made of leather. Beatings ceased except when a dog attacked another. Mackintosh was noticeably more sympathetic to the animals' predicament than he had been earlier in the journey. Getting up on hearing one of the dogs loose, he

> found it was Tug who had eaten through his leather thong – they all do this now poor brutes, yet we are giving them more biscuits than Scott did, although we can't afford pemmican. I later found that Major had eaten the straps off my glasses![58]

However, there was nothing he could do to relieve the animals' plight. At times their paws were bleeding from travelling over very rough sastrugi, and some were suffering from snow blindness.

As he slumbered on the morning of 20 February, the Skipper had a dream: 'I had been awakened by a policeman who had been moving me off from the side of the tent I was lying on, and was struggling in the bag to get to the other when, on coming in contact with Joyce's bag, I realised I was not in Piccadilly!'[59]

With the aid of a northerly wind and the dogs pulling well, the party made its final southwards march of twelve miles on 20 February, the last six being achieved in just three and a half hours.

Mackintosh had originally planned to depot 220 pounds of provisions at 80° South but, such were the difficulties of the task, he had only 135 pounds left.[60] Any more travel would further deplete the supplies, and time was running out, so he decided to leave the supplies about seven miles short, at 79° 52' S.[61] He reasoned that this would be close enough for Shackleton to see the depot on a fine day from the planned position.

His men allowed themselves a celebration of this significant achievement, Mackintosh writing:

> We have toasted 'Sweethearts and Wives', it being Saturday. We came over a remarkable surface, longer masses of heaped up sastrugi, in places as much as 4 ft in height with a razor edge. This helped the sledge along better than if the surface had been an even snow one, which is not an advantage as the snow adheres to the runners. Joyce has been ahead steering making an excellent course; the way he does this is to make a mark of some fixed cloud ahead which I direct him on to the course by compass. Owing [to] the mountainous surface we have named this camp the 'Rocky Mountains'. I write this sitting up in my bag while the primus is going as an extra luxury the heat from this keeps the interior quite warm but we shall suffer in the morning owing to the freezing of the condensed water in the tent. The sling thermometer registers at 8 p.m. –8° . . . We are snug and warm inside though, in fact hot! We have done quite well, taking the journey as a whole, this being our first long journey, we cannot be far off the position of One Ton camp. We have brought 3 weeks full provisions equal to 135 lbs. In the morning we intend building the depot and two of us laying one at every mile a flag for 5 miles at right angles to our course.[62]

On the journey south from the Bluff, the party had placed cairns at every 1.5 minutes of latitude (one and a half geographical miles),[63] a technique used by Amundsen on his return journey to the South Pole three years earlier. Mackintosh's decision to mark the depot by placing cairns to the east and west of it was another Amundsen technique.[64]

On 21 February, Joyce and Wild took the dogs and a light sledge and laid cairns and flags every mile for five miles eastwards,[65] attaching a note in a tin to the flagstaff of the end cairn to give the position of the main depot.[66] Mackintosh endeavoured to fix the position of the depot by theodolite but only succeeded in freezing his whiskers to the instrument, which, to make matters worse, malfunctioned. '[The] axis of the telescope is loose and does not remain fixed when clamped in a horizontal position so am only able to get rough angles.'[67]

After lunch on 21 February, four weeks after they had set out from *Aurora*, the Skipper's party built the main cairn, a solid square of snow blocks eight feet in height, on top of which was placed a bamboo pole of twenty feet, stayed up with lampwick. 'On a clear day this depot could be sighted at a distance of 12 miles and almost impossible to miss coming from the south.'[68]

On that same day the ice-trapped *Endurance* reached the southernmost point of her drift in the Weddell Sea, at 77° S, 35° W. Shackleton would later write: 'The summer had gone . . . I could not doubt now that the *Endurance* was confined for the winter . . . The land showed still in fair weather on the distant horizon, but it was beyond our reach now, and regrets for havens that lay behind us were vain . . .'[69]

Thus the farthest south point reached by the Imperial Trans-Antarctic Expedition was achieved by the men of the Ross Sea party.[70]

CHAPTER SEVEN

Support parties – autumn 1915

W HEN Spencer-Smith, Gaze and Jack said farewell to the 80° South party
at the Bluff on 11 February 'amidst mutual cheers',[1] the two Australians were disappointed to lose Joyce. They blamed the Skipper for breaking
up what Jack termed a 'happy little party . . . We have been sledging together
now for nearly three weeks under the capable leadership of Joyce. We have
had a most delightful trip. We were looking forward to a quick return to Hut
Point and another long journey together with sledge to lay the third depot.'[2]
Jack queried whether Mackintosh was 'a very capable leader and if Shackleton's
selection was a very wise one'. Gaze expressed a similar sentiment:

> This was a rotten slap in the face – we didn't want to lose Joyce and he didn't want
> to go with the Skipper . . . four miserable dogs to help us along and 70 miles to go
> with 7 days provisions. Deadly – not that we minded having A.P. because we didn't
> . . . It felt awfully funny without old Joyce, he was absolutely the best of compan-
> ions, and kept us in good spirits the whole time.[3]

Mackintosh had little choice but to send the Padre, whose feet were in a
bad state, back to base, and he was put in charge of the two Australians. With
a load of 400 pounds, the returning party had to average ten miles a day to
reach Scott's Safety Camp, about a mile from the edge of the Barrier. If they
did not meet the motor party en route, they trusted that the camp had the old
provisions they had uncovered three weeks earlier.

The snow surface was often sticky, making man-hauling arduous, but a floor
cloth was rigged as a sail to take advantage of southerly following winds and
achieve an estimated average speed of three miles an hour.[4]

Their four dogs were in a weak and emaciated condition. Duke, a discard
from Mackintosh's original team, was set free on 12 February, to 'follow if he
would', but he was soon lost to sight. The next day it was blowing hard with
heavy drift. Gaze reasoned: 'I expect this blizzard will fix Duke – anyway he was
no earthly good, and it's a painless death.'[5]

KK, one of the lightweight dogs that had started so promisingly, also succumbed four days later. The Padre wrote remorsefully: 'I am sure that he gave of his best each day.' This left Towser, the 'lightweight' collie, and Gunboat, a 'heavy brigade' reject from the other team, as the only survivors of a nine-dog team. The pair were ravenously hungry but kept pulling, helping the party sledge to achieve up to twelve to thirteen miles a day. Spencer-Smith wrote: 'Even three hours of [KK's] pulling in the morning is worth a good deal, especially when the going is heavy.'[6] The combination of dogs and men combined as one pulling team was again put to good effect.

Mackintosh's decision to send Spencer-Smith back was increasingly vindicated. 'A.P. properly fagged,' wrote Gaze on 14 February, and, three days later, 'A.P. awfully fagged out.' On 16 February, the Padre recorded: 'I am a little strained on the left side intercostals, I hope not heart – and shall have to be careful.' To add to his discomfort, he snapped a gold tooth off, 'the nearest dentist being in New Zealand!'[7]

Gaze had a badly blistered heel from his oversized boots but obtained some relief from wearing finnesko. His diary for 16 February describes a typical day:

> Up at 6 a.m. sharp . . . it was not until our usual 3 hours were up, that we got a move on . . . After breakfast we have 30 minutes spell (generally a read and smoke) then comes packing up etc. and stowing of the sledge; fixing of skis and donning of harness (hauling) and finally a last look at the dogs to see that everything is o.k. with them – then off we go. Our morning's trek was jolly hard going; we were at it for four solid hours & did about 7 miles. We also built 3 cairns (these take roughly 15 minutes each); so you see we kept up a good slogging pace the whole time. (Lunch at 1.15 p.m.) Had 2 hours for lunch and started off again determined to put in a record afternoon's work. The going became worse and worse though, and although we put in 5 hours solid graft we only managed to do 6 more miles making a total of 13 for the day . . . Had our supper at 9 p.m. (Bonzer) & turned in immediately afterwards. (Jolly tired.)[8]

By 17 February, having finished the last of their kerosene and down to their last day's rations, the Padre's men thought they were within fourteen miles of Safety Camp.[9] They had no wish to fall back on dog biscuits, which at times appeared to be a possibility.[10] The night temperature fell to –18°F and it was bitterly cold in the tent, a world away from Australia and the 'cool of a summer evening on the lawn' that Jack wistfully dreamt of.[11] An increasingly homesick Spencer-Smith wrote: 'People at home are just finishing their after-church supper. One always wonders if they are thinking of us – and how the war is proceeding.'[12]

On the following morning they saw the motor party close by and hurried on ski to meet them. Gaze observed: 'It appears they had had a very hard time of it, and were relaying the whole time. The load was over the odds – 2 sledges each weighing over 900 lbs – 1800 lbs, with 6 men to haul – no wonder we haven't met them before, I think they've done jolly well.'[13]

The meeting of the retreating Bluff depot party and the advancing combined motor party not only saved the two dogs from starvation but was a welcome chance for the men to relax.

> We will be alright for food now, they are giving us a full week's supply of everything – it will save the necessity of our broaching Safety Camp . . . Everything seems to be A1 with the party, they've had a few squalls it appears amongst themselves, but nothing serious. It bucked us all up tremendously to meet like this, it seems ages since we left them. (4 weeks practically.)
>
> Didn't have lunch until the motor party had got their first full load up to our camp at 4.30 p.m. . . . The weather conditions had got far worse now, so it was decided to camp together for the night – this was A1. – We had a jolly good talk & told our experiences. A.P. spent the night with Stevens and Cope, and Hooke came over to us – he's an A1 chap. Gave the dogs a jolly good feed; some of the new biscuits brought along by Cope – they did bolt them. Turned down our bags at 7.30 p.m. – had a good old yarn, and then to sleep – it was a jolly pleasant day.[14]

It was decided that the struggling Stevens would return with Spencer-Smith and Gaze to Hut Point, and that Jack, who was proving himself one of the fittest men on the expedition, would turn south again with Cope, Hooke, Ninnis, Richards and Hayward. Gaze thought Jack's decision was generous. 'This was a very sporting thing for Keith to do in my opinion – specially as he was looking forward so much to getting back again'.[15]

Stevens immediately benefited from a change in diet and could now better digest his hoosh. Unlike Cope's party, which was using Bovril pemmican, found on *Aurora* after Mawson's expedition, Spencer-Smith's party had seemingly superior Beauvais Copenhagen pemmican left over by Scott's second expedition.[16] The Padre noted: 'It will make all the difference to his comfort (warmth) and vitality generally.'[17] Gaze, relieved at returning to base, found the new arrangements convivial and noted: 'Stevens is far more at ease with us he says.'[18]

The retreating party reached Safety Camp two days later and, on Mackintosh's written instructions, dug down for further supplies, but at five feet came only to pony fodder.

The men were apprehensive about the hazards of crossing eight miles of soft sea ice between the edge of the Barrier and the shore of Ross Island. However, their luck held because cold night temperatures and 'a glorious day, clear all round' ensured that the sea-ice surface was passable. Gaze wrote: 'For the most part we kept to our (Joyce's) old tracks, but came in closer to Cape Armitage when making for the hut.' The two dogs still worked hard but sometimes pulled backwards and gave other trouble. Such was the Padre's frustration that he gave

Gunboat 'a good thrashing' when they were just an hour or two from the hut.[19]

The prospect of staying in the *Discovery* hut was not attractive and the party hoped to get back on board *Aurora*. Spencer-Smith wrote: 'Apart from the creature comforts I am not looking forward to the icy interior of the hut.' They avoided the open water around Hut Point and reached the building at 4.15 p.m. on 22 February. Gaze described it as being in 'a fearful state of filth', which could not be removed because it was frozen in, and he lamented: 'Can see no sign of the ship, so expect she's away looking for winter quarters, and that we'll have to live at Hut Point for quite a time – hope we don't.'

While Stevens cooked porridge and hot scones on the blubber stove, the men spread out their sleeping bags on senna grass[20] and used old tents as makeshift mattresses. Spencer-Smith wrote: 'Before turning in, we went up to Vince's Cross to see the sunset (one can really distinguish the evening now): a golden-red glory behind Mount Discovery: every tender shade from luminous violet to translucent green to the north – mystic, wonderful beyond description.'[21] To his cousin Irvine Gaze, it was the most beautiful sight he had ever seen. 'Away to our left stretched (looking north) the Western Mountains bathed in beautiful colourings of green & gold impossible to describe.'[22]

Within a day the sea ice was rapidly breaking up. 'Great 1000 ton blocks are swinging in a heavy swell and grinding at the edges they have just left. The vibrations can be felt in the hut . . . Thank God we got here safely yesterday!'[23] Soon there was open water southwards to the edge of the Barrier, access to which would now be by a more difficult route, over Hut Point Peninsula near Castle Rock and thence by negotiating difficult ice slopes.

Any expectations of returning to the Barrier were thwarted by the conditions. The men slept, ate, read and enjoyed long discussions on such topics as the exact nature and definition of a verb, whether there is such a thing as 'an honest person', and the Oxford theological movement.[24] A tally of stores indicated there would only be enough for a dozen men for four weeks. There was little fuel and, with an absence of sea ice, no opportunity to hunt for seals to provide further blubber. The hut-bound men fired a rocket to try to signal the ship, but this was considered a failure when it ascended only about a hundred feet. On 2 March, the sound of voices was heard and Ninnis, Richards and Hooke appeared at the hut.

The story of their venture to the south was soon told. On 19 February, Cope's party of six men, without dogs, had made slow progress. Jack, the new man in the party, complained that their load was excessive. 'It is most exhausting work this relaying . . . the load this party is hauling seems to me to be very absurd and far too heavy for a team of untrained inexperienced men.'[25] They tried different methods to increase their daily distances in order to reach the Bluff, 60 miles away, without using up the supplies they were meant to be placing there in a depot.

After travelling a distance of less than two miles on 20 February, they dropped off 277 pounds of provisions, making a depot at '2nd cairn from Joyce's Corner Camp', and tried to proceed with one sledge of 1,288 pounds, including seventeen bags (750 pounds) of food rations.[26] Jack gives the position for this depot: 'at bearings summit Mt Discovery 92.95 Erebus 154.5 Terror 214.5 . . .' This became known as Cope's No. 1 depot. The party had to give up after a short distance: Richards said a hundred yards; Jack about half a mile. The load was then distributed between two sledges and the party made 'reasonable speed on foot though on ski each is rather heavy', according to Jack. In this way, Cope, Hooke and Jack achieved five miles 600 yards on 22 February, but Richards, Hayward and Ninnis found their load too much and stopped at a cairn almost two miles behind. The reason for their stopping, according to Jack, who skied back to lend assistance, was that 'Ninnis had strained himself as the result of heavy pulling yesterday, and Richards' rupture is troubling him a good deal'.[27] Despite these discomforts, both men felt they could proceed further south.

Jack then suggested to Cope that the party should be split and that the 'two weak men . . . and one very light weight [dog]' should return to Hut Point. This would have the added benefit of allowing Ninnis, once back at base, to repair the motor sledge, and Hooke to help with the wireless installation on the ship. Richards supported Jack's proposal, and Cope agreed, putting Richards in charge of Hooke and Ninnis, with instructions to proceed to Hut Point and 'there place [his] party in the charge of Spencer-Smith'.[28] The appointment of Richards as leader of the returning party would be the only time in the entire expedition that a non-Briton was appointed to lead any sledging group.

The fittest men in the party were now left in the field, and they re-stowed the sledges and deposited some stores at what Jack termed the 'blue flagged depot'.[29] This became known as Cope's No. 2 depot.

Richards led his returning group, with only seven days' provisions, in determined fashion, pressing on whenever possible so long as it was clear that they were on the correct route. Within four days they were at the Barrier edge, only to find the sea ice gone and killer whales disporting and 'blowing the whole night through' in water that looked 'black and dismal'.[30]

The party set up camp 200 yards from the shore in the hope that *Aurora* might 'put in an appearance' and to give 'those around Hut Point a chance to see us'.[31] A full inventory of stores revealed a satisfactory position in the short term:

Oil on reduced rations 5 days' supply. Biscuits – 20 whole 37 part, at 12 per day 4 to 5 days. Pemmican half a bag therefore ¾ pannikin per meal. Oatmeal twenty spoonsful or 4 to 5 days. Chocolate 24 bars 1 bar per day per man. Sugar 150 lumps – 10 per man per day – 5 days. Tea, salt, and glaxo – enough for a week.[32]

Ninnis made a possible sighting of a ship but concluded that this was a mirage. Richards and Ninnis returned to Safety Camp and 'Seal Meat Cairn' to see if Spencer-Smith had left a note indicating his planned route to the *Discovery* hut, but found nothing.

On 2 March, the trio set out for the hut, taking with them an ice pick and two coils of alpine rope they had picked up from the 'blue flagged depot' a week before. Richards describes the nineteen-hour journey that followed:

We struck camp at 10 a.m. and set out along the Barrier edge past Seal Meat depot. After three hours march we halted at a place where it was possible to get on to the sea ice from the Barrier. Here we camped for one hour and before leaving the Barrier erected a cairn with our intentions outlined in a note. We found good surface on the sea ice but inshore there were several cracks. A two hours march brought us to the steep face to the right of the gap. Here we had some troublesome pressure ridges to negotiate with the sledge. The ice was groaning very persistently. It was judged impractical to scale the gap and a trail was made by Ninnis and self to climb the steep face of basalt. We managed about 70 ft. and then gave up the attempt. An investigation showed a possible snow track to the right and Ninnis investigated this while Hooke and I saw to the sledge. On his return Ninnis reported favourably and after considerable trouble the sledge and gear was hauled up with alpine rope to a ridge about 300 feet above sea-level. Here we managed to level a patch of snow – which was very thin – and pitched camp. The tent was secured with lumps of rock in place of snow, of which there was not a sufficient quantity to seal down the edges. We had a meal about 3 a.m. and then turned in. Awake again at 10 a.m. and had breakfast – half rations continue. We intend to go in search of a route to Hut Point.[33]

On breaking camp they found a relatively easy track down to the hut and reached it in two hours. To welcome them, Stevens turned on a sumptuous meal of porridge, sardines and coffee, 'and they eat it ravenously, especially dear old Hooke!'[34] Richards confessed that 'after our reduced rations I am afraid I made a beast of myself'.[35]

The three men then headed back to their camp in the hills to retrieve their gear. They slept the night there, and the following day, with a 'howling cold wind blowing', brought the sledge into the hut, with one man at its head and the other two steadying it on the rope.[36]

Thus ended the only sledge journey of any consequence undertaken by Ninnis and Hooke. The former, whose normally extensive diary entries had all but ceased three weeks before, wrote for Wednesday, 3 March: 'Hut at last.

11 p.m. in bag, full of food.' Six men were now safely back at the *Discovery* hut, and six were still out on the Barrier. 'God guard them!' prayed the Padre.

Those at the hut had little to do as they waited for some sign of *Aurora*. Spencer-Smith wrote on 3 March that a 'journey south would be senseless as we could not carry out stores in any useful quantity. A seal-killing expedition might be carried out a little later. Decision is very difficult in the absence of knowledge of Sten's orders, and of the present position of the barrier folk.'[37]

Bleak conditions confined the men to their sleeping bags for extended periods. 'So jolly cold can't scarcely hold a pencil,' wrote Gaze on 6 March. Ninnis and Richards shovelled out an estimated two to three tons of ice and snow from the hut doorway. Until this task was completed, the inhabitants had been entering through the 'lee' window, which had also been used during the *Nimrod* expedition.[38]

Ninnis and Richards sighted *Aurora* on 8 March, the shore party's first evidence that she was safe, when they climbed to the highest point on Hut Point Peninsula to search for an inland route to Cape Evans and to look out for the parties on the Barrier. 'We had a magnificent day – climbed to Castle Rock 1310 feet sheer from the sea. Found great ice fields on top of hills . . . [*Aurora*'s] crow's nest only was visible over the headland at Cape Evans 13 miles away and took quite a bit of picking up (with glasses).'[39] They lit a fire to signal the ship, and although this was apparently not seen on board, Chief Engineer Larkman had noted four days earlier: 'Believe I see smoke from Hut Point.'[40]

On 11 March, the expedition ship moored near the hut in 'Discovery Bay' (as described by both Thomson and Ninnis but known since the *Discovery* expedition as Winter Quarters Bay). An elated Gaze commented: 'It was a very battered and storm ridden vessel too – looked as if she had come through some great old gales.'[41] Stenhouse sent in a whaleboat with provisions for twelve men for about two months.[42] Thomson wrote:

> [We] had great difficulty in approaching the shore near enough to get a line ashore. We could not make the boat fast alongside as we had to keep the boat off to keep her from getting under the ice foot and then most surely getting smashed up and there would have been no chance of a man in the water ever getting out again so steep to and overshot was the icefoot.[43]

Eventually the boat was able to take the six men from the hut, plus two dogs, aboard. Spencer-Smith wrote: 'The boat's crew did not recognise me until I spoke! [We] received the warmest of welcomes from Sten and all the others. We are all thoroughly thankful to be "home" again.'[44]

The ship's cook served a special meal of seal-steak stew, soup, plum pudding, and pancakes with whisky to follow, after which Larkman provided 'warm water in the stokehold' and the shore men had their first bath for almost two months. In the late afternoon the ship left Hut Point and headed towards Cape Evans.

Gaze's diary of 11 March recorded the frustrations that *Aurora*'s crew had experienced: 'They had had a devil of a time of it since we left (6 weeks) could not get a sheltered anchorage and had to ride out the gales and blizzards as best they could and just trust to luck to get them through safely.'[45]

Mackintosh's verbal instructions to Stenhouse as to the relief of the sledging parties and the mooring of the ship had necessarily left the first officer considerable discretion.[46] Shackleton had ruled out the use of Winter Quarters Bay, the only proven harbour in the vicinity to winter a ship, and had insisted that *Aurora* not be moored south of Glacier Tongue. Stenhouse had written on 7 February:

> I had hoped to find a suitable place to winter ship off shore to N. of Captain Scott's Hut (at Cape Evans) but abandoned the hopes when I saw the ice coming into the Bay. There is fairly good holding ground off the Hut but to moor ship we would have to lie anchors down to the NW and stern moorings from shore – there is little shelter from South'ard and to lay with stern to prevailing gales would be out of the question.

Nor was Thomson impressed with Cape Evans as a suitable place to winter the ship: 'It is completely open to the NW to wind and swell and icebergs drive into it all sweet will, but in my opinion it is as good a place as there is at present offering and beggars can't be choosers.'[47]

Stenhouse next tried to get alongside Glacier Tongue, some four and a half miles south of Cape Evans. At first sea ice blocked the way and *Aurora* rode out a southerly gale in the shelter of Hut Point Peninsula.[48] By 13 February the ice had cleared sufficiently and Thomson was soon able to report: 'We are laying snugly under the lee of the Glacier and I feel more like home than I have done since we arrived in this White windswept country.'[49] Ice from Glacier Tongue provided fresh water for the tanks, but even with the aid of three ice anchors the mooring was not equal to the force of a blizzard that struck two days later. Stenhouse manoeuvered the ship off Tent Island. He recorded in the ship's log: 'Strong gale; rough sea; heavy floes about; everything obscured near to ship.'[50]

The ship was now unprotected in hazardous water. Thomson wrote:

It [was] very dangerous manoeuvring ship to stop her striking an iceberg or going ashore, and to make it more exciting we do not know what water we have under us anywhere and in clear weather we keep the lead going near the land. But in this blizzard we are nearly on top of it before we know we are so close. I will be very glad when we get into safe winter quarters and frozen in and I think everyone else will echo my opinion on this subject. The strain continually is beginning to tell on everybody.[51]

Again Stenhouse headed the ship in towards Castle Rock and found temporary shelter. On 20 February, he tried to reach Hut Point because those on board the ship thought they had seen smoke from that direction, but the intervening two miles of water was covered with heavy pack ice.[32]

The storm had carried out much of the ice in the bay and allowed Stenhouse to try Glacier Tongue again as a possible wintering berth. Paton, the most seasoned of hands, had throughout been sceptical of the idea.

It is behind this place that Capt. Mackintosh instructed Mr Stenhouse to winter the ship. After we were fast, Mr Stenhouse said 'Well Bo'sun; what do you think of this place?' . . . I told him straight out I did not like it, in fact I told him he could never winter the ship here. I condemned it . . . he did not like what I said, of that I am certain, because he looked straight at me and said 'Don't be pessimistic.' I know this place well, however, we shall wait and see.[53]

Despite his concerns, this was an improvement on the first attempt to moor *Aurora* at Glacier Tongue. Paton noted that the ship was 'much further up' towards the edge of Ross Island, 'but we will have to get much further yet before we can find a place to winter the ship here, as there is 200 fathom of water under our keel'.[54]

After a couple of fine days, even the sceptical bosun was optimistic: 'I cannot help admitting that it certainly looks an ideal place.' However, his first judgement was vindicated on 24 February when the wind shifted to the northwest and a heavy northerly swell returned to the bay much of the ice that had been blown out in the preceding days. *Aurora* was now caught between Glacier Tongue and the icebergs. As the ship rose and fell with the swell, her stern crashed down on the ice, 'grinding and crunching her stern post and rudder against the glacier'.[55] It was Thomson's belief that a lesser ship would have foundered in these circumstances.

In the midst of the battering Paton noted that 'there was some talk of landing the stores on the Tongue as it was feared she would not stand much more'.[56] Thomson recorded that 'the ship looked in a very dangerous position',[57] and Stenhouse ordered all hands to put on extra clothing and prepare to abandon ship and land on the glacier.[58] Larkman wrote: '[W]e quite thought rudder and screw both gone but we survived it all right.'[59] *Aurora* owed her survival to a sudden subsidence of the swell, but this crisis ensured that no further attempt would be made to find a winter mooring at Glacier Tongue.

By evening on 24 February, the ship was again moored off Cape Evans, which by default now became the winter berth for the ship, despite Stenhouse's earlier dismissal of the site as a suitable mooring.

Paton, however, favoured another possibility:

> Mr Stenhouse has decided to winter the ship here and again asked me what I thought of it, and told him I was not in love with it, that the only place in the straits that I thought fit for a ship to winter was Backdoor Bay and that was fully 8 miles from here. He said that Captain Mackintosh would not hear of such a thing so that ended the discussion.[60]

Backdoor Bay, on the southern side of Cape Royds, was perhaps more exposed to southerly storms than Winter Quarters Bay, but it did offer the protection of solid land as a bulwark against the northerly flow of ice. Such an anchorage would have separated the base and ship, although the *Nimrod* expedition hut was nearby. The separation of base from ship had already been countenanced by Mackintosh because his first overwintering choice, Glacier Tongue, was a similar distance to the south of Cape Evans. Shackleton's *Nimrod* had moored at Backdoor Bay to embark and disembark the 1907–09 party, although no vessel had wintered there.

In the event, Stenhouse found himself bound both by Shackleton's command not to winter in 'Discovery Bay' and Mackintosh's instructions. Captain J. K. Davis would later suggest that this was 'one of those rare occasions when such a refusal [to accept an order] would have been amply justified'.[61]

If Shackleton's original plan for the ship to return to Australia had been followed, it is likely that *Aurora* would by then have been well out of the Ross Sea. However, Mackintosh had announced in Sydney in October 1914 that Shackleton had decided that *Aurora* would remain 'the whole year round in the Antarctic for reasons of economy'.[62]

Paton and Thomson were critical of Stenhouse's apparent delay in deciding on a suitable berth for the ship, and the bosun fretted about dwindling coal supplies: '[Our coal] is half gone now, what shall we do when we are coming out of the ice next year, or the year after, tis then we shall need it more.'[63]

Thomson now urged Stenhouse to settle on Cape Evans as a winter mooring, and also lamented what he regarded as wasteful use of coal:

> This is the place I have been advising the C/O to come to now for nearly a month and all the worry of steaming, drifting and making fast to the sea ice might have been saved, not mentioning incidentally an amount of coal . . . 45 tons . . . 60 tons . . .

so vital to our return trip. I do not see how we can have enough to steam home and we will have to depend on poor sails to a big extent especially with fair winds . . .[64]

Stenhouse had been requested by Mackintosh to call at Hut Point on 20 March,[65] but the first officer decided to go there on 11 March because conditions were suddenly favourable and he considered it unwise to further delay mooring the ship. 'The shortage of coal and smallness of the crew rendered investigation for a harbour and the manoeuvring of the ship extremely difficult.'[66]

It was evident that the substantial cache of petrol and coal earlier deposited high on the beach at Cape Evans was no longer intact. Thomson noted on 2 March that only one case of benzine remained out of 78 landed, and 30 out of 43 bags of coal.[67] There was no mention in his tally of the twenty cases of kerosene, which had apparently vanished. He concluded that the cache had been 'washed over either by a very high tide or by a large wave caused by the overturning of a large berg or some other mysterious cause'.

When Keith Jack learned of the capsized-iceberg theory, he doubted that the offending berg would have been big enough, but Ninnis was to note in a diary entry on 7 April:

> During the afternoon . . . a most unusual vibration occurred . . . with marked movement and roll of ship . . . it split up most of the remaining ice and caused a sudden 'sea' which washed over the ice foot and bumped that ice against us heavily. Perhaps that's how our 750 gallons of petrol and oil got washed away.[68]

Over following weeks Paton, too, would observe 'submarine upheaval, eruption or earthquake'.[69]

The 30 bags of coal had effectively disappeared and Stevens later presumed that they were 'largely removed and covered up in gravel'.[70] The remnants had become frozen solid and submerged in ice and snow, and were quite unsalvageable except as occasional lumps.

Richards would later state that 'we never saw the coal or oil again',[71] and some six decades after the event he was still mystified:

> The 20 tons of coal landed. This loss has always been a mystery to me. The coal was bagged and rowed ashore and I was one of the boat party . . . It was put ashore well above the tide mark well on the dark gravelly beach. I remember we thought the mate was making us haul the heavy bags an unnecessarily long way up the beach. I have never fathomed how the coal disappeared.[72]

On 24 February, Stenhouse had dropped *Aurora*'s bow anchor in 23 fathoms of water, about three cables from the Cape Evans beach.[73] The ship yawed in strong winds and at times was 'ranging about like a mad horse'.[74] Paton reported: 'All hands are now put on day work except the firemen who are still keeping their watches and will do so, as long as we are lying under banked fires.'[75]

Stenhouse could not relax in case the ship was carried away, and Larkman wrote on 1 March: 'We have a full head of steam in case anchor drags.'[76] Steam was also necessary for Thomson to work the windlass to adjust heavy mooring cables and anchors.[77]

On 2 March, Stenhouse finally decided that the ship would winter at Cape Evans.[78] He sent a party of seamen ashore and ten seals were killed as a start towards establishing a stock of blubber and meat.[79]

Thomson was despatched in charge of a ship's boat to survey the ocean floor off Cape Evans because Paton reported that *Terra Nova* had struck a rock there. The second officer satisfied himself that no such rock existed and concluded that Scott's ship had grounded on the same shoal, north-west of the proposed mooring place, that *Aurora* had struck six weeks earlier.[80]

Thomson supervised the construction of a raft from empty drums from the hut to float ashore two anchors, each weighing about a ton, to be used when mooring the ship for winter. It took a full day's effort to land these on the beach.

> [It was] a sufficiently rough day as we had been working over our boot-tops in the surf, in a continuous fall of snow and everybody including myself felt wet and miserable and in no very pleasant mood as it was beastly cold. The wind began to increase and by midnight it was blowing a strong wind and looked like a blizzard brewing.[81]

By the time the storm abated three days later, the anchors had been buried in ice from 'the continual freezing of the surf as it ran over them'. Thomson and four sailors dug them out and brought them 'about 50 to 60 feet in shore'.[82] The following day an attempt was made to bury the anchors in the beach using picks and shovels, but the gravel was frozen by permafrost. Thomson recorded: 'This was very hard stuff and we could not have got any deeper without drills and powder, so we made that do and buried them at that depth which we had already got to. I was very satisfied with these anchors and was feeling sure that they would hold until they broke.'[83] He had no illusions as to the importance of securing the ship. 'These anchors were expected to play a large part in our winter quarters as they were required to hold us against the south easterly blizzards.'[84]

The task of provisioning Hut Point and retrieving the party there still had to be attended to. However, heavy pancake ice delayed that final pre-winter voyage.[85]

On 9 March, with the weather threatening, Stenhouse reduced steam to two hours' notice for the main engines. In the early hours of the morning of 10 March, *Aurora* dragged her anchor and began to drift in a southerly gale. The ship almost collided with the end of the Barne Glacier to the north as she was carried along in heavy seas, beam on and 'hove down to bulwarks by the wind'. Thomson described the near-calamity. 'The wind in this blizzard was blowing with hurricane force and hove the ship over until she was nearly on her beam ends.'[86] The anchor cable was left out in an attempt to steady the ship, which became 'fairly manageable' when steam was available. 'This blizzard was a continuation of squalls each one seemingly heavier than the last . . . it was extremely dangerous . . .'[87] By evening the weather had moderated, the lost anchor was retrieved and the ship steamed towards Mt Discovery to the south.

Stenhouse was on deck continuously for 22 hours throughout this emergency,[88] during which *Aurora* had been carried 30 miles to the north-west and had narrowly escaped destruction.[89] The storm had, however, also blown out the sea ice from Erebus Bay, south of Cape Evans, and the way was now clear to rendezvous with the men at Hut Point.

The same storm that had carried *Aurora* away on 10 March had buffeted the two parties still out on the Barrier. Mackintosh, Joyce and Wild had finally reached the Bluff depot on the return from near 80° South and were precariously placed, still 80 miles from Hut Point, at a late stage in the season.

Seventy-five miles north, Cope, Hayward and Jack were able to get some benefit from the southerly winds and rigged a sail as they neared Safety Camp on the edge of the Barrier. When they reached the water's edge in the afternoon of 11 March, Jack wrote: '[The] sea ice had all gone out and what was on our outward march solid ice was now a seething mass of surging dark water . . . Altogether the scene presented a most forbidding and angry aspect . . .'[90]

If Cope and his men had reached the Barrier edge even half a day earlier, it is likely they would have seen *Aurora* as she steamed slowly towards Hut Point and they might have been picked up. The ship's log records on 11 March: '9.45 a.m. Stopped engines ½ mile n.w. of Hut Point & cleared anchor.' At this point *Aurora* was some four miles from the Barrier. Although Hut Point and the *Discovery* hut would have been initially obscured by Observation Hill and Cape Armitage, the course of the ship had been 'towards Mount Discovery', which would have brought it into view of sledging party.[91]

Writing about this day two years later, Ninnis would note: 'The various rockets we fired were not observed and they did not make any signal fire to tell us of their return.'[92] There is no other record of these rockets.

After the storm of 10–11 March passed, Cope's men may have been visible to the Padre's party, then still at Hut Point, if they had looked from the Gap, especially with the use of binoculars.[93] The unexpected arrival of the ship on the morning of 11 March and the consequent evacuation of the men and dogs from Hut Point meant that no such check was made.

When *Aurora* left Hut Point at 6 p.m. on 11 March, it would seem that she headed directly for Cape Evans, and there is no record that any attempt was made on that day to check for signs of sledge parties. When Jack learnt of the movements of the ship, he despaired: '[Had *Aurora*] only steamed up to the Barrier beyond C. Armitage [they] would probably have seen our camp at Safety Camp.'[94]

Of the party that so nearly reached the ship, Hayward would not see *Aurora* again, and Cope and Jack had to wait until January 1917 to meet the survivors of the six men (other than Hooke) picked up from Hut Point on 11 March 1915.

Since they had said farewell to the northbound party of Richards, Ninnis and Hooke on 24 February, Cope, Jack and Hayward had made desultory progress, at least on the outward trail. Cope had showed little inclination to make an attempt to reach the Bluff, and once he was with Hayward and Jack progress became virtually non-existent. He camped at the slightest hint of deteriorating or thick weather, and would lie in his bag reading novels while his companions prepared the morning breakfast of tea, pemmican and biscuits. On occasions he refused to sit up when served his pemmican, objected to holding out his hand to take the mug and complained when the pemmican consequently got cold.

Jack could not believe the turn of events. At first the conviviality of the tent, with Cope talking about English university life, and Hayward about his Canadian experiences, impressed him: 'We form a happy little party and I hope it remains one till the end.'[95] However, within a few days he became frustrated and annoyed at Cope's attitude, which differed markedly from that of Joyce on the journey to the Bluff. Jack wrote on 27 February: 'I don't feel Cope shows the best qualities required in a leader of a party & I think is much inclined to be lazy.' The following day: 'Cope does not relish unpleasant conditions.' And on 1 March:

> was awakened by Cope asking what time I thought it was ... replied it was all right wherever the sun was & we could push on. He made a very uncomplimentary remark to which I replied pretty shortly and which he did not answer, and probably just as well for I have given Cope a good deal of assistance & for little thanks too. I have studied him in many ways but he unfortunately exhibits little sign of appreciation & I am becoming tired of his at times really insulting ways ... We have just finished breakfast. Cope as usual lying in bed but Hayward lending me help now & then in preparation of the meal.

Even taking account of a heavy load of 690 pounds, plus skis and sticks (25 pounds),[96] the distances achieved by Cope's party were minimal.

On 25 February, when the party led by Richards, a few miles to the south, marched for nine and a half hours, Cope's men did not travel. On 26 February, they achieved two miles in thick weather before Cope convinced Hayward to stop sledging, and they stayed in camp the following day even though the weather cleared in the evening. By comparison, Richards, Ninnis and Hooke marched all day. On 28 February, Cope stopped for the day at the lunch camp after only two hours' travel, though Jack felt they could have proceeded, given his knowledge of the route and of marked cairns. On 1 March, they managed only one and three-quarter miles over a difficult surface, then just one and a quarter. After Jack told Cope that they were 'not making good enough headway',[97] they travelled eight and a half miles on 3 March, despite the fact that Cope and Hayward had suffered a restless night.

Finally Cope took some initiative when the party was laid up the next day. He got out of his bag, assessed the week's provisions and filled the cooker with snow. However, he was suffering from skin irritation and asked Jack to examine his lips for scurvy.

By 5 March, rather than covering just sixteen miles in nine days since leaving Richards, Cope's men could have been to the Bluff, still 50 miles away, and back to their present position. Jack recorded that Cope told his colleagues that 'he felt quite done up and if he could not get sleep he could not possibly go on'. It was then decided that the party should immediately depot three weeks' supplies for three men, rather than carrying on to the Bluff to depot a week's worth. Cope wrote a report to the Skipper and a depot (Cope's No. 3) was built at the bearings 'Bluff 71.5°, Summit of Mt Discovery 114° (uncorrected)'.[98]

The three depots laid by Cope were potentially important for a north-bound party, but the quantity was excessive given the relatively short distance to Hut Point. None of the supplies left at these depots was relayed further south in the following season.

The return journey, albeit with a lighter sledge, put their previous efforts into perspective. In two days (including one when they were tent-bound in a blizzard) they reached the point where Richards had left them on 24 February.

In 1920, Shackleton was to describe the part Cope had played:

> The man from all records and diaries . . . is shown to be inefficient, lazy and incompetent . . . the one independent piece of work he had to do was to lay a depot . . . he failed to do this because he used to camp at the slightest pretext and read novels in his sleeping bag until late in the morning instead of marching though the men with him urged him to proceed.[99]

The cold March temperatures made sleep difficult and the sleeping bags were, according to Jack, 'as hard as boards' and only slowly thawed with body heat. The men slept fitfully with their heads under the bags to avoid the cold. Jack wrote: 'Every morning we wake to find the bags covered with a thick layer of white hoar frost on the outside. What would I give for a good warm bed.'[100] On 8 March, they made almost ten miles on a bad surface. The following day they halted at 8 p.m. in a thick mist of ice particles after eleven and a half miles. Jack recorded: 'Bitterly cold tonight and as usual I expect we shall have but little sleep.' Cope felt 'very irritable'.[101]

When the party reached Safety Camp on 11 March and, soon after, arrived at the Barrier edge, they found open water across towards Hut Point. Fearing that the shore might carve away and carry them out with it, they returned to the camp. Jack and Hayward then travelled by ski to try to find a safe route for the next day.[102]

Cope's men eventually made their way across to the hut by the route near to that taken by the Richards party nine days earlier. On this hazardous trip they relayed and hauled their sledge '800–900 feet'[103] up an icy slope that, according to Jack, was 'really a glacier forcing its way down and breaking off on the Barrier ice'. They camped there for the night and 'had a most glorious view of the sunset, the Barrier, Western Mountains bathed in gold and Erebus in its mantle of snow towering to the east'.[104] No longer was there perpetual daylight, so they lit a candle at night in the tent and left the Primus stove on for warmth.

Like Richards and his men before them, Cope's party abandoned the tent and sledge and made a dash for the hut. Jack wrote:

> After a precarious and exciting and at times dangerous climb we were delighted to see Observation Hill capped with Scott's Cross open to our view and shortly after were able to detail the hut lying at the foot of Vince's Hill. Part of our march had been over most precipitous slopes ... and one false step at times would have probably entailed the loss of possibly the whole party of three, for the spikes in our boots were worn and afforded little grip on the ice ... There was grave danger of being hurled into the sea or dashed to pieces on the rocks below. However we reached the hut about 4 p.m. and felt extremely thankful. Here we had first of all a good feed and smoke ... the ship had very kindly left a quantity of stores ...[105]

These stores included tobacco, a towel and soap. Because Cope's men had left their sleeping bags in their last camp, there were now only two available at the hut. However, Jack sewed together long strips of blanket, which, together with 'a couple of empty coal sacks and an old pony rug', made a 'tolerably warm bunk'.[106]

For most of the next ten days a severe blizzard kept the party inside. On

23 March, they took a walk through the Gap, below Observation Hill, and thought they could see the tent of the Skipper's party near Safety Camp. The following day Hayward and Jack retrieved the gear left at their last camp. They lined up a distant dot between two ski sticks and found it to be moving, thus satisfying themselves that this sighting was indeed Mackintosh's party.

From their vantage point Hayward and Jack looked out to White Island and beyond to Minna Bluff. It was a 'beautiful day' and the sun beat down on the striking panorama of brilliant white and blue. In this emotion-charged moment the Australian and the Briton stood and 'simply clasped hands in mutual satisfaction' that the overdue men were safe.[107]

CHAPTER EIGHT

'The dead dog trail'

THE RETURN JOURNEY from the depot laid by Mackintosh, Joyce and Wild near 80° South started on 24 February. The men had been at their southern position for four frustrating days because of bad weather, prior to which they had succeeded in laying cairns five miles eastwards of the depot, but only a single cairn one and a half miles to the west. Mackintosh wrote: 'It's very exasperating but these are some of the trials we have to put up with.' The Skipper listed the stores they had placed in the depot:

2¼ tins Biscuit (each tin 42 lbs.)
3 weeks provisions (1 unit 3 men)
3 tins oil.[1]

The laying of the depot was a significant achievement, even though it was short in distance of the intended latitude and short in quantity of the intended provisions. Mackintosh's men now had ten days' supply of provisions for the 60-mile journey back to the Bluff, which provided only a small margin of safety given that the southern journey had taken eight days.

Two of the nine dogs had died during the blizzard. Briton had been a passenger since the party left the Bluff, but the loss of Tug was a shock. Mackintosh lamented: 'We had no idea. He was one of our good dogs. We are left with seven now – I wish we could give them more biscuits.'[2] The dog rations of a pound of biscuits per day were quite inadequate and the hunger-ravaged animals were susceptible to hypothermia and death in the colder temperatures.[3] As early as 25 February, Mackintosh could see that the dogs were doomed:

We are giving them three biscuits daily which really is supposed to be sufficient: yet they are ravenous. Shacks . . . having demolished all his harness, canvas, rope, leather, brass and rivets! He is the best dog we have. I am afraid they will not pull through, they all look thin and these blizzards don't improve matters.[4]

Shacks succumbed four days later, a day after Pat died. Joyce noted: 'I don't know how I refrain from giving Mack[intosh] a bit of my mind. Will have to keep that until we get back, he will have enough to think about until we get to Hut Point.'[5]

After only four and a half miles, with the depot still in sight before the weather closed in, the party was further delayed for three days. At Joyce's urging, he and Mackintosh returned to the depot to remove a week's provisions. Joyce wrote in his diary: 'Mack is feeling the strain. We went across to the depot. The sun is out at last. We left Wild behind to lay out the sleeping bags, they may dry somewhat. It seems hard after depoting stores to rob it again.'

As the old month made way for the new, the sun dipped below the southern horizon for the first time, heralding the approaching winter. There were scenes to savour as the sun's rays illuminated the clouds and the moon added to the grandeur, in stark contrast to the 'ugliness, misery and pain there is when the blizzard obliterates everything'.[6]

The Skipper's men found themselves only a third of the way back to the Bluff depot in the time it had taken them to make the outward trip. Wild's companions restored circulation to his big toe, which had become badly frostbitten as a result of inadequate boots. Mackintosh wrote: 'It is black and blue like a bruise. I bandaged it up and smeared it over with vaseline.'[7] Even disregarding wind-chill factor, the temperature was plummeting to −15°F (47° of frost) at noon in the warmest part of the day.[8] The men's discomfort was accentuated by inadequate clothing, causing Mackintosh to rue: 'I had no idea we should be out in such low temperatures . . . We ought to have had more clothing.'[9]

Tuesday, 2 March, was calamitous, as Ernest Wild's diary records: 'Today we did four miles. First Nigger then Pompey, Major and Scotty fell out. So now we have only got Pinkey left. He has had a good feed tonight. We shall have to call this the dead dog trail.'[10]

Mackintosh, too, described the painful events of that day:

> After lunch our time has been disastrous. We went off fairly well for half an hour, then Nigger commenced to wobble about, his legs evidently giving under him. We let him out of his harness and let him travel along with us but he was given us all he can, and now poor brute can only lay down. After Nigger my friend Pompey collapsed; the drift, I think, accounts a good deal for his. Pompey has been splendid of late, pulling steadily and well. After Pompey – the bachelor and quite one of the best dogs – Major fell down, and followed in the tracks of the others, then the last but one, Scotty. They are all lying down in our tracks; one thing [is] they have a painless death, for they lie curled up in the snow and fall into sleep from which they never wake again.[11]

The victims included two of best dogs: Nigger, leader of the heavyweights, and Major, leader of the lightweights. As the men sledged north, they could see the black inert forms of the dead dogs for some distance behind them. Several times severe wind gusts caught a makeshift sail they had erected, and capsized the sledge. On one occasion the Skipper fell and was run over by the sledge, but escaped injury.[12] Mackintosh likened their predicament 'unto a cold hell', in contrast to the beautiful evening scene.[13]

At times their man-hauling efforts could not budge the sledge:

> Started with great hopes this morning and found we couldn't move the sledge so we took the double runners off during which I broke my knife. Then we made another attempt. Joyce forgot to hitch his harness on and while the Skipper and I were struggling, away he went saying 'By Gollams this is better already.' I shouted out to him and he came back and hitched on and then we couldn't move the sledge so we set off [on] ski and pulled that way. We went about 2 miles in four hours pulling the hardest we have pulled before. After lunch we took everything off the sledge and capsized it and found the runners covered with some sticky stuff. With only one old table knife between us we had to scrape both runners. The temp. between 20°–30° below zero, 60° of frost.[14]

To compound the party's difficulties, Joyce suffered frostbite to his legs and hands, and his companions had to massage the affected parts in the shelter of the tent during a spell of two hours, also spent cleaning off the sledge runners.

The men built a cairn and placed there all surplus gear, including dog biscuits and harness, allowing them to make better progress, but often only at a speed of about a mile an hour. By 5 March, they were just past the halfway mark back to the Bluff depot.[15]

Pinkey, the party's last dog, was given full rations and a 'busman's holiday riding on the sledge',[16] but on 6 March:

> About 4 p.m. Pinkey, our last four-legged supporter, gave in! So he shared the fate of the rest and now we are without one of our dogs! We did think he would last out, especially as he has been having his full rations . . . they have all given in when the drift has been on . . .[17]

Noting the parallel to Scott's experience 'in this latitude... in 1902 [when] Captain Scott lost all his dogs', Joyce was critical, but just how he considered the depot might have been better laid is unclear. 'This could have been avoided if common sense had been shown for the time we were at the Bluff.'[18]

Mackintosh's party did not reach the Bluff depot on the return journey until 10 March, two weeks after setting out from near 80° South. Over the week from 3 March they averaged just five miles a day, including one day when a blizzard prevented any progress. Although marching by day made them 'more or less warm',[19] the bitter conditions, accentuated by darkness from 6 p.m., made it a hardship to write up their daily diaries in the tent at night.[20]

When, on 10 March, the party finally reached the intended position for the

Bluff depot, with 'the corrected peak of Discovery in line with peak on SE of Bluff in transit', they decided to shift the stores back to that point.[21] Joyce could see the depot flag through binoculars[22] and, taking an extraordinary gamble with the elements, they decided to leave the tent and sleeping bags at the correct depot position and set out in fine weather with a light sledge on a return journey of perhaps fifteen to twenty, even twenty-two miles.[23]

The Skipper wrote:

> In spite of the sledge having nothing in it we found it quite a hard pull. There must be something radically wrong with the sledge. After a hard 4 hours pull over a rough surface we got to the depot flag and found it and the cairn intact. In fact all had been left as if no time had intervened . . . We can't make out why no other parties have been up, it's puzzling for they should be here by this time at least. We loaded the sledge with the stores, placed the large mark flag in the sledge and proceeded back to our tent which of course now is out of sight – indeed it was not wise to come out as we have without tent or bag but we have taken that chance and the weather has promised fine, yet that is no criterion in these parts. As we proceeded it grew darker and darker and eventually we were travelling by only the light of stars, the sun having dipped. After 4½ hours we sighted the little green tent. 'Be it ever so humble there's no place like home.'[24]

That evening the men had an extra thick hoosh, which they ate by the flickering light of an improvised lamp made from a tin burning methylated spirit. They turned in at 2 a.m., shortly before a blizzard enveloped the tent. Wild noted of the day's activities: 'We risked our lives and went for it with an empty sledge.'[25]

After a day lying up in the blizzard, the party built the depot to a height of twelve feet, over which they 'lashed and stayed 3 bamboos, the height in all 27 feet'.[26] Mackintosh recorded that they placed there '6 weeks biscuits, 3 tins of oil, and 3 weeks full rations'.[27] Joyce described it in slightly different terms: '6 weeks biscuits, 3 weeks provisions for 3 men and 4 weeks oil.'[28]

The principal work of the season now complete, Mackintosh's men headed north with one week's supply of food to get them to Safety Camp, 50 miles away.[29] They anticipated meeting the support parties, who so mysteriously had not arrived at the Bluff, or at least coming across depots left by them. Although they felt buoyed at having achieved their task, the rapidly decreasing temperatures created daily agonies, as the Skipper wrote:

> Getting away in the mornings is our bitterest time, the putting on of the finneskoes being our regular nightmare for they are always frozen stiff and we have great struggles trying to force our feet into them, the icy sennegrass round one's fingers too is another punishment that causes much pain. We get no comfort until we are actually on the move then warmth returns with the work.[30]

Both Joyce and Wild were afflicted with frostbitten toes, and Mackintosh described Wild as 'a mass of sores as the after results of frostbites'. The Skipper himself suffered a frostbitten nose and observed that the frozen bags by night offered little respite. 'You will find one or other of us groaning and cussing trying to bring back a frozen toe or rub some part of the body that has been cooled.'[31] Joyce wrote in his diary: 'Our circulation must be at a very low ebb, the first bites to occur in our sleeping bags.'[32] A good trick, noted Mackintosh, was to place socks and other clothing inside jerseys 'and produce them when required. Wild carries a regular wardrobe in this fashion.'[33]

The Skipper's injured right eye, a legacy from the *Nimrod* expedition, gave him much discomfort. Gaze would later recall that 'with the winds . . . his glass eye had to be covered. It did freeze up and eventually he had to take it out and leave it out – it was a great handicap to him, but he had plenty of guts . . .'[34] In Joyce's opinion, 'Mackintosh never ought to have left the ship. His eye is very painful.'[35]

Three miles north of the depot a blizzard once again delayed the party, this time for two days. The phenomenon of temperatures rising during blizzards resulted in dampness and discomfort in the tent. The reindeer-skin sleeping bags became putrid, and meals were forgone to save food. On 13 March, Mackintosh wrote: 'Having been without a meal since yesterday evening one's insides begin to feel hollow. The wind howls outside, the hoosh we are having sends a glorious tingle right through one.'[36] Drifting into a restless sleep, the Skipper dreamt he 'was strolling about outside when a paperboy came rushing to me to say Erebus was in eruption 1000 lives lost. Smoke was coming out of Castle Rock!' He awoke to find himself in his wet clothing and 'dampness all round'.[37]

As the blizzard passed, barometric pressure rose and the men's wet garments and bags turned to ice. After a relatively satisfactory day's progress of some twelve miles on 15 March,[38] the temperature fell to an estimated –50°F and the shivering men found sleep impossible. As if this were not enough, Mackintosh developed severe toothache and moaned and groaned through the night. Joyce left the comparative shelter of his frozen bag to check the medical case, but

> there was nought to ease him. My thoughts could only think of methylated spirits a bottle of which we kept for starting the Primus. This I passed to him together with cotton wool. During the evolution of putting the spirit on the cotton wool his fingers went. He placed the cotton wool on the tooth, a second elapsed and then a yell, the sound of which must have penetrated to Cape Evans. The toothache was cured, the inside of the [mouth] raw. The temperature of the spirit was the same temperature as the air, 82° [*sic*] of frost. It had the same effect as boiling liquid.[39]

With the party some 63 miles from Hut Point, the familiar landmarks of Erebus and Terror were prominent to the north in clear weather. Mt Terror was in direct line with the travellers' northern trail and they steered by it as a point of reference.[40] Of the three men, Wild was in the worst condition. Joyce observed of his friend: 'Wild in agony with frostbites, difficulty in trekking on hard ice with raw feet.'[41]

For the next four days they averaged ten miles a day, despite Wild's crippled condition. By 19 March, they reached a point where the route turned towards Castle Rock. They sighted a red flag that Mackintosh assumed marked 'Joyce's Corner Camp',[42] but he did not investigate because Joyce had not left supplies there and had merely indicated the outward trail near White Island with flags.

In fact, if Mackintosh had inspected the cairn at Corner Camp, he might have found it to be the depot laid there by Cope, Jack and Hayward on 5 March, and their food worries would have been over.[43] As it was, they had gone on to reduced rations on 16 March to make their supplies last until they reached Safety Camp. By 21 March, the Skipper noted that they were down to 'close on half rations, and have two days left to take us in'.[44]

Equally critical was a shortage of matches, the use of which they decided to ration to lighting the Primus, using an improvised methylated lamp.[45] Now that they were approaching Hut Point, thoughts turned to more civilised comforts: 'I look forward to seeing the ship and enjoying the luxury of my own little cabin . . . Here we are frostbitten in the day, frozen at nights, no sleep, what a life![46]

They were travelling over very high rough sastrugi that, because of mirage, would at times appear to be dancing 'like some ice goblin'. The men had managed most of the journey on ski, but with difficult surfaces they proceeded on foot in finnesko. 'It makes the sledge go better, but it's not so comfortable travelling as on ski,' remarked Mackinstosh.[47]

Yet another blizzard held them up on 23 March. Although they had only half a full meal left and could not afford to be delayed for long, the men attempted to left their spirits with a singsong following a makeshift hoosh of biscuit crumbs and water mixed with chocolate. The Skipper wrote: 'How one longs to be out of this infernal region – the dear ones at Home what are they doing? . . . But food is our one thought, what will we eat when we get back? Even dog biscuits now would be a luxury.'[48]

They ate the last of their food and left at daybreak on 24 March. Joyce wrote in his diary: 'Poor Wild is on his last legs, his feet are causing him terrible pain',[49] and added that if he and Mackintosh had not been so weak they would have pulled their crippled companion on the sledge. Their anxiety lessened when, after two hours' hauling, Joyce spotted the flag of Safety Camp. The men were soon eagerly consumming pemmican thickened with sweet porridge.

As Wild was lighting the Primus in the tent in readiness for the feast, his hands lost their feeling. Mackintosh wrote of his desperate companion: 'To stop this and bring the circulation back he put them over the lighted Primus – a terrible thing to do – the result he was in agony, tears rolling down his cheeks.'[50] In addition, Wild's frost-affected ear had turned a pale green colour.

The Skipper's men learnt from notes left by Spencer-Smith and Richards at the camp that all was well with the other parties, despite the failure of the motor sledge.

Like the two preceding parties, Mackintosh's men now had to make their way along the Barrier edge to find a route to Hut Point. They headed towards Castle Rock but, near Pram Point, prospected their way down through some 'curious undulations on the surface, high hills of ice running in waves parallel to the coast'. These pressure ridges, up to 30 feet in height, formed a valley that led towards newly formed sea ice. The men depoted their sledge and travelled light.

> We soon made our way across the Bay, and found ourselves off Pram Point and here we saw the old pram, the boat the *Discovery* Expedition used and left here after which the point was named. About here we were able to scramble up the cliffs, leaving our ski on which we had been travelling . . .[51]

Joyce's diary records that 'on inspection the ice was thin and therefore treacherous. We decided to climb the hills . . .'[52] Carrying only ice axes, they made their way through the pressure ridges and thus saved themselves the extra distance that the parties led by Richards and Cope had travelled. Joyce described the final stages of their trek:

> We assisted Wild up the gradual slope. His feet still very painful. Reached the summit of the hills which leads down to a plateau between Cape Armitage and Hut Point. I remarked 'Let us play chance – slide down and see where we land'. We let ourselves go, in two minutes we found ourselves at the bottom and about ten yards from the edge of a drop of about thirty feet. Our breath exhausted.[53]

Within half an hour they were at Hut Point.

Despite every effort by Mackintosh, Wild and Joyce, their journey back from the southern depot at 79° 52' S had taken them nine days longer than the outward journey of nineteen days, in addition to the four days when bad weather had delayed them at the depot. This preliminary yet important achievement by the Ross Sea party, in life-threatening conditions, has been underrated and largely forgotten.

CHAPTER NINE

Sanctuary reached

D ESCRIBING HIS PARTY'S arrival at the *Discovery* hut on 25 March 1915,
Mackintosh recorded:

> We shouted – no sound – again, presently a dark object appeared; this turned out
> to be Cope who was by himself, the others of the party having gone out to fetch
> gear off their sledge . . . The ever-required meal was soon prepared . . . We found
> even a blubber fire luxurious but what a state of dirt and grease. However warmth
> and food at present our principal objects, all else considered as ordinary. The mys-
> teries of sledge parties were now explained; while we were having our meal Jack
> and Hayward appeared – more shaking of hands, more yarns. Late in the evening
> we turned into dry bags for the first time for over a month.[1]

John Cope, the medical man in the absence of a qualified doctor, immediately set about treating the injuries, one of his first tasks being to lance several
throbbing frostbite blisters. The conditions in the hut were far from sanitary,
with blubber soot and grease everywhere. In his diary Joyce paid tribute to the
'good management of Cope who was working under extreme difficulties'.

Mackintosh had come through the best, with only slight frostbite to his
feet, hands, cheeks and nose. Joyce's feet and hands were in bad shape, his knees
were swollen (almost certainly early signs of scurvy) and a big black blister extended across his cheek and covered his nose. Wild was in the worst state and,
in Joyce's opinion, could not have travelled another day.[2] Jack observed that
Wild's ear was 'dripping viscous matter continuously and [his] toe looks almost
gangrenous'.[3] Joyce recorded: 'Part of his left ear came off. It was a couple of
weeks before our faces straightened out again. It was painful to laugh . . .'[4]

Jack, normally a full diarist, made remarkably little comment about the
return of the Skipper's party and their achievements, this possibly being a carry-
over from some animosity and bad feeling from when he was at the Bluff.

Although anxious to recover the sledge and equipment abandoned at the
Barrier edge, Mackintosh decided this task could wait for fine weather: 'after all,
why should we go and endure more battering about?' (On 22 April, the day the

sun finally dipped below the northern horizon for the winter months, he would lead Joyce, Hayward and Cope to retrieve the sledge via Cape Armitage.[5])

After their extreme exposure on the Barrier, the recently returned men recuperated in the security and relative warmth of the hut. The Skipper, himself convalescing, observed: 'J[oyce] and W[ild] are progressing well with their frostbites, it's only a matter of time. Joyce feels the cold very badly at all times.'[6] It was three weeks before Joyce walked any significant distance from the hut, on the first seal-hunting trip, and Wild did not venture out until the middle of May.[7]

The six men divided themselves into two watches, alternated use of the sleeping bags and shared cooking duties.[8] Initially the hut seemed a mansion, as evidenced from Mackintosh's account three days after returning from the Barrier:

> Yet, I feel how glorious it is to be warm, sheltered and assured of sleep – food too as much as we can please. Here we are 3 of us huddled up alongside of stove, applying lumps of blubber as the last piece gets burnt away . . . the blubber gurgles and splutters, the delightful sound of heat which one gets to know besides the feel; we have one sack of coal – this mixed with the blubber makes it last longer and we thus economise its use.[9]

Then, four days later: 'One consolation we always have, we are sheltered here, we can keep warm, frosts and blizzards can predominate outside, but here we're warm for ever.'

However, the Skipper's heaven soon became more like purgatory. The fastidious Mackintosh detested squalid conditions. Only a few days after his party's sledging ordeal had ended, he wrote: 'The dirt – it's too terrible . . . oh! this filth – when will we be released?'[10] And added a day or two later: 'What a crowd of utter tramps we look; long matted hair, uncropped straggling beards, grease all over ourselves, clothes – dirtiness personified.' In early April he ordered a general clean-up.[11]

Southerly blizzards regularly broke up the fragile ice and frustrated the men in their desire to return to Cape Evans. They remained virtual prisoners in the hut. The Skipper fretted: 'We do so hope the sea will soon freeze over and release us.' He was not expecting to see *Aurora* back at Hut Point, as his directions to Stenhouse had been fulfilled, albeit nine days early, when the ship picked up the Padre's party on 11 March. Joyce maintained in his diary, written some months later, that he argued with the leader over the subject: 'Although we are heated in our arguments it is forgotten soon after.'[12] He would add in his 1929 book that they 'decided to taboo the subject', but it is more likely that Mackintosh told him not to raise it again.

When the sea froze, temporarily as it turned out, Mackintosh, Hayward and Jack prospected for a route close to the shore beyond Castle Rock towards Glacier Tongue, but to no avail because open water blocked their path.[13] As the days turned into weeks, and the weeks into months, Mackintosh became increasingly impatient at their marooned condition.

Jack wrote:

> Mackintosh talks about 2 or 3 making a dash for Cape Evans without a sledge or other equipment. I maintain it would be madness . . . he is rash to a degree and fails to learn from any experience. Had only got in from our walk for a short time and it came on [with] heavy drift.[14]

The extended sojourn at Hut Point depleted the supply of seal blubber, vital for heating and cooking. On one occasion it ran out completely and the men burnt wooden cases they found lying around the hut.[15] They were forced to become hunters again but, because of difficulty of access, had to ignore some seals that appeared on 6 April north of Hut Point by the abandoned motor sledge. A week later they killed five seals near Cape Armitage, ensuring a ten-day supply of fuel. They would daze an animal by hitting the tip of its nose and then use one of the two available knives to slit its throat. Mackintosh wrote: 'At first I detested the job, especially when the seals looked beseechingly at one with their large eyes, but after starving in the tent I am afraid the tender instincts, if any, in us vanish.'[16]

Jack and the Skipper developed ugly finger infections, and Cope's legs became covered in ulcerated sores, such that for some days he could only hobble about.[17]

Although there were fine periods, blizzards frequently confined the men indoors. In cramped and dark conditions, petty disputes sometimes arose. On one such occasion, Mackintosh told Cope to consider himself 'disrated'.[18] On another, the Skipper refused to lend Wild a combination suit after he had fallen through the sea ice up to his waist. Wild remonstrated in his diary: 'I can't understand the people here at all, they've got no business down here at all. I don't know what they came for (with one or two exceptions). I mean the people on the ship as well.'[19]

Other arguments, especially over cooking, were good-humoured. The men played ludo and draughts on makeshift boards using cubes of sugar and pieces of biscuit for pieces.[20] When the supply of candles became depleted, Jack made simple but effective blubber lamps from old tins and seal bones.[21] These gave a flickering light in the dim atmosphere of the blackened hut, two-thirds of which was filled with ice and snow.[22]

On 26 April 1915, the moon appeared at Hut Point for the first time that winter. This offered sufficient light for the hazardous crossing to Cape Evans, but the sea ice was far from ready. On 6 May, a blizzard set in that lasted for a week. Although Cape Evans was only fifteen miles away, a drama was unfolding there of which the men at Hut Point were as unaware as they were of events elsewhere in the world.

Almost two months had passed since 11 March, when *Aurora* had left Hut Point for Cape Evans with the six men and two dogs of the Padre's party. For Stenhouse and Thomson, charged with the duty of mooring the ship for the winter, it had been a time of great anxiety. No sooner had they dropped the ship's anchors again at Cape Evans than *Aurora* was again carried away in a blizzard. Bosun Paton wrote:

> Just after midnight it began to blow furiously and the ship ranged heavily at the anchors. I altered the helm several times during the night to see if that would ease her but this blizzard proved the hardest one we have had this year, she yawed and tugged at her cable until 6 a.m. just as I was going below and she was off like a racehorse down the straits . . .[23]

With steam available, Stenhouse raised the anchors and attempted to manoeuvre the ship. Again *Aurora* passed close to the Barne Glacier. The engines were put astern to clear Cape Barne and then Cape Royds. The ship was broadside to the wind with a heavy list to port and would not answer the helm as the officers tried to bring her head up. Concerns that *Aurora* would founder on the shore were compounded by midmorning when the wind increased to gale force and driving mist and spray reduced visibility to a few hundred yards. Thomson wrote of

> . . . tremendous squalls which threatened to tear the masts and spars out of the ship and heave her down on her beam end. Besides we could not tell which way we were drifting for certain as we could not see and was nearly blinded with the frozen spray as it dashed over the deck . . . there was a higher sea running through this gale than I thought possible.[24]

By midday the wind was at storm force.[25] This was a terrifying experience not only for the ship's crew but for the landlubbers of the Padre's party, who were 'all sick with the pitching and rolling of the ship'.[26] By late evening the wind moderated and Thomson noted that *Aurora* 'began to drift through large fields of pancake ice which kept the sea from breaking and acted like oil upon it'.[27] Thomson had been on deck for over twenty hours without a break, except for snatched meals. By morning *Aurora* was off Beaufort Island and, after steaming through pancake ice all day, she anchored off Cape Evans at

6 p.m. It was Saturday night and, and with the danger apparently gone, the men's morale improved. A relieved Padre noted:

> A great singsong after dinner tonight, gramophone first, and then piano: all sorts of songs, solos and chorus – 'The Wearing of the Green,' 'Auld Lang Syne,' 'Three Fishers,' 'Old Folks at Home,' 'Little Grey Home' 'Where my caravan has rested' etc.[28]

For the first time the ship was moored stern to the shore in readiness for winter. Over two days five wire hawsers (later increased to seven) were rowed ashore and attached to the anchors on the beach. In addition, there were two bow anchors and a chain cable was later attached to the shore anchor outside the hut. The bosun led the working party at the capstan to the call of slow shanties, the favourite being 'Reuben Ranzo'.[29]

The men on the ship realised that the recent storms had probably delayed the Skipper and the other five men they hoped would be at Hut Point. Larkman wrote: 'We are not justified in leaving safe moorings with the risk of not picking them up again.'[30] Stenhouse considered it safe to finish with steam on the main engine and, after the ship was pumped as dry as possible, Thomson recorded: 'The fires were drawn and the boilers blown down.' Coal supplies on *Aurora* had reduced to 118 tons from the 472 taken on in Australia. The ship's engineers supervised the opening of all drains and sea cocks, sealed the boiler and funnel, and generally made 'the engine room snug for winter'.[31]

Thomson concluded that he was 'perfectly confident that [the two shore anchors] will not drag out although they may break or else the bits to which the moorings are fast may drag out of the ship'.[32] The experienced bosun thought that 'nothing can shift her'.[33] The ship's moorings were constantly adjusted to maintain tension depending on wind and ice conditions.

On 27 March, as recorded by Thomson, a 'slight south easterly breeze' caused the whole of the ice in the bay to break away from the shore and put very heavy pressure on the starboard side of the ship and 'also the port moorings were kept at breaking strain'.[34] Ice formed in the bay, then was carried away by southerly storms on at least seven occasions over the next month or so.

On 7 April, one of the port stern moorings parted and, three days later, two more gave way. Thomson contemplated creating an island of ice around *Aurora*:

> The ship and moorings was [*sic*] holding all the ice in North Bay ... extending to about a mile and a quarter out from the hut. Quite a piece of ice to be hanging on to our moorings in a strong wind with signs of increasing to a strong gale. The only hope I can see for us is to saw off as much of the bay ice as we think we can hold comfortably and keep it free from the rest which is rather a large job but could be done.[35]

On 25 March, he retrieved two ice saws from the hut in case they 'may be of service at a later date'.[36]

By 25 April, four of the seven wire hawsers holding the ship to the shore anchors had snapped. This left two four-inch wires, one two-and-a-half-inch wire and the heavy chain cable holding the ship to her moorings.[37] Thomson supervised the moorings and crew members were also engaged in other work, principally setting up wireless masts on the ship and rigging a temporary aerial to the hut, a task completed on 3 May.

Stevens, Gaze, Spencer-Smith and Richards, all designated shore-party members, had moved from *Aurora* to take up residence in the Cape Evans hut on 23 March. Ninnis often worked ashore but elected to keep his sleeping quarters on *Aurora*, near his lathe and workshop equipment.[38] The Padre wrote of life in the hut:

> It is very cold, but nice to be on one's own and a good sleeping bag makes up for much else. Stevens and I have the corner formerly occupied by Evans and Wilson: nice and private and next to the darkroom: plenty of shelving too. Our books and beds make it look furnished and I have mother's photo too.[39]

Richards soon set up his meteorological programme and, according to Ninnis, was

> usually to be seen at stated times when he goes to take the meteorological readings at the seven instruments on the hillside. Today he was quite entertaining. He made a dash from the hut door up hillside but the wind caught him and swept his feet away, he went to leeward a few yards, flying in the ice and snow. Twice he was blown over like this and then he reached the rubble slopes. Here he dashed for the screen, head down and got blown some yards to leeward of it. It must have been cold handling and resetting the instruments. He is quite the most energetic of the 'science' party.[40]

Stores and equipment landed over the following six weeks included 56 pounds of butter and 75 pounds of sugar, medical and sledging stores, including Bovril rations and dog pemmican, Streimer nut food and Trumilk.[41] The shore party received only five bags of coke of the 60 requested from the ship.[42]

A set of *Encyclopaedia Britannica*, presented by Captain Davis, and an HMV gramophone, on loan from *Aurora* for six weeks, were welcome additions to the shore base.[43] Regular issues of tobacco, cigarettes, liquor and other weekly requirements such as tea, condensed milk and matches were made from the ship. At the request of Stenhouse, the shore party listed its requirements for two months. Thomson noted ironically: 'I received a very pleasant note from the Shore Party . . . with a request for several useful foods and also wanting a stock of toffee and chocolates to be sent ashore to them with a sprinkling of bottles of whisky and rum. I expect that they are thinking that they are missing their share.'[44]

No extra clothing was unloaded; in fact some items in the hut were taken to the ship. Ninnis noted on 26 March: 'All have swooped on cast off clothing of Scott's party. Boots chiefly in demand and the felt boots in particular. I have a pair marked RFS . . .'[45] Although there was not an abundance of clothing on board, Thomson listed on 21 March garments such as lambskin mittens, Burberry pants, blouses and helmets, sheepskin vests, sleeping stockings and socks, much of which was clearly meant for the sledging parties.[46]

Further important sledging equipment, such as tents, reindeer sleeping bags and sledges, some of which had been removed from the hut, remained on the ship. Stevens wrote in his post-expedition report: 'Stenhouse stated that he had been ordered to land no stores at Cape Evans, and later Mackintosh confirmed this.'[47]

Uncertain of the predicament of the Skipper's party, Stenhouse attempted to signal the men at the *Discovery* hut by means of rockets and a blue flare when the ice to the south of Cape Evans looked sound.[48]

On 16 April, Ninnis, Hooke and Gaze prepared to sledge to Hut Point with contingency plans for a search in case the six men were not there. The location of the food depots was now brought into sharp focus, with some criticism of Ninnis, presumably because of the non-performance of the motor sledge and the shortfall in distance of the depot from the Bluff. The Padre, who was not in favour of the Hut Point trip, counselled Ninnis that it would be futile and foolish to search beyond the depot they had laid. If the Skipper's party was lost, 'every life that remains becomes doubly or trebly valuable in view of next year's work'.[49] The search party could not set out from Cape Evans because the sea ice was constantly carried away. Instead, they set up a 40-foot rope ladder, made by the ship's crew, on the south side of Cape Evans to give access from the sea ice in case the route around the end of the cape was impassable. At the top of the ladder they left their fully laden sledge as a depot.

Meanwhile, life in the Cape Evans hut was pleasant and the four men were free to pursue their own interests and establish their own routines. Spencer-Smith adopted the darkroom formerly used by Herbert Ponting of the Scott expedition, and also used it as a chapel and study. He wrote on 15 April: 'Darkroom very comfortable now with oil stove. Temp. about 41°F. It is nice to be able to sit here and write – a private sitting room in the Antarctic an unheard of luxury.'[50] Stevens cooked most of the meals, Richards did his scientific work, the Padre spent much of his time reading, and Gaze was occupied with general duties and tending the remnants of the dog team, four sledging dogs and two bitches. (Two sickly dogs that had not sledged, Buller and Tiger, had died when put ashore in late March.)

Coal and coke were taken ashore by sledge as required and used in preference to blubber, although some seals were killed and left on the shore, a practice that drew adverse comment from the men on the ship. Sometimes the half-frozen sea ice prevented a boat passing from *Aurora* to shore, yet was not thick enough to cross on foot or ski. On Sunday, 2 May, some of the crew visited the hut. The Padre enjoyed the companionship and wrote in his diary:

> Ginger [Kavanagh], Atkins, Glidden, and the Bo's'n each made several visits & there was much tobacco and talk round the fire. I went on board about 5.30 to fetch a plum-duff presented by the cook, who seems rather better, and stayed to have yarn aft – all in good spirits . . . By invitation went over again at about 8 and played for a singsong aft. Hymns first of all. 'Lead Kindly Light' – 'Nearer my God to Thee', 'Eternal Father', 'Adeste Fidelis', 'The Church's One Foundation', 'Old 100th', 'Rock of Ages' and many other old favourites, in which everyone joined. Then we had some songs, mainly by Sten, and I did not come ashore till 10. Had a cup of cocoa with Irvine and turned in at 11 for a short sleep, tired but happy.[51]

On 30 April, the wireless mast on *Aurora* was sent aloft, the crew having previously extended the fore and mizzenmasts by twenty feet with the temporary receiving aerial rigged to the hut. On 4 May, Hooke came ashore and listened in vain for four hours for signals from the Macquarie Island station.[52] He left a wireless set, described by Ninnis as 'a small set of gear . . . capable of being rigged as sending and receiving', at the hut for use in emergencies.[53]

Over the previous two months the ship's personnel had observed four eruptions from Mt Erebus, each accompanied by loud explosions and emissions of steam and black smoke.[54] They had also seen on four occasions (sometimes coinciding with the volcanic activity) sudden and unexplained heavy swells under the sea ice. These subsided after a short period.[55] On 21 April, Paton wrote:

> Mt Erebus continues still to belch forth huge columns of black smoke and has still a very angry appearance. At 7.30 p.m. there was a strong submarine upheaval which caused a nasty sea to get up making the ship roll unmercifully accompanied by a dull hissing sound. The whole thing did not last more than five minutes, but it was quite long enough to set us thinking, and now as I am writing this, everything is calm and peaceful, the sea is as smooth as glass, and new ice is making rapidly.[56]

Stenhouse recorded something similar on 5 May:

> 8.45 (p.m.)
> Noise heard at ship (apparently from Erebus) – followed by heavy swell under ice causing great disturbance.[57]

On 6 May, the crew worked on the wireless masts until midafternoon, when a party was sent ashore shortly before darkness to fetch ice for the water supply. There were unmistakable signs of a blizzard advancing from the south-east. The ship's carpenter, Charles Mauger, was 'all spruced up and ready to go' to have tea with Stevens in the hut, but the weather deterred him. By 8 p.m. the wind had freshened to Force 4 and there was heavy strain on the moorings.

CHAPTER TEN

❖

'A glimpse of hell'

A T 9.45 P.M. on 6 May 1915, the entire ice in the bay north of Cape Evans 'broke away in Body from the shore'.[1] With it was carried *Aurora*, locked in the frozen sea with her stern moorings still in position behind her but snapped from the shore anchors embedded in the beach.

Mauger likened the loud reports of the mooring lines parting to 'a six inch gun',[2] and Thomson said the sound was 'like the report of guns'.[3] All hands were called and the crew tumbled out of their bunks fearing that the groaning of the decks and hideous noise of the grinding ice spelt disaster. Hooke wrote: 'We rushed up on deck and now knew we were adrift in the sound. The ship swung on her bow anchors, which at once dragged'.[4] The light in the hut ashore was soon swallowed up in the snow and darkness. The mournful sound of bagpipe music wafted from the ship's forecastle. In case there was any doubt about the turn of events, Paton 'rushed along with his hurricane lamp and shouted "She's away wi' it." '[5]

Stenhouse ordered steam, knowing that this would be many hours off because the boiler fires were out. There was little the crew could do except apply relieving tackles to the two bow anchors, which were each on 75 fathoms of chain cable, to reduce the immense pressure on the bow and the windlass. Thick ice pressed up against the ship to the height of the rails. The wind was blowing at gale force and struck the ship even more savagely when the shelter of the land was lost.[6] There was a heavy list to port, then the floe in which *Aurora* was stuck fast began to break up and the ship entered the loose pack.[7]

At about 1 a.m. on 7 May, the moon emerging through the clouds revealed the ship to be eight miles north-west of Cape Barne, well clear of Ross Island, in contrast to the two previous break-outs. Stenhouse later recalled the experience. 'In that "homeless" time, I, keeping watch . . . hard pressed to know what to do, in the circumstances had a glimpse of hell.'[8]

The dim two-hour twilight, with the ship approximately eighteen miles from Cape Evans, confirmed to the men of *Aurora* that she was not in any immediate danger.[9] Perhaps because the ship had been blown out twice before, there was no great alarm on board and the crew was put on 'balance watches', which left them 'liable to be called on deck for any work at any time during the day or night'.[10] Stenhouse hoped that when steam was raised they would return and moor to the edge of the fast ice near Glacier Tongue in order to replenish their fresh water, which was reduced to two days' supply. He reasoned that, despite the difficulties experienced in trying to moor the ship south of Cape Evans two months earlier, the ice would eventually be stabilised by nearby islands and allow a safer anchorage than at the cape.[11]

The ship's engineers worked tirelessly to reassemble the disconnected engine-room fittings in 50 degrees of frost, which caused unprotected skin to stick to metal. The sea-cock was frozen solid, so Larkman and Donnelly drilled a hole and fed in iron rods heated with blowtorches until the water flowed.[12] 'After getting as much water into the boiler as the ship's draught permitted (being fast in pack ice she could not settle lower), we made up the 8 inch deficiency by passing blocks of ice into the top manhole . . .'[13] By 5.30 p.m. on 7 May, fires were lit in the furnaces, which Stenhouse described as 'the first blow in our defence against the terrific forces of Nature in the Antarctic'.[14] The canny bosun, however, was not cheered. 'We were then frozen in harder than we have ever been with no hope of getting out again . . .'[15]

At 3 a.m. on 7 May, Richards left the hut at Cape Evans to take meteorological readings.[16] He turned instinctively to look seawards and was amazed not to see the masts of the ship showing above the drift in the moonlight. Walking down to the water's edge, he found the broken hawsers and cable, but no ship.[17] He then went back into the hut and woke his three companions. More than six decades later, Irvine Gaze would recall the poignant message: 'Oh Gazey, the ship's blown out . . .'[18]

Richards and Gaze went outside, but in the limited visibility they could see only open water. The day passed with no news of the ship, the Padre noting: 'All rather gloomy at dinner.' An attempt was made to signal *Aurora* by flashing a lamp, but there was no answer.[19] At first the men in the hut thought that the ship could well return in the next day or two, as the blizzard of 6–7 May had not seemed too severe. When they then experienced their worst blizzard, which lasted for three days with winds over a hundred miles an hour, they feared the worst, thinking the ship had gone down.

It was immediately apparent that many items required for depot laying were still on the ship. This was also noticed aboard *Aurora*, where Thomson wrote: 'If we are at all handy we will try and send them in by sledge journey next spring or at least as soon as it is light enough.'[20]

Over the following weeks Hooke made repeated attempts to contact Cape Evans on the ship's wireless, with aerials now rigged from the masts to the sea ice.[21] The men at the hut had practised sending and receiving Morse code, but there is no record of any regular attempt to listen on the elementary wireless set left there. Half-hearted attempts to signal the ship received no response,[22] though faint, unreadable signals, thought to be from a 'northern station', were heard on *Aurora* on three consecutive days during the second week of June.[23]

When the ship was four days out from Cape Evans, the storm that caused concern at the hut struck *Aurora*, measuring Force 12 and the worst that Paton had experienced.[24] Stenhouse instructed the crew to prepare sledges when the spectre of having to abandon ship became a distinct possibility.[25] Although the storm passed without mishap, the ship's predicament and position, estimated to be west of Beaufort Island and 50 to 60 miles from Cape Evans, indicated that there was little chance of returning to Cape Evans.[26] Instead, those on the ship hoped she would soon break free of the ice and they would be able to return to New Zealand to get more coal and other equipment.

Thomson noted: 'We are better off for gear than we would like to be as we have a fair amount of clothing which should have been left with the people at Hut Point and C. Evans.'[27] A few days later, he found even more clothing that had not been taken ashore. Much of this was kept aside for the sledging parties and extra clothing for the crew was largely improvised.[28]

Steam, raised in the hope that *Aurora* would soon be in open water, was of use only for raising the stern mooring chain and the bow anchors. These were hauled through a hole made in the ice, four and a half feet thick, using saws, crowbars, picks and shovels.[29] Both anchors were damaged and quite useless, 'so we are practically without any anchor at all excepting a very small kedge anchor'.[30]

With little prospect of the ship's breaking free, and coal being at a premium, Larkman and Donnelly blew down the boiler again on 17 May.[31] Thomson recorded the crew's prospects: 'I do not expect . . . to break adrift from the pack . . . before August by the look of things at present but one can never tell how this ice is going to act . . .'[32] Gone was the reassurance of smoke emitting from the chimney-stack and the sound of steam. A silence descended on the ship, reinforcing the reality that *Aurora* was beset.

It was cruelly ironic that at the same time *Endurance* was trapped in the Weddell Sea, where Shackleton wrote in his diary:

One feels our helplessness as the long winter night closes upon us. By this time, if fortune had smiled upon the Expedition, we would have been comfortably and securely established in a shore base, with depots laid to the south, and plans made for the long march in the spring and summer. Where will we make a landing now? . . . Time alone will tell.[33]

Although Shackleton could call on his second-in-command Frank Wild, *Endurance*'s captain Lieutenant Frank Worsley and four officers for advice and leadership for his party of 28 men, responsibility for the welfare of *Aurora* and her crew of eighteen lay principally with two young officers, Stenhouse and Thomson.

A week after the break-out, Stenhouse suffered from pains in the abdomen. Ninnis wrote: 'Chief Officer seems to be feeling the effect of things and also of the change of water being a bit seedy tonight. It is no wonder, he has stood the most exhausting strains unflinchingly.'[34] His affliction highlighted the absence of a ship's doctor and, although Stenhouse soon recovered, the symptoms would return some weeks later.

The poor-quality water posed a general health risk because little snow had fallen and the sea ice was suitable only for cooking. Larkman and Donnelly rigged up a condenser in the galley and small quantities of fresh water were produced, but with what Thomson described as 'the horrible taste of oil'; Larkman called it 'bilge water'.[35] However, the condenser was soon operating more efficiently and a welcome snowfall on 23 May also boosted the water supply.

Shortly after the break-out, all six occupants of the aft berths were affected in their sleep by 'sulphur fumes' from the wardroom stove, a problem that had occurred twice before, despite remedial attempts.[36] Replacing the stove with one that had been removed from the Cape Evans hut proved such a success that it brought about a general thaw and subsequent dampness. Much of the ship, however, was akin to an ice chamber such that metal cutlery could not be used. Ninnis's blankets had frozen to the wall, and parts of the crew's quarters had iced up like limestone caves.[37]

Repeated attempts by Hooke and Ninnis to send 'All well' wireless messages remained unsuccessful. A month after the break-out, Thomson wrote: 'We expect [the hut party] should be listening for us.'[38] Hooke tried to earth the equipment by lowering a copper wire with weights through the sea ice, then the wireless motor was restarted for the first time since the voyage south, in an attempt to transmit messages to Cape Evans, Macquarie Island (at a distance of 1,340 miles) and beyond. However, the aerials shorted, giving out a blaze of lights, and Hooke received a shock 'of about 9,000 volts' when he leant over a wireless transformer. Incredibly, although this made him sick, he escaped death or serious injury.[39]

The crew's spirits were generally good, despite some restlessness and minor quarrels, which Thomson usually sorted out. On one occasion this resulted in a 'rough up' when he was showing 'a little authority physically [which] met with some resistance'.[40] Writing of a complaint about breakfast, 'Thomo' said: 'You would think one was in the Hotel Cecil instead of on a ship adrift in pack ice in McMurdo Sound and not knowing we will not [*sic*] go ashore and break up or not.'[41] Shaw, the powerfully built engine-room trimmer, suffered fits and insomnia. He was seen as a threat to others, and Stenhouse suspected that he had been dismissed from the Hobart police force on account of his health.[42]

Ninnis did not get on well with Larkman, and Stenhouse inadvertently compounded the problem by, without first consulting Larkman, appointing him in charge of motors to take some of the load off the chief engineer.[43]

In case of having to abandon ship, Stenhouse had set contingency plans that allowed for four teams, each with a sledge (some with two), a tent, clothing and food for 28 days. The ship's boats were readied and provisioned, and the crew made up eighteen sets of man-hauling harness and improvised field bags from wardroom tablecloths and a tent left over from the Mawson expedition. One plan envisaged making for land to the west, from where six men and a sledge would endeavour to return south down the coastline to Cape Evans, as had a party from Scott's second expedition after spending the winter of 1912 on Inexpressible Island in North Victoria Land. The remaining twelve men from *Aurora* would follow this party, but with no forced marches, and would kill penguins and seals to make depots in case of emergency retreats.

If the ship did not drift further north, an alternative plan was to send a party of three with a month's rations to Cape Evans. A third contingency, if the ship broke free by September, involved *Aurora*'s sailing to New Zealand to obtain an extra officer and four volunteers, and take on coal and further provisions. She would then return south to a point two miles east of Cape Crozier and land all necessary stores and equipment. From there a sledging party would depot stores at Corner Camp and proceed to Cape Evans. This plan also allowed for Stenhouse's party to lay out the depot to the Beardmore Glacier if the men at Cape Evans had not carried out the task.[44]

At first, *Aurora*'s position in the middle of a very large floe protected her from the worst of the ice pressures. After a month or so, ice leads broke out near the ship and lumps of sea ice – standing on their ends and likened by Thomson to tombstones – created a spectacular effect, though they were uncomfortably near the ship.[45]

Owing to these dangerous ice conditions, the men were largely confined to the ship. At times, especially during the night, 'loud cracks and squeaks . . . in the darkness' awakened them.[46] The ice movement reached an estimated three to four knots, but the pressures on the ship seemed less than when she was moored at Cape Evans. Two weeks of mild weather belied the usual rigours of an Antarctic winter, and frequent displays of the aurora australis, together with the claimed sighting of a comet by Ninnis, helped relieve monotony.[47]

The ship's company celebrated King George V's birthday on 3 June by indulging in what Thomson termed 'a big spread at dinner time'. The king's health was toasted in a wardroom bedecked with flags, and a 'stiff tot of rum' was served to the crew.[48]

One of the crew, always on the lookout for wildlife, mistook Stenhouse, who was walking out on the ice in the midwinter gloom and darkness, for an emperor penguin. 'Kavanagh gave the penguin call ... This is the first time that I have been hunted by man. Luckily Kavanagh had no gun.'[49]

Thomson estimated there was less than half of the necessary supplies required to sustain eighteen men for 'nine and three quarter months' – until March 1916.

> The figures [are] about as follows roughly Fish 896 lbs, Tinned meats 1854 lbs, Ham and bacon about 188 lbs. Fresh mutton about 200 lbs. Total 3138 lbs requirements for 18 men for 9½ months at present rate of consumption is 6840 lbs so this 3138 is considerably under half.[50]

The eagerly anticipated Midwinter's Day, 22 June, featured football on the ice in the moonlight and, according to Larkman, 'for a wager Hooke raced right for'd and back in his birthday suit'.[51]

Hooke wrote:

> We have been looking forward to this day for months. At last we sort of feel homeward bound. We are halfway through the darkness, a feeling that we are daily making, not losing, light is fine ... The wardroom is decorated with flags and at dinner actually used china dishes again, but a downcast air seemed prevalent, due no doubt to the absence of ten shipmates been [sic] ashore. They will be able to make some sort of spread, but nothing to compare with this.[52]

A fine meal, prepared by an inebriated Wise (who 'eclipsed himself in more sense than one', according to Hooke), included mock turtle soup, roast mutton, boiled ham, plum pudding and liqueurs donated by Herbert Ponting, photographer on the *Terra Nova* expedition.[53]

Thomson wrote:

> After the afternoon tot, the cook seemed to be getting into difficulties so I had to delay the sending along of the rum for the sauce until about 4 p.m. so that if he drank any he would be sober enough to get dinner served up. I am very glad I timed everything so nicely as he got the men's tea at four thirty instead of five ...

I sent him forward with a bottle of whisky for the crew and he had a peg out of it, this brought him near collapse. But he held on until we got dinner on the table and then we sent for him to drink his health and that was the last straw. He folded up soon after reaching the galley and a very useful days work was thus brought to a close. We had a very excellent dinner . . .[54]

Following toasts to their separated comrades 120 miles south at Cape Evans, and to the health of the expedition, there were 'a few songs and stump speeches' before the men were dismissed, according to Thomson, 'all very happy and mostly very full'. Hooke wrote: 'The most commended items were a ragtime song by the seamen, others who had plenty of volume, a French song by the steward of which I understood but little, and a duet "It's a long way to the Antarctic" by Ginger [Kavanagh] and the bos'n.' The 'men aft' then had a little concert on their own until midnight.

The midwinter conditions created some surreal effects. On 26 July, Thomson wrote:

It is full moon and it is as good as daylight to look over the ice . . . we are resting on top of a high pressure ridge aft, and all around is a confused mass of upturned floes. Like a graveyard struck by lightning.[55]

In early July, as the crew outfitted lifeboats with sails and loaded in provisions, Thomson observed that these craft offered

a very poor chance of salvation . . . but . . . about our only chance now, as sledging to the shore from here would be about impossible as there are numerous cracks in the ice which would be very dangerous. The only thing I can see to do in a case like this is to camp upon some floe with all possible provisions and hang it out until the ice breaks up and then try to get clear with the boats and try and make Macquarie Island or New Zealand as circumstances would permit. A very poor chance.[56]

Thomson's prediction of camping on the floes and waiting for the ice to break up before clearing the boats and making for land would not be tested by the Ross Sea party but by the men of *Endurance* in the Weddell Sea, who were facing a similar future.

The route westwards to the coast would be fraught with hazards of rough ice, open leads and a north-easterly ice drift of one to ten miles a day. Progress would be further impeded if the men dragged the ship's boats, and yet to abandon them would be to eliminate one of their few survival options.[57] They could take food to last only a matter of weeks, and would have to resort to killing wildlife. In Ninnis's view, rescue could not be expected 'till the summer of 1916', still eighteen months off.

The men on *Aurora* had constant hopes of an imminent break-out, owing to the steady northern drift of the ship. In early July there was a promising lead some 50 or 60 yards wide away on the port side. Soon the ice pressure became more intense and made, wrote Thomson, 'a noise like a soul in torment'.[58] To ensure the pumps would not be useless if the ship did break free, Larkman and Donnelly cleared the suction pipes with blowtorches and were ready to give steam at about 30 hours' notice.[59]

On 16 July, with temperatures at −30°F, there was a series of 'sharp cracking noises' in the ship's timbers. During a rising blizzard the pressure on the ship increased to the point where everybody rushed out onto the deck, fearing the worst, but *Aurora* remained intact.

Given this emergency, and with the last case of whisky now broached, Saturday night festivities came to a sudden end and the card players abandoned their game. The 'Old Hooker,' to use Thomson's term for *Aurora*, continued to creak and groan,[60] and the following day everyone again rushed to the deck when the ship sounded as if it was being 'torn in halves'. As the ice cracked and moved, the gangway was taken on board. The night of 18 July was the most anxious yet spent, with ice acting 'like a nut cracker' on the hull. In hope as much as in recognition of the sturdy work of the shipbuilders in Dundee and shipwrights at Cockatoo Island, Thomson wrote:

> The way [the ice makes] the timbers of this old ship cry out is pitiful to listen to, especially when one is so much interested in the ultimate end of this struggle for supremacy. The old ship is now about our only hope and if she goes back upon us we are about as good as cold meat. But I am a believer in fate and do not think this is the time this old ship is to finish her Antarctic wanderings.[61]

In the early morning of 21 July, *Aurora* was in an open pool of water 'about 100 feet wide', as observed by Stenhouse. This narrowed during the day because of heavy pressure, and by early evening the stern was forced against thick ice floes. The crew attempted to save the rudder and propeller with relieving tackles to counter the strain, but the ship was now held fore and aft and pushed upwards like a bent ruler. Eventually the rudder bent to starboard and smashed. 'Solid oak and iron went like matchwood,' noted Stenhouse. In this dire predicament the ship was 'visibly hogged' and the pressure threatened to break her back.[62]

The crew was kept on standby and normal duties were not assigned. Dinner was punctuated by the creaking and jarring of the stern post against the ice only four feet from the end of the wardroom table. Ninnis wrote:

> We did not enjoy the meal at all and after it I got together a small stock of extra clothing and necessaries into the pillow case. The others all did similarly. An evening of great anxiety followed. Sledge food was got up ready on deck, a small stock of clothing was apportioned out ready for distribution and each changed into clean,

warm underwear and just remained fully clothed henceforth . . . We finally managed to turn in fully clothed still with the Wardroom light left burning, all cabin
doors left open lest they got stuck . . . sleep I think was quite impossible, for every
footstep on deck, every bang of a door . . . and every creak of the hull put us ready
for a bolt to the deck with our gear.[63]

Hooke also described these momentous events:

Since turning in last night, a few bumps and noises have been heard and the mate's
and bosun's footstep were far too constant over head to permit of sleep. At about
10 the mate came down and called Thompson [*sic*] saying that the wires were to
be cut as the ship was broadside in channel. These were our original moorings
from Cape Evans, which had frozen into solid ice, making it impossible to get
them out. A few minutes later the bosun rushed down 'All hands on deck, smart'.
We all thought the long expected had happened and we were bound on the longest
sledging trip on sea ice yet taken. On deck we found the ice in a general state of
breaking up with the main channel some 200 feet wide. On the forecastle head we
cut the wire through with cold chisel and sledgehammer and now are standing by
dressed in case we are again wanted.[64]

The men of *Aurora* assembled their most precious belongings. Larkman
cut out and saved the pages from his diary and offical work log.[65] Those aboard
realised that if they had to take to the sledges there was practically no hope of
survival, and that Thomson's plan of drifting on an ice floe and then sailing the
lifeboats north offered only a slim hope.[66]

Hooke's diary entries describe the dire situation:

22 Jul. Shortly after nine 'All hands' were mustered and told off to sledges. In my
sledge is second engineer [Donnelly], cook [Wise], Arkins [Atkin] and Grady. All
stations and duties are arranged to save any panic. All day was spent packing the
sledging and arranging things, ropes are ready for and after (with planks) to get on
to ice at the better end. The sledges are packed outside the galley and spare clothing is piled under canvas. After five things quietened . . . Some of the doors are
jammed with the squash. With deafening crashes the ship is between two floes
fore and aft, and the enormous pressure the strength of which it is impossible to
estimate pushes her more hard up on the other. The ship is perceptible [*sic*] 'hogging'. All hands are on deck as it is thought she might break at any moment.

23 Jul. The whole crew is like a crowd of school girls, our nerves are absolutely
shattered. The dropping of a book or the slamming of a door brings us all up with
a start. Things are quieter and hope to have some sleep. Listened on the aerial till
midnight but heard nil. In case of leaving ship we will endeavour to make to Cape
Adair [sic], some 150 miles away. The position of the trans-continental party is
now a serious matter. Should we be lost or even succeed in making the mainland,
no relief could be expected for two years and the possibility of the depots would
not be laid. The rudder is smashed beyond repair.[67]

Although the carpenter Mauger remained optimistic that the ship's stout oak planks, which visibly buckled and jumped, would withstand the strain, the prospect that the vessel and all hands would be lost was all too real. Thomson summed up their predicament: 'I think I have never been in a [more] serious position before in my life.' *Aurora* was forced up 'a foot or two several times', and Thomson thought the ship might 'jump right out of the ice if she receives a very heavy nip beam on'. Sulphuric acid was poured on the ice to try to break up the floe, but to no avail.[68] Stenhouse wrote: 'Ship jumping, straining and listing badly.'[69]

Hooke attempted to send distress signals by wireless, and even messages to King George, which were repeated frequently over a number of days but failed to gain any response:

> ... ship in precarious position at present 90 miles S.W. of Coulman Island, Ross Sea. Ships company prepared for abandonment in case of disaster to ship to proceed land Cape Adair [*sic*] or coast to southward. As safety of southern depot party doubtful I pray your Majesty if ship does not reach New Zealand port by Nov 1st, to permit a relief ship to proceed with haste to the relief of the southern depot party at Cape Evans with relief party, clothing and stores and to meet the Trans Continental Party at Beardmore Glacier in Feb. Your Majesty's humble and devoted subject J. R. Stenhouse Master *Aurora*.[70]

The wireless messages disappeared as if into a void. Hooke believed that 'the failure [of the wireless] is entirely due to the abnormal conditions that appear to prevail in the Antarctic'.[71] He had expected the equipment to be effective to transmit approximately 1,200 nautical miles distance to Macquarie Island, but concluded that the insulators and aerials were not equal to the power of the Marconi transmitter. There was a huge loss of energy as the aerial system sparked and hissed aloft in the winter's darkness. Thomson noted: 'On one occasion an old rope lying on the deck started smouldering, a considerable fire hazard due to the benzine and spirits stored nearby.'[72] Hooke reasoned that moisture was causing the wireless halliards to earth, so he coated the insulators with shellac, bitumen paint and paraffin wax, to no avail.[73]

By the end of July, the immediate danger to the ship was over, although severe ice pressures occurred from time to time. The men again drank to sweethearts and wives, and to their comrades in the south.

❖

CHAPTER ELEVEN

Crossing to Cape Evans

B Y THE TIME *Aurora* broke away from Cape Evans, there was some concern as to the whereabouts of Mackintosh, Joyce, Wild, Cope, Hayward and Jack. On occasions the sea ice near Glacier Tongue appeared firm enough for a possible crossing to the cape, and there was considerable uncertainty about whether all of the southern party had returned from the Barrier.

Meanwhile, Mackintosh's men were biding their time in the *Discovery* hut and thankful to be indoors in bad weather. A fierce blizzard struck for four days in early May, the same storm that carried away and buffeted *Aurora*. The men took to their sleeping bags, housed around the stove on platforms raised off the floor. The small makeshift room, partitioned by provision cases and remnants of the winter awning from the *Discovery*, had been assembled during the *Nimrod* expedition and enhanced during Scott's second expedition. Much of the rest of the hut was deep in ice and snow. Water froze, even when close to the fire. However, the blubber stove and feeble blubber-fed lamps brought some degree of comfort despite the pungent sooty smoke.

The hut was a welcome refuge while the southerly wind howled off the Barrier, but when the weather permitted, the men went out in the weak twilight of noon to catch seals. Their coal was finished and the supply of blubber meagre. Four seals caught early in the month provided fuel for eleven days, and on 12 May a large seal was taken. With Cope laid up because of his ulcerated legs, the five able-bodied men accounted for a further ten seals during May, one of which was caught by a lasso and held by Mackintosh while being slaughtered.[1]

Newly formed sea ice to the north was repeatedly swept away with the next southerly blow. Jack wrote on 19 May: 'Had our usual inspection of sea ice. A wide lane of open water exists now . . . our term of imprisonment is again to be extended.'[2] Following Wild's fortunate escape when he fell through the ice (his clothes being 'frozen as hard as boards' before Joyce assisted him back to the hut),[3] Jack also broke through the ice up to his waist. He had been overtaken by a blizzard while prospecting with the Skipper for a route towards Cape Evans on 23 May.[4]

On 27 May, Mackintosh announced his intention to make the crossing two days later. Jack recorded: 'There were no dissenters for all will be glad to get to more comfortable quarters. The burning question is, shall we be able to make Cape Evans this moon?'[5] The full moon was necessary for safe passage over the sea ice in the midwinter darkness. However, a blizzard prevented the proposed trek at that propitious time.

The men whiled away time playing various games. As the month ended, Jack wrote: 'Had dinner at 9.30 p.m., a most aristocratic hour ... Played draughts until 4 a.m. and then turned in.' The next night they played ludo until 1 a.m.[6]

The opportunity to make the dash across the ice came on 2 June, with the moon on the wane. After a breakfast of pemmican, the six-strong party left the *Discovery* hut at 10.45 a.m. After a long pull into a strong north-east wind over what Jack described as 'a fair but in places much broken and rough surface due to ice pressure' they reached the Cape Evans hut at about 10.30 p.m.[7] Their route had taken them between Tent Island and Razorback Island to the ice cliffs at the foot of Mt Erebus. There they found the flag planted by Hooke and Gaze on 24 April, directing the party to the access ladder and depot half a mile further on. Jack recorded:

> However Skipper decided not to avail himself of depot but to make for the ship. We could not however pick her up in the now dim light (for it had clouded over). We could not even locate Cape Evans but ultimately we heard the barking of dogs and so turned in to the land, making for a dark spot which fortunately proved to be the hut.[8]

As a result of Mackintosh's flawed decision, the party had in fact headed around Cape Evans into North Bay before coming back to the hut. The twenty-mile journey had taken almost eleven hours and the travellers had been sustained with only occasional snacks of chocolate and biscuit.

The extreme blizzard conditions that had struck early in May had caused the four men left at Cape Evans to wonder not only about the ship and its crew, but also about the sledging party presumably then sheltering at Hut Point. The Padre noted: 'Irvine [Gaze] is really the only sanguine one among us.'

Apart from meteorological readings taken on nearby Wind Vane Hill at four-hour intervals, usually by Richards, the men rarely went out into the winter darkness.[9] On clear days there was limited visibility between 11 a.m.

and 3 p.m. Spencer-Smith wrote on 25 May: 'Went out with R[ichards] to take readings. Our daylight is almost a minus quantity now. Just a glow – patent green to deep red, behind the Barne Glacier.'[10]

Some time was spent tallying the stores left by the Scott expedition – inside the building, on the outside of the southern wall and at a large cache on a knoll to the south-east of the hut. It was an inexact task because cases were often frozen into the ground or snow-covered, but hours of fossicking often brought the reward of supplies such as tinned meats and jam.

The Cape Evans men estimated that they had enough of most items to last two years, 'if the worst should happen to the ship'.[11] Milk and sugar were the principal shortages, and although there was tinned meat, it was necessary to procure supplies of fresh seal meat, which even the Padre was now beginning to appreciate. In addition, seal blubber was an essential source of fuel to supplement the small amount of coal remaining from that unloaded from *Aurora* and nine bags left by the Scott expedition.[12]

Like the men at Hut Point, the Cape Evans party found the killing of seals a grim business. The Padre was especially repulsed. 'R & Irvine went out for a moonlight walk between 4 & 5, but soon returned for the gun saying that there were 5 seals on the shore. These they killed – a ghastly scene – moonlight, two lanterns, knives & pools of blood! – and skinned while I came back and prepared dinner. The blubber is especially a great acquisition.'[13] A few days later, Ernest Wild rode seals bronco style, creating a bizarre scene in the flickering lamplight.[14]

The four men adopted a basic routine. Gaze stayed up until 11 p.m., then called Richards and Stevens, who used the 11 p.m. to 3 a.m. watch to take meteorological readings. Spencer-Smith took the 3–7 a.m. watch and then prepared breakfast. Lunch was a scratch meal prepared by 'the first man who was idle or hungry'.[15] Dinner at 7 p.m. was often cooked by Stevens or Gaze. The Padre described their existence: 'We smoke, eat and talk and work. Except for our natural anxiety about the ship, life is smooth enough: plenty of music and, as R said today, food surprisingly good for bachelors.' The homesick Spencer-Smith spent much of his day reading in his bunk.[16] He relocated his sleeping quarters to the central area of the hut after finding his blanket frozen to the wall and his mattress 'thick with frost underneath'.[17]

By the end of May, the sea ice had largely gone out again and the men at Cape Evans assumed that with its departure went any chance of the missing sledging party arriving from Hut Point, or themselves going there. The Padre wrote: 'The chance of a visit to or from Hut Point seems likely to be postponed for another month.'[18] They were sure they were marooned for at least a season, with the probability that the ship had been lost with all hands.[19]

Spencer-Smith, Gaze, Richards and Stevens had just turned in for the night on 2 June when the six dogs began to bark. It was thought that the sound of the gramophone had worried the dogs, so Gaze went out to settle them down and found the Skipper and his party just arriving. The Padre celebrated: 'Thank God they are all safe . . . they are all very dirty and hairy and the hut looks like a low down pub full of Anarchists tonight and there is a tremendous noise, of course.'[20]

After enduring weeks of semi-darkness the newcomers were blinded by acetylene light in the hut, from a system originally set up by the Scott party, and put on snow goggles. Joyce wrote: 'The hut looked like a palace. A lovely coal fire was burning and the hut party looked very clean, our party looked like scavengers. We had been out practically 129 days, laid depot to 80° and travelled 288 miles. A good breaking in for the coming sledging season.'[21]

Mackintosh and his five companions were startled to find the ship gone, but the Skipper 'seemed assured of her safety'.[22] Tobacco and liquor, though in short supply, had not yet run out at the more northern base. As a tobacco substitute, the men from the *Discovery* hut had improvised with a concoction known as the 'Hut Point Mixture'. Later at Cape Evans, the men smoked dried herbs as well as 'tea coffee sawdust saennegras different kinds of dirt scudding about etc'.[23]

After dinner on 3 June, on his first day back at Cape Evans, Mackintosh made a short speech outlining the routine to be followed for the rest of the winter. Joyce and Wild would be principally responsible for making up deficiencies in clothing and footwear, but the problem of a lack of spare underclothing probably had no answer. Hayward and Gaze would be the seal hunters, with help from Joyce and Wild. Because coal had virtually run out, a steady supply of blubber would be necessary. This quartet would also be responsible for gathering ice for the water supply and exercising the dogs. Stevens, Cope, Jack and Richards would carry on their scientific duties, with Stevens also taking principal responsibility as chef. Spencer-Smith would be free to get on with his darkroom work. It was to be hoped that *Aurora* would show up again with replacement clothes and equipment. Although scarcer food items such as sugar would be rationed, they could be grateful that much of the sledging supplies had been offloaded from the ship and, with the leftovers from the previous expedition, it should be possible to complete the task of laying the depots.[24]

Wild and Joyce made crude but serviceable trousers, jackets and outer boots from a Willesden cotton tent left from the Scott expedition. These were to replace the Burberrys still on the ship and the boots left behind at Hobart.

Fur boots were made from old sleeping bags, with lampwick ties, a desperate expedient for men with the task of walking many hundreds of miles in the months ahead. Old tents were patched and well-used Primus stoves and sledges overhauled. Paraffin oil for stove fuel was in good supply, with 138 gallons on hand. Flaps were sewed on the sleeping bags to remedy a problem experienced in the first season's sledging, especially by the taller men, Gaze and Spencer-Smith.[25] The greasy Burberrys from the previous season were washed in benzine and put away for the spring sledging. Hair was cut and water heated for a rare, luxurious wash.[26]

After the day's work was over and the dinner dishes were washed up, the men would sit around 'yarning', listening to the gramophone and sometimes singing shanties. Fierce arguments raged over such matters as the relative greenness of grass in Australia compared with England, politics, motorbikes, tennis – any topic, according to the Padre, 'that promises excitement irrespective of reason or convictions!' Wild, Joyce and others spent endless hours over the bagatelle table, and on most evenings a rubber of bridge was played in the galley area with cards made by the Padre. As the men settled down into their bunks at night, curious noises came from different corners of the hut. 'Wild and Joyce are terrible rumblers,' reported Spencer-Smith.

Stevens and Mackintosh had some kind of difference at the dinner table as to the role played by the scientists in the first season's sledging and their lack of opportunity to get on with research.[27] Jack wrote: 'Stevens announced to Richards & I [sic] today that scientific staff were to devote time solely to scientific work and not to be hampered by routine work.'[28]

Most of the scientific work was undertaken by Richards and Jack, with Stevens having limited duties as a geologist and spending much of his time in the galley, where he was assisted by Cope and Spencer-Smith.

The scientists had to improvise in their work, despite having laboratory equipment remaining from the Scott expedition, and were hampered by a lack of tools. They tried to make up such items as a Wilson cloud chamber from an inverted flask for analysing the dust content of the atmosphere, and a Cary Foster bridge, in an attempt to make an electrical micro-thermometer to record air temperatures. Both experiments failed because of lack of proper components. They also endeavoured to measure the rate of sea-ice formation and ablation, and the rate of evaporation from freshwater ponds near the hut.[29]

Cope, who was only slowly recovering from skin infections to his legs, undertook some biology, including the dissection of a baby seal. He also started to study the fauna of the ponds, but 'his preparations were disturbed and his apparatus broken, so he gave up in disgust'.[30]

Spencer-Smith spent many days developing films, both stills and cinematograph, taken during the previous sledging season. He also photographed the hut by moonlight, and interior scenes and portraits of his companions with the aid of a magnesium-powder flashlight.[31] On some Sundays he converted the darkroom bench to an altar and celebrated Holy Communion or Mass (he used both terms), often with only one other person present. Mackintosh, Stevens, Cope and Gaze each attended from time to time. One of the men, after counselling from the Padre, made his confession.[32]

In preparation for Midwinter's Day on 22 June, Gaze and Richards created prizes such as 'an ounce of tobacco, worth its weight in gold', according to Spencer-Smith. They held a series of competitions in which everybody won a prize. Stevens prevailed in a spelling game, Wild won a potato race (using tins of potted meat as a substitute), Richards a card gamble as well as 'donkey's tail', Gaze a water game, and Cope the 'billiard handicap', played on the bagatelle table. Booby prizes were also awarded.[33]

Cope and Stevens cooked what the Padre described as 'a magnificent dinner', comprising rice soup, tongue, potatoes, salad, meat pates, cabbage, plum pudding, trifle, raspberry or vanilla jelly, followed by coffee and cake, whisky, cigars and cigarettes. The pudding was topped with 'Scott's holly' and berries made from sealing wax. At the end of the dinner the Padre said grace.

> We drank to the King and the Boss and then sat around singing shanties, partially improvised. These included 'Ranzo', 'the Yankee Ship' (Blow, boys blow), 'Farewell, Spanish Maidens' (We'll rant and we'll roar), 'Grace Darling', 'Pull for the shore', and other fragments. Cope told one or two stories and recited 'The German at the phone' . . . the last revellers went off to bed at about 3, leaving Cope and self on watch to clear up . . . if only the ship is safe somewhere – God keep them and bless them, as he has kept and blessed us.[34]

On *Endurance*, held in the ice of the Weddell Sea and out of sight of any land, midwinter celebrations included an after-dinner concert in the wardroom with speeches and toasts, then 'God Save the King' and 'Auld Lang Syne' were sung and the men sat down to a midnight supper.[35]

Mackintosh, who had spent much of his time writing and planning the following season's sledging, discussed his plans fully with the men at Cape Evans in late June. All accepted the need to carry on. Lessons had been learnt, including that sledge loads should not be excessive. Rather than endure March temperatures on the Barrier, the Skipper considered it would be better to make an early start, even as early as 1 September. He considered that although the four sledging dogs and two bitches were proving their worth around the base, man-hauling would be the basic means of transport. Possibly the motor sledge could be repaired and prove useful. Somehow the depot-laying parties would have to improve on the slow progress of the last season to finish by the end of February. Spencer-Smith recorded his response to the proposals:

> Spent most of the morning discussing the sledging problem with Joyce, Wild, Irvine &c and it's a pretty big problem, too, tho' I think the O.M. [Old Man] has a good solution already worked out . . . if his weights are correct, the job will D.V. [God willing] be done, tho' there'll be 10 very much played out men at the end of it. It's all in the game . . . We shall have a very tough time for five months, especially at the beginning and the end but D.V. shall get through all right.[36]

The men exercised outdoors when the weather and light permitted. Wednesday, 14 July, was a typical day, as recorded by the Padre:

> Turned in, very weary, at 8.30 & slept well till about 11.30. Rather an idle day, finishing two packs of cards, after I had been out for a short exercise on ski with S[tevens]. The band of daylight to the NW seems extending. The dogs always gather even for the shortest walk and are friendly, usually to one another, as well as to us. A little tea-party in my darkroom & plans for home! Richards & Jack are busy on stores weighing: Joyce & Wild on clothes: all in argument.[37]

A favourite pastime was to walk or travel on ski around a large stranded iceberg, south-east of Cape Evans, estimated by Spencer-Smith to have a surface area of 300 to 400 acres.[38] On 17 July, Cope and Stevens produced a sumptuous meal complete with menu cards made by the Padre for 'Hôtel Babbleön, Cape Evans', as named by Spencer-Smith from a book title in the hut.[39] However, Wild's birthday on 10 August went uncelebrated because of a lack of fuel. From early August the shortage of fuel meant only one fire was kept alight. The Padre wrote: 'Owing to long blow, we are short of blubber & so, with only one fire going, the hut is cold, ink frozen hard & there's little to do except wait for the next meal.' Richards, however, would look back upon these simple and uncomplicated days, usually tempered by good-natured banter around the galley stove, as some of the happiest of his life.[40]

CHAPTER TWELVE

Aurora *under siege*

THROUGHOUT THE EMERGENCY aboard *Aurora*, Stenhouse had little chance for rest. Paton wrote: 'It has been found necessary to provide him with stimulants so as to keep him from breaking down altogether . . . His services are invaluable . . . he has proven himself a capable Officer . . . we hope that he may retain his health.'[1] Thomson hesitated to tax his superior with proposals about a replacement rudder. 'I think I could design stay and rig an ordinary rudder which would steer almost as well as the damaged one used to. But I have not been asked so will hold my tongue until I am asked for my idea of the matter.'[2]

However, four days after the crisis the pair had a long and satisfactory talk 'about everything in general and what we intend to do'.[3] Responsibility for the ship weighed visibly on Stenhouse, who wrote in his diary: 'This is Hell and one must appear to be happy and take interest in the small happenings of shipboard.'[4]

Grady, who had broken a rib from a fall down the engine-room ladder while the ship was moored at Cape Evans, was back on duty by mid-June. Atkin was laid up for some days with lumbago. Larkman, a conscientious worker who spent long hours in the engine room, suffered two frostbitten toes and was forbidden to return to work until they healed, Stenhouse noting: 'I think he has probably overdone things, lately, working overtime . . .'[5]

Stenhouse and Thomson did their best to keep the crew occupied, with only a limited number of jobs to be found. The seamen were allocated different duties: Atkin was put in charge of sails and canvas; Warren, tarpaulins, lead lines and stove fuel; and Kavanagh, ropes, cordage and rigging stores. Downing looked after general stores, and Glidden, a lamp trimmer by training, was responsible for 'lamps, oils, paints and small stores'.[6]

Thomson encouraged the men to exercise, whether with a football on the ice or by taking extended walks or even runs when ice conditions and a full moon permitted. He wrote on 26 July: 'The crew did practically nothing today except a couple of small jobs to give them a little exercise as they would remain in the forecastle for a month on end if they did not get any work to do. There is [*sic*] a couple of signs amongst some of the party that they are developing nerves ...' Ninnis, who seemed to have little in common with most others, responded to the midwinter darkness and enforced confinement by withdrawing to his bunk to escape 'a colonial concert of very questionable merit' in the wardroom.

> It is difficult at times to preserve composure down here. Even little things cause the greatest irritation now ... the wardroom is usually the resort of the officers of the ship and these are as often understood to be gentlemen. Our conversational standard and general tone is many shades below a Dockhead public bar ...[7]

He would often retire after dinner for a chat with 'the C.O.', a respite that offered a reminder of 'the gentlemanly side of life being still existent somewhere', and recorded that the effect of his 'dark spell' was so bad that he 'would never come to face it again'. However, both Ninnis and Stenhouse were sure that the party would come through the ordeal safely. 'We seem to be shepherded about among all these grinding fields and see them being torn up and thrown about and still we are kept safe.'[8]

The need to replace the smashed rudder provided a welcome activity for all hands. Thomson proposed an 'ordinary rudder' suspended vertically from the overhanging stern with a giant tiller in the form of a ship's spar over the deck. The ship's wheel would be attached to steering wires to the end of the spar and from bollards direct to the rudder near the waterline. This would require simple rigging at 45 degrees to the stern to give additional stability, while the rudder was to be weighted with plate iron.[9]

Stenhouse's design was triangular, capable of being hoisted above the level of the deck. It would be constructed from boat skids and the main derrick and weighted with reinforced concrete and two iron plates. Wires would also be used to provide stability and for lifting.[10] Thomson preferred the chief officer's design to his own: 'I think it will be a success, it looked good.'[11] Ninnis opined that there was 'the prospect of inspecting the propeller by lowering an electric lamp in a bottle through a hole in the ice',[12] although there is no record of an attempt to do so.

All surplus spars and timber were assembled to construct a jury-rigged rudder based on Stenhouse's design.[13] One spar that had been on board since Mawson's time took a full day to extract from below decks and necessitated the shifting of a large number of stores. Paton noted on 30 July: 'The crew were employed today at the gear for the jury rudder which the carpenter is constructing. The spanker boom, gaff, fore-top-gallant yard also two boat skids are being used to make the rudder.'[14]

Larkman and Donnelly, assisted by Grady and other crew members, drilled through three-quarters of an inch of steel sheathing to sever the old rudder. 'We had to spend many hours simply forging and tempering drills because of the low temperatures in which the work was done.'[15] The cold temperatures and treacherous ice made the task difficult but finally, on 24 August, the old rudder was lifted clear and left on the ice. Stenhouse was rueful – 'I don't like to part with 5 tons of good oak and iron'[16] – and he subsequently organised its dismantling and salvage. Mauger, the ship's carpenter, had the difficult task of constructing the jury rudder on the quarterdeck, 'in low temperatures and exposed to biting blasts', according to Stenhouse. Six bags of cement, fortuitously aboard the ship, were mixed with the aid of boiling water to form the concrete weighting for the rudder, which in Thomson's estimation 'would steer a 10,000 ton steamer'.[17]

The new rudder could not be put into position until the ship broke free of the ice, and in anticipation of this Mauger dismantled the aft rail. Once he had finished the jury rudder, a job commended by Stenhouse, the carpenter repaired the stern timbers that had been fractured by the ice pressure on the rudder. The ice having forced the ship up, Mauger had the opportunity to make the repairs without water entering through the damaged hull. It was as if the ship were in dry dock.[18]

There would be a parallel on *Endurance* just a few weeks later, days before that ship was abandoned, with Frank Hurley writing in his diary on 24 October: 'The ship's stern post is seriously damaged . . . rapidly making water . . . the carpenter set to work on a coffer dam in the shaft tunnel in the hope of sealing off the damaged stern of the vessel.'[19]

Because the men on *Aurora* were at a more northerly latitude, they witnessed the return of the sun some three weeks before their companions at Cape Evans. On 6 August, Thomson recorded:

> The Chief Officer was the first to see the sun rise and I was the second to see it. We were so delighted to make its acquaintance again that we called all hands upon deck and served out a tot of rum all round and gave three cheers to the old sun. I then sent the crew upon the ice to kill the first seal or sea leopard that we had seen since leaving Cape Evans . . .[20]

Only a day or so before, they had seen their first snow petrel and Adélie penguins for some months. As the pack ice moved northwards, the imprisoned *Aurora* made steady progress in her drift, and by 6 August was near Cape Adare, at the north-western extremity of the Ross Sea and 350 miles from Cape Evans.

On the following day the ship was subjected to further extreme ice pressure reinforced by hurricane-force winds. Over a period of hours she listed 35 degrees to starboard and then a similar amount to port.[21] Thomson noted:

> At about 2 a.m. we were called out to lift up the whale boat as the ship had listed
> over until the whale boat which was hanging lashed in the davits on a level with
> the rail began to rest her keel upon the ice which was pressured up alongside the
> port gangway . . . the angle which the ship's deck had taken considerably hampered
> this operation.

Despite his time in square-rigged ships, Thomson had never before experienced 'the horrible screaming that is going on on deck now. I have never before been held so steady with such a wind blowing.'[22]

North of 71° and 40 miles from Cape Adare, *Aurora* was slowly skirting the Antarctic coastline in a north-westerly direction.[23] Day and night were nearly in equilibrium. Paton wrote on 10 August after the storm subsided:

> A very quiet and peaceful night was passed last night. Not the slightest movement
> of the ice was visible and day broke at 5 a.m. without a change. The sun rose at
> 9 a.m. and though it has been much colder everyone agrees it has been one of the
> loveliest days they have seen for some time. All hands have been employed today
> getting snow on board . . . as the ice may break away at any time we require a good
> supply of fresh water to bring us back to port. Three very large ice bergs were
> sighted ahead today, open water can be seen ahead (but how far it extends we have
> no means of ascertaining) . . . the sun set at 3.15 p.m. . . . the *Aurora Australis* rose
> from the horizon in the NNE shooting upwards and westerly till it reached the
> NW where it ascended up into the Heavens and gathered into a grand glare of
> light . . .[24]

It was not long, however, before a further storm brought heavy snow, which drifted to the height of the ship's rail. Thomson wrote:

> I am beginning to believe something of Mawson when he says he struck the windiest
> place on earth somewhere about the latitude which we are now in about 70° S
> . . . it was impossible to move about the decks without holding onto something
> . . . I think if one had to abandon ship on a night like this it would not be worth
> the trouble trying to save one's life. The wireless masts are still aloft . . . They are
> bent over like whip-sticks and look like going over the side every minute.[25]

Hooke's painstaking efforts with the wireless yielded 'sounds of life, through his receiver' on 3 August, and a fortnight later he picked up Macquarie station sending a weather report to Hobart. A week later, he heard Macquarie and Bluff (New Zealand) stations exchanging signals.[26]

The aerials on *Aurora* were extended with 70 feet of wire, but despite the pitch coating for the insulators, again there was extensive sparking aloft.[27] Hooke and Ninnis could not understand their lack of success in transmitting messages. The latter noted on 31 August: 'We are now practically at the same distance as Dr Mawson's station and with practically the same installation.'

The predicament of the southern party was never far from the minds of those on the drifting ship. Thomson expressed both concern and optimism: 'But now time is beginning to press and we are anxious to get out of here . . . to get down again . . . to lay all depots to the Cloud Maker should anything have happened to the Captain's Party.'[28]

Thomson was hard-pressed to keep the crew occupied on a five-and-a-half-day working week. 'We are at about a standstill now for work until we begin to make sail.'[29] However, with each successive blizzard, men spent many hours shovelling accumulated snow, often to find that their work was undone by the succeeding winds.

On 5 September, *Aurora* experienced her worst storm yet. Thomson wrote:

> I found it impossible to walk anywhere . . . you would go sailing down to leeward and unable to stop yourself. At 2.15 p.m. while I was waiting for Mr Hooke to come up and give me a hand to secure the stove funnel, we heard a sharp report followed by a crackling noise . . . I found that the mizzen wireless mast and the top part of the topmast or topgallant mast had snapped off carrying the aerial with it . . .[30]

Paton observed that the mast 'snapped like a carrot at the heel or thick part and flew out over the ice till it was brought up suddenly by the wires and stays'.[31] When the storm subsided, the crew retrieved the broken parts and set about repairing the fractured mast. Stenhouse noted that during the storm 'the ship gave a slight jump and righted'.[32] The crew now had plenty to do, with an estimated 120 tons of snow lying to the level of the ship's rail, and Stenhouse was concerned that the weight of this threatened his vessel's safety.[33] A day or so later, Thomson observed the ice surrounding the ship subsiding 'due to the weight of snow drifted up around the ship added to the ship's overweight and a melting effect caused by the water being much above freezing point and therefore rotting the ice away underneath'.[34]

On 5 October, Stenhouse was overcome by fumes from the stove in his cabin and lost consciousness on the floor of his cabin, an incident that, in Larkman's words, 'nearly killed him'.[35] Stenhouse described what happened:

> I awoke with the room full of smoke and my lungs full of sulphur; the stove was working badly so I told the Bosun, at 5 a.m. to let it go out . . . in the going out [it] nearly finished me, for when I turned out I 'went out' and must have laid on the floor of the room for twenty minutes before coming to. I remember feeling horribly sick and cold (Room temperature $-11°$) and endeavouring to pull myself together. I have been out of action today in consequence.[36]

Although Donnelly installed a new chimney, it was not entirely successful. In February 1916, a similar incident would again render Stenhouse unconscious, this time in his bunk. 'The Bosun apparently could not awaken me and called Thompson [*sic*] who administered a "peg" which pulled me together. I must have fainted and the Poor old Bosun got a shock.'[37] Paton's 'strict attention to duty' in making his early-morning rounds almost certainly saved Stenhouse's life.[38]

In the absence of a ship's doctor, Stenhouse looked after the men's medical needs. 'The Chief Officer is having a fairly busy time with his medicine chest,' recorded Thomson. 'I do not think I would have so many patients as my cures would not be of a very pleasant nature,'[39] the droll Australian added.

Larkman was excused duties for three months because of two gangrenous toes on his left foot, but by November the risk of amputation was averted.[40]

Stenhouse also played the part of dentist. He wrote of one attempt to remove an abscessed tooth from Larkman: 'Had two heaves and after nearly heaving his head off desisted as he was on the point of swooning. It is cruel work and old L. must be a brick to stand it.'[41] He later successfully pulled the tooth, as well as one of Shaw's,[42] and also sutured Atkin's hand after he cut it to the bone while working on a seal skeleton.[43]

As temperatures warmed, particularly from early November, Mauger measured and recorded the level of water in the pump well, and attempted to seal gaps in the hull by caulking the seams with spun oakum (made by fraying rope).[44]

The sea ice became less secure as the days lengthened and temperatures rose. On the warmest day of spring, Glidden, the youngest seaman aboard and a keen hunter, went out alone onto the ice without permission. When he had not returned after three hours, a search party was assembled, but Thomson climbed the crow's nest and saw him 'about 2½ miles away driving a seal back'.

Glidden then went through the ice up to his waist. Thomson wrote: 'The C.O. sent Ninnis and Hooke out to tell him to leave the seal, and come in without it. For this neglect he will forfeit his liberty of leaving the ship again while we are in the Antarctic and serve him right.'[45]

This seaman was also involved in a minor scandal that erupted when Ninnis's camera, doeskin mitts, sheath knife[46] and a pair of pliers[47] disappeared. Ninnis suspected the culprit was Glidden but initially played a waiting game and posted a reward, hoping the missing articles would turn up. Eventually he confronted the young man and gave him an hour to find the items or 'an official note would be made of its theft', with the likelihood of a search to follow. Glidden handed over the camera, with the film missing, and Ninnis discovered the knife half buried in the snow. A Brownie camera, lent by Atkin to Ninnis when his went missing, was also found in a pool near the ship and retrieved by Shaw.[48]

Thomson recorded the consequences:

The C.O. sent for Glidden O.S. almost at once and he came aft protesting that he did not do it . . . He adopted rather an offensive attitude towards the C.O. . . . and said he would not be blamed and would shoot himself rather than that . . . 'If I am blamed I will put a bullet through myself. F— you, so there!' This brought me into the argument as I caught hold of him and forced him back against the starboard rail with my hands at his neck. The C.O. came along and took the responsibility of punishing him for his insult and made him apologise on his knees which he richly deserved.[49]

Of this incident, Stenhouse wrote: 'I accused him of this despicable action and he threatened to shoot himself and becoming excited swore at me for which I gave him a thrashing.'[50]

On the following morning Stenhouse repeated an offer to Glidden that if he would confess he would get another chance. At first the seaman refused. Stenhouse wrote: 'This is a miserable affair. It would be different if we were in surroundings where a thief could be weeded out but here one has to live with the canker in the ship.' By evening Glidden had relented and owned up to the theft of the camera but denied throwing the other articles over the side. Stenhouse reflected: 'Poor beggar! I don't think he can help it. He has had no home life and is more to be pitied than blamed . . . He has sworn to try to run straight in future. I shall endeavour to help him to do so when he leaves the ship if possible.'[51]

Stenhouse expressed his dismay and frustration as ice in the rigging melted and the snow turned to slush:

The ship has lost much of her wintry appearance and although she is in fairly good condition & order she looks like a neglected hulk. I shall be glad when we get her under weigh again. This is ghastly! What a waste of humanity, & money, 18 men eating their heads off like prisoners.[52]

The melt also revealed the quantity of rubbish littering the ice around the vessel. Thomson wrote in mid-December: 'When the sun is shining brightly there is a distinct stench arising of [*sic*] the garbage which is strewn around the ship on the ice. We should have taken more precautions with it. But it might easy [*sic*] become a danger to health.' The men also had to cope with human excrement from the open-air lavatories designed to empty directly into the sea.[53] Rats, too, became a serious problem, destroying new clothing and stores such as rubber boots and oilskins. One rat caught in a trap was found to have been partially cannibalised. Gradually the ship was scrubbed down and cleaned in the early-summer conditions, which at times allowed men to work aloft stripped to a singlet.[54]

Spring and then summer brought a rich fare of wildlife. Two whales spouted in an open pool as early as 16 November,[55] and sooty albatrosses occasionally soared nearby. The hunters aboard *Aurora* shot two giant petrels on successive days, and other species such as Cape pigeons, snow petrels and storm petrels provided target practice. Mollymawks frequented the outer fringes of the pack ice.[56]

The hunters became even more active with the appearance of seals and penguins in reasonable numbers, adding important fresh meat to the crew's fare. One splendid emperor penguin, with a girth of three feet nine and a half inches and a height of three feet three and a half inches, weighed in at 95 pounds.[57] Another, subsequently nicknamed 'Kaiser Bill', was spared and kept on board for the amusement of the crew.[58] An attempt was made to use an 'ice block' to manoeuvre a seal sufficient to feed the ship's company two meals a day for ten days.[59] By contrast it took three Adélie penguins to provide a meal.[60]

In late October, hunters captured a newly born leopard seal by lasso and hauled it to the ship, thereby attracting the cow, eight feet long with a girth of five feet. Both were killed.[61] However, Stenhouse did spare a crabeater seal (which he described as 'a beautiful specimen with a silver sheen on his coat') the men came across as they played an improvised game of cricket on the ice floe, using a pick handle for a bat, a cardboard tobacco box for wickets and needle-stitched canvas for a ball.[62] Thomson noted a similar incident of animals being spared: 'A couple of chaps went out for Emperor penguins but found them to be a family of seals. Mother, Father and calf, so did not bring them in.'[63]

Thomson estimated in mid-November that, including sledging pemmican and meat pastes, *Aurora*'s supplies included 'enough [meats] to last six or seven months. So why worry.'[64] But as the ship's entrapment continued into December, Stenhouse and Thomson sought every opportunity to add to the supply of fresh meat, which they salted down for preservation, as freezing the carcasses on deck was no longer an option.[65] A group of Adélie penguins approached the ship, 'apparently attracted by the wail of the carpenter's melodion', wrote Stenhouse. He rued the fact that all twelve were taken for food: 'It seems a cruelty to kill these quaint little chaps after making friends of them.'[66] By year's end, the men of *Aurora* had added the carcasses of 59 Adélies and twenty emperor penguins to supplies.[67]

Underlying frustrations resulted in occasional arguments, such as one that occurred over dinner between Stenhouse and Larkman in late November. 'Made things a bit uncomfortable,' noted Thomson.[68] However, there was also a lighter side to events, as observed by Ninnis on 12 December: 'In evening hands playing quoits on deck in light attire and two comedians, one with melodion and a broom crutch, the other with a false stump arm and a begging hat and flute, caused great fun and got photoed too.'[69]

In mid-December, the sails were hoisted for the first time in almost a year and were found to be in good order, owing to the extreme dryness of the polar atmosphere.[70] Over Christmas the men enjoyed three days' holiday from regular duties. They washed and shaved, cut one another's hair, and cleaned the ship down.[71] The cook produced a sumptuous Christmas dinner featuring 'roast Aptenodytes forsteri' (emperor penguin), as listed on the coloured souvenir menu produced by Ninnis. Wise also baked bread, a novelty because of fuel economies, and all hands assembled in the wardroom to drink toasts. Larkman gave a rendition of his song ' Life in the Southern Pack'.[72]

On 29 December, the crew started lime-washing the holds, the bosun observing 'an operation which will make our old packet smell healthier and sweeter after everything being closed down during the winter months'.[73]

During the last four months of 1915, *Aurora* had drifted 490 miles, and by year's end she was north-west of the Balleny Islands.[74] Sturge Island, the southernmost of the group of three, had come into view on 22 September and provided a welcome landmark that helped to fix the ship's position, as the Antarctic continent was now only distantly visible.[75] For two months the islands had remained sporadically visible to the north and east. Young Island was seen for the last time on 23 November, the day after *Aurora* crossed the Antarctic Circle.[76] Curiously, on the same day, land to the south, thought to be 'Cape Hudson',[77] could also be seen, but within a day it too had disappeared and the ship's navigators were without any landform against which they could measure their progress.

Stenhouse and Thomson continued to be despondent because of lack of progress, and worried about the Shackleton party, now expected to be near the South Pole, and also the men left at Cape Evans.

Despite Paton's predictions in early September that it would be 'late in December or about the beginning of January before we get free of the ice',[78] at the end of December *Aurora* was still stuck fast. On 30 December, Stenhouse wrote: 'Our hope of early release and return to the Sound are becoming meagre but still we stand a chance. If we had only to think of ourselves there would be little cause for anxiety.'[79]

Stenhouse still hoped that, if the ship broke free of the ice by 15 January, he might still have time to go north 'for rudder, anchors and coal' in time to return to Cape Evans to pick up those on the ice. 'After that date we can only attempt to go south in our crippled state and short of fuel, with nine days coal on board we would have little chance of working through any Ross Sea pack . . .'[80] Thomson recorded 60 tons of coal, approximately ten days' supply, on hand on 14 December.

Thomson, unrealistically as events turned out, relished such a challenge. On 1 December, he wrote: 'Nothing would please me so much as to try our luck as sailing this old barge south again without going into port for help of any kind.'[81] Earlier he had written: 'But it is taking a big risk, as we might possibly get caught again in the pack next year and that would mean certain starvation. But if we are in doubt as to the ability of the party to carry out the depot laying which has been arranged for it would be almost as well to take the risk.'[82]

Thomson considered this scheme was possible even if they were held fast until February. 'My plan if we break out in February the first or second would be to run north until getting Westerly winds, sail due east until on the 178° to 180° E then shape a course for C[ape] Crozier expecting plenty of S.E. wind as fair wind and I think we could make there under sail.'[83]

The men on *Aurora* celebrated New Year's Eve in style, Stenhouse recording:

> Towards midnight, there was much noise and unrest for'ard which was accounted for at midnight by a march aft of a 'fou fou' band which had been rehearsing under the forecastle head. A melodium [*sic*] (broken winded), marlin spikes for triangles, kerosene tin for drum and a mouth organ were the band instruments and a more motley crowd than the bandsman [*sic*] would be difficult to imagine . . .

While the band played, the bosun sang 'Britannia' and 'God Save the King'. After 'good wishes for a better year' were exchanged, cigars were handed out and toasts drunk. 'We in the Wardroom had a very enjoyable sing song which last[ed] well into the New Year,' wrote Stenhouse.[84]

CHAPTER THIRTEEN

'A new heaven and a new earth'

THE NEW SLEDGING SEASON started on schedule on Wednesday, 1 September 1915, when Mackintosh, Richards and Spencer-Smith left Cape Evans at 7.25 a.m. for Hut Point with a load of 390 pounds. Joyce and Cope gave them a push for about four miles, and the dogs danced around in noisy excitement. It seemed a good omen that the surface was good and the pulling easy. At the halfway point they pitched the tent, ate lunch and, to relieve sore heels, changed their boots for finnesko. When they reached Hut Point in the middle of the afternoon, the doorway and window on the northern side were snowed up, but after an hour's shovelling they entered to find the interior of the hut 'clear and well arranged'. Four-month-old hoosh, frozen in the pot, and salmon and biscuits comprised the evening meal.

On the following day, Richards examined the motor sledge, the condition of which he found 'better than expected'. The men gathered up the old clothes in the hut and tallied the stores, which had gained considerable significance now that the shore party was apparently marooned. The trio returned to base on 3 September with a stop-over at the halfway tent now christened 'the Pub'. The Padre wrote: 'Glad to be back and free from blubber smoke and cold backs. Filthily dirty!'

On Sunday, 5 September, he heard a confession and gave absolution, and at 5 a.m. the following morning, before the second journey south, celebrated Holy Communion with Mackintosh, Stevens and Cope present. A week later, while sledging to Hut Point, Spencer-Smith was to recall the first anniversary of his ordination in Edinburgh: 'Thoughts full all day of last year – thankful for it all . . . God Bless all the good folk in Edinburgh.'

The entire party except Richards, who was left on duty at Cape Evans, set out on 6 September with two laden sledges and five dogs in harness. It was the first time during the expedition that Hayward, one of the specialist dog-drivers, was called upon to take charge of a team.

Some lessons painfully learnt from past experience were evidently forgotten.

The men departed in fine weather, but by the time they reached 'the Pub' a blizzard was upon them. Gaze's raw and cold feet had to be massaged by Cope. Gaze was wearing leather boots from the Scott expedition, though it had been found that these did not give sufficient warmth and should be discarded for finnesko.[1] Spencer-Smith forgot to take his Burberry helmet and, like Mackintosh, suffered frostbite to the face.

A fight among the dogs resulted in the laming of Oscar, who then dropped behind out of sight. The sledgers got their bearings by steering towards the coastline in reduced visibility and were pleased to get into the *Discovery* hut by evening. The Padre wrote of his cousin: 'Irvine's heels shockingly bitten . . . huge watery blisters which Cope has to lance with a pocket knife. Hut very cold but enjoyed dinner and turned in directly afterwards.' The main purpose of this journey was to retrieve the motor sledge. However, a blizzard laid the men up in the hut, where they had 'little to do except eat and play bridge' with improvised cards.

The party returned to Cape Evans on 9 September, with Gaze lying in his sleeping bag on the back of the dog sledge. Although Oscar was retrieved, there were only four fit dogs. Seven men hauled the motor sledge but had to give up after a mile, and thereafter all hands helped with the dog sledge.

Back at Cape Evans, Richards had managed to kill a seal and, with the help of Cope and Joyce, 'soon put together a good meal of tomato soup, seal liver and vegetables and open jam tarts'. Gaze was incapacitated for weeks with frostbitten heels.

There had been some positive aspects of this initial foray. Significantly, the men and dogs had pulled together as one team, and an injured member of the party had been pulled back to safety.

The dog team was back in harness three days later when Joyce, Wild, Hayward and Richards set off with about 600 pounds of oil to the 'the Pub'. The full party, with the exception of Gaze, picked up the load with the dog team the following day and took it on to the *Discovery* hut. After resting up for the night, the men made their first foray of the new season on to the Barrier, where they found Safety Camp in good order and left as a depot a 'biggish load'. On 15 September, after killing eleven seals for blubber, most of the men went back to Cape Evans, transporting the motor sledge with its snow wheel mounted on the end of a hauled sledge. Travelling with the dogs, Jack and Hayward completed the thirteen-mile trip in just three and a half hours.

Richards and Gaze repaired the Girling's burnt-out clutch in a makeshift workshop in the Cape Evans stables. A leather plate was designed to operate at right angles to the flywheel on the Simplex motor, to give a gradation of speed from the centre to the outside. In the absence of suitable tools they used a red-hot nail to make about 50 bolt holes around the clutch.[2] The pair eventually succeeded in making a ten-minute jaunt on 28 September to an iceberg aground off Cape Evans, a trial run that raised hopes that the sledge would be of some value on the main journey.

As a preliminary to the third journey to Hut Point, 600 pounds of stores were sledged to 'the Pub' on 20 September by five men, and Mackintosh, Cope and Hayward sledged a further 370 pounds to that point the following day. Meanwhile, other members of the party were taking advantage of pleasant weather and the sudden increase in wildlife that the spring heralded. The Padre wrote:

> Stevens and I went out to fetch blubber. Found a colony of eight seals which S. attacked while I went on to look for the old hide. Saw a large band of emperors (31) away west, hurrying to inspect me – first in mass, then in line ahead, then in columns of ½ companies, with a Captain and two Lieutenants ahead. One of the latter saluted me first and got pecked by the Captain for his pains.[3]

After rough weather caused a delay of two days, a party of eight travelled to Hut Point on 24 September, leaving Richards, who continued to work on the motor, and the injured Gaze. The following day, after what the Padre estimated to be a trek of nearly twenty miles, 'a good load' was added to the stores dropped off eleven days earlier at Safety Camp. Pulling two empty sledges, and en route demolishing 'the Pub' encampment, they returned to Cape Evans on Sunday, 26 September. This trip took six hours from hut to hut, including an hour to rest and eat.

Although the men could feel pleased with their efforts since 1 September, Richards had not succeeded in resurrecting the motor sledge as an operational unit. As Ninnis had discovered the previous January, excessive vibration caused rivets and bolts to loosen and 'even the sledge wheel began to break up'.[4] The Girling was finally abandoned on the beach outside the stables at Cape Evans.

On 27 September, the party had a meeting to settle plans for the next stage of sledging. It was agreed that Gaze would stay alone at base during the first journey to the Bluff and then would be relieved by Stevens, 'unless someone else is really badly laid up'.

The men mended clothes, assembled equipment, bathed and shaved. Wild modified and fixed the Padre's sleeping bag and gave him two pairs of socks. On 29 September, the day before the main sledging was due to start, the Padre celebrated Holy Communion with Mackintosh, Stevens and Cope attending.

Spencer-Smith concluded his winter diary on 30 September. 'No start – still things to finish off – rather a relief to us all especially as it's bitterly cold

−27°F.' Mackintosh took the opportunity to write references 'in case of any accident befalling myself'. Of the Padre he noted:

> During the winter which has been passed under the most severe conditions Mr Spencer-Smith has been the mainstay of the party. His influence over the other members of the party has had a great effect on it being passed, possibly in a manner in which it would not, had he not been with us . . . Finally I can only state that Mr Spencer-Smith's services to this section of the Expedition have been such, that no money could buy, or could I speak too highly.[5]

The party set off from Cape Evans man-hauling three sledges on 1 October. The load of 1,700 pounds proved too much and, in the face of deteriorating weather, the men cut loose the rear sledge and arrived at the *Discovery* hut at 9.30 p.m. after a trek of eleven hours.[6] There they were laid up there for a week by rough weather.

During lulls they brought in the jettisoned sledge and stores, killed seventeen seals and took two loads of supplies out to Safety Camp.[7] In their leisure time, Richards, Hayward and Jack climbed Observation Hill to view the jarrah cross erected in memory of the Scott party. Two days later they walked via the Gap to Pram Point to examine the old 'pram' from the *Discovery* expedition, derelict with its side staved in. An oar from this boat was used as a stunning hammer during sealing.[8] Back at the hut the nicotine-starved men found some old butts, enough for what the Padre described as 'a very thin cigarette each'.[9]

The journey to Mt Hope was to be achieved over two stages. The first task was to get the bulk of the supplies to the Bluff depot, a task originally planned for the first season. From there the entire party would proceed to lay the southern depot at the foot of the Beardmore Glacier and return rapidly with light sledges, a journey made with apparent ease by two of the returning teams on Scott's second expedition.

As in the first season, Mackintosh divided his men into two parties. The Skipper led his original sledging mates, Wild and Spencer-Smith, while Joyce commanded Jack and the four members of the former motor party, Richards, Stevens, Cope and Hayward. The dogs were to be brought up later by Gaze.

The two parties left the *Discovery* hut on 9 October. Unlike in the previous season, when the journey had commenced in midsummer, the travellers did not have to contend with difficult and dangerous sea-ice conditions. On the first day, despite heavy going, they managed to reach south of Safety Camp after covering a distance that had taken many days to achieve earlier in the expedition. The loads, however, were proving difficult to manage by man-hauling.

At first the nine men attempted to pull three sledges with a combined weight estimated by Joyce to be 2,000 pounds.[10] Then they split into teams of three men, each pulling a sledge. Joyce wrote in his field diary: 'Distance done during day about four miles – I don't think in all my experience down here I have had harder pulling – temp −18° turned in wet through.' That night they soon became aware of the discomforts of sledging on the Barrier early in the season, as the temperature dropped to −36°F and wet clothes turned cold and clammy.

In the privacy of his diary Joyce was critical of the Skipper, who 'won't take good solid advice' and failed to appreciate the advantage of making rapid journeys with lighter loads. Even if an extra trip to the Bluff were needed, Joyce reasoned, the toll on the men would be less. 'Hearts are willing but strength will not avail . . . I suppose he will learn to his regret.'[11]

However, the Padre recorded: 'Joyce's chariot seems to drive heavily, tho' we relieved him of 40 lbs. of oil . . . We took on Joyce's very heavy sledge and found it was not too bad after all.'[12]

The following morning Joyce confronted Mackintosh, who announced that his party would shed 60 pounds and push on, while Joyce was to use his discretion and carry on to the Bluff the best way he could. The Skipper had clearly lost patience with his companion, and Joyce questioned: 'Why he is deserting this party which is supposed to be the weakest no one knows.'[13] Jack, too, anticipated that there would be 'a mix up with the stores in the not too distant future',[14] and disclaimed responsibility to Mackintosh.

The normally taciturn Wild had strong views on the matter: 'We pulled [the] heaviest sledge and the others couldn't keep up. It's the foreigners that do it. They give everybody a bad heart.' The following day he added: 'We've left the others behind with poor old Ern in charge. I'm sorry for him but d . . . d glad to get away from the remainder. Very cold temp −32°.'[15] His sledge-mate Spencer-Smith became despondent as the temperature dropped: 'Very sick of life. Too cold to write more.'

During the afternoon of 12 October, Mackintosh's men moved ahead of the others, who started to relay on a bad surface. Soon the Skipper arrived at Cope's No. 1 depot off White Island, where he left an alpine rope and an ice pick he considered to be surplus. The party altered course two points to the southwest, 'so may meet crevasses but it will save us a few miles of agony'.[16] Spencer-Smith soon observed that 'many little crevasses got in our way – from 6 inches to 2 feet wide. I counted about 18 and fell into most of them, including the widest one which seemed of great depth and to widen out as it deepened.'[17]

Wild was fired up: 'I want to get to the Bluff with this load because the others reckon we can't. Cope says he knows we can't. However wait and see.' Ever hopeful, he dug down at 'one of Scott's bamboos, but alas there was no tobacco'.[18]

Their daily distances improved, including fourteen miles on 18 October, the day before they reached the Bluff depot, where they left another three weeks' food for three men plus nineteen pounds of biscuits and a similar amount of oil, a total of 178 pounds. Jack itemised the supplies:

> 2 tins biscuit (82 lbs.), 4 tins oil (40 lbs.), 2 packets Tru Milk (2.7 lbs.), 1 box sugar (14 lbs.), 3 bags Oatina (2.7 lbs.), 3 bags pemmican (31.5 lbs.), 3 bags cocoa (2.7 lbs.), 1 bag salt (0.5 lb.), 2 bags matches (0.5 lb.), 2 boxes lime juice (1.5 lbs.).[19]

The journey to the Bluff had taken only ten days and, aided by light sledges, the party arrived back at Hut Point five days later.

Joyce's men also made good progress, at times using the tent floor cloth for a sail, and reached the Bluff just two days after the Skipper.

Despite the efforts in stressful circumstances of Mackintosh, Joyce and Wild the previous season, the depot was still wrongly placed. Richards sighted it at some eight to nine miles distance in a mirage, but was surprised to find it was not in the expected position: '30 miles off the Bluff with the Bluff and Mount Discovery in transit'. He continued: 'Altogether it has to my mind been very badly placed . . . Thought Joyce would have known the peak for he was with Mackintosh when he re-established the depot last March . . .' Joyce made no mention of the apparent error in his field diary.

When the second party found that the Skipper had arrived ahead of them, Jack acknowledged: 'Unquestionably this is a fine piece of hauling for they have carried out three weeks food per unit in eight days to our two weeks food in ten days – a fine performance if it can be kept up without his party knocking up . . .'[20]

Joyce's party left 273 pounds of stores and a sledge at the misaligned Bluff depot before turning north for the homeward run. This represented the farthest south to date reached by Richards, Hayward, Cope and Stevens.[21]

North of Corner Camp where, according to Joyce, 'Richards gorged, Cope revelled',[22] the men discovered an upturned sledge with a note in a Kodak film tin, written on 16 March 1912 by Apsley Cherry-Garrard on his return from One Ton depot. They also found several cases of Spratts biscuits, which they replaced for later use, and some Wolseley motor oil.[23] Jack recorded: 'We shall take the oil to Hut Point for illuminating purposes in case the ship does not appear to relieve us in March next.' He also added: 'A note from Apsley Cherry-Garrard to Captain Scott and dated March 13 [1912] was attached to the bar and Hayward took same as a memento.'[24]

This old depot yielded more than one discovered six days earlier, which 'consisted of two . . . bamboo poles lashed together with lampwick and surmounted by a tattered piece of faded bunting and projecting above snow about 12–14 feet . . .' That depot was buried eight feet down, but there was nothing to be found apart from a 'few crumbs of biscuit' and the smell of lubricating oil. Jack concluded it was 'probably one of Scott's or Shackleton's motor depots',[25] and Joyce claimed that he 'found it to be the depot I made in 1908 for Shackleton'.[26]

As the party neared the edge of the Barrier, Stevens suddenly disappeared and Hayward raised the alarm: 'He's down, he's down, lookout, he's gone, he's disappeared.'[27] He was discovered suspended by his harness down a crevasse. The rescuers had no alpine rope but managed to tie their harnesses together and haul Stevens, minus his fur mitts, to the surface.[28]

After a hard struggle in the face of strong northerly drift, Joyce's men reached the *Discovery* hut, where a 'good brew of hoosh, seal liver, onions and cocoa was ready for us'.[29]

Meanwhile, the recuperating Gaze had spent a month at Cape Evans enduring a

> rotten, lonely and very miserable time. I had the records to look after, also two loads of stores to get over to Hut Point . . . and blubber to get in. Very nearly failed to do the last two things, owing to the dogs disappearing for 11 days – thought they'd gone for good – luckily however they reappeared on the 22nd, and as the weather held beautifully fine I managed to get through with the job.[30]

Over six decades later, he would recall loathing the slaughter of seals, because they were 'so docile'.[31]

Gaze's feet had healed by the time he was joined at base on 25 October by Wild, who had come from Hut Point to fetch a groundsheet and other items, and to help with the dogs. The pair proceeded together to Hut Point, where Gaze was pleased to find all the party 'in A1 condition, but their gear had suffered especially finnesko, so that several days will have to be spent here at Hut Point "making good"'. Fresh seal meat provided a welcome change from the sledging rations of previous weeks.

The entire party, including the dogs, was now assembled at Hut Point. As events were to unfold, this was to be the only time all members of the shore team were together at the southern base. Plans were formulated to make two further trips to the Bluff and then proceed south to Mt Hope. When the Skipper proposed to Joyce that the dogs should now be used as part of the sledging teams, 'the latter didn't take it kindly', noted Gaze. 'There seems to be something wrong somewhere, there's no "pulling together".'[32]

Despite the work accomplished already in the second season, Mackintosh still hoped for reinforcements from *Aurora* and left a letter at the hut for Stenhouse, damning all but three other members of the party:

Hut Point
27 October 1915

Dear Stenhouse

. . . Now if you can land that party – Stevens who is remaining behind better be in charge as he will probably know the routine better otherwise you can select who you wish but I should keep your ships crew intact as possible . . . will you send each a coat of Burbury and also a pair of finnesko of which they will be in need.

The rest as before – Spencer-Smith and Wild are the only people who are fit and prepared to tackle a hard job, they never trifle, the harder the work the more they do of it – of the remainder I am despaired and so would anyone – I don't include Stevens poor chap, as he is not at his best. We are hand patching up of clothes and starting off again immediately.

Looking forward to meeting you, & to get clear of this God forsaken country forever.

Yours sincerely

A. L. A. Mackintosh[33]

This letter, disclosing a contingency plan whereby Stenhouse would, if necessary, muster another sledging team, underlines the ill-feeling that existed between Mackintosh's party and the others on the ice.

While Joyce and his men remained for a further six days, Mackintosh, Spencer-Smith and Wild left the *Discovery* hut (described by the Padre as a 'foul' place) on 29 October for what would be the last time. They picked up 326 pounds of stores at Safety Camp and made running repairs to the hoop of their tent, which had been damaged when the sledge capsized.[34]

The Skipper's party reached the Bluff ten days later, by which time Spencer-Smith was nursing a painful left Achilles tendon. This was a most unwelcome affliction with perhaps almost 800 miles yet to travel on the depot-laying expedition.

On the return journey to Safety Camp they had yet another narrow escape with the crevasses, as Wild recorded:

Passed over a lot of crevasses & went right down one nearly sledge as well. At least Smithy went right down to the length of harness. I got caught up just under the arm pits & the Skipper was lying across it somehow behind me. However we got out alright . . .[35]

Although the Skipper had asked Joyce by letter at the *Discovery* hut on 28 October to leave at Safety Camp 'a small amount of cooked seal meat also other provisions that could be used there such as jam, butter and some fancy biscuits', Wild 'couldn't find any fresh meat but had jam and onions extra'.[36]

After resting for four days at the camp, Mackintosh's men headed south again on 18 November and sledged 23 miles to Cope's No. 2 depot. Here they left 278 pounds of supplies, which completed the requirements for Shackleton's trans-continental party at this position, 'except for seven weeks biscuits and 40 lbs. oil'.[37] They were back at Safety Camp again on 23 November, somewhat mystified that they had not seen Joyce's party.

By stopping at Safety Camp and not proceeding on to the *Discovery* hut, Mackintosh, Wild and Spencer-Smith deprived themselves of the opportunity to eat more fresh meat.[38] They had now been in the field for almost four weeks without fresh food, and the Padre's ankles were increasingly giving him trouble. Mackintosh was keen to get on with depot-laying, conscious that 'the lives of Sir Ernest Shackleton and his party are to a great extent in our hands', and his party left the camp for the last time on 25 November.

Meanwhile, Shackleton had watched *Endurance* finally disappear beneath the Weddell Sea ice on 21 November:

> She went today: I was standing by H's sledge at 4.50 saw the funnel dip behind a hummock suddenly: ran up the lookout: at 5 p.m. she went down by the head: the stern the cause of all the trouble was the last to go under the water: I cannot write about it . . .[39]

The day before leaving Hut Point on his second journey to the Bluff, Mackintosh had left detailed instructions for Joyce:

> Hut Point
> 28th October 1915
>
> Dear Joyce,
>
> The plans for you to carry out for your next trip to the Bluff depot will be as follows – Stores to be left at the Bluff by each unit (3 men) to be 159 lbs. To enable you to undertake this five of the dogs will be used each day to pull a weight equal to 70 lbs., their ration to be 1.5 lbs. per Diem. To enable two efficient sledge parties, they should consist of yourself (in charge) Hayward and Gaze. For the other party, Richards, Cope & Jack with the dogs. The party under you then can pull the load according to the programme (560 lbs.), while the other party with the dogs should easily manage that amount or I hope over without undue overloading. The above is what I require you to do, anything you can do to better this or to accelerate the speed (3 weeks out & back) will be to your credit. After this trip the partys [*sic*] will arrive and leave from Safety Camp. Trusting this will be plain to you . . .
>
> I remain
> Yours sincerely
>
> Æneas L. A. Mackintosh
> In charge Ross Sea Base

... For the dog pemmican Stevens and another could take the dogs to C. Evans &
bring a load ... While you are in this hut, I hope, as there is no one in charge of
provisions, you will see these are used with economy, there is no reason to starve,
but certain items of which there is a small amount should be used sparingly.[40]

During the week that followed his leader's departure, Joyce detailed his men
to carry out the preliminary tasks laid down by Mackintosh. Hayward and
Stevens, possibly with 'Doctor' [Cope],[41] went to Cape Evans with the dog team
and brought back a load of pemmican. Stevens, however, incurred Joyce's wrath
for not retrieving an aneroid barometer as requested. 'Stevens did not bring
back the B— as promised. I can't express words on this man, but will do so in
front of Shackleton.'[42]

While others in his party retrieved ten cases of stores from the sea ice, together with the blubber of a dozen seals to augment autumn fuel stocks at the
hut, Joyce overhauled sledging gear. In a significant entry in his diary (though
curiously not included in his book), he wrote: 'We are all feeding up well, a
sort of taking in provisions for the trip.'[43]

Stevens remained at Cape Evans when Joyce's party (including five dogs)
started on their second journey from Hut Point to the Bluff on 5 November,
travelling on ski because of the soft surface. At Safety Camp they took on three
weeks' provisions for themselves plus a further seven weeks' rations and 102
pounds of oil to depot at the Bluff. Gaze noted: 'We ought to be able to get a
move on as we are all pretty hefty. Rather funny to be under canvas again, but
much prefer it to that rotten, dirty, blubbery hut.'[44]

The heavy load of 1,500 pounds was carried on two sledges, and men and
dogs were harnessed to the same trace, a technique successfully used earlier in
the season. Gaze, however, had doubts about this arrangement: 'Dogs are working pretty satisfactorily but not nearly as well to my mind as if they had a sledge
to themselves and weren't mixed up with us.'[45]

The route to the Bluff was now well trodden. In the previous month both
parties had made a return trip and Mackintosh was now a week ahead of
schedule on his second trip. Despite the cairns and marker flags, some left from
the previous season, the route taken by Joyce's differed from that of their first
journey. A depot of food they had offloaded then was discovered some two
miles from their current course.[46] Hayward and Richards took the dogs and
retrieved the 200 pounds of supplies, which were added to their already-heavy
sledges.

Like Mackintosh, Joyce also risked travelling through the crevasses off
White Island in order to shorten the journey. When his men reached the Bluff
on 14 November, they placed in the depot 624 pounds of supplies. Gaze had the

pleasure of anticipating the Skipper's response: "Won't the "Old Man" get a shock. It's about 200 lbs. over what he's expecting.'[47]

Before leaving the Bluff, Joyce wrote to his leader:

Bluff Depot
Monday 15 [November]

Dear Sir

Can you let me know what there is to bring out after the next trip which I suppose be the last to Safety Camp? I will try and bring out something after the same load as before, weather and surface permitting.

I remain
Yours sincerely
Ernest E. Joyce

To
Captain Mackintosh,
(Leader),
Ross Sea Base

P.S. Kind regards to Wild S. Spencer-Smith & Self hoping you are in the Pink[48]

Laid up in a blizzard two days later, Richards and Joyce discussed completing the task ahead:

[We] decided if dogs are fit on the 4th journey to take on south & sacrifice as I think they will be the mainstay of the work on ac[count] of the good work they done coming out. Richards & I quite agreed and worked out the plans that is the Skipper & party work from 80° to 81° our party carry all stores to 80° & then on to 82°. If not! Well? I think we shall carry it out just the same . . .[49]

Richards and Joyce had reached a vital conclusion concerning the importance of the dogs in laying the main depot at Mt Hope.

The 70-mile journey from the Bluff to Hut Point was made by Joyce's men in just four travelling days. In threatening weather and poor light, they cut across ice with frequent crevasses at the north end of White Island in an attempt to reach the hut. Joyce noted in his field diary: 'Suddenly Jack fell through. Could not alter course, or else we should have been steering along them, so galloped right across them. We were going so fast that the dogs that went through was [*sic*] jerked out . . .' Although Jack had a reprieve, his leader suffered snow blindness, possibly because he was wearing makeshift goggles – a piece of leather in which a slit had been cut.

Once back at the hut both Joyce and Hayward had their eyes bandaged for three or four days, and Cope administered cocaine and sulphate of zinc. Later, Joyce wrote: 'Put snow on them, cocaine does not seem to have much effect . . .

having rather a bad time.'[50] Richards was complaining of toothache,[51] but he and Jack managed to trap a couple of skua gulls by use of a looped cord, and the birds were soon plucked and devoured as an entrée to the main fare of fresh seal meat and onions. Gaze's improvised leather sandals to counter chaffed heels were copied by Richards and Jack, the latter noting that 'Irvine also has pair which he wore throughout last trip and found very satisfactory'.

The same morning, 25 November, that Mackintosh headed south from Safety Camp, Joyce and his party of five men and five dogs left the *Discovery* hut on their third journey to the Bluff. At Safety Camp they found letters written that morning from Mackintosh, who was puzzled that he had not seen them for almost four weeks and wondered if they had suffered an accident. Joyce wrote in his field diary: 'Letters from Skipper usual whining tones etc.', and Gaze was outraged:

> Expect we'll meet the Old Man at Bluff and hear all about it anyway – he's only got a days start he'll have to be pretty careful or else he'll get his head punched – there was a direct insult offered to Joyce in the note he left and I for one wouldn't take it from the little Swine.[52]

Mackintosh also stated that he now did not intend to return to Safety Camp until the end of the main journey in March, a change of plans that pleased Joyce's men, who considered that the Skipper needed all available time to reach Mt Hope and return.

The two parties met up at Cope's No. 2 depot on 28 November. The Padre, who had been without the company of dogs for almost two months, wrote: 'Dogs look splendid.' Joyce recorded an apparently acrimonious conversation with Mackintosh:

> Sighted what appeared to be cairns but turned out to be Skipper and Smith who sighted us 4 miles off. Came on us 10.30. Smith returned. Skipper came into our tent. Richards and I gave him a really good working plan to go on, but as usual he thinks he knows best, but will find out before long he is in the wrong – & on one occasion he tried to ride the usual high horse but I wasn't having any then he practically accused our party for [*sic*] spoiling his plans but apologised. I told him straight, he would be getting into trouble one of these days through his foolishness, after a lot of talk he said he was making a 21 hour day that is sleeping 8 meals 3 and travelling 10 – I at once told him he would be laying himself up. He left us at 12 o'clock agreeing on the 1st part of our programme and we meet again on the 23rd December what then? – I never in my experience come across such an idiot to be in charge of men!![53]

With the dogs pulling strongly, Joyce's party reached the Bluff with a full load of 1,400 pounds on 2 December, three days ahead of the Skipper. After leaving at the depot 729 pounds, a hundred more than on their previous journey, they turned northwards.[54]

In contrast to Joyce's method of pulling a single heavy load, the Skipper shifted supplies between the depots in smaller lots by relaying.

At the Bluff, Joyce was moved to write a rambling and colourful letter addressed to 'My dear Paton and Bhoys'. After describing the first sledging season, when his men laid 'a depot past Captain Scott's grave', and the difficult and harrowing time they experienced, he continued:

> When we arrived at Cape Evans and found the ship gone, oh my! as it was the only clothes I had was a singlet [?] shirt Drawers 2 pair socks 1 pair finscoes [*sic*] 1 cardigan what a prospect to look forward to I think the worst hit of the lot is No Tobacco. Wild and I made trousers for party out of canvas and boots out of old sleeping bags. We started sledging 1st September that was to get 4500 lbs. of stuff on to the Barrier. I forgot to say all the dogs gave in when we laid the last Depot, we had the 6 left they gave us a good hand. We got the last load on the Barrier 1st week in Oct. during that time the temperature were very low. The Skipper is running one Party, Wild, Spencer-Smith and himself and I have Hayward, Cope, Richards, Jack and Gaze and 4 Dogs as both bitches are up in the Bunt, every little helps and the dogs are doing well. We are often wondering what became of the ship and what you are all doing. I am now taking out the last load, and then we proceed South. I think we shall just be able by a stroke of good fortune to carry out our programme that is lay a depot at 83° 30' I suppose it will be really the biggest thing ever been done. Here we are sledging, the last bath and shift of clothes I had was Jan. 20th 1915 on the ship in the Galley, the last pipe of tobacco in April, ah well! we will make up for the lost time if we get through.
>
> Our programme now after we get out to Bluff there will be 44 week provisions, then to 80 (2 loads) 81 (2 loads) and then right on to 83 30, The party who goes on last will turn about the 1st week in Feb., that will be 3 men. The remainder turn 1st Feb. so practically all parties will arrive together about 7th March. If Shackleton crosses I expect we shall be back earlier. Well lads that is all the news I can give you at present I am writing this in a hurry, as I meant to do it before and I know how hard it is for the crew to receive any news. All hands are well up to date I think the roughing it a bit will make some of them buck up.
>
> If possible get me a couple of Emperor Skins and 2 Adelies whoever skins them I will pay them for it on arrival in Civ Well Paton old Bhoy kind regards to everyone including my old pal the Cook and all the bhoys.
>
> Your old Shipmate,
> ERNEST E. JOYCE[55]

One of the principal reasons for the party's returning to Hut Point for a third time was to bring up extra supplies for the dogs, which were now an integral part of the sledging team. Gaze wrote on 4 December: 'Dogs going well, though Towser is not looking too good.'

The rare warmth of an Antarctic summer allowed the luxury of what Gaze termed a 'snow wash' as they travelled in 'drawers and singlets'.[56] The heat, however, made the snow surface like a pie crust, which the men broke through up to their knees. In addition, Hayward suffered from sunburnt lips.

It was one year since Keith Jack had joined the expedition and he wondered 'where shall we be this time next year – at home or looking out for a relief ship. Then again how is the war progressing?' Inspired by the Canadian poet Robert W. Service, he was moved to compose 'The Lone South Land':

> Land of The Great White Silence, grim land of the polar night;
> Land of the blighting blizzard, ice fields glistening bright;
> Land where the white fanged mountains, nameless, & clearing the sky,
> Whisper of unknown spaces as the drifting clouds sweep by – . . .
> Where the endless day continues with its ceaseless, pitiless glare,
> Scorching the sight with its brightness driving one to despair –
> Where the shimmering mirage dances o'er billowy Barrier plain . . .
> And the lone sledge trail leads onwards into the vast unknown . . .[57]

When one of the two Primus stoves gave out, meals for the six men had to be prepared on one cooker, a time-wasting frustration. At Safety Camp they picked up a case of Trumilk and two cases of sugar for use at the *Discovery* hut.

The party arrived at the hut on the evening of 7 December to find 'much change owing to melting of snow and ice'. The following day Gaze and Jack walked in the hills behind the hut for about two hours.

> It was good to have a roam around the hills after nothing but snow for so long. Found two or three varieties of moss. Also came across a couple of pools – in hollows in hills the result of a thaw . . . Cope announced that dinner was ready. By jove it's good to get fresh meat . . .[58]

That evening's meal included three skuas.

The men took the opportunity to wash clothing in benzine and repair sledging gear. Stevens failed to arrive from Cape Evans as scheduled to pick up the dogs, and only Bitchie, almost due to have a litter of pups, would now be left behind, tethered at the hut with a supply of biscuits and seal meat.

Joyce's party left on their last journey south on 13 December, taking a newly repaired cooker and fried seal meat to supplement the diet of the men and dogs.

Within a day of setting out, Gaze and fellow Australian Jack were at odds with Joyce and Cope. An argument erupted and several punches were thrown, but no damage resulted. Gaze noted he could not stand Cope 'at any price', and that Joyce displayed a 'high and mighty attitude towards Keith and Self'. Joyce, in turn, recorded that Gaze 'had to be taken down a peg' and Jack was 'like an old gossiping washerwoman'. Joyce wanted a medical case left at 'Petrol Depot', but the Australians were insistent that it be taken south. To further aggravate matters, Cope had removed much of the case's contents. Richards tried to settle the combatants down, and eventually both sides saw what Jack admitted to be 'the absurdity of the quarrel'.

Joyce had hoped to reach the Bluff depot by 19 December, but his party was delayed by blizzards for a total of nine days and finally reached there on 28 December. Christmas Day was a disappointment for the men, as had been Joyce's fortieth birthday on 22 December, with nothing to drink or smoke. Celebrations consisted of a third of a mug of lemon juice, used to toast 'absent friends', and 'a small piece of cooked seal meat . . . a welcome change from the eternal hoosh'.

Mackintosh's party was more fortunate, enjoying Christmas at the Bluff depot. After meeting up with Joyce's men at Cope's No. 2 depot on 28 November, they reached the Bluff for the third time a week later, stopping for extra food before continuing on towards the depot laid the previous year 60 miles away near 80° South.[59] The Padre wrote: 'So glad to get past the Bluff at last, though there is not much change of scene.' They were now on the 'Dead Dog Trail' and soon passed the 'Box Cairn' and 'Sledge Runners'. They reached the depot near 80° South on 15 December and left about 180 pounds of supplies plus personal gear.[60] Although travelling light, it took another ten days to cover the 60 miles back to the Bluff. As happened on the outward journey, they were dogged by blizzard conditions on two or three days and were reduced to quarter rations.[61] On Christmas Day, just before reaching the Bluff, they paused:

> At lunch the O.M.[Old Man] sprung the surprise of the century on us – 4 cigars saved from C[ape] Royds – awfully generous and incredibly acceptable. We got a fright after lunch; the sky clouded right over. So we made a dash for the depot, which was only 1½ miles off and found the going rather easier. We arrived about 3 a.m. and settled down to a 'glut' . . . There is a delicious smell of tobacco: the Primus is still going to keep us warm; and hunger is far away. At lunch we sang 'While shepherds watched' and 'Adeste fideles' and Wild gave us one verse of 'Christians, awake' . . . W.P. [weather permitting] we start south for the last time on the morning of the 26th: 279 miles to go and then homeward bound, northwards all the time.[62]

Wild was equally appreciative of the Skipper's present of cigars: 'We are all smoking them in our pipes. The best smoke I've had for years and years.' However, there was something missing: 'This is the driest Xmas ever I've had and I hope it will remain so.'[63]

As Mackintosh's men rebuilt the depot and mended the tent while being warmed by the midsummer temperatures, what they had achieved in almost three months of continuous sledging veiled the dangers of their predicament. Already the party had been away from the *Discovery* hut and the anti-scorbutic benefits of fresh seal meat for over eight weeks. Although they had travelled over 500 miles since 1 October, they still had over 600 to cover to Mt Hope and back to base. Spencer-Smith, in particular, was foot-sore and his Achilles tendons continued to trouble him. Unfortunately, Joyce had not arrived at the Bluff by Christmas Day, as scheduled, and so there was no opportunity to review strategy and consider other options.

On 27 December, when Mackintosh, Wild and the Padre turned south for the last time on their journey to Mt Hope, Joyce's men and the dogs were just a few miles behind. Gaze wrote: 'Caught a glimpse of depot through glasses. Fog lifted for a while but Joyce decided to stop where we were . . .' When they reached the Bluff depot Joyce noted that the Skipper's instructions 'were more reasonable than the others', and that he had thanked the other party for the sterling work done in getting the stores out to the Bluff. Mackintosh instructed that they were now to take on ten weeks' supply of depot provisions – some 530 pounds – to 80° South, plus 230 pounds of dog food, sufficient to proceed to 82° South. They were to make one trip under this new arrangement, instead of two as previously planned.[64] This met with general approval in Joyce's camp, but Gaze warned: 'We'll have a damned heavy load by the time we've finished, about 2000 lbs. Hope surface improves – it's too awful for words at present.'

The two teams sighted each other on 30 December, a day after Joyce's men found the feathers of a skua, a 'Christmas turkey' that had been captured and cooked by Wild for the Skipper's party,[65] and on New Year's Eve they met in good humour and fellowship. Joyce's men brought gifts of books, seal meat, butter and tinned paste. Private recriminations and cherished misunderstandings were cast aside. 'All are A1,' noted Gaze of the Skipper's party. Joyce wrote: 'Had a pipe of tea with Ern and a long talk with the Boss . . . came to a mutual understanding (at last). I think it is nearly time he woke up. We had a nice cup of tea together to drink the peace.'[66]

CHAPTER FOURTEEN

Journey to Mt Hope

T HE JOURNEY TO Mt Hope was the *raison d'être* of the Ross Sea party. The southern depot was to laid be at the Gap, at the foot of the Beardmore Glacier, discovered by Shackleton on his southern journey in December 1908. Scott's parties had also passed this point, a well-defined feature at the juncture of the Great Ice Barrier and the Queen Alexandra Range.[1] It meant that Shackleton's transcontinental party planned either to descend the Beardmore Glacier en route from the King Edward Plateau,[2] or take a more eastwards descent while tending westwards to pick up the depot. Additionally, Mackintosh was to lay a depot at every degree of latitude between the Gap and the Bluff.

New Year's Day 1916 found Mackintosh, Spencer-Smith and Wild a short distance behind Joyce, Gaze, Hayward, Richards, Cope, Jack and the dogs. Jack wrote: 'What a great way to spend a New Year, hauling sledges in this God forsaken country.' The absentee was Stevens, who was at the base at Cape Evans, his only companions being two bitch huskies and a litter of pups.

The travellers were again reminded of the 'Dead Dog Trail' of the previous season as they picked up two sets of harness from a cairn.[3] The welfare of the remaining four animals, employed in a unique man-and-dog combination, was now paramount. Joyce noted on 2 January: 'Con and Towser not in the best of trim, so had to dose them. We are giving them as much food as they like to eat . . .' Joyce took the ailing dogs in as tent-mates, and Richards made them a 'hot feed', to the apparent annoyance of Oscar and Gunner, who had to be 'squared with a piece of seal meat'. A hot hoosh of pemmican, seal meat and biscuits soon became regular fare for the dogs.

As Joyce's men approached the depot near 80° South, so arduously laid in cold autumn temperatures the previous season and recently further provisioned by the Skipper's party, Gaze, Jack and Cope made a 'rotten discovery'. As Jack noted on 3 January: 'Primus wearing in the gauze . . . three days ago, two holes only had gone while today we find the corrosion has extended about ½ to ¾ inch around the lowest ring of holes. This is a serious matter . . .' It was the second of the old Scott expedition cookers to burn out. Gaze rued: 'We brought out a spare Primus but the Skipper collared it – his own had gone in the same way.'[4]

The three men attempted some makeshift repairs and fitted a wire ring inside the burner, but the next day they found further damage. This time a piece of tin was successfully fitted to block off the lower holes. Jack wrote: 'It did not reduce efficiency of the lamp for it cooked our hoosh in 19 minutes tonight, the specified time being 20 . . .'[5]

Joyce discussed the problem with Richards, then came to the others' tent and, according to Jack, 'announced we would be returning to Hut Point at 80° S depot owing to collapse of our Primus. We (Irvine and self) replied . . . would see how it looked when reach the depot and talk about it then.' Gaze recorded that they

> objected strongly against this, and suggested that we went on and if the worst came to the worst we could all (6 of us) do on one Primus. – Joyce wouldn't have this or anything else we suggested at any price . . . Cope is coming back with us (in place of Hayward) – just as soon have him, there's precious little to choose between them.[6]

When Gaze and Jack (with Cope) met Joyce at the depot near 80° South the next morning, they hoped for a reprieve, but as Jack noted: 'Joyce, Richards and Hayward immediately began preparing their sledge to go on.'[7]

Joyce designated Cope as leader of the returning trio:

> I am very pleased to get rid of Gaze and Jack, as they have not been playing the game very much but Cope has been rather good, always willing and doing his best. But as the strongest have to go forward for the relief and I had to send him back in charge of the others.[8]

This left Hayward and Richards as Joyce's tent-mates. Almost seven decades later, Richards would recall Hayward as 'a pretty stolid chap with little sense of humour . . . an inscrutable man who said little. His thoughts were a sealed book.'[9]

Jack and Gaze doubted Joyce's motives and felt he was intent on keeping ahead of Mackintosh, and not turning back as had been planned at 82° South. Jack noted: 'I believe Joyce intends to make for 83° 30.'[10]

Gaze was indignant. '[Joyce] intends to push and try and meet Shackleton first, intending the Skipper to do "Hack Work" filling up the depots. – sincerely hope . . . the Skipper goes on (as originally intended) to the Farthest South and meets Shackleton himself – sending Joyce back as intended from 82[° South].'[11]

To the surprise of the returning party, Mackintosh was only a short distance behind. Gaze took the opportunity to confide in Spencer-Smith. 'I gave

A.P. a pretty good account of what Joyce's intentions were – that he was out to play dirt on the Skipper.' As a parting gift, a pound of onions was transferred to Mackintosh's party, a token offering to counter scurvy.[12] This was the last time Gaze would see his cousin.

After a brief discussion, photographs were taken with the depot near 80° South in the distance and the parties bade each other farewell.[13] Joyce's decision to send the three men back was thereby endorsed by the Skipper. Like Joyce, Mackintosh apparently ignored Cope's role as the acting medical officer, as there was no examination of any members of the party for early signs of scurvy or of physical ailments such as strained tendons, ligaments and the like before he continued north.

Spencer-Smith recorded on 7 January: 'The Skipper has been going all day with a sore knee, ricked yesterday.'[14] The Padre, too, had been having difficulties. He and Wild had been Mackintosh's sledging-mates over two seasons, and it would seem that in the Skipper's mind there was no question of this trio not remaining together regardless of fitness.

One of the men returning north was among the fittest in the party. The doughty Keith Jack, a slightly built man of medium height, had proved himself over two seasons as an efficient sledger. Methodical and conscientious – traits that did not necessarily endear him to others – he was impatient of slow progress. Some days later he would record of himself, admittedly at a time when hauling minimal weights: 'Am in splendid form . . . [it is] simply wonderful how one becomes adapted to the work of hauling and plodding through deep snow, hour after hour, day after day, without fatigue.'[15]

Cope, Jack and Gaze, travelling light, made the return journey to Hut Point in just seven days. They were without an effective compass, Gaze noting: 'We had to get along as best as we could by steering with the sun.'[16] Cope had no snow goggles and suffered badly from snow blindness. They came close to catastrophe on 13 January, as Jack recorded:

> Cope suddenly disappeared down a very bad [crevasse] to a depth well over the length of his harness . . . both sledge and myself narrowly escaped following Cope. Both Irvine and self fixed up a number of loops on a long piece of rope which at the last moment of leaving I had got from Joyce . . . eventually we landed him safe at the top.[17]

It was a narrow escape, and Gaze concluded: 'I think we can count ourselves very lucky getting out of the thing as we did.'

The three men were greeted at the hut by Beechy, 'bristling like a she devil'.[18] For safety's sake they entered through a window and discovered a litter of eight pups. The thaw had turned the hut into a stinking hovel. Gaze wrote: 'All the filth shows up in its nakedness – by jove it "hums".'

The following day they put the pups in a box, hitched up the dog to a sledge and set out across the soggy sea ice to Cape Evans. With open water nearby, they had little time to spare if they were not to be trapped at the *Discovery* hut until the winter. Their progress was soon aided by a southerly wind, which they harnessed in rough fashion by the then-familiar technique of erecting a makeshift sail. This same wind also threatened them because the rotten sea ice started moving. Twice they were forced to 'ferry on a couple of floes' across open water. The life-threatening risk seemed worth the prize, and they arrived at Cape Evans in the early hours of 16 January. Jack wrote: 'Surface simply shocking and sledge dragged terribly. Stevens . . . immediately turned out in surprise and got a rattling good meal of penguins breasts, vegetables, scones etc . . . 4 a.m. before we got into our bags . . .' The hut was in a mess and dead skua gulls littered the area. Gaze noted: 'Stevens has been busy with the gun.'[19] There was no sign of the ship.

Cope, Gaze and Jack, like Stevens, would take no further part in the sledging.

Meanwhile, the Skipper's men approached 82° South after leaving 183 pounds of supplies at 81°. These were listed by Spencer-Smith:

Biscuit 86 lb., oil 30 lb., pemmican 31.5 lb., tea 2.625 lb., milk 2.625 lb., Streimer 8.1375, salt .25, Oatena 7.875 sugar 14 total 183.0125. 3 weeks with 23 lbs. of biscuits and a tin of oil extra.[20]

Joyce's and Mackintosh's parties joined forces on 7 January, within a day or two of Cope's party leaving them near 80° South. The Skipper's men were struggling with a load of 620 pounds, of which 50 were transferred to Joyce's sledge. This party with dogs now pulled, according to Joyce, some 1,350 pounds. It was then found that the combined efforts of the six men and the four dogs hauling two sledges hooked together achieved better progress, although they frequently broke through the 'pie crust' surface.[21]

Joyce, usually steering in the leading trace, suffered more than his companions from snow blindness. Wafers of cocaine from the medicine chest were applied to relieve his intense pain,[22] but on occasions he had to relinquish the front spot and march with his eyes bandaged. On 12 January, he wrote: 'I had several bad falls owing to the blindness. It seemed like a holiday pulling behind the Padre. Nothing to worry one, except pull and keep your feet.'

The dogs also suffered: 'Con has a touch of sun blindness. At the halts likes to have his head heaped over with powdered snow: he lies still with head extended until the restart.'[23]

Frequent stops were made to build cairns, which were marked by a small piece of black cloth (cut from a pair of trousers belonging to Richards) attached to the southern side. The combined party maintained a policy of always keeping two cairns in sight, with Richards using a prismatic compass to take back readings to each cairn.[24]

When the weather lifted, the mountain peaks of the Queen Alexandra Range to the west and south slowly came into view. Spencer-Smith wrote on 10 January: 'Last night we had a glimpse of Mt Markham, 135 miles away. This morning we could scarcely see 100 yards. But by the back cairn method we carried on.'[25] At over 13,000 feet, Mt Markham soared over the Nimrod Glacier and, although somewhat north of the expedition's goal, this peak seemed a glimpse of the Promised Land.

Mackintosh, Spencer-Smith and Wild had been without fresh seal meat since they had left the *Discovery* hut on 29 October, and it soon became apparent that they were in distress. Joyce recorded ominous signs on 10 and 11 January: 'S[mith] still not pulling . . . 'S[mith] still painful to watch.' Mackintosh, too, was failing. 'Boys behind told me the Skipper had hardly been pulling the whole afternoon and he looked quite done up.'[26]

The Padre, uncomplaining by nature, appeared to ignore his problems, noting instead items of a domestic kind:

Tues. Jan, 11. A gruelling day – rather overcast. Trek 10 m. 150 yds . . . We borrowed Hayward's glass in evening & trimmed beards &c. We were all horrified at our phizes. Lip very sore and looks nasty.[27]

Although Joyce, Hayward and Richards were scheduled to turn back at 82° South, like those already sent back to base they were in better shape than the Skipper's men. However, the prospect of returning the ailing Mackintosh and Spencer-Smith with a companion in support does not seem to have been contemplated. The 81° South depot, laid on 12 January, was more or less a midway point between the Bluff and Mt Hope, and a party turning north there would have been spared 300 miles of sledging. This, though, would have left the Mt Hope party with no reserve Primus, and would have involved prematurely placing in a depot some of the stores needed for Shackleton's men.

On 16 January, with the travellers just two days short of 82°, one of the two remaining Primus cookers broke down. Richards tried to effect repairs, but it continued to cause problems. Wild noted: 'Primus not very grand' and 'Primus working rotten'. Richards made another attempt to remedy it, this time with some success: 'Primus working, all "bands" now.'[28] In fact, this cooker became central to the 'politics' of what happened at 82° South, reached on 18 January.

Tent-mates Joyce, Richards and Hayward decided that if the Skipper's men proceeded by themselves as planned, they would almost certainly be doomed. By now Mackintosh was lame, as was the Padre, whose legs and arms were stiffening badly and he was in considerable pain.[29] They pressed their argument, as testified by Richards, 'with the greatest vehemence',[30] and used the defective Primus as the reason why the party should go on as one.[31] Richards and Joyce tried to convince Mackintosh, whose leadership was being undermined by his rapidly failing health, that he should change strategy: in the interests of all six men and the expedition as a whole, the sledging party should remain together. The Skipper sensed mutiny but had little choice but to go along with the pleas of his sledging companions or, depending on one's viewpoint, his subordinates' demands.

At 82° South, Mackintosh called Richards to his tent to discuss a legal matter. He explained that all the other members of the expedition had signed an agreement with Shackleton, but none of the Australians had. 'I want you to sign this agreement,' he instructed Richards.[32] As Mackintosh dictated, Spencer-Smith wrote out his statement:

IMPERIAL TRANS-ANTARCTIC EXPEDITION

The Great Ice Barrier
18 January 1916
Lat. 82°S

I R. W. Richards at present serving as a member of the above expedition under the command of Sir Ernest Shackleton CVO do in consideration of the salary by me of £ per annum, undertake to obey the lawful commands of the above named Sir Ernest Shackleton CVO or those appointed by him. I also undertake to hold secret all work in connection with the above Expedition – as regards publishing on the return to civilisation – of news, diaries, photographs, or other material such as I now have, or shall have, as a member of the Expedition in my possession such property as above mentioned, to be considered as belonging to the above expedition. This to hold good for a period of two years after the return of the Expedition to civilisation.

Æneas A. L. Mackintosh   (signed) R. W. Richards
Commanding Ross Sea Base.[33]

Mackintosh, distrustful of Richards, felt the need to extract an expression of his allegiance. It added nothing to the status quo and the deal was struck without any fuss on the Australian's part. This curious incident is not mentioned in any of the three surviving diaries, but it seems it enabled the Skipper to agree to the Joyce camp demands to proceed as a single team to Mt Hope. It was to be Mackintosh's last assertion of leadership on this journey: thereafter the Ross Sea party's decision-making was effectively by consensus.

If the Skipper had taken into account his own dangerous state of health and that of the Padre, the discussions at 82° South might well have focused on how the party could most safely split. Common sense would then have required that the invalids turn for home. Given the Primus problem, there would be a risk whatever choice was made. Perhaps one fit man and two of the dogs could have accompanied Mackintosh and Spencer-Smith on a slow trudge homewards. If they did not make much ground, the returning Mt Hope party would eventually have caught up with them.

At least two of the men now back at Cape Evans could have replaced either or both of the sick men and been substituted for Mackintosh and Spencer-Smith near 80° South. However, the make-up of the party and the attitude of the Skipper had prevented any useful dialogue on contentious subjects since sledging began twelve months earlier. Stubbornness and misguided pride on the part of Mackintosh and the Padre now imperilled the party. Neither man acknowledged his dangerous symptoms, and both remained determined to get to Mt Hope.

Spencer-Smith noted on 16 January: 'The land to the west looks huge and there is also land dead ahead.' Although almost 2,000 pounds of supplies – some three weeks' provisions – were placed at 82° South on 18 January,[34] Wild wrote: 'Still sledges don't seem to go much better.'[35]

In fine weather the sledgers hoisted sail before a northerly tail wind and, between 19 and 21 January, averaged over thirteen miles per day. Joyce generally led on the end of a 25-foot rope, followed by Mackintosh, Spencer-Smith and Wild attached to this rope by harness, with the four dogs (Con, Oscar, Gunner and Towser) harnessed behind them. Richards and Hayward were usually tied to the sides of the sledge with eight-foot ropes.[36] Richards later described a variation to this unusual man-and-dog sledging arrangement: one man followed by two dogs, then two men followed by a further two dogs, with two men hitched directly to the sledge.[37]

By 19 January, the Padre was rapidly failing and complained of his knees 'being bad'. Joyce observed in his diary: 'He has not been doing much pulling. I think the Skipper and him ought to have gone back with the other party. Now they are with us they will have to leg it out or camp until we come back. Time is too precious to waste . . .'[38]

It had been, however, Joyce's decision near 80° South to send back three fit men, including the acting medical officer of the party, without waiting to confer with the Skipper. Nor is it likely to have been feasible for a party of just three men, even with dogs, to have proceeded from there in order to depot the necessary provisions as arranged with Shackleton.

On 20 January, matters reached crisis point. Joyce noted: 'Sk[ipper] and [Spencer-Smith] walking along like old men.' A day later: 'S[pencer-Smith] serious, legs are worse. I expect it will mean carting them on the sledge.'[39]

Late in the middle of a sunny morning, the Padre sat down and said he could go no further. For two days he had been feverish: '. . . cold and un-comfort[able] knees . . . feeling rather seedy; head hot; eyes ache.'

> Dreamt last night that the war was over – that all German rivers were now English rivers . . . Nearly fainted at 11 a.m. and had to tell at lunch how weak I am: much sympathy and an extra Bovril cube all to myself. Heart rather ricked, I fear, and knees bad – swollen and like a great bruise above and below knee, especially the right.[40]

The Padre finally accepted defeat on 22 January:

> After about 2½ hours' struggle this morning, with the knees and above and below getting heavier, hotter and more painful every step, I had to ask the Skipper to depot me here and carry on to Mt Hope without me. Eheu! But it's no use howl-ing. It is about 3 p.m. now and I reckon on getting 2½–3½ days complete rest before they return. They have gone on with one sledge and 5 weeks' food: and they rattled off at a tremendous pace; with the dogs scrapping en route. Skipper and Wild most sympathetic: The others kindly [left] me a bottle of lime juice in case my complaint is some form of scurvy – which I doubt altogether . . .[41]

Wild felt sorry for his congenial tent-mate: '11¼ miles. A short day. We had to leave poor old Smithy behind, he has got a bad leg, so we are rather jambed up with five in a tent. Wrote a letter to Frank.'[42]

As Wild wrote to his brother, whom he expected to be in the trans-continental party, Shackleton's second-in-command was at 'Patience Camp', stranded with the *Endurance* party on the sea ice of the Weddell Sea. Both sections of the ITAE were about to become part of the fabric of the heroic era of Antarctic exploration.

One of the two sledges was left with Spencer-Smith, whose tent was in sight of the mountains to the south. Joyce urged the Skipper to rest up also, but Mack-intosh was not going to give in at this point.[43]

The travellers thought they could identify Mt Hope 'right ahead, about 30 miles off'.[44] With luck they would be at their destination within a couple of days. However, a few miles further on a blizzard held them up for a crucial two days. These circumstances put all five men together in one tent for the first time and there was an atmosphere of camaraderie. Wild wrote: 'Had a game at Auction Bridge this afternoon. We lost. The Skipper was my partner.'[45]

The morning of 25 January dawned fine and the party made a record seventeen and a half miles. Wild wrote: 'We haven't quite reached Mount

Hope. There are crevasses all round us and we couldn't find a passage through them.' It was a year to the day since they had landed from *Aurora*, and for Ernest Wild it was the longest time he had been off a ship for over twenty years.[46]

On 4 December 1908, as Shackleton had approached the feature he named the Gap, he had written:

[We] eventually, at 5 p.m., reached the head of the pass, 2,000 feet above sea level. From that point there was a gentle descent towards the glacier . . . The pass through which we have come is flanked by great granite pillars at least 2,000 feet in height and making a magnificent entrance to the 'Highway of the South'.[47]

Joyce, Mackintosh and Richards negotiated the way through the maze of crevasses on the morning of 26 January. Joyce recorded: 'Such a scene one can't imagine. Thousands of tons of ice churned up and the depth about 300 ft.'[48] They could see a great glacier ahead, but the chart seemed to have Mt Hope in the wrong position. Joyce recorded in his diary:

We nearly arrived at the ice foot when Richards saw something to the right, which turned out to be two of Captain Scott's sledges. Then we knew for certain this was the place we had struggled to get to. So we climbed the glacier on the slope and went up about 1¼ mile and saw the great Beardmore Glacier stretching to the south. It is about 25 miles wide, a most wonderful sight.[49]

Richards lay down and examined the surface of the glacier below with field glasses. For a moment he thought he saw Shackleton's tent.[50]

The three men trekked six miles back to the tent and the party then advanced the camp to the two Scott sledges. That evening the Mt Hope depot was laid: 'Wild, Hayward and myself [Joyce] then took the depot up the glacier. A fortnight's provisions. We left it lashed to a broken sledge and put a large flag up. I took two photos of it. We did not arrive back until 10.30.'[51]

At 11.45 p.m. Wild also recorded the momentous events of the day:

We've made Mt Hope depot at last. 7 miles from where we were last night. 2 weeks provisions and 2 full tins of oil so they ought to be alright. We found two sledges here that had been left by Scott's party. The depot is 2 miles from here. Joyce, Hayward and myself laid it and came back here for supper. The ice pressure around here is tremendous. The Beardmore Glacier looks very rough from the Gap.[52]

Of all the entries in Wild's diary, this is the most crucial and gives better detail than Joyce's account, which does not make it clear whether the depot was laid at or near the Gap. Wild's description proves the party was at a pass overlooking the Beardmore Glacier.

After Joyce, Hayward and Wild returned to camp, the Skipper thanked his men for their sterling work.

CHAPTER FIFTEEN

Aurora *breaks free*

A S MACKINTOSH'S PARTY turned for home, *Aurora* was still held in the outer fringes of the rotting pack ice, the ship and the ice moving northwards at some eight to ten miles per day.[1] In exasperation, Stenhouse wrote: 'No change in prospects!'[2] Any chance of the vessel's returning to Cape Evans that season had by then gone. The formerly buoyant Thomson conceded: 'The best we will be able to do . . . will be to save our own skins.'[3]

On 5 January, Thomson had recorded: 'We only have about 90 lbs. of tinned meats and about 60 lbs. of tinned fish and 10 hams remaining on board . . .'[4] Soon after this observation Stenhouse decided to reduce meals to one per day. 'We have plenty of flour and butter on board but little else.'[5] Thomson must have reappraised matters and was more optimistic on 19 January: 'We are not as well off for seal meat as we would like to be but I am sure we would be able to hang down another year with a bit of trouble.[6] They still had considerable stocks of such items as soup, pemmican, jam, honey, meat paste, fruit, sugar, tea, salt, rice and beans.[7]

Stenhouse made renewed efforts to capture every available seal or penguin. Frequently the prey eluded the somewhat clumsy would-be captors, who floundered in the melting ice floes. A moulting call-bird, soon nicknamed 'Archiebald' [*sic*], positioned near some discarded tins close to the ship, lured some of the prey. The hunters took 233 Adélie penguins, seven emperor penguins and six seals during January and February.[8] Stenhouse berated those men who made little or no contribution to these efforts, and Ninnis called them 'the absolute work-shirkers'.[9]

The hours of darkness markedly increased as *Aurora*, locked in the ice, tracked north of 65°. This latitude gave more chance for successful wireless transmission, free of solar interference. The aerial was re-rigged on the ice and sent aloft to a height of 95 feet, from where it was stretched out to a flagstaff rigged on a high hummock some distance from the stern of the ship.[10] Hooke hoped to communicate with Macquarie Island, but in fact the meteorological station there had been closed down two months earlier as a wartime economy measure.[1]

The ice floe that had imprisoned *Aurora* split open on 12 February. Ninnis wrote: 'Momentous day. Ice broken up at last . . . At 5.40 I was on bridge, saw a crack open, an old one, then another . . .' The bosun recorded the breakout in these words: 'The ship bumped heavily and trembled from stem to stern, rolling heavily from side to side, finally steadying herself with a heavy list to starboard. Great excitement prevailed . . .'[12] As she settled in the ice, *Aurora* soon made 'over 4 feet of water'. The crew formed a bucket chain and baled as the engineers worked to free the frozen pumps. They only just managed to rescue the cache of seal meat alongside the ship before the gangway, according to Ninnis, 'fell into the pond'. The aerial was hauled on board, 'a ghastly tangle of wires'.[13]

By nightfall on 13 February, there were no bergs in sight. The crew was placed on Kulassi watches[14] while the ship made an erratic course through the floes. In 36 hours *Aurora* made about five miles to the north-west.[15] When a large floe blocked the way ahead, they attached an anchor to it and warped the ship free.[16] Fortunately, the propeller was undamaged, but it was not yet time to use the engines.

The squalor of the wintering site disappeared as old and notorious landmarks, such as the offal heap with its foul stench, drifted away on previously trapped ice. As a farewell gesture, an idle marksman shot a feasting giant petrel.[17]

Aurora celebrated her liberty by moving ahead through the ice floes, rudderless and without steam, over the following days and nights. At times the southerly wind carried the ship along without sail, with the yards positioned to give some direction. Setting the sails, with the 'yards braced to keep ship off wind', sometimes had dramatic results, as one instance recorded by Larkman: 'The pack to starboard again drifted downwind and hemmed us in till 3.30 a.m. when the ice opened, the ship paid off to SSW and started off like a racehorse. 'Twas a pleasing sight to see how she made her way through the floes without a rudder.'[18]

The morale of the ship's complement lifted as they found themselves freed from their ice prison and and suddenly witnessing a majestic scene. Larkman was inspired to write: 'What a beautiful blue the water is.'[19] Whales, seals and seabirds seemed plentiful.

For a fleeting moment Stenhouse thought there might be a chance to achieve his appointed task: 'Have hopes of getting to McMurdo Sound if luck holds. Cannot burn short supply of coal. Must endeavour [to] make southing under sail and keep coal for emergencies . . . Will have to be very careful of snow [fresh water] supply.' Three days later he accepted the inevitable: 'Nights are dark and getting long now but if we can get out we must strive to get south although it is an insane thing to attempt in our condition and so late in the season.'[20] The state of the ship and the lack of coal and supplies, not to mention the stress of the last nine months, all pointed to the need to get to port.

Although floating, *Aurora* soon became jammed in the dense pack ice. Stenhouse wrote on 15 February: 'No open leads visible from crow's nest, appearance of open water on northern horizon, no bergs in sight.'[21] However, the swell of the ocean pressing through the ice brought hope of progress. The crew constantly worked the hand pumps and managed to keep the water level below the 45 inches recorded on 13 February when the ice broke up.[22] From the crow's nest they caught tantalising views of distant leads through the pack ice. The appearance of the sky was also promising. 'Open water sky is visible to east and south but no actual open water can be seen,' Stenhouse recorded on 20 February.[23] Curiously, the ship was pointing south.

Icebergs towering many times the height of the ship progressed rapidly through the pack, constituting a new danger. The need to preserve coal added to the lead time necessary to make an escape, as it took at least 30 hours to raise steam. One of the roughest nights was 29 February. Paton wrote:

> Massive ice floes hurled after us and battered up against our sides and making her tremble from stem to stern. Mr Stenhouse and another of the crew have been on deck with me all night and we have had our work cut out putting fenders over, and shifting them about to meet the ice . . .[24]

Ninnis described the same event:

> A heavy swell from north west was running and of quite astonishing size. As each crest passed under ship she was heaved up and heavily bumped against the other floes whilst the weather side floes hammered as heavily . . . A modern ship, or any iron or steel ship, would be cracked like a nut . . . about 25,000 cubic feet of solid ice battering us. In ones bunk it is impossible to sleep . . . when a large flow cracks into side and we hear the side give and timbers creak and crack . . .[25]

The engineer reported a leak near the propeller shaft, an old trouble spot into which the ship's carpenter packed 'cement, stockholm tar and oakum'. He also caulked another leak under the boiler.[26]

With a large overturned berg in the pack four miles to the north, and another like a pinnacle to the east also causing concern, Stenhouse decided it was time to get clear of the dangerous pack ice. He ordered the engine-room fires be lit for the first time for almost nine months: 'We *must* waste our coal before the ship is smashed up. With the lighting of fires, while still in the pack, goes our last chance of relieving the people south. I have been loath to raise steam.'[27]

Larkman cautiously increased pressure in *Aurora*'s boilers, and the main engines were put into use 29 hours after the order was given. Almost three hours later the ship had made a distance of only 'one cable' to westwards, with repeated stops to avoid damaging the propeller on under-foots of ice.[28] Significantly, before 'ringing off' engines for the night and banking fires, Stenhouse steamed on to an ice anchor he had affixed from a floe to the starboard bow and manoeuvred the ship's head to the north. Like the throb of the engines, the sound of water being pumped through the bilge pumps and the billowing smoke from the chimney-stack, the reorientating of the *Aurora* was a reassurance that normality was returning and soon the ship would be on its course to New Zealand. In the distance could be heard 'the long roll of the sea over the ice'.[29]

The crew rigged a spanker-gaff weighted with a mooring chain to gain steerage, and on 3 March the ship made five miles westwards.[30] However, hopes of quickly steaming clear of the pack and the dangerous icebergs were thwarted, as the following day *Aurora* was held up with the fires banked to preserve coal. Paton wrote:

> 5.30 when daylight was good enough to see, I went aloft with the glasses to have a view of our surroundings. It was a beautiful morning and a lovely sight was to be seen. The open sea was plainly to be seen from N. to W. and 17 large icebergs had worked their way right up to the edge of the pack. One berg was fully 5 miles long, another 3 miles – dangerous customers to come in contact with on a dark night. These fellows can work their way into the pack, even when we are powerless to move, so a careful lookout has to be kept. The crew are now on sea watches . . .[31]

On 5 March, noted Paton, 'after an hour's hard steaming she would not budge an inch', and six hours of steaming on the following day failed to achieve any progress. 'We cannot get her to go in the right direction. Unable to use either our jury rudder or the spar, even the use of ice anchors we have tried to turn her head but cannot get her round. We have been going to the east instead of the NW where the open water is.'[32]

A northerly swell again set in and for three days *Aurora* bumped heavily against the pack.[33] By 7 March, the ship had made no progress, despite her crew's determined efforts. Oddly, open water previously visible to the north and west now could be seen from the south around to the east. Everywhere else there was nothing but ice. Paton observed: 'Although we have been steaming to the north and west, my opinion is that we have been going further into the field as the whole field was gradually turning round . . .'[34] Stenhouse shared this view: 'The ship is apparently driving down with the pack.'[35]

By daybreak on 10 March, after a heavy battering overnight, *Aurora* was in immediate peril. Two bergs to the east were only two miles away and drawing nearer. Ninnis wrote: 'Steam had to be raised from dead low fires and the tightly packed ice had quite locked our propeller.'[36] Even to the experienced bosun, the bergs were 'great monsters, the tops of them towering high above our masts . . . A desperate attempt was made to get free, we did not stop to think of our propeller blades . . .'[37]

By 8.30 a.m. the nearest berg was 'about 2 cables from the ship'.[38] Stenhouse renewed his attempts to escape. Slowly the ice opened and the ship started to make headway. The bosun recorded their escape: '. . . we had just broke free then, the bergs were quite close but we were slowly crawling away. It was a lovely sight but one I have no wish to see again.'[39]

Beyond the bergs to the east, great lanes of water were observed. Still not able to use either of the temporary rudders because of ice, Stenhouse and Thomson skilfully drove *Aurora* to the north. Stenhouse wrote: 'We made good progress with the swell and wind on the port bow – jibs set, to counteract effect of screw . . . Pack opened during afternoon and we came thro' wide stretches of open floes (small) and brash.'[40] By 11 March, Paton estimated they were barely a quarter-mile from the sea and could hear the clear sound of the 'wash of the sea over the ice'.[41]

Again, *Aurora* became stuck fast in heavy ice and the crew could not turn her towards the gap that led to the open water. The following day, however, they did manage to move her slowly through the heavy pack into a 'huge lake' where the steering spar was used successfully.[42]

Describing the night of 12 March as 'a weird scene', Ninnis wrote: 'In the darkness of fog all around us can be heard the sucking roar of the sea around the foot of bergs . . . a rising wind.'[43]

Stenhouse held *Aurora* under steam all night, noted Paton, with 'the engineer standing by the throttle ready to go ahead or astern so as to avoid the heavy growlers and huge ice bergs'.

> It was not till 2 a.m. when the greatest danger threatened us. We had just cleared one big growler by not more than 30 feet which passed from port to starboard across our stern and travelling at a great pace to windward when another huge berg appeared dangerously close on our port bow. To clear it we had to go astern, but could not go far as we were coming back on the growler, to go ahead again only brought the berg back on our lee bow, so we had to keep backing and filling until we find ourselves once more in the pack, the safest place.[44]

On the afternoon of 13 March, *Aurora* slowly half turned and made what Ninnis described as 'a diagonal run for the sea'.[45] By 10.30 p.m. she was close to the fringe of the pack. The crew spent another anxious night dodging 'huge bergs' and 'ugly growlers' and were thankful when day began to break at 3.30 a.m. and they found that the ship was in a big bay.

The bosun's account continued: 'We thought we were hemmed in but on scouting from aloft we could just see a faint line of open water beyond the ice, and our spirits began to rise again.'[46] The ship was steered north into a neck of ice and cleared the last narrow belt of the pack at just after midnight on 14 March 1916.[47] Stenhouse noted the position as 64° 27.5', S 157° 32' E. All that remained before *Aurora* reached the open sea was a further belt of brash ice.

Stenhouse wrote: 'Spliced the "Main Brace" and blew three blasts of farewell to the pack with the whistle.'[48] Making the final entry in his diary, Ninnis wrote on 15 March: 'At 6 p.m. we sounded 3 blasts on our steam hooter as a farewell to the ice, long looked for.' [49]

It was almost twelve months since *Aurora* had been moored at Cape Evans, some 1,200 miles to the south, in readiness for the 1915 winter and to await the arrival of Shackleton and his party from the Weddell Sea.

Aurora in the open sea was a different vessel to *Aurora* in the pack ice. Ninnis observed the 'noise of creaks and groans is ten times that whilst lying in ice'. There were many leaks and the bilge pumps were constantly in use.[50] Occasional growlers and icebergs were soon left behind, as were the familiar cries of the Adélie penguins, which 'rapidly diminished and [were soon] lost to us'.[51] Paton, however, reported hearing the birds after leaving the ice behind: 'Just before midnight the harsh calls of a mob of Adelies were heard, they were travelling north for the winter.'[52]

The ship proceeded slowly under a combination of sail and steam, frequently labouring with 'insufficient steerage way'[53] in heavy seas. Stenhouse delayed using the big jury rudder and found the smaller spar rudder adequate in most conditions.

By 21 March, the ship was at 58° 33' S.[54] Stenhouse ordered 'steam shut down' and sailed under canvas alone for the next five days. The coal was needed as much for ballast as for fuel. From 21 February until early March, *Aurora* had used just six to seven tons of coal, leaving 80 tons – eight days' supply at full speed. Although ashes were being stowed as ballast, their weight was only fifteen per cent that of an equivalent volume of coal.[55]

Aurora made 90 miles to the north in the first day clear of the pack, 'not bad for one mast only and a propeller dragging'.[56] Taking advantage of a favourable wind, Stenhouse sailed on through the autumn night with all hands on call. With a contrary wind, he hove to until daybreak.

On 25 March, support wires on the jury steering spar (the lighter of the two jury rudders) carried away and the crew hoisted the makeshift steering device on board. It was not used again.[57]

The ship sailed on rudderless before a southerly wind for 26 hours, and by noon on 25 March she had covered 92 miles. Paton wrote: 'We have been making a splendid course all day with no hand to guide her, what I have never known a ship to do before.'[58]

As if in a bizarre reaction to the sudden change in fortunes of *Aurora*, and when only a few days out from port, D'Anglade, from the galley, and then Shaw, from the engine room, refused duty.[59] Both had been somewhat isolated characters: D'Anglade as a Frenchman among English-speaking shipmates, and Shaw's fits and unstable behaviour had made him the butt of many jokes. Paton referred to them as 'mutineers'. The French steward seemed to have acquitted himself well until this point, and on New Year's Day 1916 had even written, 'in broken English', letters of appreciation to the wardroom officers and to Stenhouse. ('His wishes are conveyed with such poetry that it seems strange that one should have never before credited him with such thoughts.'[60]) D'Anglade remained off duty for the rest of the voyage, but Shaw returned to work after two days. Stenhouse announced that the pair would be disciplined when the vessel reached port.[61]

The first hint of success with the wireless came when, on the night of 22 March, Hooke picked up a signal, 'too feeble to be read, of uncertain origin and direction' but thought to be from a coastal ship.[62] The next night he established contact with Awarua station, near Bluff, 590 miles away, and with Hobart, at twice that distance.[63] Awarua, opened in December 1913 primarily for defence purposes,[64] picked up *Aurora*'s Morse signal on its nightly listening service. Hooke also made contact with the Chatham Islands and continued sending and receiving messages all night.

The reappearance of *Aurora* captured world headlines. Stenhouse telegraphed the expedition's copyright holders, the *Daily Telegraph*, whose story occupied most of the front page of the 25 March issue, and King George V was also informed.[65]

The wireless on *Aurora* brought news that was unexpected and depressing. Paton wrote on 25 March: 'After midnight the ship's business being finished they sent us all the latest war news . . . from Wellington N.Z. At 4 a.m. when day began to break work ceased, then all the war news was posted up forward for the benefit of the crew.'[66] Hooke learned that his brother had been killed in action with the Australian Expeditionary Forces.

As the ship neared Campbell Island, Stenhouse decided it was time to call for steam and to launch the jury rudder, which proved to be successful, if difficult to handle.[67] Paton explained the technical details:

> . . . in rigging up the jury rudder the top portion of the decapitated mizzen mast
> has been used, being lashed across the deck as a shaft to give the necessary leverage

when steering. The actual rudder itself is made of a 12 or 15 ft spar to which heavy beams weighted with ferro concrete and bound together with iron plates, have been affixed horizontally . . . For the purposes of steering . . . is connected with 2 sets of block & pulley tackle, with each side of the vessel.[68]

Two helmsmen together controlled the rudder, which 'surged and jarred heavily'[69] and gave a 'heavy kick' as seas struck it. While at the helm, Downing suffered a suspected broken rib, which was to result in his being hospitalised when the ship reached port.[70] To ease the helmsmen's difficulties, Stenhouse reduced boat speed by taking in the square sails and proceeding by steam alone.[71]

A sharp lookout was kept for the breakers indicating Campbell Island, but there was no sighting.[72] The ship's chronometer, checked against time signals received by wireless from Wellington, indicated they were 150 miles farther south than previously calculated.[73] On 28 March, Aurora passed the Auckland Islands.

Despite his desire to reach port unaided, Stenhouse decided to accept an offer of assistance from the New Zealand government and cabled the Prime Minister, William Massey: 'Owe deep debt of gratitude [to the] Otago Harbour Board for generous offer. Would appreciate services of tug approaching land. Expect arrive thirty-first.'[74]

Aurora became increasingly disabled in heavy seas and a westerly gale. Under sail alone, the crew struggled in the darkness to lift and securely lash the unmanageable jury rudder as they maintained some kind of direction and 'hoped for the best'.[75] Following international convention, the ship displayed red lights from sunset and black discs by day to indicate that she was 'not under command'.[76] On 30 March, Aurora cleared the Snares Islands but was only four miles from The Traps, recognised as 'very dangerous rocks only four feet above sea-level, just south of Stewart Island'.[77]

The newly commissioned steam-tug *Dunedin*, with a crew of 24 and two youthful passengers, left Port Chalmers under the command of Captain D. Spence, whose previous command had been of a full-rigged sailing ship. The round-bottomed vessel encountered heavy seas off the exposed east coast of the South Island, the tall funnel at times shipping water.

The men on board *Aurora* were heartened by the news of their pending rescue, even though *Dunedin* had to put in to the southern port of Bluff for repairs to its wireless set, a last-minute addition. The limited range of this meant that contact with the Antarctic ship was relayed through the Awarua station.

Shortly after midnight on 2 April, a searchlight from the tug was seen on *Aurora*, and Stenhouse sent up flares at hourly intervals.[78] By 3.30 a.m. *Dunedin* was almost alongside and Captain Spence hailed that he would stand by until daylight.[79] Paton wrote:

At 5.30 all hands called and at 6 a.m. we had our mail, also fresh provisions of bacon and eggs, and many other luxuries sent out by friends and we were soon following after the tug. I received a cable telling me of my Mother's death which took all the joy out of my homecoming. At 10 a.m. we sighted the New Zealand coast . . .[80]

Stenhouse lowered the jury rudder one last time as *Aurora* proceeded under tow and her own steam towards Cape Saunders, at the entrance of Otago Harbour. A cheer went up from the crew when the harbour pilot, accompanied by a doctor, a customs official and a representative of the *Daily Telegraph*, came aboard. Entering the heads, *Aurora* was greeted by the signal station welcoming her to New Zealand. The mayor of Port Chalmers turned up in a launch, followed by a boatload of local dignitaries on the old tug *Plucky*. They were not allowed on board *Aurora* for fear that a premature leak of the story might breach copyright arrangements.

As *Plucky* pulled alongside, Mr J. Dickson, chairman of the Otago Harbour Board, announced that *Aurora* could have the use of the dock and the freedom of the port. Stenhouse expressed his thanks and his frustration:

We had hoped that when we came back it would have been with all our party on aboard. I am sorry that Sir Ernest Shackleton is not with us. As to the party we left ashore, we know nothing about them at present, but they were all well when we left. Owing to adverse circumstances we have been hindered from carrying out the work we intended to do. Bur Sir Ernest Shackleton is the finest leader I know, and the most courageous of men, and I am fully confident he will win through. I thank you most heartily for sending your tug to give us the last leg home. We hope to look on Port Chalmers as home for a time.[81]

The crew marvelled at the green of the grass and native bush after what Ninnis described as the 'terrible white monotony' of Antarctica. Fresh fruit and food, fresh faces and voices, fresh sights and colours and smells could hardly be believed. Ninnis wrote: 'Words fail to describe the novelty of hearing other people speak and seeing so much life and real civilisation, including a real bowler hat once more.'[82]

The anticipated arrival of *Aurora* generated considerable interest among the port's 2,500 residents, and many of Dunedin's 55,000 citizens came by train to witness the event.

With only occasional help from the tug, *Aurora* navigated the harbour's narrow shipping channel under her own steerage. As she came into view of the assembled throng on the wharf, her jury rudder now hoisted and most of her personnel on deck, sustained cheering broke out. Late on that autumn morning, the Ross Sea party's ship berthed at the port, her perilous voyage over.

'The Skipper', Æneas Mackintosh, RNR, leader of the Ross Sea party and master of *Aurora*, December 1914 – January 1915. His appointment followed his loss of an eye through a deck accident while on the *Nimrod* expedition. Some said that Shackleton felt sorry for his old friend and rewarded him with the leadership of the support party of the Imperial Trans-Antarctic Expedition. It would prove to be one of the toughest assignments in the history of polar exploration.

Stenhouse collection, copy by David Yelverton, courtesy Patricia Mantell

Richard Walter Richards at Cape Evans, June 1915. Photograph by A. P. Spencer-Smith. Richards played a crucial role in the return of the sledging party from Mt Hope. During the second winter he suffered an emotional and psychological breakdown and was a 'derelict' when rescued in January 1917.

Middleton collection, Canterbury Museum

Joseph Russell Stenhouse, RNR, first officer of *Aurora* and master from January 1915 when Mackintosh took up sledging duties. He was unfairly criticised in some quarters for his decision to try to moor the expedition ship *Aurora* at Cape Evans and the damage it received when drifting for ten months, necessitating a major overhaul in New Zealand.

Otago Daily Times, courtesy John Mauger

Victor Hayward was selected as a member of the Ross Sea party for his experience as a dog-driver. He died in May 1916 when he accompanied Mackintosh on an attempted crossing on the sea ice from Hut Point to Cape Evans.

Copy by David Yelverton, courtesy Derek Bolton

John Lachlan Cope, a graduate of Cambridge University, was medical officer for the Ross Sea party in the absence of a qualified doctor.

Frank Hurley photograph from Shackleton's *South*

Right: Aubrey Howard Ninnis, had an Admiralty background and was appointed as 'motor expert' in charge of the pioneering Girling motor sledge. He was a member of the 'motor party' during the first season of sledging and was on *Aurora* both during the drift and on the relief voyage.

Middleton collection, Canterbury Museum

Above: Alexander Stevens, geology graduate from Glasgow University. An inveterate smoker, he was particularly deprived when the marooned party's tobacco ran out. He was resident cook at Cape Evans over many months of the party's confinement there.

Gaze collection, Canterbury Museum

Right: 'The Padre', the Reverend Arnold Patrick Spencer-Smith, BA, in the grounds of Merchiston Preparatory School 1914. Inappropriately retained in the Mt Hope sledging party, he died of scurvy before his companions returned to Hut Point.

Fraser collection, Canterbury Museum

Lecture programme, SS *Ionic*. Eleven members of the Ross Sea party sailed from England to Australia on the White Star liner as the early stages of war unfolded in Europe in late 1914.

Fraser collection, Canterbury Museum

Aurora in Rose Bay, Sydney 1914.

Jack collection, La Trobe Library, State Library of Victoria

The Ross Sea party on board *Aurora* in Sydney Harbour 1914. John Cope is second from left at rear, with Victor Hayward (arms folded) beside him. Joseph Stenhouse is central, with arms folded. Æneas Mackintosh is centre, in a light-coloured jacket. Clarence Mauger is fourth from right, and Alfred Larkman on the extreme right. Sydney Atkin is third from left in the middle row. James Paton, in a peaked hat, is centre. A. ('Shortie') Warren (left), S. Grady and W. Mugridge are in the front.

Jack collection, La Trobe Library, State Library of Victoria

Expedition members on board *Aurora*, voyage south, December 1914.

Middleton collection, Canterbury Museum

Left: Ernest Edward Mills Joyce, a veteran of two Antarctic expeditions, using the cinenatograph camera during the voyage south. Spencer-Smith looks on. In his 1929 book, Joyce seriously misrepresented the terms of his appointment to the Ross Sea party.

Jack collection, La Trobe Library, State Library of Victoria

Below: A rare photograph of the Girling motor sledge, at the start of the first season's sledging. The runners can be seen to the rear. The front mounted 'crawl wheel' dug into the snow and resulted in the leather friction drive clutch burning out.

Richards collection, Canterbury Museum

Climbing from the sea ice onto the Barrier, 30 January 1915. The party encountered a crevasse on this short stretch. Mackintosh is in the foreground.

Stenhouse collection, copy by David Yelverton, courtesy Patricia Mantell

Harnessing dogs (one muzzled) during the first season's sledging. The only tent landed from *Aurora* is seen in the background. Designed by George Marston, of the *Nimrod* expedition and with Shackleton on *Endurance*, it proved an efficient and essential shelter during two seasons of sledging.

Joyce collection, Canterbury Museum

The depot near 80° South, the southernmost point attained during the first season's sledging.

Stenhouse collection, copy by David Yelverton, courtesy Patricia Mantell

Aurora, with seamen preparing the ship for winter, in newly frozen sea ice, was secured by wire ropes and a chain cable to two anchors embedded in the beach outside the Cape Evans hut. The Barne Glacier is in the background.

Joyce collection, Canterbury Museum

Barne Glacier and North Bay with the Cape Evans hut in the foreground, December 1971. *Aurora* was moored north of the hut before being carried away in a storm on 6 May 1915. The ship reappeared near the glacier on 10 January 1917, to the disbelief of the Ross Sea party survivors.

Richard McElrea

A winter view from the south-east of the hut at Cape Evans.
A rare photograph during occupancy by the Ross Sea party.

Gaze collection, Canterbury Museum

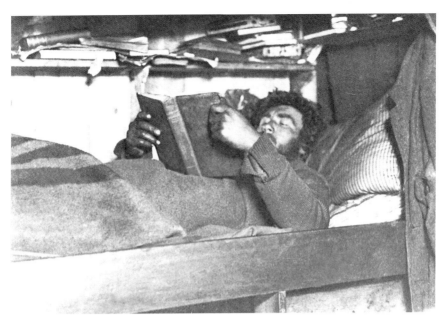

Physicist R. W. Richards in the Cape Evans hut. The book he is reading,
Elements of Meteorology, was found during hut restoration in 1960–61
and is now in the Canterbury Museum.

Richards collection, Canterbury Museum

Spencer-Smith's communion table in the darkroom at Cape Evans.

Gaze collection, Canterbury Museum

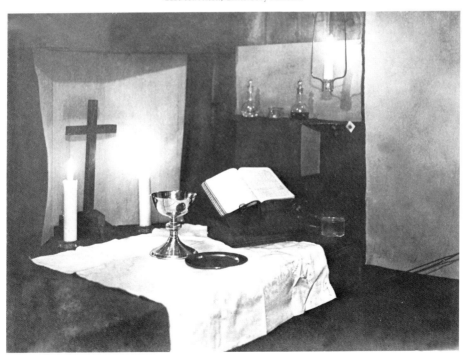

Right: John Cope photographed by Spencer-Smith in the darkroom at Cape Evans 1915. A raconteur and wit, Cope could tell 'funny stories without repeating himself for months and months'. During the second winter he became a recluse.

Gaze collection, Canterbury Museum

Below: The kitchen area of the Cape Evans hut, 1971. Richards would look back with fondness on times spent around the galley stove during the first winter (1915).

Richard McElrea

Aurora, with funnel covered, in the pack ice of the Ross Sea. Carried away in a storm on 6 May 1915, she survived major ice pressures and finally broke free of the ice on 14 March 1916. Meanwhile, the other ITAE ship, *Endurance*, was trapped by ice in the Weddell Sea.

Middleton collection, Canterbury Museum

Aurora by moonlight, drifting with the Ross Sea pack ice. Photographed by Howard Ninnis using a half-hour exposure.

Stenhouse collection, copy by David Yelverton, courtesy Patricia Mantell

An Australian who joined the expedition in Hobart, Leslie Thomson was one of only two officers during the drift of *Aurora*. He was a key man in supporting Stenhouse and getting the ship back to port.

Otago Witness, Hocken Library

Alfred Herbert Larkman, chief engineer of *Aurora*, 1914–17. With second engineer Adrian Donnelly, he worked in 50° of frost in the engine room to reassemble disconnected fittings before raising steam, after the ship was carried away in the ice. Their names, and those of three others from the drift of the ship, are remembered in the Aurora Nunataks, five peaks in the region of the Beardmore Glacier.

Larkman collection, Canterbury Museum

In the wardroom during the drift of *Aurora*. The sign on the wall reads: 'Life is just one damn thing after another.' From left: Adrian Donnelly, Lionel Hooke, Joseph Stenhouse, Leslie Thomson (partly obscured) and Aubrey Ninnis.

Royal Geographical Society

Midwinter's Day was celebrated on 22 June 1915 during the drift of *Aurora*. 'We had a very excellent dinner,' wrote Thomson.

Royal Geographical Society

Aurora's cook, E. Wise, taken on in Hobart, often proved erratic in his work owing to inebriation. At times, however, he excelled in difficult conditions.

Royal Geographical Society

Stenhouse at work on the chart table.

Aurora about to rendezvous with the tug *Dunedin* east of Stewart Island, 2 April 1916.

Right: Clarence Charles ('Chippie') Mauger, ship's carpenter, with a year's issues of the *Otago Daily Times*, thrown from the tug *Dunedin*.

Otago Witness, courtesy Norma Barrett and John Mauger

Below: Ship's personnel on *Aurora* following her arrival at Port Chalmers on 12 April 1916. At left is Leslie Thomson, first officer during the drift in the sea ice and voyage under jury rudder to New Zealand. Boatswain James Paton (with pipe) is towards the right, in peaked hat, and 'Ginger' Kavanagh behind.

Otago Witness, courtesy John Mauger

The jury-rigged rudder raised at the stern of *Aurora*. Paton and Kavanagh are at left. Mauger is second from right.

Otago Daily Times, Otago Harbour Board, courtesy John Mauger

Shipping the new rudder, Port Chalmers. *Aurora* spent 59 days in dry dock.

Otago Witness, Richards collection, Canterbury Museum

A party preparing to leave Cape Evans at the beginning of the
second sledging season, October 1915.

Gaze collection, Canterbury Museum

Sledging party in the vicinity of Hut Point, October 1915.

Joyce collection, Canterbury Museum

The view to Mt Hope, in the vicinity of which a depot was laid on 26 January 1916 by the Mackintosh party, completing a line of food supplies as instructed by Shackleton. The photograph is taken from the east. Mt Hope (835 metres) is the highest point on the dark landmass beyond the crevassed lower reaches of the Beardmore Glacier (foreground). The Gap is beyond Mt Hope. The sledging party's route, from upper right of photograph, was approximately parallel with the mountains of South Victoria Land, now known as the Trans Antarctic Mountains.

US Navy, courtesy Dr Charles Swithinbank

Arnold Spencer-Smith being dragged on a sledge on the party's return from Mt Hope. The four dogs, Oscar, Gunner, Con and Towser, played a vital role in the journey to and from Mt Hope.

Joyce collection, Canterbury Museum

Æneas Mackintosh enfeebled with scurvy after the journey to Mt Hope.
'At this time he could only walk with difficulty with the aid of a stick,
as he was going downhill rapidly with scurvy' (R. W. Richards).

Richards collection, Canterbury Museum

Members of the Mt Hope party at the end of their trek. From left: Hayward, Joyce, Wild and Richards, with the dogs Gunner (at front) and Towser.

Joyce collection, Canterbury Museum

The survivors of the depot-laying journey outside the *Discovery* hut after their return from Mt Hope on 18 March 1916, nine days after the death of Spencer-Smith. This is almost certainly the last photograph of Mackintosh (centre rear) and Hayward (right front with cord to camera). Richards stands behind the seated Wild, and Joyce is at rear on the right.

Joyce collection, Canterbury Museum

The unique man-and-dog harness used by the Ross Sea party in laying the depots south to Mt Hope in early 1916, recovered at Cape Evans in December 1971 and identified by R. W. Richards, a veteran of the party.

Richard McElrea

Preparing to leave Cape Evans to place a cross on Spencer-Smith's grave. Joyce, Wild and Gaze set out with six dogs on 17 December 1916. They cut short a proposed detour to Cape Crozier and returned on 3 January. Richards (facing) is talking to Joyce or Wild. Behind is Wind Vane Hill, where a cross to the memory Mackintosh, Hayward and Spencer-Smith was erected as a final act before the party left on the relief ship a few weeks later.

Joyce collection, Canterbury Museum

Joseph Kinsey (left) and John Mill at Port Chalmers in 1916. As members of a working committee they successfully oversaw the refitting of the ship and the appointment of Captain J. K. Davis as master of *Aurora* in place of Joseph Stenhouse in controversial circumstances.

Canterbury Museum

Members of the relief expedition. Morten Moyes is left rear, Frederick Middleton front left, next to Sir Ernest Shackleton and Captain Davis (central front). Howard Ninnis is standing second from the right. The dog Oscar is at front.

Middleton collection, Canterbury Museum

Aurora in McMurdo Sound, January 1917.

After picking up the survivors on the relief voyage.

Six of the seven survivors approach *Aurora*. From left: Alexander Stevens,
John Cope, Ernest Wild, 'Richie' Richards, Irvine Gaze and Ernest Joyce.
Davis later wrote: 'They were literally blots on the virgin landscape. Anything
more remote from normal civilised human beings would be hard to imagine.'

Joyce collection, Canterbury Museum

Survivors of the Ross Sea party at the point of rescue, about to come on board *Aurora*.

Joyce collection, Canterbury Museum

Cope after his first bath and change of clothes in almost two years.

Middleton collection, Canterbury Museum

Above: John Cope in tattered clothes black with soot, photographed by Aubrey Ninnis aboard *Aurora* after the rescue on 10 January 1917. The clothes were disposed of overboard and formed a greasy slick on the water surface.

Middleton collection, Canterbury Museum

Right: Australian Frederick Middleton, medical officer on the relief expedition. He found there were surprisingly few physical problems in the health of the rescued men, given their deprivations. He noted that Shackleton, who had accompanied the relief expedition, was greatly affected by the death of his three comrades.

Middleton collection, Canterbury Museum

Ernest Henry Wild after the rescue. A former petty officer in the Royal Navy and brother of Frank Wild, Shackleton's second-in-command of the *Endurance* party, Ernest Wild was a member of the Mt Hope sledging party and, along with Richards, Joyce and Hayward (posthumously), would receive the Albert Cross for gallantry in saving life. He died of typhoid in Malta in 1918.

Middleton collection, Canterbury Museum

Irvine Owen Gaze on *Aurora* after being rescued. A quietly spoken Australian, he was described in May 1915 by a fellow castaway as 'the only sanguine one among us'. Gaze survived being shot down from 18,000 feet as the pilot of a two-person Bristol fighter in the closing weeks of the First World War.

Middleton collection, Canterbury Museum

Right: Alexander Stevens on rescue. In 1928, he wrote to H. R. Mill of a 'party at odds all through when Mackintosh was lost. On reaching home I was disgusted with the whole affair, with the general behaviour and attitude of Shackleton and glad to shake free of the whole thing and get on to other matters.'

Middleton collection, Canterbury Museum

Below: Andrew Keith Jack with mail after two years. An Australian appointed as a physicist to the Ross Sea party, his fitness and methodical skills were under-estimated in selection of sledging parties by Mackintosh, who favoured fellow Britons regardless of their aptitude and physical condition.

Middleton collection, Canterbury Museum

The rescued party refreshed and reclothed, on board *Aurora*.
From left: Keith Jack, Alexander Stevens, 'Richie' Richards, Ernest Wild, Irvine Gaze,
Ernest Joyce and John Cope, with Sir Ernest Shackleton and Captain John Davis.

Aurora in Wellington Harbour at close of the relief expedition, 9 February 1917.

Undisturbed for almost 40 years, the meal abandoned by Wild, Jack and Shackleton in January 1917 was photographed by John E. Fletcher of the *National Geographic* through a window of the Cape Evans hut in December 1955. Ice and snow filled most of the hut, but only a relatively small amount (left) had entered the kitchen area. The scene was irretrievably changed a year later when unauthorised entry was made to the building.

John E. Fletcher, *National Geographic*

The Cape Evans hut from the north-east, December 1971. Abandoned by the Ross Sea party in January 1917, the hut was entered by personnel from USS *Glacier* in December 1956 through the window above the stable to the right.

Richard McElrea

The interior of the Cape Evans hut, blackened by the blubber smoke of the Ross Sea party, photographed in 1971 from the galley or kitchen end. The darkroom also used by Spencer-Smith as a chapel is beyond Scott's former 'wardroom table'. The hut was substantially filled with ice and snow before a New Zealand party excavated it over two months from December 1960.

Richard McElrea

CHAPTER SIXTEEN

Return from Mt Hope

SEVEN YEARS BEFORE Mackintosh's party started their return from Mt Hope on 27 January 1916, Shackleton, Dr Eric Marshall, Lieutenant Jameson Adams and Frank Wild had been at the same spot after turning back at 88° 23' South on the Polar Plateau. Shackleton wrote: 'We marched along till we were close to the Gap, then had lunch. At 1 p.m. we were through the Gap and on to the crevassed and ridged Barrier surface.' Just before leaving the Beardmore Glacier, Shackleton had plunged into a hidden crevasse and was saved by his harness. After an arduous journey, his party reached Hut Point 36 days later, on 5 March 1909.[1]

Scott's three returning parties had covered the return from Mt Hope, a journey of some 370 miles, with varying degrees of ease and difficulty. Cecil Meares and the Russian dog-driver Dimitri Gerof,[2] with two teams of dogs, left the Lower Glacier Depot at the foot of the Beardmore Glacier on 11 December 1911 and reached Hut Point 24 days later. Their trip was so uneventful that it scarcely rates a mention in any polar literature.[3] Only navigation difficulties and the summer temperatures restricted progress to fifteen miles per day.[4]

Dr Edward Atkinson, Charles Wright, Apsley Cherry-Garrard and Patrick Keohane returned from the top of the Beardmore Glacier, reaching the Lower Glacier Depot on or about 28 December and the *Discovery* hut 29 days later.

The last party, comprising Lieutenant Edward Evans, Thomas Crean and William Lashly (the latter pair veterans of the *Discovery* expedition), left Scott's polar party at 87° 32' S on 4 January 1912 and reached the Lower Glacier Depot on 22 January, by which time Evans was showing severe signs of scurvy. By early February, after a hundred days in the field, he was in great pain. Lashly wrote: '[W]e were forced to put Mr Evans on his ski and strap him on, as he could not lift his legs.' At 80° South, as they approached One Ton Camp on 7 February, the faithful Lashly wrote: 'We have got to help him in and out of the tent . . . it is difficult for him to stand.' And a day later: 'Mr Evans have [*sic*] passed a good deal of blood today.'

After another week, with about 70 miles to go, Evans could walk no further. Crean and Lashly jettisoned everything they could and put their companion on the sledge. By 17 February, their circumstances were even more desperate. '30 miles from Hut Point . . . Mr Evans is getting worse every day, we are almost afraid to sleep at night as he seems very weak.' When he collapsed, Lashly and Evans decided to camp while Crean hurried on to the *Discovery* hut to get help. There he found Dr Atkinson, with Dimitri and the dogs.[5] On 20 February, Lashly was able to reassure his ailing friend: 'Hark! Yes it is the dogs near.' Two days later, the party was at the hut, the return from the bottom of the Beardmore having taken 31 days. Crean and Lashly were awarded the Albert Medal for bravery in saving Evans's life.

On 27 January 1916, Mackintosh's men on their northward march had first to negotiate the heavily crevassed area near Mt Hope, with hidden dangers beneath a mantle of snow from an overnight blizzard. Joyce took the lead but soon suffered severe snow blindness. For the next day or two, with his eyes bandaged, he stumbled along behind Mackintosh, using the Skipper's trace as a guide rope. The party reached the Padre's tent two days later.[6]

Spencer-Smith was a complete invalid. Alone for a week, he had spent part of his time delivering a lecture and a sermon, 'both in execrable French'. Mackintosh massaged the Padre's knees, which were giving him great pain when he tried to walk.[7] He was put into a dry sleeping bag and placed on a second sledge. Wild wrote on 29 January: 'Picked up Smithy this afternoon. He is still crook, so we had to put him on the sledge. I'm afraid that will make us rather longer getting back. Still it can't be helped . . .'[8]

Joyce wondered whether Spencer-Smith was suffering from scurvy: '. . . limbs swelled up and black. It may be scurvy but I do not think so as his gums and eyes do not shew it.'[9]

Mackintosh's party was near the end of its fifth month of sledging, and Wild hoped that 'another month will finish it'. They would have to achieve fifteen miles per day to get back to base by the end of February, perilously late in the season given the state of the party.

Just a day after they had picked up the Padre, a blizzard halted the party's progress for 36 hours. However, the travellers made eight miles in the afternoon of 31 January before setting up camp at five o'clock. Mackintosh wanted to make up time in the extended daylight, but his wishes did not prevail, he no longer being in a position to assert his authority.

Joyce noted in his diary of 31 January that before long 'it is almost certain we shall have the Skipper on the sledge'.[10] This prospect threatened calamity for the party, with the dogs now assuming even greater importance.

Some six decades later, Richards would write:

> . . . the decision to take them was most providential. They proved their worth. None of the men who made the southern journey will ever forget those faithful friends of the dog world – Con, Gunner, Oscar and Towser. Without them the party would not have got back. Oscar and Gunner weighed 110 and 112 lb. respectively, while Con and Towser between 70 and 80 lb. Some of the four had a touch of the wolf in their pedigree. They disliked going indoors rather violently.
>
> Con, the leader, third in weight, was a misfit among the other three, a Samoyed with a completely different temperament, a gentleman, while the others were hoboes. He was clean-living while the others showed some of the less lovely aspects of humanity. He was fast and agile and liked hunting, whereas the others were sluggish and cared nothing for annoying seals and penguins. The other three resented him . . . he was the lead dog on the trace and I reckoned that he knew he was different from them. He was a good, agile fighter, cleverer, and managed to come out on top many times, and that was why he lasted so long.[11]

In an interview in 1980, he recalled:

> . . . we took [the dogs] too much for granted, but they really were marvellous. Just simply four dogs and we didn't take them for a start because we thought we couldn't possibly accommodate their pace of pulling with men trudging in snow . . . one foot is not more than 12 inches ahead of the other in snow . . . we thought they couldn't possibly pull in harness because they like a sort of loping gait, but they turned out to co-operate absolutely marvellously . . .[12]

Joyce's rewritten diary records his companions' ailments: 'Skipper black like Spencer-Smith and his gums are badly swollen . . . ankles are twice the size. There is one thing he has plenty of pluck. Haywards gums are black and protruding . . . Wild Richy and self gums turning black . . .'

It was obvious that the men could not make the necessary progress if they were to continue with two sledges, so despite Mackintosh's misgivings the choice was made on 2 February to stow everything on a single sledge, with the Padre in his bag on top. Over the following days all gear considered surplus, such as shovels and ice picks, was jettisoned. Few decisions in the saga of the expedition would be more important. The sledge-meter was discarded after it broke down on 12 February.[13]

The party passed the 82° South depot the next day and picked up a week's provisions,[14] which 'left 2 weeks [provisions] for the Boss'.[15] Forced marches sustained a rapid advance and within ten days, including a lay-up for a day because of a blizzard, they covered over 143 miles. A sail was set to good effect to catch the southerly wind. A further week's rations were collected at the 81° South depot on 7 February and, four days later, a similar supply at the depot near 80° South.[16]

As part of the daily routine, Spencer-Smith was lifted in his sleeping bag from the tent floor and placed on the rolled-up bags on the sledge, where he was tied on, often with his face covered. Still in his bag, he was removed to the shelter or the tent at each lunch and day's end stop.[17] Sometimes the sledge would upset, 'but without damage to me or it', he wrote on 12 February.

The Padre accepted his lot when reduced to using a boot for a pillow. An outraged Wild, usually a man of few words, recorded of Mackintosh on 4 February: 'He's still as selfish as ever. Letting Smithy lay on a boot while [he] has got two big bed-fur mitts for pillows.'[18]

In his position hitched to the sledge, Richards heard Spencer-Smith 'wandering quite often, and then he would come back to sensible talk again. He was a very, very sick man . . .'[19] Sometimes he would recite a prayer in Latin and find comfort in recalling happier times. 'Uncomfortable morning but pleasant afternoon in South Square, Gray's Inn. If only the dream could come true . . .' A few days later he wrote:

> Dreamt of Christmas day at All Saints last night – Procession of the Blessed Sacrament, hundreds of candles, incense etc, the organ crashing out the first few bars of 'Adeste Fideles'. The wretched 'Oscar' loose outside woke me up – nor could I recapture the Vision.[20]

Wild tended and nursed his sick friend, who would at times cry out in pain. On 17 February, Wild wrote: 'Hope to reach Bluff depot tomorrow. Smithy still keeps pretty cheerful. He doesn't howl much, like I should. He is still very weak.'[21]

Mackintosh, too, was close to collapse. Joyce noted as early as 28 January: 'Skipper still weak on the pins . . .' Six days later: 'S not very well but will have to stick it.' And the following day: 'Hayward, Wild & Richy, splendid condition. S – rotten.' At first, Joyce seemed to have little sympathy for his debilitated leader, whose strength was rapidly failing. He railed on 1 February: 'Skipper is still not pulling a dam.' A fortnight later, ignoring Mackintosh's enfeebled state: 'I would not mind if we all putting our weight in but I am afraid not.' And then on 17 February: 'Surface very rotten, sinking in up to the knees. S pulling about the same 1 rat power . . .'[22]

Despite the tone of his diary entries, Joyce maintained an outwardly respectful demeanour. Almost 70 years later, Richards remarked that Mackintosh was always 'Sir' to Joyce, and 'neither he nor Wild would ever forget their years in the Royal Navy before the turn of the century where the ingrained respect for authority was instinctive'.[23]

Mackintosh soon began bleeding from the bowels – a likely indication of scurvy. Richards wrote in late February: 'The Skipper from 83° 30 S . . . has kept up bravely but is useless. He is continually wrenching his strained leg and appears to be going to pieces.'[24] Mackintosh's condition was obvious to his men, but they did not know that the Padre was also bleeding internally. Richards later explained: 'Never knew that Smith was bleeding at the bowels then for we never saw his stools. It was Mac who displayed this for we often saw the result when he bogged in the open.'[25]

As the men approached the depot near 80° South, they often sank in the soft snow up to their knees, and the dogs up to their bellies. It was by far the worst surface they had struck. The Padre observed on 8 February: 'It took about a dozen hoicks to start [the sledge].' Joyce called it the 'hardest afternoon we have experienced'. Despite these gloomy observations, the party managed eleven and a quarter miles that day.[26] Richards wrote: 'The surface has been very heavy between 79° 30 S. and 81° 30 S. while here (79 to 79.30) it surpasses anything I have seen for difficulty . . .'[27]

Eventually, reassuring signs of home appeared. Wild observed on 12 February: 'Sighted Old Discovery and the Bluff; so we are getting among familiar places again.'[28] They passed 'Sledge Runners' and 'Box Cairn' of the previous season, on 'Dead Dog Trail'. At this stage the four dogs were still going strong and were fed with hot hoosh every second day, with an extra or double-extra feed of dog pemmican and biscuits whenever possible. Great care was taken to tether the animals out of reach of one another.[29]

Clearly buoyed up at the thought of reaching another milestone, the Padre wrote on 17 February: '. . . given light we should be at the Bluff tomorrow afternoon. *Domine Deus exaudime.*' There, with luck and as had been pre-arranged, would be news of the return of *Aurora* and possibly a relief party from the ship. 'I can hardly dare think that there is no good news at the Bluff.'[30]

Towards evening on the afternoon of 17 February, with what Joyce described as 'heavy clouds flying around' and a low drift blowing, the party lost the line of cairns. Using his prismatic compass, Richard had laid these 'every half hour' on the outward trail to a height of four or five feet. The men pitched camp ten miles short of the Bluff depot, relaid closer to its true position by Mackintosh, Joyce and Wild on 10 March 1915.[31] Thanks to this correction, the homeward-bound party was not confronted with a nineteen-mile march.

Because the party still had provisions for three days, there was not a great deal of concern when a blizzard set in on the night of 17 February and continued unabated the next day.

Joyce wrote: 'One day's lay up, although against our plan . . . will not harm us especially Skipper, he is keeping up pretty fair, better than we expected.' The Padre, however, seemed to find something sinister about the storm: 'The wind

– still howling – seems about the strongest I can remember and almost carries a note of personal animus.'[32]

As the blizzard continued, rations were reduced to one meal a day and a hole was scraped inside the tent to serve as a lavatory.[33] Drifting snow soon banked to the top of the tent and bellied in against the walls. Occasionally the men in Joyce's tent heard 'a burst of song from Ernie [Wild]', which at least reassured them that their companions 'were in the land of the living'. The cheerful Wild adopted a pragmatic approach to the party's predicament: 'Shall have to make more holes in my belt . . . Have had two biscuits and a chunk of snow.' Fuel for the Primus was virtually finished, so Richards improvised a spirit lamp that took half an hour to melt a mug of water but offered a little warmth.

All the men were getting dangerously weak and the dogs' food was finished.[34] On 22 February, the fifth day of forced encampment, Joyce, Richards and Hayward decided that they would have to make a start the following day or else they would 'be sharing the fate of Scott and his party'.[35] Realising that the party may not survive, and doubting the likely accuracy of Joyce's records, Richards started to write his own diary.[36]

On the following day there was a break in the clouds and the sun briefly showed through. 'She's breaking!' was the cry from Joyce's tent. The men had some hot Bovril, kept for the occasion, and prepared to leave. Joyce wrote: 'One would hardly credit how weak we were. Two digs of the shovel, you were out of breath.' With the Padre tied to the top of the sledge, and the five men and four dogs, so much weaker now than when they stopped six days earlier, once more in their traces, the party set off. Mackintosh was too sick to pull and barely able to stand. He tied his trace to the back of the sledge but collapsed after half an hour.[37]

Richards described his leader's pathetic state:

His face was changed [and] he could scarce[ly] walk and in a broken voice he said he would have to tie on to the sledge instead of pulling trace. We all had an awful struggle that afternoon – blinding drift and deep soft snow to walk and pull through and we [were] weaker than ever. Then the Skipper's collapse. I caught him from falling. He seemed to me to be almost delirious. He kept saying 'Oh my hands are gone' and then: 'I'm done' over and over again and again. 'I don't care what happens.' I tried to comfort him a little . . .[38]

Joyce noted in his diary: 'He sung out "Stop Joyce, I cannot go any further. Just wrap me up in a deck cloth, let me lie there in the snow."'[39] Decades later, Richards verified this defining moment, recalling Mackintosh's words as: 'Leave me with a tent cloth, wrap me up and go on.'[40]

Faced with this further crisis, the party had no alternative but to unload the sledge and pitch camp. It was decided that Wild would remain with the two invalids while Richards, Hayward and Joyce went on to the Bluff depot to bring back food and oil. Richards wrote: 'Poor Wild I was sorry for. I don't think he wanted to stay. But it was necessary to have one whole man to look after the two weak ones. And so he stayed.'[41]

Wild noted: 'Made a start about three o'clock, then the Skipper went crock [*sic*] so we had to stop again. After a bit of a palover [*sic*] the other three went on.' Spencer-Smith noted that he and his two companions were left with 'a few biscuits, a few sticks of chocolate, ? "meals" of oil, a ¼ tin of methylated and a few oddments, vegetables, Bovril and lime juice tablets'. However, he was grateful for Wild's company. 'We had a great and glorious cup of tea (Te Sol!) to warm us up and sat talking pretty late, the wind still howling.'[42]

Over the next six days there were three significant periods of calm, when the horizon was faintly visible and Minna Bluff was apparent. Wild built a new cairn, marked by black bunting because the tent was now buried to within a foot of its peak.

Sensing disaster, Mackintosh made a formal record that had striking similarities to Scott's 'Letter to the Public' and included a frank admission as to why his men had succumbed to scurvy earlier than Joyce's had:

> I leave this record in the event of anything happening to this party. Today we have finished the last of our food. A blizzard has been blowing 11 days with exception of one day when wind fell light ... we were left here 4 days previously in order that Messrs Joyce Hayward & Richards could travel with dogs and light sledge to Bluff depot ... I take precaution to leave this should I later become too weak, and the cold make it harder to write. Smith and myself are stricken with scurvy – the former being helpless and weak. I am able to stand about yet becoming more feeble daily. Wild has signs of scurvy but is still able to move his hands and feet and with a meal could travel – [O]ur present position ... has not been through any lack of organisation. We have done the work we came down to do the laying of a depot at Mt Hope 82 81 80 for Sir Ernest Shackleton. We made splendid progress homewards travelling as much as 18 miles a day and this with Sm[ith] on sledge. We filled up with a fortnight's provisions at 80 ... Instead of doing the trip in a week we have been [held?] 17 days – getting to within 9 miles of our big depot on 18 Feb. – since which date we have been camped ... With the exception of Smith we were all able to travel until the blizzard came upon us when we laid up 6 days. After that period when we made a fresh start I had to admit defeat, owing to my inability to stand the strain – our lay up making me weaker, legs black & blue, gums swollen & black ... Wild who could have gone on preferred to remain & help us – the good, unselfish fellow that he is. It must be explained that with exception of first trip to Bluff we have had no fresh food since October 9 hence the disease has taken a stronger hold of us than the other party who have had opportunity of reaching H[ut] P[oint].

Yet I leave it on record here that all have done their duty, nobly and well ... if it's God's will that we should here give up our lives we do so in the true British fashion as our tradition holds[us] forever to do. Good bye friends. I feel sure our people, my own dear wife and children will not be neglect[ed.]

Æneas A Mackintosh
Commdr Ross Sea Base.[43]

Mackintosh wrote farewell letters to his mother, his sister Bella and, almost certainly, to his wife, Gladys.

Spencer-Smith smoked a couple of pipes of tea while the Skipper had two cigarettes, small comforts to desperately sick men but a welcome distraction from the cold and the wetness, and their weakness and pain. As they lay in the tent, the wind blew fiercely and visibility was again reduced to zero.[44]

For Richards, Joyce and Hayward, the dash to the depot became a merciless trial of their strength and will. The fuel was almost exhausted, the dogs had no food and there was little for the men, who were becoming progressively affected by scurvy. The blizzard, which had blown since 17 February, scarcely paused, night and day.

After leaving Wild and the invalids at what Richards called 'Blizzard Camp' on 23 February, the trio managed to cover about three miles before camping. Richards noted: 'Hayward, Joyce and self are weak and feel the effects of lay-up. Our gums are swollen and slightly black – mine seem to be shredding.'

In these adverse conditions they were not aware of whether they were to the right or the left of the line of cairns laid on the outward journey. Richards would recount over six decades later:

> We worked through pea soup – the howling blizzard. There was nothing you could see. North was the same as south and we had lost our line of cairns the previous night, but we thought we were pretty close to it. And I happened to have the bearings of all the cairns in my diary at that time, taken about every half-hour on the way out. We worked on the fact that we would be parallel to the line if we were not exactly on it. I would take a bearing on the wind, which was coming over my right shoulder. Joyce was in front on a long lead. I would put him on line with the wind and then put the prismatic compass away because it was pretty damned cold trying to read it. We'd keep him on that bearing as long as we could and perhaps in another 20 minutes I would say, 'We'll take another look,' and try again with the same bearing.[45]

The following morning they came across one cairn in the blinding snow-storm.[46] Richards wrote: 'With difficulty pitched camp owing to extremely heavy wind and snow. Our tent is torn and threatens to run at any time.'[47] In spite of the urgency of their journey, they could not face the weather and had to stay in camp for the rest of the day. Meals consisted of a quarter of a biscuit each and a cup of tea. Ironically, when the wind dropped in the evening and it came on to snow heavily, they were still immobilised because they could not steer a course in the absence of visibility or wind to give direction.[48]

The dogs had been without food for two days, and Con, the Samoyed lead dog, was 'groggy'.[49] Joyce wrote: 'If we cannot soon pick up depot and save the dogs, it will be almost impossible to drag our two invalids back the 100 miles which we have to go.'[50]

In later years Richards acknowledged how, when three of the dogs were losing heart, 'in the crisis the massive Oscar just lowered his great head and pulled as he never did when things were going well'.[51]

> Normally Oscar was a lazy sort of dog but this time he seemed to know that there was food at the end of it perhaps, and he used to put his big shoulders down and every now and then he'd give a heave and try and get a little bit of weigh on the sledge, which was empty by the way, and he'd bite the heel of the dog in front of him.[52]

On 25 February, they struck camp at 4 a.m. and struggled for another three miles in extreme conditions.

> Heavy wind and heavy snowfall. Steering difficult and we do not know how we stand in regard to depot or whether in the weather we have strayed from course. We are very weak. Our pace is possibly 1 mile an hour . . .[53]

Richards would later estimate they were travelling at between a quarter and half a mile per hour. With the weather thickening and the wind very strong, the men were forced again to camp because of the considerable danger that they might overshoot their destination.[54]

Shortly after a 2 a.m. start on 26 February, they saw the depot three-quarters of a mile ahead. Joyce wrote: 'The dogs sighted it which seemed to electrify them. They had new life and started to run but we were that weak that we could not go more that 200 yards and then spell.' Richards would recall:

> We had no sledge meter then – we had chucked that away – and we had to figure out how fast we were going. I reckoned it was about G of a mile an hour I think. And we were pretty right in the long-run because it took us three days to get the ten miles. And when we stopped after it cleared a bit we saw we were not far from the Bluff depot.[55]

Soon the dogs were eating their first meal in four days. Richards wrote: 'Decided to halt here till dogs have had couple of meals as it would be fatal to them to turn too soon and we depend on them for the lives of Mackintosh and Smith.'

The three men struggled to erect the tent, and at first they could not eat:

We occupied today in short rest and several meals, very light in amount but at fairly short intervals. Strange that when we arrived we had difficulty in forcing a biscuit down – practically past hunger. Joyce spent afternoon in mending tent. This was most pressing job as if we need to pitch camp again in a blow, tent would rip to pieces before we could get it up. Hayward & self arranged depot stores and stores to take back to other party. The depot was in an untidy condition and took considerable digging out. Weather at present is dull and heavy wind and drift continue . . . Hayward complains of stiff legs under knees. This was where the others (Smith and Skipper) first felt symptoms of their disorder. I hope for our sakes he has nothing of this sort. We must go carefully.[56]

Patches were sewn on the tent by Joyce, on the inside, passing the needle through the fabric, and the others pushing it back from the outside.[57]

Joyce wrote: 'We decided to have Oatina and milk for a start, which went down very well and then a cup of tea. How cheery the Primus sounds. It seems like coming out of a thick London fog into a drawing room.'[58]

Expecting to set out the following day to collect the Skipper, the Padre and Wild, the men were desperately frustrated by the conditions:

Rose at 5 a.m. Wind hurricane force and heavy drift. Impossible to see anything. We are now sitting on our bags waiting for the wind to ease. Dogs and men could not face this even if a course could be steered. This is awful – held up here helpless, knowing three men are starving and worse deathly cold 10 or 12 miles back. But we can do nothing. This is the 10th day of the blizzard. Our gums are all swollen this morning – especially Hayward's. His knee he says is a bit better but he can hardly walk.

[Later] . . . signs of a break appeared at 10 a.m. Had a meal and commenced to get under way at noon or thereabouts.[59]

They took the precaution of picking up an extra sledge from the Bluff depot, knowing they would have to haul back two of the invalids. The rescue journey began dramatically with the dogs refusing to face the weather coming from the south, so 'we started them north and gradually worked them around'.[60]

Richards wrote:

Took a good deal of time in starting the sledges. Heavy wind blowing and drift. Dogs have no heart. Sledge took H hr to start altho' very light. Cleared runners and made it a little easier. Dogs unsettled and two fights occurred before starting. We got them apart in time however. Worked till 11 p.m. One of the hardest days I have put in. Dogs have no heart for south journeys now. Hayward I am afraid is not in good form. He is painfully stiff. When we camped too dark to steer. Weather dull but wind dropped.[61]

Pondering on events, Richards wrote:

The pity of it [was] that Mackintosh did not realise his folly in passing 81° S with Smith. I . . . can see the two of them in my mind's eye neither able to pull much and both walking as I have now seen Hayward and as I fear will shortly do myself – stiff, horribly stiff in both knees.[62]

Despite the anxieties and exertion of the day, Richards found time to massage Hayward's legs for half an hour that night and a quarter of an hour the following morning.[63] Joyce noted that this 'did him a world of good', but there remained the awful realisation of what a third invalid would mean to the party: 'If he [Hayward] were to crack up now I should not know what to do.'[64]

Richards, too, had ominous symptoms, though he hoped they did not indicate scurvy: 'I am sorry to find that I have the dreaded black appearance on the back of my legs . . . I don't know whether it's scurvy or not but remembering that Smith, Skipper & Hayward each was taken there first it makes for unrest.' Joyce again suffered frostbite, which was not helped by footwear that comprised 'finnesko with more hole than boot' and quickly filled with snow.[65]

Continuing their rescue mission southwards, the three men camped at lunchtime on 28 February, knowing they would be near the Skipper's tent. In the hope of making contact they shouted together, but their voices were lost in the unremitting howl of the wind. They were extremely nervous and weary. Richards wrote: 'We can only sit still and wait for a clearance. We are looking out at intervals of 10 minutes. I fear what we may find on arriving.'

The afternoon passed with heavy snow and moderate wind. As Joyce and Hayward tried to snatch some sleep, Richards fretted 'with the thought of these men starving and cold within perhaps a very short distance of help – one keeps wondering how it will all end'. He thought back on the previous weeks, recalling how his old tent-mates had

joked sometimes about the humour of [Mackintosh and Spencer-Smith] being taken to see the laying of the Beardmore Depot by us – confident then of our full strength. How I wish we had more of it now. Then the long march back towing Smith, the obvious agony of the Skipper during some of the long marches . . . Then the great blizzard . . . that layup searched out our weaknesses – shortened our wind – knocked Hayward in the legs and smashed Skipper completely . . . And then our nightmare in making the depot – starved. And thro' all the continued blizzard never or practically never easing. And now we are here waiting waiting waiting for this blizzard to cease! And this seems to be the end of Mackintosh's folly in going south when done himself and with the company of another done man. Truth was that neither M[ackintosh] or S[mith] were fit for the job. M. not the type of man [and] always too well looked after in civilisation . . . even first year sledging M. suffered from bleeding very copiously from [the] bowels and that has continued ever since. Smith too was done last year after a short journey to Bluff. I have written down these thoughts more to keep my mind occupied than anything else . . . and now it's too cold on fingers and so I'll stop.[66]

The bunting placed by Wild on the cairn as a marker for the returning party was seen from their campsite on 29 February when visibility improved. The dogs reacted by barking and pulling for the first time in a while. Suddenly Wild appeared out of the tent door. He and his two companions had scarcely eaten for the six days they had awaited rescue, a Bovril cube in heated water comprising a day's rations.[67] On seeing the rescuers, Wild reached for his harness on top of the tent and staggered out to help them in. Richards summed up the common feeling in his diary entry for the day: 'Thank the fates all alive.'[68]

CHAPTER SEVENTEEN

Death of the Padre

A N ENFEEBLED and emotional Mackintosh struggled from the tent to greet the relief party. In his field diary Joyce recorded the historic encounter: '[He was] very weak & as much as he could do to walk, saying: "I want to thank you for saving our lives."'[1]

Spencer-Smith rejoiced:

[N]ow we are bursting with thankfulness and food ... We have had the closest of close calls – *Deus det incrementum* ... I was sunk at least a foot into the ground at Starvation Camp – and very wet. We have three weeks of food now, so all seems well.[2]

Wild was typically pragmatic:

Full belly once more ... Saw the others at 12.30 & they got up to us about 2.15 p.m. We had our feed & started on our way again. I'm not so weak as I thought I should be. Thank goodness. I think seeing them was the most welcome sight I've ever seen.[3]

Joyce found that the Padre, immobile for six days, had been partly entombed in the ice. 'When we lifted Smith we found he was in a great hole which he had melted through.'[4]

The reunited party wasted no time in turning for home and, by the end of the day, had travelled almost three miles north. Richards, in his typically matter-of-fact style, wrote in his diary for 29 February: '9 p.m. Picked up party at striking camp ... Wild in good condition considering. Returned made good headway back for 2 hours on a much improved surface.'

The Skipper made a gallant attempt to hobble along in a semi-squat position with the aid of two sticks,[5] but it was obvious he could not continue on foot. 'We had to put the Skipper on the sledge. Luckily they brought a spare sledge from the Bluff ...'[6] Perhaps hoping that his ride was only a temporary expedient, Mackintosh initially refused to be put in a sleeping bag.[7]

On the evening of 1 March, the party reached the Bluff depot, where they were dismayed to discover that their tent poles had fallen from the sledge. Fortunately, these were spotted in the distance with the aid of the binoculars, so Richards trudged back and retrieved them. However, this incident did not rate a mention in his diary entry, which read: '. . . straining to pull the 2 men is very severe. My legs are in fair condition so far. Hayward finds difficulty in walking. Dogs in good condition.'[8] He would later describe the day's work as 'the hardest I have ever put in'.[9] As the three fitter men heaved on their traces, the Padre, in his sleeping bag on one of the sledges, called to Richards: 'Pull up Richy, [or] you'll bust your heart.'[10]

Once at the Bluff depot their immediate anxieties about supplies were eased, although they were desperately in need of fresh food.

The men's tentative skiing efforts during the previous season had not been persevered with, and the absence of skis now proved a severe handicap to their progress in soft conditions. For a day or two, however, a southerly wind came to their rescue. 'Sledges went well in the afternoon sometimes carrying four men so strong was the wind. One sail only set.'[11]

On 3 March, the party was laid up in heavy wind and drift, but the relatively able-bodied Richards, Wild and Joyce resolved to proceed the following day regardless of weather. The Primus stove, essential to their survival, required constant maintenance. Wild recorded:

> March 4th Sat. 11.0 p.m. 10 miles in a blizzard. Haywood [*sic*] is done now so we have got three men to pull three more. I have just been making a new Primus. That is why I am so late.[12]

Richards ignored any blizzard, merely noting in his diary: 'Fine wind fair progress.'

During that day's travel the Skipper fell off the sledge two or three times, prompting Joyce to tell him that 'if he did not shout as soon as he fell he would be left behind. He said it would be a good job.'[13]

In the same diary entry Joyce recorded Hayward's symptoms:

> Gums very swollen and turning black. Joints and legs swollen and black. Feet – cannot hardly press on them. Elbows stiff and sore. Pupils of eye enlarged – so no mistake it is scurvy and the only possible cure is fresh food . . .[14]

As if this were not enough, his dire predicament seemed to be affecting Hayward's mind. Richards would later recall: 'Joyce, Wild and myself were the only ones capable of pulling. Hayward had become somewhat unbalanced mentally. Skipper was in a daze and Smith unconscious part of the time.'[15]

On 6 March, Wild noted: 'Poor Smithy seems a bit worse', and Joyce also expressed his concern: 'He has not hardly moved for weeks, he has to have everything done for him.'[16] The Padre was administered two grams of opium from the medicine chest to counter 'bad gripes'.[17]

On the following day, Spencer-Smith dedicated what was to be his last diary entry, to one 'F', presumably the same 'Freddie' whose birthday he noted a year earlier. The abbreviation includes what is presumed to be the birthday saluta-tion, 'Many happy returns of the day'.

> Tue. March 7 To F.M.H.R.O.T.D. A bitterly cold night: bag frozen stiff & in a bad condition. Glorious weather but only about 3 miles, as the wind dropped. Decided to depot O [ld] M.[an] [Mackintosh] tomorrow and push on to H.[ut] P.[oint] with the invalids – Hayward's legs are very bad now and even Wild has a touch in the teeth. H.[ayward] and I will be left at H. P. and the others will come back at top speed with seal-meat and C. and fetch the O.M. – with whom we leave 3 weeks' food.[18]

The reference to 'C' is likely to be to Cope, the acting medical officer. Unfor-tunately, he and his companions were effectively marooned at Cape Evans, with no passage possible across the sea ice.[19] Inscribed on the inside of the front cover of Spencer-Smith's diary is the adage: 'It's all in the game. Plug on.' Inside the back cover is a clipping of a letter that reads: 'Ever your loving Tony xxxx.' The meaning of this personal note is unclear.

Wild's unusually lengthy diary entry for 7 March describes the party's situ-ation:

> 3 miles after a desperate struggle. We did one mile this forenoon & then decided to depot the second sledge & everything possible. So we did. Then we had lunch & with the Skipper & Hayward hobbling along, the Skipper riding a little way, we just managed to go about two miles. We have now decided to leave the Skipper here & struggle into Hut Pt with the other two & then come back for the Skipper. I think that's the only way we can possibly do it . . .[20]

The men were so weakened that they found it difficult to proceed without a following wind. Mackintosh and Hayward had courageously battled on.

Over 60 years later, Richards recalled that 'their legs were bent and they couldn't straighten them. You couldn't see their teeth for the swollen lips and gums and oh they were really sick men . . .'[21] Because of the Skipper's serious condition, responsibility for the party lay with the fitter men, Richards, Joyce and Wild.

Joyce wrote, with greater sympathy for his leader's plight than he had often expressed:

> Hayward and Skipper going on ahead with sticks [at a] very slow pace but it will buck them up and do them good as I think exercise is one of the cures if one could only get some fresh food . . . I told him when we camped what we proposed to do

. . . He said 'do anything you like with me, Joyce' . . .It seems hard only about 30 miles away and yet cannot get any assistance. Our gear is absolutely rotten. No sleep last night, shivering all night in wet bags. I wonder what will be the outcome of it all after our struggle. 'Trust in Provi.'[22]

Richards wrote:

M.[arch] 7. We are all rapidly going down with scurvy. Hayward particularly bad. Decided to depot S.[kipper] here & march in to H. Pt & out again as soon as possible.[23]

Leaving Mackintosh with three weeks' provisions, the others said farewell and on 8 March headed north, stopping for lunch at Cope's No. 2 depot, four and a half miles on. Richards wrote: 'Hard going. Hayward just staggering.' The wind backed around to the north and slowed progress, but when they camped at 6.30 p.m. they had covered a satisfactory eight or nine miles for the day.[24] As the Padre was passed from the sledge that had carried him for almost 40 days to the tent into which the five men huddled in the gathering dark, it was early morning in Edinburgh, where he had been ordained eighteen months earlier. In the Christian calendar it was Ash Wednesday, the first day of Lent.

Arnold Spencer-Smith died at about five o'clock the next morning.[25] His head was out of the sleeping bag, his eyes closed and jaw dropped.[26] Richards would recall that ice had formed on the dead man's eyelashes and beard.[27] The diary entries of his companions eloquently describe the pathos of the Padre's final hours. Wild wrote:

Woke up this morning and found poor Smithy dead at 6 a.m. He asked me the time at 4 o'clock and spoke to Richards afterwards. It was very cold last night, that, and all the hardships he has come through, did it. −29°.

Later he added:

Smithy had a little joke with me after 4 a.m. He asked me 'if I'd lost my bearings' because I was looking round. Afterwards he said to Richards: 'I say Rich, if your heart is behaving funny, what is the best thing to do, lie down or sit up.' Richards after thinking about it said he really didn't know, but he thought the best thing to do would be to lie still . . . It's a great pity him dying within twenty miles of Hut Point . . . He was complaining about the cold during the night but we couldn't do a thing.[28]

Richards wrote:

All night he had been restless but he expressly told us not to take notice of him the night previously. He had been suffering from pains in the stomach for some days and took say 10 tabloids of opium all told. The night before he died he had a severe attack and took 4 tabloids. We have pulled him helpless for 40 days. A distance of over 300 miles. He had been laid up for 47 days and complained some 10 days previously. He should never have been allowed to pass 81° S.[29]

The night the Padre died would be etched in the memory of Richards for a lifetime. Sixty years later, he recalled Spencer-Smith as

a very sincere Christian although not a demonstrative one. I was only in the tent with him on the last two nights of his life . . . he had no idea his death was so near. In the tent after camping on those two nights his thoughts were fixed with eagerness in getting in to Hut Point in the next night or two and was quite cheerful about it . . . the night he died was very difficult. We were crowded 5 men into a three man tent. It was pitch dark and very cold. The sleeping bags after six months of sledging were full of ice and all in all it was the worst night I have ever experienced.[30]

He was a very, very sick man . . . at one stage I noticed he had given a very severe kick or something of that sort. By the time it got light we could see . . . he had been dead for an hour or two and there was frost over his eyelids and he was obviously dead.[31]

The Padre's final agony is also recorded in Joyce's diary:

Smith was groaning and singing out practically the whole time as he was in pain with gripes for which he was taking opium. 4 o'clock a.m. he asked Wild the time and started laughing at him and asked him if he had lost his bearings . . . I turned out at 5.45 and Richards said 'Joyce I think he has gone.' After examining him I found he was dead . . .[32]

Joyce, Wild and Richards dug a shallow trough at the side of the tent, pulled the tent down and rolled Spencer-Smith into the grave, his sleeping bag serving as a coffin.[33] Richards wrote in his diary for 9 March: 'We buried him at 9 with cross on cairn. (Erebus 184° Observation Hill 149° Discovery 93°.)'[34] Later he would comment: 'When Smith died we were so close to Hut Point it wouldn't really make much of an impression because he'd be so ill and we'd expected it so long, we had so much on our plate we just thought we would bury him straight away and get into Hut Point.'[35]

Cardinal Newman's *Dream of Gerontius*, a copy of which the Padre carried on the sledge journey, seems an appropriate epitaph to this young clergyman. The long poem starts:

Jesu, Maria – I am near to death.
And thou art calling me; I know it now.
Not by the token of this faltering breath,
This chill at heart, this dampness on my brow . . .
'Tis this new feeling, never felt before,
(Be with me, Lord, in my extremity!)
That I am going, that I am no more . . .

And later:

I went to sleep; and now I am refreshed.
A strange refreshment: for I feel in me
An inexpressive lightness, and a sense
Of freedom . . .
                        How still it is!
I hear no more the busy beat of time,
No, nor my fluttering breath, nor struggling pulse;
Nor does one moment differ from the next,
I had a dream; yes: – some one softly said
'He's gone' and then a sigh went round the room . . .

The poem concludes with the Angel saying:

Farewell, but not for ever! brother dear,
Be brave and patient on thy bed of sorrow;
Swiftly shall pass thy night of trial here,
And I shall come and wake thee on the morrow.[36]

The Padre's grave was in a unique setting. Passing that way the previous season, he had written:

> . . . it seems a shame that we are not outside enjoying the scenery – Western Mountains and [Mt] Discovery behind; Observation Hill and C.[ape] Mackay to our left. Black, White and Brown Is[lands] on the right; and far ahead C. Crozier and the Barrier. These all form a vast wall surrounding an immense snow plain, bediamonded by the sun . . . Erebus and Terror look grand . . .[37]

Before leaving base he had written to his parents:

Cape Evans
Sept 30 1915

My dear Mother & Father

Owing to various misfortunes . . . we are setting out for the season's sledging under rather precarious conditions; equipment poor, time of year too early, loads heavy &c. So there seems an unusual element of risk – wherefore a short note to say 'au revoir' in case I should not come back. We've had a pretty stiff time, taking it all round, but I can't feel any regret about it all, except that I should have liked to have been with you all during the hour of the war. Believe me that if anything does happen to me I will face it cheerfully as I can – with a hope that is really 'sure and certain' of seeing you all again with everything unworthy in myself done away with. I have tried to 'be good' and to do good without preaching – & even so I don't feel worthy of you two dear ones.

Goodbye for the present
I am, your loving son,
Arnold.

Please keep the communion vessels in the family.[38]

Spencer-Smith had confided to his old headmaster from Merchiston Castle Preparatory School that he had been 'doing his bit' by going south. Because he was in holy orders, his role in combat would have been limited, but by taking his place on the expedition he had freed up another man (reputed to be Sir Philip Brocklehurst, Bart., of the *Nimrod* expedition) to fight in the war.[39]

The Padre died eight days short of his thirty-third birthday. To his companions who had nursed him and cared for him through everything, his death was a bitter and ironic blow. Joyce reflected: 'I think the irony of fate was poor Smith going under a day before we got in.'[40]

The party reached Safety Camp, near the edge of the Barrier, the day after Spencer-Smith died, and the *Discovery* hut the following day. Attaining this haven was a bittersweet experience. On 10 March, Wild recorded:

> March 10. Friday. 14 miles. Reached Safety C.[amp] at five o'clock. After stopping there about ½ an hour we went to the Barrier edge & to our joy saw the ice was in as far as Cape Armitage. So away we went across it, we saw some pressure ice where we got close up & what looked like water, so we decided to go back and try the 'gap.' On reaching there we couldn't find a place to climb up so, at Richards' suggestions we went to where his party got up last year. Well we got there & after the most strenuous work ever I've done in my life we got up there. I've never been more done up. I took my sleeping bag up last, & after every two steps, I fell on top of it & had a spell . . . We finished at 11.30 p.m. all done in.

And on 11 March:

> Hut P.[oin]t at last. Richards and I had a walk round on top of the hills after breakfast and found the ice was in right to Ht Pt. So we went back to the tent and packed up and got round here at 2 p.m. Richards & I killed & cut up a seal for eating while Joyce made a vegetable lunch . . .[41]

Increasingly, since 26 February, Hayward had been so sick that at best he could hobble along, but for much of the time had been carried on the sledge, falling from it at times. According to Joyce, 'all his limbs [were] swollen and black. Gums very prominent.'[42] The sea ice, which gave access to the hut and at least saved Richards, Wild and Joyce the effort of manhandling him over the hills to the hut, was soft and dangerous. The rough shelter was half full of snow, but the three men soon gained access and got Hayward inside. The agony of the homeward struggle over, Joyce recorded that Hayward could hardly move.[43]

The four men briefly rested to gather strength before the fittest of them tried to bring in the Skipper. They eagerly devoured seal meat, mended gear and sheltered from a passing storm.[44] Wild, with classic understatement, wrote: 'We've all got a touch of scurvy and are on fresh food now trying to get rid of it.'[45] Richards later recounted: 'As we neared the hut several seals were lying on the ice foot . . . I experienced the strongest desire to kill at once, and I am sure that I would have eaten the meat raw had we not been in a position to cook it immediately.'[46] Joyce wrote: 'Wild went down to the bay and killed a couple of seals . . . we turned in at about 11 o'clock full in the tummy and too full in fact.'[47]

With no news of the ship and no sign of Stevens, Jack, Cope, Gaze and Ninnis, it would be up to Joyce, Richards and Wild to turn south again to rescue their leader. On 13 March, they 'cooked sufficient seal meat for our journey out'.[48]

Alone from 8 March, the Skipper somehow managed to stay alive. Rotting clothes hung from his emaciated and bent frame, his teeth were sunken into black and swollen gums, and his remaining eye was grotesquely distended. With great courage, he still managed to hobble about the campsite, his legs swollen and black, and spent eight nights shivering in a wet and foul bag. He constantly hallucinated and 'found himself talking to supposed people in the tent'.[49] Meagre rations, coupled with his will to live, somehow saw Mackintosh through.[50]

After recuperating for four days, Joyce, Richards, Wild and the dogs left Hut Point in fine cold weather after lunch on 14 March. They spent the night near Safety Camp, where the temperature plummeted to −30°F, passed Spencer-Smith's grave late on the morning of 16 March and soon sighted the Skipper's tent. Joyce wrote: 'Looking through the glasses found him outside the tent much to the joy of all hands as we expected him to be down. Picked him up at 4.15, broke the news of Spencer-Smith's death and no ship . . .' The Skipper's relief at being rescued was immense. Joyce continued: 'He said it was the best time of his life to see us.' He was dazed and in very bad shape,[51] and thus the news of Spencer-Smith's death 'did not seem to impress him much'.[52] The four men immediately departed for Hut Point, leaving the trail of depots southwards to Mt Hope behind them for the last time.

As they camped that night, Joyce wrote in his diary: 'We gave the Skipper a banquet of seal, veg[etables] and blackcurrant jam, the feed of his life.' On the following day the party lunched 'a few yards past' Spencer-Smith's grave on 17 March, and made twenty miles before spending their last night on the Barrier, 'with wet bags and clothes rotten'. The intense cold woke them before dawn but, on a good surface, they reached Safety Camp at 4 p.m. and found the sea ice passable.

Three hours later they were at the hut, where Hayward was 'still about the same'.[53] Wild rejoiced: 'Hut Pt again, Hooray.' Joyce wrote: 'We made a good dinner and all hands seemed in the best of spirits.'

An examination of the party, recorded by Joyce, confirmed symptoms of scurvy. Mackintosh had 'a heavy blue and hard swelling from his right hip bone down to knee' as well as discoloration of his lower leg, swollen gums, 'white of eye distended', but an extraordinarily good appetite. Hayward's gums were swollen and black. 'Knees cannot bend at all, not swollen – just slightly black, walks like a bent up old man.' The others fared better. 'Richards right leg and gums slightly swollen. Wild's right leg behind knee black, slightly swollen. Gums very swollen. Myself, right leg behind knee stiff, and gums slightly swollen.'[54]

The Ross Sea party had been sledging for 170 days. Richards calculated the distances travelled (geographical miles) in that time:

Mileages for main sledging season

5 trips to Hut Pt (C. Evans)	130
4 trips to Bluff	380
Bluff to Hope and return	560
One additional journey to 80° S and return	120
Blizzard Camp to Bluff and return	20
Hut Point to Mack and return	60
Relays	60

1330 = [1531] statute miles

There remained one important duty for Æeneas Mackintosh. Joyce wrote: 'Before turning in Skipper shook us by the hand with great emotion thanking us for saving his life and said his wife and children will bless us.'[55]

Richards also recorded the occasion: 'Mar 18 Hut Pt – H.[ayward] safe & Sk[ipper] thanked all hands for what had been done and we shook hands all round.'[56]

Richards' final diary entry was for the following day: '. . . fixing hut for winter – rubbed M. and H. with spirits to ease their legs. [Skipper] brighter. H. less cheerful.'

Having laid the depots to Mt Hope, the Ross Sea party had achieved the goals set by Shackleton. This was by any measure an heroic journey, for which Joyce, Hayward, Richards and Wild would be awarded the Albert Medal.

CHAPTER EIGHTEEN

Deaths of Mackintosh and Hayward

COPE, GAZE AND JACK had joined Stevens at Cape Evans on 16 January 1916 after making their hazardous crossing from Hut Point on disintegrating sea ice. Once there, they had been largely confined to the cape region because the summer thaw made passage over the ice impossible.

Earlier, Stevens had made three trips alone to Cape Royds 'to observe the penguins and to obtain eggs',[1] and one trip to the *Discovery* hut. 'On 15 [December] I went to Hut Point to fetch the dogs, but only the black bitch was said to be there in pup. She was not to be seen.'[2] Joyce and his party had left Bitchie tethered at Hut Point on 13 December, expecting Stevens to arrive imminently, but she had been retrieved by Gaze, Jack and Cope on 16 January.

Mackintosh had sent instructions through Cope that, if *Aurora* turned up in time, 'one week's stores were to be removed from the Bluff depot and placed in a depot half way to 80° S'.[3] This task could have been given to the party of Cope, Gaze and Jack that Mackintosh had sent back to base from near 80° South on 6 January, but for some reason the Skipper chose to ignore this opportunity. However, the absence of the ship meant that the instructions could not be followed. An intermediate depot could have greatly aided the Mt Hope party on its perilous retreat, as would have a relief party of 'fresh legs' from the ship. The four men at Cape Evans had no instructions to try to mount any relief out on the Barrier.

The main concern of the Cape Evans party was to get in sufficient supplies for the winter. There were no available sledge dogs to haul in the seal carcasses, about fifteen of which, according to Jack, 'were lost at a depot on the sea ice'. Despite this, the men killed and retrieved 34 seals during March, and by winter they had laid in the bulk of the 40 or so carcasses that they estimated would be needed for the two months of darkness. These were stored in racks in the outer passage of the hut.[4]

After the disastrous 1915 season, when all but six dogs had perished, there was a welcome addition to the dog population when each of the two bitches kept at Cape Evans had litters. Nell, never a favourite, destroyed three pups of Bitchie's (herself one of the earlier pups by Con) and was shot by an uncharacteristically impetuous Gaze.[5] Jack recorded on 15 March: 'Nell killed pup last night . . . Told Irvine and he got up and shot her.'[6] Gaze was to kill another dog when, while hunting seals with Richards in the winter, he 'hurled a steel and hit it in the haunches'.[7]

Hunting forays regularly took the men to the tip of Cape Evans, a short distance from the hut, where they would scour 'Coal Beach' for remnants of the cache unloaded from the ship a year earlier. They loaded stores from nearby dumps left from the *Terra Nova* expedition and endeavoured to chip out ice-locked stores from around the hut and in the stables.[8] Throughout all of this Cope did little but lie in his bunk, sometimes emerging for a meal. Stevens noted: 'His stomach appeared to give him trouble, and he seemed to fear appendicitis . . . He was very difficult.'[9] Jack wrote similarly. 'Cope still remains in bed the greater part of the time – some days simply getting up for one meal and then turning in again. He says he is not ill and if this is so it seems a most unnatural existence.'[10]

Stevens and Jack worked constantly at the meteorological gear set up on nearby Wind Vane Hill. The anemograph, recording the direction and force of the wind, required constant attention.

Some minor professional skirmishes occurred between the two men. Jack was sceptical about Stevens's record-keeping and general scientific approach. For his part, Stevens was apparently reluctant to give the Australian details of the meteorological readings he had undertaken when alone at the base. Because of his work the previous season, Jack claimed priority over ablation experiments at a nearby pond known as 'Skua Lake'.[11]

With Shackleton's party expected to cross the continent at the latest by 20 March,[12] and the rest of the Ross Sea party still unaccounted for, the men at Cape Evans observed the condition of the sea ice to the south with particular concern. By early April the sea had frozen over, but it was clear again of ice by 18 April after several days of blizzard.[13] In the ghostly half-light of autumn Stevens observed what appeared to be a ship at the end of the Barne Glacier, but this turned out to be a phantom, a mere shadow.[14]

The sea froze over again and on 8 May, Jack remarked alongside his 11 a.m. reading: 'Cloudless – Clear – Still – Ice well set.'

❖

Having stumbled exhausted and physically impoverished into the *Discovery* hut on 19 March 1916, the five survivors of the Mt Hope party experienced enormous relief just to be there (as had three of them the previous season) and to have a chance to rest after the arduous months of sledging. Mackintosh and Hayward had undoubtedly been on the brink of death.

The men all craved fresh meat. Fortunately, they found seals more plentiful than in the previous year and often present on old sea ice clinging to the shores north of Hut Point. After a mid-April blizzard, hunting became much more difficult. Wild wrote on 23 April: 'It's no joke walking 10 or 12 miles a day after seals in the dark, and not getting one.'[15] He and Richards would often walk five or six miles before breakfast, and a similar distance before the next meal, and not find one seal.[16] As the winter darkness came on, the hunters found it hard to see the animals and were reduced to searching around tide cracks between the sea ice and the land. By 23 April, they had taken 28 seals and a number of emperor penguins. Wild's diary entry for 8 May offers an extraordinary snippet of their cavemen-like existence: 'Richey and I got two more Emperors last week. We skinned them and we are going to try and dress the skins for clothes.'

The *Discovery* hut, though a rough shelter by any estimation, provided great comfort to the men so recently exposed to the hellish autumnal conditions of the Barrier. During an extended blizzard that lasted from 11 to 24 April, drifted snow piled up around the door, keeping Richards and Wild constantly busy with the shovel.[17] Betweentimes, hair was cut, whiskers were trimmed and yarns swapped.

The men were confined to the north end of the building, partitioned off with empty cases and tarpaulins, the centrepiece being the fireplace comprising a sheet of iron over bricks, around which they sat, ate and slept. They laid sleeping bags across planks resting on old provision boxes, clear of the melted blubber that oozed from the fireplace across the floor before being scraped up and reused as fuel. Pungent smoke permeated the building, although there was some relief at night when the fire was allowed to go out. Bones and other refuse were thrown out a window, forming a heap that slowly rose to window level.[18]

A mass of blue ice encased the rest of the interior of the hut. There were some stores, although a shortage of dripping meant the party 'would have to have more stews but many of the provisions were beyond their reach, imprisoned in ice as hard as cement', which they had little means to tackle.[19] Richards would comment in later years: 'It was dark in the hut with only the feeble glimmer of improvised blubber lamps and I guess we had enough to do to keep alive.'[20]

With a steady diet of seal meat, Mackintosh and Hayward soon regained a measure of health. Meals were seasoned with salt obtained by melting sea ice, a cookerful of which gave 'about 1½ lbs of good salt'.[21] The invalids rested, read and walked in the environs of the hut while Joyce, Richards and Wild cooked and generally looked after them.[22] After a month of recuperation, the legs of both men still had some residual discoloration and, with the party confined indoors for long periods in April, there was little chance for them to rebuild their stamina.[23]

Richards would recall:

> The effect of seal meat is simply miraculous. That is all we had at Hut Point because there was virtually nothing else there. I think there were some old moth-eaten biscuits from Scott's 1900 expedition, a pallid imitation of biscuits that you wouldn't eat, but we had seal meat for morning, afternoon and night and nothing else. No vegetables. The diet of seal meat was simply wonderful for its recuperative powers.[24]

The first possibility of escape to the north came early in April when the ice northwards of Hut Point froze for the first time that season. However, a blizzard soon carried all the newly formed ice away and Joyce reported: 'I walked out for 4 miles over the new ice . . . and found it about 2 inches thick and in about 2 days would have been able to travel to C.[ape] Evans but fates forbade . . . The ice has gone out within ½ mile of the hut.'[25]

An overland route from Hut Point to the cape, if it existed, was ruled out as an option. As Richards said: '. . . to attempt the journey by land was much too hazardous in the dim light that now prevailed.'[26]

The sea again froze in the first week of May. Joyce was to testify:

> On the 7th May weather being fine I took a walk as far as Cape Armitage with Capt. Mackintosh and V. Hayward. They both informed me they had been to the North the day before and found the sea ice bearable and they thought of going north on the next fine day. After arriving back at the Hut they took a stroll again to the North for 2 miles and . . . found [the ice] about 4 inches thick and bearable, but on account of the salt, very sticky and unfit for a sledge.[27]

It was generally thought that a continuation of this weather would enable the full party, with dogs and sledge, to cross the ice on about 16 May. This strategy would make use of a full moon but depended entirely on favourable weather.[28]

On the evening of 7 May, Hayward approached Joyce and asked if he should make a trip to Cape Evans with Mackintosh. Joyce replied that he should not, because the ice was unsafe.[29]

Richards, who first learnt of the Skipper's plans from Wild when sealing on the sea ice on the morning of 8 May, was to testify: 'At about 10 a.m. all was clear and calm and Mackintosh announced his intention of crossing to Cape Evans with Hayward. He was advised strongly not to go.'[30]

Wild recorded that, before breakfast, he and Richards had been 'out look-ing for seals and when we got back to the hut, the Captain and Hayward had packed up their few belongings and told us they were going to Cape Evans. It was fine then but looked thick to the south.'[31]

Crucially, and for a reason that remains unclear, it was not until early after-noon that Mackintosh and Hayward left the hut, a delay of some three hours from the time the Skipper made his announcement. It would seem that he was uncertain, because he again asked Joyce what he thought of the idea. 'I told him he could please himself but I thought it was not a day for it but still they shoved off.'[32] Joyce elaborated in a signed statement some months later: 'I went out and examined the weather and strongly advised him not to take the risk as it was coming up thick from the South.'[33]

Mackintosh too went out and had a look around, then came in and said he thought it would be all right, according to Joyce, 'no doubt urged on by our uncomfortable quarters'.[34] It is, however, likely that the Skipper made his deci-sion to go because the blizzard was approaching, not in ignorance of it, and believed that he and Hayward could make the dash in time. If the weather did get up rough, the ice might disappear and, with it, the chance to get out of the cramped and squalid existence he detested. As Joyce later acknowledged, the party lived 'like animals at Hut Point'.[35]

Without the three-hour delay, the south-easterly blizzard that did strike would then have occurred much later in the pair's journey. Once past Glacier Tongue, there would have been some shelter afforded by that formation and the Dellbridge Islands, but more importantly the sea ice there was much more secure. Stevens would write some months later:

> This part of the ice has as a rule been more permanent, occupying as it does an area more or less enclosed by the Dellbridge Islands...A large tabular berg stranded some few hundred yards south of Cape Evans helped to retain it...A party making the trip from Hut Point to the Cape Evans Base on the 8th of May and reaching the neighbourhood of Tent Island, would in my opinion be safe.[36]

Jack echoed this observation, stating that in the neighbourhood of the islands 'the ice appeared solid and had [Mackintosh and Hayward] succeeded in reaching either of the Razorbacks they could have found their way to Cape Evans itself'.[37] A rope ladder, positioned during the previous season, gave access from the sea ice on the south of the cape.

Although the return journey from Mt Hope had increasingly welded the men into a coherent team, as a measure of good health had returned to the party, so the divisions of the old sledging parties began emerging again and Mackintosh sought to exercise his authority. Of all the men, Hayward had spent the most time with the Skipper since reaching Hut Point and now went along with his leader's decision to make the crossing in doubtful conditions.

Joyce, Wild and Richards felt that they had an investment in suffering and hardship in saving the lives of the Skipper and Hayward. That Mackintosh was ready to risk his hard-won life and that of his subordinate on a whim caused the trio bitterness and brought back all their old reservations about the Skipper's quality as a leader.[38] Richards wrote over 60 years later:

> He was a weak character but headstrong. We did our best to dissuade him and Hayward from making the needless crossing in May 1916. I remember as if it were yesterday Joyce coming in after having a look at the weather to the south around Minna Bluff. 'You might call me "Old Cautious", Sir, but I would not go to Cape Evans today for all the tea in China.'[39]

A year earlier, hemmed in at Hut Point, Wild had noted with amazement:

> [Mackintosh] has got some daft ideas about getting back to the ship. One is he wants to start back to the ship himself or with one companion and try and walk back taking nothing with them. If it comes on a blizzard he says they will lie down and cover themselves with their burberrys till it's over. I don't know what he means. He had got all sorts of 'impracticable schemes'.[40]

Joyce, Richards and Wild were resigned to what they considered a foolhardy plan.[41] Richards reasoned: 'There was not much we could do about his decision. Mackintosh was in charge of the party and short of forcibly restraining him we could only urge them not to go.'[42]

At 1 p.m., in fading light, the Skipper and Hayward left the hut.[43] In favourable conditions the thirteen-mile trip to Cape Evans could take as little as two or three hours, but more often it took five to six hours, or even longer.[44] At best, the pair had only two or three hours of daylight left. Joyce made up a bag of seal meat and chocolate, their only food.[45] The men remaining at the hut extracted a promise from the Skipper that, if the weather grew worse, they would turn back. In later years, Richards gave several accounts that Mackintosh and Hayward stated that they would 'make for land if it blows'.[46]

Wild would later tell an inquiry: '. . . they started away soon after 1 p.m. when the light was fading. We went to the top of the hill and saw them off. The last I saw of them they seemed to be going straight for Cape Evans.' Joyce too said: 'The last sight of the watching party on the hill gained of them was when they were about a mile away – close to the shore, but apparently making for C. Evans.'[47]

Ominously, the weather that had been seen to the south soon struck. Joyce would record: 'At 3 p.m. a moderate blizzard was raging which later on increased in fury and we then had many misgivings for their safety . . .'[48]

Mackintosh and Hayward would not be seen alive again. As the two men progressed around the lee of Hut Point Peninsula for a mile or so before making a course for Cape Evans, one figure was seen to be keeping closer to the shore than the other.[49] With the approach of the bad weather from the southeast, the sky quickly clouded, further reducing visibility in the fading light. The newly frozen surface was uneven and sticky, and the travellers' finnesko footwear was worn and gave a poor grip. As the pair left the shelter of the shore, the wind started to drive the snow from behind.

About two miles out from the hut the travellers encountered fragile young ice. With the wind rising in force this would have been their final opportunity to turn back, as the Skipper had promised he would. It is likely that, before he could make such a decision, events overtook them.

With no shelter out on the ice, as the storm increased, so did the difficulty of retracing their steps. Wild had experienced similar conditions in much the same place a month earlier. He had written on 23 April: 'I was out in the wind this morning and it was as much as I could do to stand up against it. I couldn't see two yards on account of the drift.'

The wind suddenly increased above 40 miles an hour, enveloping them in driving drift, and visibility was reduced to zero on the shifting ice.[50] Just two months earlier, stricken with scurvy and facing death on the Barrier, Mackintosh had written to his mother: 'Trust God to keep my Beloved Ones in his Safe keeping. Goodbye.'[51] He is unlikely to have contemplated that, having survived the hazardous return trek from Mt Hope, the plea in the letter would be so soon invoked, but in circumstances of his own making.

Three years earlier, on 28 April 1913, a trio of Scott's men – Wright, Keohone and Gran – had set out from Hut Point to cross to Cape Evans with a stove, food and a tent. Their experience on the newly formed ice suggests why the poorly equipped Mackintosh and Hayward did not survive.

The Scott party had taken eight hours to make the crossing, arriving at the cape at 6 p.m. after they had 'struggled for dear life all day'. Shortly after leaving Hut Point the three men ran into a belt of thin new ice, but found a strip of stronger ice along the coast beneath Castle Rock. By midday, thick snow began to fall and the wind was rising. They suddenly found the ice begin to give way but managed to scramble to old sea ice in the vicinity of Turtle Rock. On the north side of Glacier Tongue they camped for lunch of pemmican and tea. One of the party, Gran, suffered frostbite in his fingers and a frozen foot after breaking through the sea ice. When they reached Cape Evans in bad visibility and near darkness, they had difficulty finding the best place for climbing the ice foot.[52]

As the weather deteriorated during the early afternoon of 8 May 1916, the unease felt by Joyce, Richards and Wild quickly turned to a conviction that their companions had walked to their deaths. Wild wrote:

May 8th. Monday . . . The Skipper & Hayward have gone on a foolhardy attempt to get to Cape Evans. I don't know why. It will be a wonder if they got over there without getting a wetting. The ice has only been frozen for about four days, so it isn't very safe. We others (Joyce, Richards & myself) have stopped here. There's nothing to be gained by risking our lives in going over there now. If the other two get lost I shall be very sorry. We humped them back here, over the 'Barrier'. However let's hope they get there alright. We have killed 38 seals up to date, but we shall want more than two more. We mean to stop here till it is quite safe to go to C. Evans. We shall not be much better off there than here.[53]

Joyce was equally damning in his diary entry for 3–10 May:

I don't know why these people are so anxious to risk their lives again . . . half an hour after leaving it came on a howling blizzard. Whether they got there or not they deserved to be badly frost bitten or lose their lives. After dragging them back from death they seem to think they can court it again. Ah well, such is life & what fools we [have] got to put up with. Carried on blowing and still the same outside, open water to the N. Perhaps they have gone out on a floe . . .[54]

The worst fears of the hut trio were all but confirmed on 10 May when the weather cleared and they followed the travellers' footsteps on the ice. Wild was to recall in January 1917:

One set of marks was much nearer the land then the other. There were two sets of them going to Cape Evans, & one set returning, which had been made on the 7th. Both sets of marks stopped suddenly about two miles from Hut Point, and we could see that the ice had all gone out from there, after they had passed . . . We thought they might have got safely over before it broke up . . .[55]

Joyce stated:

Their footmarks were seen clearly enough raised up on the ice and these were followed for about 2 miles in a direction leading to Cape Evans. Here they ended abruptly and in the dim light a wide stretch of water very lightly covered with ice was seen as far as the eye could see, no doubt one night's freezing. It was at once evident that part of the ice over which they had travelled had gone out to sea.[56]

And Richards explained that

On 9th May a wind prevented anything being done but by 10th the three remaining members walked over the ice to the north tracing the footsteps in the soft slushy ice. These ended abruptly in a sheet of water very lightly frozen as far as the eye could see – The footsteps often keeping in to land for a little suddenly turned heading directly for Cape Evans as though a sudden decision had been taken . . .[57]

Because of the ice and very cold weather conditions, the three men left at

Hut Point could not take advantage of the full moons of May and June to cross to Cape Evans. Their store of seal meat dwindled to almost nothing, and when Joyce took stock of other remaining supplies in mid-June, he recorded: 'We have plenty of flour but out of everything else.' They read books, some for the third time, played cribbage on a makeshift board, and rationed the remaining seal meat and blubber.[58] They noted, but could not specially celebrate, Midwinter's Day. Wild wrote on 8 July:

> Still at Hut Point. We are getting fed up with this place now . . . We got a seal today
> (the first one for six weeks,) & that has saved our minds a bit. We have been burn-
> ing all the wood we could find, & one piece of blubber per day, & it has not been
> very cheerful. We put [in] a good deal of time in our sleeping bags . . .[59]

The stranded party's chance to cross the ice came with the next full moon. At 10 a.m. on 15 July, in calm and very cold conditions, the three men and four dogs set off with a sledge. They initially encountered a difficult, churned-up surface but, once past Glacier Tongue, soon came upon an area of more permanent ice. They were surprised to find the moonlit night slowly turning into darkness as a lunar eclipse occurred. Wild recorded this surreal event: 'I thought we were going to be left in darkness but a very little bit of the rim remained to light us.'[60]

The men at Cape Evans had expected the party across from the *Discovery* hut for some weeks. Jack had written on 22 May: 'Still no sign of anyone from Hut Point and this too in spite of fact there has been fine, beautifully calm for last 8–16 days and the ice to all appearances is firmly set and fixed for the winter . . .'[61] He had earlier noted that, following a storm on 8 May, the ice had blown out. At 7 p.m. on that day, about the time Mackintosh and Hayward would have been due at Cape Evans, he had recorded in the meteorological records: 'Blizzard – Ice gradually creeping out, now about five yards off shore.'[62] This entry gives the most compelling clue to the fate of the two travellers. By the following morning the ice 'along the shore south of Glacier Tongue' had gone out.

Those at the Cape Evans base did consider travelling to Hut Point to find out what had happened, 'but scarcely think it would be advisable to leave Cope alone as he is at present', wrote Jack.[63] Cope was in fact badly affected by the forced idleness and circumstances of his second winter as a castaway. Gaze and Jack took over his meal duties and, fearing for their hut-mate's safety, kept poisons out of his reach and dismantled the harpoon gun. They closely observed him to ensure that he did not leave the hut without their knowledge.[64] Stevens too was suffering the effects of deprivation and spent some time in bed, often with recurring toothache (later an abscess), and suffered from rheumatism.

On 20 May, there was a brief moment of hope that the men from the south had returned when, before dinner, Gaze thought he heard the 'heavy sound of footsteps outside . . . thinking it was the party from Hut Pt. But it was only Cope who had gone outside without [his] knowledge.'[65]

Despite concerns for their missing companions, Midwinter's Day was a time of some celebration for the four men at Cape Evans:

> Stevens prepared a right royal dinner. Menu – tomato soup (Heinz's), stuffed olives, tinned salmon, roast Adelie penguin with potatoes, beans, celery, plum pudding, custard, pineapple, coffee. I surprised the company by bringing forth a small tin of Capstan tobacco as my contribution and oh how it was appreciated, Irvine and Stevens almost weeping tears of joy . . . very dark all day and tonight the wind appears to be getting up again.[66]

Frequent blizzards kept the party confined to the hut for days on end. Apart from regular meteorological forays by Jack or Stevens, the principal outdoor activity was hunting seals and collecting blubber from a nearby cache. An indoor lavatory was set up in one of the pony stables in the lean-to on the north side of the hut,[67] and primitive but effective fur boots were made to replace those worn out during sledging.[68]

On 15 July, the dogs started barking about 5 p.m. Jack went outside but could see nothing, then: 'In a short time the barking recommenced and on going out I saw with much surprise a sledge party about 100 yards from the hut. Rushed back again and shouted to others in hut, then ran down to the new arrivals.'[69]

Richards, Joyce and Wild and the four dogs, veterans from the journey to Mt Hope, rounded Cape Evans in the midwinter darkness to an eerie welcome:

> When we got near the Cape we could see quite a number of dogs, which ran for the high land round the Cape. With the moonlight behind them you could see the prismatic colour in their fur. They were barking and making a terrible to-do. They were the pups which had been born before we went away and which now had become big dogs.[70]

Oscar, the powerful leader of the sledging pack, broke his harness and gave chase to the scattering prey.[71]

Jack, Stevens and Gaze greeted the Hut Point party at the edge of the sea ice. 'Where is Captain Mackintosh?' Jack enquired. 'They first thought I was joking.'[72] This is a slightly different account than that of Richards, Joyce and Wild, each of whom said their first enquiry was: 'What had happened to Mac and Hayward?' Stevens would later observe: 'I think that on both sides, surprise was tempered by expectation of misfortune.'[73] The Cape Evans men had, according to Jack, 'half expected' the loss of all of the southern party, so the return of three of their number was a considerable relief. 'The people here had given us all up,' wrote Wild.[74]

The terrible truth concerning Mackintosh and Hayward was now apparent: '... the poor fellows had succumbed to the horrors of the region', wrote Joyce.[75] Wild was less sympathetic: 'After all our trouble with them, they have slung their lives away. If they had done it on the Barrier we might have got Smithy back.'[76] The news of Spencer-Smith's death was a further blow to the welcoming party, particularly the Padre's cousin, Irvine Gaze.

The emaciated figure of Cope then appeared from the hut and joined the group in the moonlight. 'How are you, Copie?' Richards asked his old friend, who replied, 'I'm not much good, I've got appendicitis. I'm shitting nanny goat turds.'[77] Cope's erratic behaviour caused Joyce (for no known reason) to push at him and he tumbled down a snow slope as he uttered: 'I've shit myself.' Cope continued to act strangely and Richards concluded that he 'did not possess all his marbles'.[78] Many years later, Richards would dismiss the incident involving Cope and Joyce: 'There was nothing significant in it. They were the best of friends after.'[79]

Joyce was relieved to get inside the hut, which 'although black and grimy, was like the Carlton'.[80] Over a good meal prepared by Stevens, the southern party recounted the events of the last six months. The Cape Evans men were deeply moved by their tragic tale. Jack wrote:

> Am more convinced than ever of the hardships endured, and the heroism displayed by all. When we returned from sledging both last season and this I thought we had suffered considerably but all we encountered pales into insignificance when compared to the suffering of the six comrades we left at 80° S.[81]

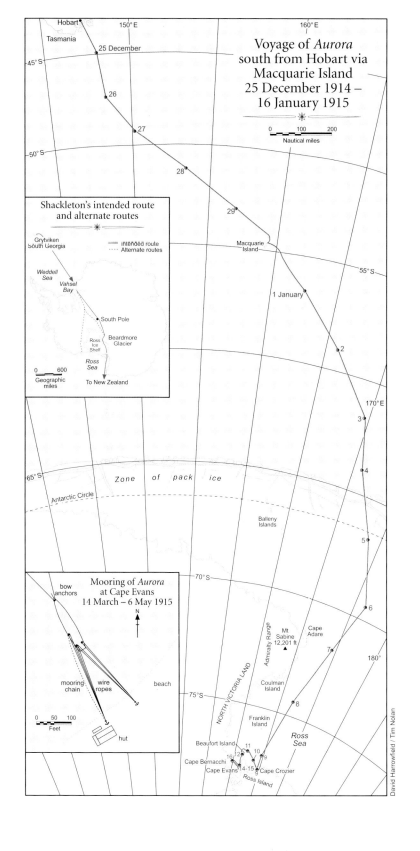

Voyage of *Aurora*
south from Hobart via
Macquarie Island
25 December 1914 –
16 January 1915

Hobart

Tasmania

150° E   160° E

25 December

45° S

26

27

50° S

28

29

Macquarie
Island

55° S

1 January

170° E

2

3

4

65° S   Zone of pack ice

Antarctic Circle

Balleny
Islands

5

70° S

6

Admiralty Range   Mt
Sabine   Cape
12,201 ft   Adare

7

180°

Coulman
Island

8

75° S

Franklin
Island

*Ross
Sea*

Beaufort Island

11   10

NORTH VICTORIA LAND

16   12   9

Cape Bernacchi

14-15   Cape Crozier

Cape Evans   Ross
Island

0   100   200
Nautical miles

Shackleton's intended route
and alternate routes

Grytviken
South Georgia

——— intended route
------- Alternate routes

*Weddell
Sea*

Vahsel
Bay

● South Pole

Beardmore
Glacier

Ross
Ice
Shelf

*Ross
Sea*

0   600
Geographic
miles

To New Zealand

Mooring of *Aurora*
at Cape Evans
14 March – 6 May 1915

bow
anchors

N

mooring
chain   wire
ropes   beach

0   50   100
Feet

hut

David Harrowfield / Tim Nolan

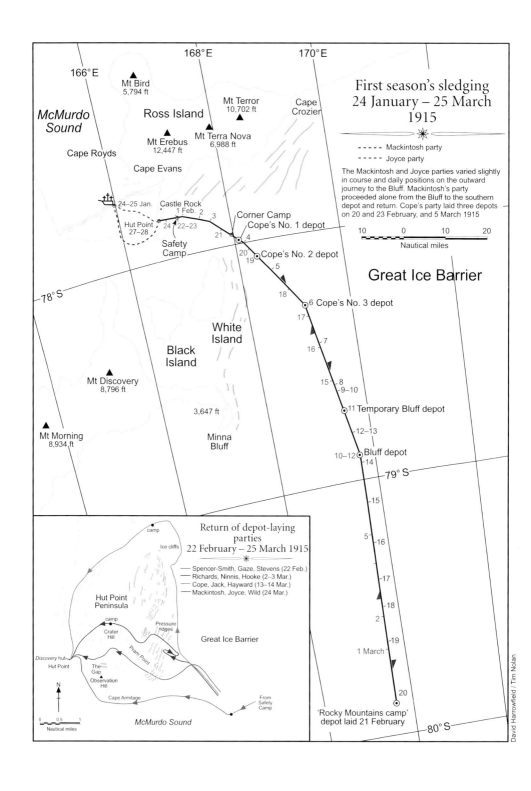

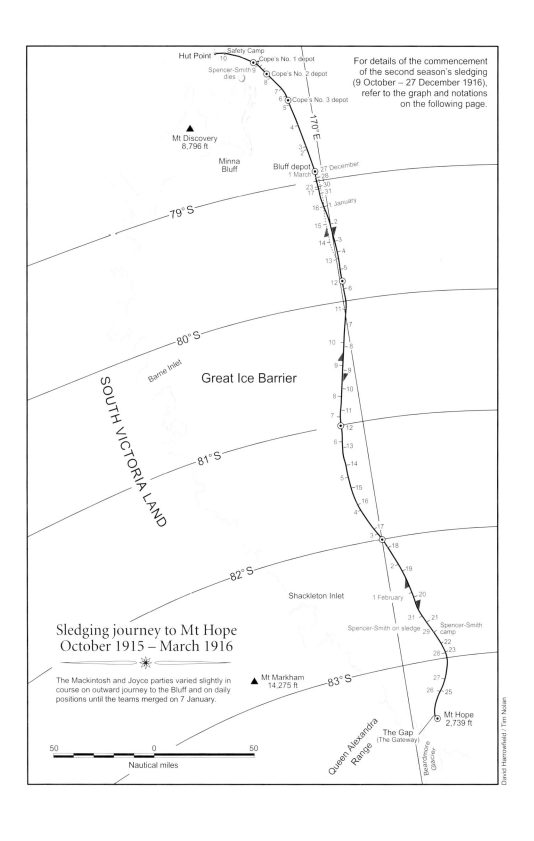

Hut Point
Safety Camp
10
Cope's No. 1 depot
Spencer-Smith 9
dies
8
Cope's No. 2 depot
7
6
Cope's No. 3 depot
5
170° E

For details of the commencement
of the second season's sledging
(9 October – 27 December 1916),
refer to the graph and notations
on the following page.

Mt Discovery
8,796 ft

Minna
Bluff

4
3
2

Bluff depot   27 December
1 March   28
23   30
17   31
16   1 January
15   2
14   3
13   4
5
12   6
11   7
10   8
9   9
8   10
7   11
6   12
13
14
5   15
16
4   17
3   18
2   19
1 February   20
31   21
Spencer-Smith on sledge 29   Spencer-Smith
camp
28   22
23
27
26   25

79° S

Great Ice Barrier

Barne Inlet

80° S

SOUTH VICTORIA LAND

81° S

82° S

Shackleton Inlet

Sledging journey to Mt Hope
October 1915 – March 1916
——— ❋ ———

The Mackintosh and Joyce parties varied slightly in
course on outward journey to the Bluff and on daily
positions until the teams merged on 7 January.

▲ Mt Markham
14,275 ft

83° S

Mt Hope
2,739 ft

Queen Alexandra Range

The Gap
(The Gateway)

Beardmore Glacier

50   0   50
Nautical miles

David Harrowfield / Tim Nolan

Second season's sledging
9 October – 27 December 1915

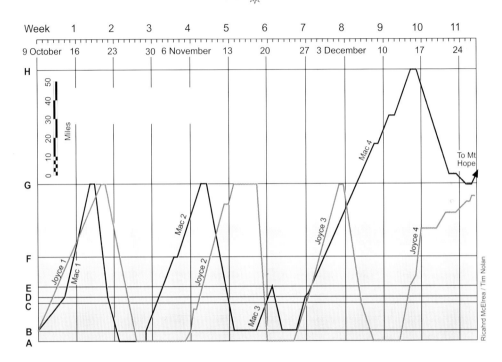

A = Hut Point
B = Safety Camp
C = Corner Camp
D = Cope's No. 1 depot
E = Cope's No. 2 depot
F = Cope's No. 3 depot
G = Bluff depot
H = 79° 52'S

Mac party of Mackintosh, Wild and Spencer-Smith made four journeys shown as Mac 1, Mac 2, Mac 3 and Mac 4.

Joyce party of Joyce, Stevens (first journey) Gaze (second and subsequent journeys) Hayward, Richards, Cope and Jack made four journeys shown as Joyce 1, Joyce 2, Joyce 3 and Joyce 4.

By returning to Hut Point on each journey, Joyce's party had the benefit of fresh seal meat. Mackintosh's party was subsequently afflicted with scurvy at an earlier stage than Joyce's.

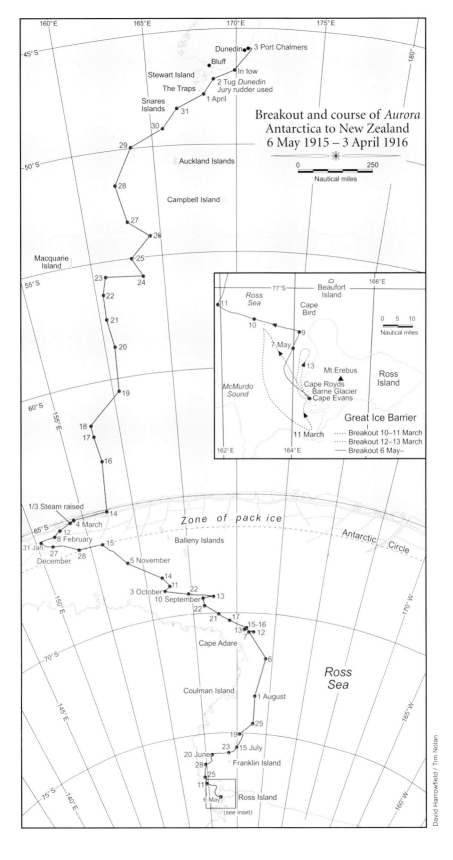

Breakout and course of *Aurora*
Antarctica to New Zealand
6 May 1915 – 3 April 1916

David Harrowfield / Tim Nolan

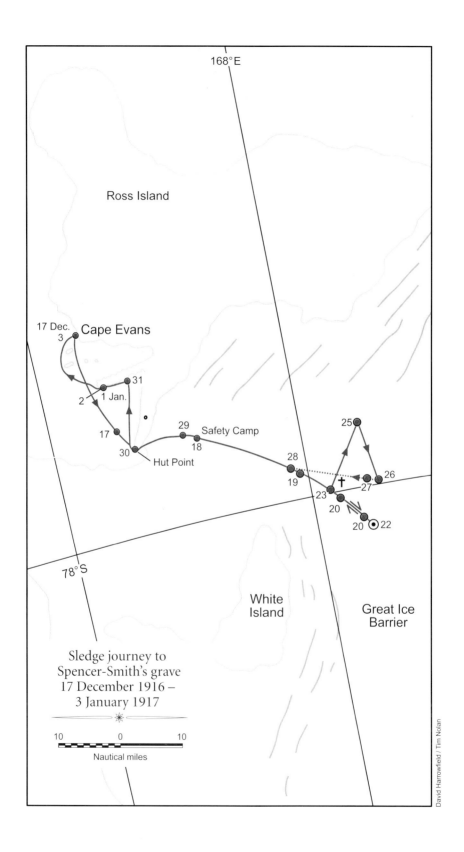

168°E

Ross Island

17 Dec.   Cape Evans
3

31

1 Jan.

2

17

30

29   Safety Camp
18

Hut Point

25

28

19   26

† 27

23

20

20   22

78°S

White
Island

Great Ice
Barrier

Sledge journey to
Spencer-Smith's grave
17 December 1916 –
3 January 1917

10   0   10

Nautical miles

David Harrowfield / Tim Nolan

Map labels:

165° E 166° E Cape Bird

77°15'S

77°30'S

Ross Island

Cape Bernacchi

Cape Royds

12 17 14

15 Barne Glacier

New Harbour

15–16

13 ■Hut

12 January

Cape Evans

13

Inaccessible Island

13

Butter Point

14 Razorback Islands

Tent Island

McMurdo Sound

Erebus Glacier Tongue

77°45'S

Hut Point Peninsula

Movements of *Aurora*
and search parties in
McMurdo Sound
10–17 January 1917

Great Ice Barrier

0 5 10

Nautical miles

78°00'S

Black Island

78°15'S

David Harrowfield / Tim Nolan

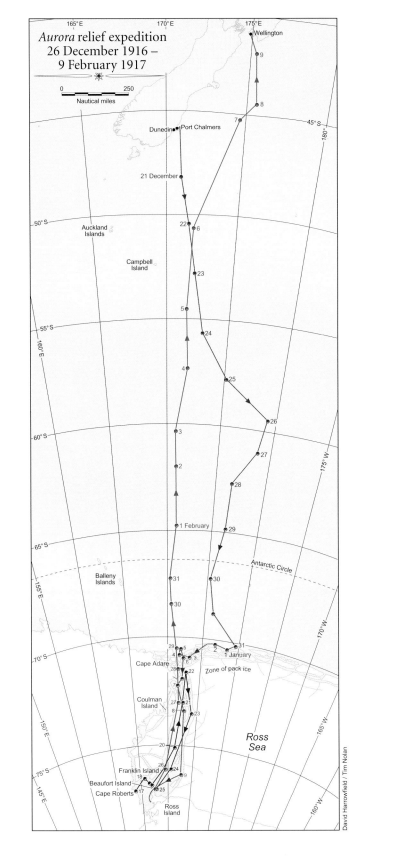

CHAPTER NINETEEN

Apparent treachery

A S MACKINTOSH and Hayward walked to their premature deaths, a drama of a different sort concerning the Ross Sea party was unfolding in New Zealand. With *Aurora* back in port, it was clear that a rescue would have to be mounted for the men left at Cape Evans, but who would pay for the repairing and reprovisioning of the ship and who would lead the relief voyage soon became matters of contention. There was no news of Shackleton's party in the Weddell Sea, and the Imperial Trans-Antarctic Expedition was in disarray.

Sir Douglas Mawson, aware of the opprobrium arising from the refit of the ship in Australia and recognising that the expedition was in effect bankrupt, quickly offered advice to Stenhouse:

> I hope that Mackintosh and the other men are all right . . . it seems to me that they may be badly off for clothes. It is impossible to say what steps will be taken to help you – anyway New Zealand should dock and refit the ship free of charge.[1]

Prominent businessman John Mill of Port Chalmers offered his services as honorary agent, and the support of the Otago Harbour Board.[2] When he found that there were insufficient funds to meet immediate needs, Mill advanced £150 to help pay wages due to the crew of *Aurora*.[3] Arthur Mabin of Levin and Company, Wellington customs and shipping agents, also offered support to a grateful Stenhouse, who replied: 'I have given your salaams to Larkman and Mauger, and Ninnis who is with us . . . it has been a very sad homecoming to us without the party aboard and a miracle that the ship arrived at all.'[4]

Stenhouse estimated that a sum of at least £2,500 would be needed to discharge the crew, pay officers' wages and make sundry payments. He urgently sought assistance from Frederick White, the ITAE's secretary in London, and received £500 on 7 April. White was shortly to be replaced in his role by Ernest Perris of the *Daily Chronicle*,[5] who on 18 April advised Shackleton's solicitors: 'Forwarding [£] two fifty expedition funds finished appealing for relief ships.'[6]

Ninnis, who had offered to serve in a voluntary capacity in any relief party,[7] noted in his diary on 17 April: 'Whole expedition seems to be in chaos at head-quarters. Cannot pay crew off, nor get any support from London, getting rapidly sick of it.' Then two days later: 'Climax reached. Cable to say we are all bankrupt, what a joy after all the hardship.'[8]

George Fenwick, editor of the *Otago Daily Times*, sought help from the New Zealand Prime Minister, William Massey, who responded: 'I quite realise that the expedition has more claim from the national point of view than many of the demands which are made on the public purse.'[9] On 5 June he telegraphed Stenhouse: 'Cabinet authorised £300.'[10] The New Zealand government contributed a further £200.[11]

Stenhouse was still a long way short of the amount needed to meet the immediate financial obligations of the expedition, and on 6 June 1916 he wrote to Mabin:

> I have already received another advance of £300 from Mr Massey, with which I will be able to pay off one more man and meet the month's debts. I will then again be lacking funds and wish that I could get the whole of the £1500 asked for, at once, so that I could lay up the ship and proceed to Australia.[12]

The rescue of the men stranded in the Ross Sea and the fate of the *Endurance* party missing in the Weddell Sea were matters of intense speculation in England.[13] *The Times* suggested that Mawson might be persuaded to command a relief ship, apparently overlooking the fact that he was a scientist, not a mariner.[14]

On 27 March, a meeting at the London solicitors' offices of Hutchison and Cuff, attended by Lady Emily Shackleton and Mrs Mackintosh among others, determined that steps should be taken immediately to organise a relief expedition to the Ross Sea.[15] The British government appointed a Shackleton Relief Advisory Committee, to be chaired by Admiral Sir Lewis Beaumont. However, the plight of the Ross Sea party, whose fortunes were at least partially known, was secondary to that of the Weddell Sea party.

On 10 April, Ernest Perris and Alfred Hutchison, in their capacity as attorneys for Shackleton, approached Captain J. K. Davis:

> A ship will have to be sent down to the Ross Sea to bring off the men there but as this is a matter of far less importance [than the rescue of the Weddell Sea party] we need not trouble you about it . . . it might be that we should request Mr Stenhouse, who brought the Aurora back, to take her down again . . .[16]

Davis replied from SS *Bonnah*:

> Provided such an expedition is undertaken by the Admiralty I have no hesitation in offering my services without conditions other than that . . . all matters pertaining to equipment and personnel shall be left to my absolute and individual control.[17]

Public speculation on the fate of the Mackintosh party was matched by informed private concern. In a fascinating exchange of correspondence, Shackleton supporter and London financier Campbell MacKellar wrote on 4 April to Scottish polar explorer Dr William S. Bruce seeking his opinion on whether it could have been possible for Mackintosh's party to have laid depots to the foot of the Beardmore Glacier during the austral summer of 1915–16. Mackellar suggested:

> I am afraid disaster has overtaken Mackintosh and his party, and in any case they could not have laid all the necessary depots, and if so Shackleton was done for Speaking privately while I think Mackintosh is excellent in many respects, I do not know that he has as great a feeling of responsibility as he might, and that he might be a little haphazard in his ways. I know him very well and like him – but in regard to his life ashore always thought he lacked foresight and a sense of responsibility – his marrying on £100 a year showed that.[18]

Bruce's reply proved remarkably perceptive:

> Naturally they would not have been able to have laid depots very far to the south during the early months of 1915, but with luck they might with an effort attained the foot of the Beardmore Glacier.
>
> It is admittedly disconcerting that Macintosh did not get in touch with the ship again by May 6th [1915], but there is no evidence to show that he did not get back to Hut Point much earlier . . .
>
> With regard to Shackleton's position, I do not see that there is any news at all that indicates that any calamity has befallen him or his party . . .
>
> The *Aurora*, of course, must in any case after necessary repairs, proceed again early next season to McMurdo Sound, with a suitable relief party on board . . .[19]

On 8 May 1916, the Australian Prime Minister, Andrew Fisher, wrote to the Secretary of State in London: 'As to Mackintosh's party it has been suggested to Ministers, organisation for rescue expedition be entrusted to local committee, in Commonwealth or New Zealand, wherever *Aurora* fitted out . . . Commonwealth Government prepared assist in matter of relief expeditions . . .'[20]

On 30 May, the British government suggested that Australia and New Zealand should undertake the whole expense of the relief expedition to the Ross Sea.[21] This was unacceptable and Australia proposed that Britain should meet half of the expenses and Australia and New Zealand the other half, shared on a population basis.[22] This formula had been aired in London by the Shackleton Relief Advisory Committee with apparent approval.[23]

By early August, the formula was adopted by all three governments.[24] Australia and Britain drew the line as to liabilities considered to be those of 'the promoters of the expedition', such as wages due to crew members.[25] The New

Zealand government, however, advanced further monies to meet wages and other expedition liabilities incurred in New Zealand.

The Australian government also countered a suggestion that it nominate a representative on a 'Home Government Advisory Committee' by proposing that a working committee be appointed in New Zealand and a supervisory committee in Australia. The working committee was to order the necessary repairs to *Aurora*, draft a scheme of action for the relief expedition together with detailed estimates and submit same to the supervising committee, which would then seek the approval of the Australian government, which in turn would consult with the New Zealand government.[26]

Stenhouse's entry in *Aurora*'s logbook for 1 June 1916 recorded a dramatic development in the ITAE saga: '*Endurance*'s crew reported safe and Sir E. Shackleton also.'[27]

This followed news that had been telegraphed to the Admiralty from Port Stanley: 'Shackleton arrived Port Stanley. 22 men left on Elephant Island . . .'[28]

Shackleton's re-emergence after his boat journey from Elephant Island and crossing of South Georgia to the Norwegian whaling station at Stromness Bay was, to his detractors, proof of the failure of an expedition that was never likely to succeed. It was now apparent that whatever Mackintosh and his men had achieved would count for nothing.

Shackleton learnt from the manager of the whaling station of *Aurora*'s 'misadventures' and that Mackintosh and his party were still unaccounted for, but he had to await until he reached the Falkland Islands some weeks later to learn more.[29]

Stenhouse found himself having to defend the fortunes of the Ross Sea party, and received an accusatory cable from Shackleton's agent in London: 'Was [Mackintosh] at Hut Point when you left, if not give your reason for his lengthy absence. Mawson gravely apprehensive.'[30]

In a letter to Fisher, Mawson uged that *Aurora*, if repaired in Australia, should become the property of the Australia government. Reminding the Prime Minister that the government should have paid off the balance of his (Mawson's) expedition debts, he said: 'The results (scientific, economic etc) from the Ross Sea affair are nil – even if it had gone off in the best possible way, there could have been no real value to the results for that is old ground – they are the fourth expedition to sit down in the same spot.'[31]

The Australian government appointed Rear Admiral Sir William Cresswell to chair the advisory committee, which included geologist and Antarctic veteran Dr Griffith Taylor and noted Australian academic Professor Orme Masson as well as two navy men, Captain J. R. Barter and Commander J. R. Stevenson.[32]

By 14 June, the New Zealand government had appointed John Mill and another prominent businessman, Christchurch shipping agent Joseph Kinsey, as the New Zealand working committee to 'proceed with repairs and other proposals at once and submit particulars to Australian committee'.[33]

Ninnis was especially pleased with the appointment of Kinsey, writing to Mabin: 'He has given real impetus to our affairs at last and I trust that it may now be a case of real progress.'[34]

A skeleton crew on *Aurora* at Port Chalmers carried out such tasks as washing decks with caustic and stripping the yards. When the ship was moored for a period at Dunedin, a short distance from Port Chalmers, Ninnis sold stuffed penguins to raise funds for the Red Cross to aid the war effort. Seaman Glidden joined up with the 'Middle Battery defence force'.[35]

On 16 May, an estimated 2,000 people inspected the ship and were treated to music from the St Clair School band. Some 3,000 patrons came the next day, paying £106 in admission fees.[36]

The seamen of *Aurora* were frequently absent without leave, at brothels and bars. Stenhouse spent a week in a nursing home suffering what Ninnis described as a bad attack of 'Barber's rash'.[37] Meanwhile, Bosun Paton took issue with Thomson about the leniency given for crew shore leave and stopped work until he could speak with Stenhouse.[38]

The Minister of Marine, Robert McNab, offered technical support to assess *Aurora*.[39] On 28 June, she was towed back to Port Chalmers, where hands were employed pumping out the ship and carpenters began work. Next day the ship went into dry dock and surveyors confirmed that the hull was severely 'hogged' and 'the stem and stern were badly strained'. The bow and stern had dropped some seven and a half inches in opposite directions, there were gaps in the planking, the starboard water tank leaked, and metal linkages between the deck and the side of the vessel, known as 'iron knees', and other fittings needed repair or replacement, as did the rudder.[40] The condition of the ship highlighted how close she had come to being destroyed or made totally unseaworthy in the pack ice.

Coal, ashes and stores were discharged and the hold was cleaned so *Aurora* could be assessed for internal damage. The surveyors recommended extensive repairs, including replacement of timber, hull plating and iron fittings below the water line, recaulking and painting. Masts, rigging and other equipment and fittings also required maintenance. The engines needed to be partially dismantled, the boiler and propeller shaft examined, and the ship's boats overhauled.

Despite the fact that Port Chalmers was busy with troopships,[41] the Otago Harbour Board and the Railways Department provided two gangs of eighteen men and use of the dock and facilities free of charge.[42] Kinsey and Mill appointed two well-known local companies, engineers and boilermakers Stevenson and Cook, and shipwrights Miller Brothers, to effect the necessary repairs 'on the basis of time and labour'. These were estimated to take 60 working days at a cost of at least £6,000.

In July, a considerable amount of material and tools was obtained for the ship, including nearly 300 pounds of black paint and 170 of white lead paint, two tons of Stockholm pitch, over 300 pounds of nails and spikes, 400 super feet of 6 x 1 inch tongue-and-groove flooring, and over four tons of iron rod and plating. Tools obtained included a 'hogging hammer'. Materials used each day were meticulously recorded.[43]

The true extent of gear and equipment that had not put ashore at Cape Evans was evident upon the unloading of the ship and placement of its cargo in a shed loaned by John Mill.[44] This included fourteen cases of private clothing, 52 Jaeger blankets, 40 sets of Burberry windproofs, nearly 70 pairs of assorted boots and slippers, 60 pairs of finnesko, 150 pairs of new socks, eight reindeer-skin sleeping bags, eight sledges, thirteen pairs of skis, five Primus stoves and the second motor sledge. There were negligable food provisions of consequence left after the eleven-month voyage – 30 pounds of dried vegetables.

Because the relief expedition could be unexpectedly detained in the south, plans were to provide 36 men with supplies for eighteen months. Kinsey drew on his experience of provisioning *Nimrod* on its second voyage to Antarctica in December 1908, and wrote to a friend in Melbourne seeking supply of 'certain things some of which it is impossible to obtain here'.[45] His detailed list included staples – 2,318 pounds of vegetables, 3,000 of potatoes, 6,000 of flour and 2,000 of oatmeal – plus such delicacies as 300 tins of whitebait and six dozen tins of oysters at eight shillings a dozen. 'Medical comforts' included one case each of whisky and brandy, and two of wine, while smokers were provided for with 43 pounds of Havelock Dark tobacco. The total cost of these provisions amounted to £1,571 6s 11d. Companies in Dunedin and Christchurch supplied clothing, footwear, medical equipment, stationery and tools, and 21 'good serviceable beds' were purchased. Stenhouse enquired into the 50 pairs of missing ski boots bought by Mackintosh from the Victor Shoe Company in Sydney, doubtless keen to use the items, albeit belatedly. Stores were purchased to provide each of the Ross Sea party, upon rescue, with a storm cap, two shirts, two drawers, three pairs of socks, a pair of leather sea boots, a cardigan jacket, two pairs of woollen mitts, a suit of heavy cloth and two blankets.[46]

On 28 May 1916, Captain J. K. Davis had been appointed to command *Discovery* during the search for the Weddell Sea party.[47] However, Shackleton's return from the south, and the fact that the rest of his men were known to be safe on Elephant Island, shifted the focus of rescue to the Ross Sea. Thus the captain's appointment was revoked on 2 June, with the Shackleton Relief Advisory Committee noting 'that there remains no suitable command for Davis and with regret have released him from his engagement'.[48]

Shackleton soon announced that, after relieving his party, he would travel to Australia or New Zealand and take over command of *Aurora*.[49] He initially received support for this proposal from the relief committee, and the Admiralty noted: '. . . in view of his knowledge and experience it is considered essential that he should be the leader of the Rescue Expedition'.[50] It was originally intended that *Aurora* be used as a back-up vessel for the attempt to rescue the men on Elephant Island by use of 'a trawler of steel construction' or the 'Chilean wooden surveying vessel *Toro*'. The Secretary of State for the Colonies opined: 'Admiralty consider ample time for *Aurora* effect rescue and return to New Zealand for Ross Sea Relief'.[51]

. Fortunately, the plan came to nothing. Stenhouse calculated that *Aurora* would take 34 days to sail a distance computed as 5,156 miles from Port Chalmers to Stanley Harbour.[52] He noted that in order to have the ship ready in time would require the services of a further twenty shipwrights from other ports in New Zealand.[53] Kinsey and Mill considered it 'a very dangerous policy to run the double risk of attempting [to] rescue both parties' with *Aurora* and, on 12 July, advised the New Zealand Minister of Marine accordingly.[54] By that time the Admiralty was arranging for *Discovery*, being fitted out at Devonport, to be towed to the Falkland Islands.[55]

On 19 July, the Secretary of State for the Colonies advised the Governor-General of Australia: 'Government of New Zealand informed *Aurora* will not be required now to proceed to Elephant Island as arrangements progressing satisfactorily to send *Discovery* from England.'[56] On 22 July, overtime ceased for the men working on *Aurora*.[57]

On 28 June, the Christchurch *Press* had prematurely announced that it was 'definitely settled that Captain Stenhouse will have charge of the expedition for the relief of Captain Mackintosh and his men'.[58]

The decision as to who would command *Aurora* on the relief voyage to the Ross Sea would normally be a matter for Shackleton as the legal owner of the ship. However, de facto control of the relief expedition passed to the three governments financing the enterprise. Although Shackleton's attorneys had at an early stage assumed that Stenhouse would command the ship, Kinsey and Mill, strongly influenced by Mawson, ensured that neither Stenhouse nor Shackleton would be in command.

Kinsey and Mill also said privately that the safety of the six men who were sledging when *Aurora* broke away on 6 May 1915 'must be very doubtful'.[59] Mawson, too, thought that the men were likely to have died in the southern autumn of 1915.[60]

In June, Kinsey persuaded Stenhouse to relinquish the ship's articles and agreement, ostensibly so that he could copy them for sending to Australia.[61] Stenhouse did not see these documents again and would later tell Shackleton of this apparent treachery: 'From my first meeting with Mr Kinsey, I knew he was extremely bitter against you and during one conversation, he made some disparaging remarks about you.' Stenhouse also suggested disloyalty on the part of Ninnis because he had worked with the New Zealand committee, apparently against Stenhouse's interests. Kinsey, however, found Ninnis a 'very trustworthy and valuable officer, in fact he comprises the whole of our clerical staff'.[62]

Early in July, Kinsey enquired as to the availability of Captain Davis 'in the event of a second vessel being chartered for either Elephant Island or the Ross Sea'.[63] On 18 July, a puzzled Minister of Marine (who supported Stenhouse as master of *Aurora* for the relief expedition) inspected the ship at Port Chalmers and told Stenhouse about this 'ambiguous' communication from Mr Kinsey.[64] According to Stenhouse's later report to Shackleton, McNab asked him if he could give any explanation and said that he and the Secretary of Marine, George Allport, were not in favour of the services of Davis being retained.

Stenhouse was later to tell Shackleton:

> At the time I did not think there was any other meaning in the note as Mr Kinsey had read part of the letter to me. Since then I can understand that this was the means he took to retain the services of Captain Davis and dispense with mine. There were many influences at work of which I knew nothing ... Mr Kinsey told me that the Imperial Trans-Antarctic Expedition had finished as far as the Relief Committee were concerned and that you had nothing to do with the matter.[65]

Kinsey urged that the officer in command of the relief expedition should 'not be under the influence of Mr Mackintosh nor Sir Ernest Shackleton' but should hold direct appointment from the 'various governments undertaking the relief work'. He suggested that Stenhouse 'would have a most difficult position to fill were he in command'.[66] McNab said he needed to be sure that Stenhouse

> be given a status that would ensure his independence of the two gentlemen already mentioned . . . [*Aurora*'s] Commander should only be passed over if we are agreed in the end that the risk of his not being able to maintain his independence is too great. That being decided I am one with you.[67]

Kinsey and Mill advised McNab that Stenhouse should be asked to accept that the expedition was solely one of relief, absolutely under the control of the countries contributing the funds, and that he would abide by instructions and duties assigned. Anticipating that he would be unlikely to agree to these terms, they urged: 'We should not lose an opportunity to secure Davis.'[68]

Initially, Stenhouse seemed to go along with the plan. Kinsey reported to McNab:

> Have had a long and satisfactory chat with Lieutenant Stenhouse . . . So keen is he to work that he offered to go south again under anyone whom we might appoint and have more confidence in than himself. I disabused his mind on the score of want of confidence. I feel relieved that a rather delicate question has been settled.[69]

By 14 August, McNab had decided that Stenhouse be given the command of *Aurora* on the conditions recommended by Kinsey and Mill. He would be responsible to 'the countries contributing the funds' and 'outside his duties as Master of the ship, for the relief of the men at Ross Sea'.[70] The Australian committee did not agree, but any response from Stenhouse was soon overtaken by events.

Arriving in Wellington on 4 August on SS *Boonah*, Davis had written to his father: '*Aurora* fitting out in Dunedin and will I suppose go south under Stenhouse.'[71] However, by 26 August his ship was in Sydney for refitting and Davis continued his filial correspondence: '[*Boonah*] will sail with 1,400 troops for Durban and Europe . . . I may have to go south in the *Aurora* but unless the invitation is a pressing one I do not wish to accept it.'[72]

Davis put his views to Kinsey:

> From what [McNab] said, I gather that you consider Stenhouse may be trusted to carry out the relief successfully. I had only a slight acquaintance with him, and certainly was not impressed with the report of their misfortunes, which to some extent appeared to me to be the result of inexperience and lack of judgement . . . Why this ship did not under the circumstances remain where she was safe and in a position to render assistance requires explanation. To go at this time of the year and in these circumstances back to anchor at C. Evans is to me inexplicable and even a slight acquaintance with the literature of the Ross Sea, would have warned them of the risk involved . . .[73]

The Shackleton Relief Advisory Committee in London now had strong views on the question of the command of *Aurora*. According to Mawson: 'We feel that the relief ought to be placed under the best and most experienced man obtainable; that we owe to the men marooned there, to our governments and to ourselves, and that no other consideration should count.'[74]

The Australian committee said that if Davis were appointed, 'Stenhouse as second in command should suit well for leader of any necessary sledge party'.[75] Kinsey and Mill immediately agreed and further expressed a wish to have Davis posted to Port Chalmers as soon as possible.[76]

On 5 September, Rear Admiral Cresswell offered the command to Davis,[77] who replied: 'If committee consider services necessary and my control is absolute and undivided accepted . . .'[78] Mawson regarded Davis as 'the best man in the world for this specific work'.[79] Three days later, Davis met with the Australian committee in Melbourne and formally accepted command of the relief expedition to the Ross Sea.

All of this was without the concurrence of the New Zealand government. On 11 September, Kinsey explained to the Secretary of Marine: 'We have not compromised ourselves with regard to appointing Stenhouse in command and we have private reasons for not having done so.'[80] A perplexed Allport responded: 'The officer agreed on is Stenhouse, and I cannot agree to change except on very good reason shown.'[81] Kinsey then suggested that the 'misunderstanding could have been avoided if the Australian Government had been advised re Stenhouse. We are not responsible for the telegram sent to the Secretary of State for Colonies . . .'[82] The offending telegram had suggested that Davis be given absolute command of the relief expedition.[83]

Eventually, McNab and the New Zealand government agreed that the relief expedition might be better served by appointing Davis.

When Mawson informed Lady Shackleton of the decision, she replied: 'It came as a great shock for me, for it seemed to me that it should be my husband's privilege and duty to effect the rescue of his own men . . .'[84] She then tried unsuccessfully to persuade the London relief committee to reverse its decision.

Davis's appointment became effective from 26 September. On loan from the Australian navy, he would receive an additional £1 per day.[85] He wrote to his father: 'Shall be just a little glad of a change of work. I do not know if S[hackleton] is coming out or not.'[86]

As late as 21 September, Stenhouse was still under the impression that he would lead the expedition. Writing to Kinsey, he said:

I shall be prepared to leave this port for the Ross Sea on or about November 15th . . . In the event of circumstances arising which will necessitate the despatch of a sledging party, I propose that a party of four men be taken for this special purpose, thus ensuring a safe working crew, for the ship, at all times.[87]

Kinsey did not immediately confront Stenhouse and was anxious that Davis should sign the ship's register as soon as possible.[88] He suggested to McNab that the appointment not be publicised.[89]

However, the news soon reached the notice of reporters. Stenhouse was sitting in the Otago Club, Dunedin, when he read the news of Davis's role in the relief expedition in the *Otago Daily Times* of 4 October.[90] He immediately cabled Kinsey, who confirmed the story and explained that he 'could not break a confidence'.[91]

Stenhouse said he was astounded that 'those entrusted with the affairs of this relief expedition should behave in such an underhand and un-British manner'. He later reported to Shackleton: 'Had I been prepared to humiliate myself and renounce my contract with you there would, in my opinion, have been no change of the command to the *Aurora*.'[92]

McNab officially informed Stenhouse of the decision on 4 October.[93] Stenhouse then cabled Shackleton, suggesting that Kinsey was responsible for endeavouring to frustrate Shackleton's efforts to join the relief expedition.[94] He was only partly correct, as Kinsey was reflecting the unanimous view of the committees in Britain and Australia. Nevertheless, Stenhouse, who had acted honourably throughout, was understandably aggrieved.

CHAPTER TWENTY

Dismissal of Stenhouse

FROM SANTIAGO, Shackleton cabled the governments of Australia and New Zealand to advise that he would personally lead the relief expedition.[1] He also notified the Australian authorities (in a cable that was misdirected and did not arrive for a week): 'Understand your Government has kindly lent Davis services for relief but as can now personally conduct rescue and consider it my duty to do so, will be able to relieve Davis on arrival Sydney. Deeply grateful Australia's consistent help and feel preparations being made will be adequate.'[2] The Australian Prime Minister's office replied on 12 October, advising Shackleton that the 'three governments financing relief expedition have made full arrangements and appointed Captain Davis in full command'.[3]

On 4 October, responding to newspaper reports that Shackleton had announced his intention of proceeding to Australia to take charge of the relief expedition, Davis offered to resign: 'I should not like to feel that my appointment is in any way embarrassing to the committee.'[4] His offer was rejected outright by the Australian committee.[5]

Rear Admiral Cresswell immediately forwarded to Davis a letter confirming his earlier appointment and orders. The committee instructed Davis 'to take control and continue all the preparations being made in refitting the *Aurora* . . . so that the *Aurora* will be ready to sail at the earliest date which, in your judgement, will be most favourable for the work . . . you are to consult with the New Zealand Committee . . .'[6]

However, Stenhouse was still the accredited officer in charge of the ship. A letter in support of Stenhouse, written by Thomson, Hooke and Donnelly to the mayor of Dunedin, was published in that city's newspapers: 'Such an action by those with an intimate knowledge of the Captain's abilities and sentiments is unexplainable . . . We also take exception to the discourteous manner in which this alteration was conveyed to the captain, whom we know to be a worthy leader in danger and difficulty . . .'[7]

Kinsey reported to the Australian committee on the resentment among some members of the ship's complement, to Stenhouse's treatment:

> The news of Davis's appointment having now become public there is, as we expected, some slight sensation. We are sorry to inform you Stenhouse is taking it very unkindly . . . three men – Chief Officer [Thomson], Wireless Operator [Hooke] and Second Engineer [Donnelly] – have also assumed a very antagonistic attitude. It is very foolish of them for we shall stand no nonsense – they will have to go.[8]

Stenhouse was to report to Shackleton that

> All of this party, with the exception of Ninnis, remained loyal to me . . . not only during the long drift but since our arrival at Port Chalmers, since when they have stood by me through all the financial difficulties . . . As Ninnis, in obeying the commands of Mr Kinsey, has ignored my authority, I, as your representative, ordered him to hand over to me all his diaries, photographic negatives and prints, sketches and also my cash books and inventory books; this he has failed to do.[9]

Ninnis, however, maintained that he

> did not know of the letter of protest until I saw it in print and in it I was pointedly ignored . . . it has been suggested that I influenced the affair (which is absurd) and this because I have been in contact with the Committee more than any other individual.[10]

Wellington solicitor Leonard Tripp was in no doubt that Stenhouse had been 'very cruelly treated' and accompanied him to see the Minister of Marine.[11] McNab stated his regret that he had not insisted on all correspondence being made through his office. Stenhouse said: 'I protested against the change in command and the discourteous manner in which it was conveyed to me.'[12] Acting Prime Minister James Allen was also present at the meeting and suggested that Kinsey and Mill were at fault in not informing Stenhouse of Davis's appointment. Tripp later said: 'I must admit it made my blood boil to think that Stenhouse had been so badly treated in New Zealand.'[13]

Stenhouse returned to Dunedin on 10 October, the same day that Davis arrived to take up command of *Aurora*. The following morning Kinsey accompanied Davis to the Custom House and Shipping Office, where the Australian signed on *Aurora*'s register as master, the document asserting that Stenhouse would revert to his original position as first mate.[14]

Stenhouse continued to stand his ground and made it clear to Davis that he (Stenhouse) was under Shackleton's instructions to remain in charge of *Aurora*. On 13 October, Davis wrote to Stenhouse:

> From the conversation I had with you last evening you expressed doubt with regard to the validity of my appointment to the command of the S.Y. *Aurora*, and I requested you to put your doubt in writing which you have failed to do. I therefore now inform you that with approval of the Secretary of State and the Governments

of the Commonwealth and New Zealand I have assumed command of the Relief Expedition. I require and direct you to resume forthwith your position as Chief Officer of the vessel.[15]

Davis visited Wellington the following day and discussed matters with the Minister of Marine.

Stenhouse received instructions from Shackleton on 15 October: 'On no consideration sign any document official or otherwise relating to ship or finance connected with ship you have no authority from my attorneys to do so. This may appear cryptic to you but will explain when we meet. I appreciate your consistent loyalty.'[16]

Tripp wrote to Stenhouse: 'You must remember the three governments are behind the committee. Don't have any row with Davis because it is not his fault.'[17] He wrote further:

> A gentleman came to see me who knows Shackleton very well . . . He considers that the Admiralty and the Australian Government have made up their minds independently that Shackleton shall not have the command of the expedition; the reason being that Shackleton is considered a bad financier and starts on his expeditions without sufficient capital, and in consequence the money has to be found by some Government or other . . . I am told that Davis would welcome Shackleton, and would be only too glad to have him on board to take command of the shore party . . .
>
> It seems to me that in any case you should go down with the boat in some capacity or other. I feel satisfied that if you talk the matter over with Davis you should be able to arrange something which would be satisfactory to yourself. When one realises that the Admiralty are insisting on having Davis, it is not good kicking against the pricks. Davis is a good man, and from what I am told he is a man you would like.[18]

Meanwhile, Tripp contacted representatives of the Merchant Service Guild, who suggested to McNab that Shackleton travel south in charge of the shore party, which should include Stenhouse.[19]

In a letter to Stenhouse, supporter and businessman Arthur Mabin explained: 'It is difficult to assess the undercurrents at work . . . the action of the authorities seems directed against Shackleton not you . . . you must go slow and do nothing to compromise yourself.'[20]

On 17 October, Davis purportedly dismissed Thomson, Donnelly and Hooke, citing 'mutual consent and with my sanction, they having failed to attend the shipping office at the appointed time'.[21] Stenhouse had countermanded the instruction to so attend.[22] On the same day, Davis reported to Cresswell:

. . . saw Mr Stenhouse and urged him to realise that the position he was adopting was in direct conflict with the interests of those in the Antarctic, whom he professed to be concerned about, and indicated that he must either resume his duties as Chief Officer, or I should have to take steps to replace him.[23]

Following Shackleton's instructions, Stenhouse replied that he was 'duty bound' to retain ownership of *Aurora*: '. . . my plain duty is to remain in command of the ship until officially notified of my owner's desire to have me superseded.'[24]

Davis cited Cresswell's orders and responded: 'I gather that you do not recognise the right of the representative of the Governments who are paying you to give you directions. I am regretfully obliged to recommend to the Committee that your services be dispensed with immediately.'[25] Stenhouse then locked the ship and refused to hand over the keys to Davis.[26] Kinsey took steps to stop payment of wages to Stenhouse.[27]

The stand-off reached crisis point on 19 October when Stenhouse again refused to hand over the ship and Davis broke the locks.[28] He sent Thomson, Donnelly and Hooke on their way. Hooke later told Stenhouse: 'Sincerely trust that leaving does not seem like desertion.'[29]

Shackleton sent yet another cable to Stenhouse: 'I order you remain in command of my steamer *Aurora* until you receive further advice from me. Retain first class legal assistance for advice but you must not give up command without my permission. Appreciate officers loyalty.'[30] Stenhouse conveyed Shackleton's instructions to Davis and notified Kinsey and Mill that he was unable to recognise their right to dispense with his services. He requested the return of the ship's register.[31]

A few days later, a frustrated Shackleton railed in a cable to the *Daily Chronicle*'s Ernest Perris about 'the damned impertinence of Australia and the cheek of Davis and that bloody old fool Kinsey'.[32]

Both the Davis camp, backed by the governments funding the relief expedition, and the Stenhouse camp, backed by Shackleton, had a strong claim to control of the expedition's ship, *Aurora*. Stenhouse was the innocent victim of the two factions.

Davis had been plucked out of the war effort to rescue a party that he thought should never have gone south in the first place. He had agreed, but on his terms: his position as leader was not to be compromised and he was to have absolute command of the relief expedition.

Stenhouse's authority was founded on his appointment as first officer of *Aurora*. He took his directions from the legal owner of the ship, until June through Shackleton's attorneys, and thereafter from Shackleton himself. However, Sir Ernest could only enforce his legal position if he had the financial wherewithal to pay creditors and fund the relief expedition, which he did not. He therefore had little choice but to agree with what Davis and his instructing governments directed.

The three governments faced a legal difficulty in that they were not the owners of the ship they had commandeered, even though they had 'right' on their side as the financiers. To avoid public embarrassment, it was desirable that they reach agreement with Shackleton.

Early in November, Sir Ernest was about to leave San Francisco for New Zealand when he was alerted by Stenhouse to suggestions that *Aurora* might sail before he arrived, a position suggested by the Australian committee but resisted by Davis. Shackleton then instructed Leonard Tripp in Wellington to act for him and, if necessary, to put an embargo on the ship.[33]

Wishing to keep a low profile, the solicitor cabled Stenhouse in Dunedin: 'Don't let anyone know that I am asked to act in a legal capacity.'[34] After visiting Davis and telling him of Shackleton's planned arrival in Wellington on 29 November, Tripp then informed Stenhouse:

> It will be no use for Shackleton to try and dictate terms. He must use tact, otherwise he will be stopped going altogether . . . [He] should accept the inevitable. He can take charge of the shore party. What I want to work is that you go with him . . . There has never been any suggestion of getting the ship away so as to block Shackleton from going . . . what we want is to avoid friction and satisfy everyone. Technically of course the ship is Shackleton's.[35]

In England, Sir Douglas Mawson alleged that 'the obstructive tactics of Shackleton and his agents [were] delaying the necessary work and are viewed with grave dissatisfaction'.[36]

A conference in London on 7 November, attended by William Massey and Sir Joseph Ward for New Zealand, the Australian High Commissioner (former Prime Minister Andrew Fisher) and representatives of the Admiralty and Colonial Office, shared Mawson's view. In response to Shackleton's announcement that he would assume command of the relief expedition, the conference delegates told him that either he must fund the whole enterprise or accept the authority of Davis and the relief expedition. They suggested that he could, if Captain Davis approved, travel south as a passenger, subject to signing an agreement to 'loyally accept and abide by [Davis's] command'. No embargo would be placed on publication by Shackleton of the story of the rescue expedition.[37]

On 8 November, Tripp cabled Shackleton en route to New Zealand:

Davis saw me last week on his way to Australia. He spoke very nicely of you and told me he felt hurt, because being a friend of yours, you had not cabled him from South America, although you had cabled Stenhouse. I told him that you probably did not understand the position and felt some diffidence at cabling thinking that the committee were working against you.[38]

Stenhouse reported to Tripp that he found himself 'an interested inspector [on *Aurora*] with little to say in any matter as everything had to be referred to Mr Kinsey'.[39] In seeking 'first class legal assistance' on Shackleton's advice, he turned to the Dunedin barrister A. C. Hanlon, who had acted for Stenhouse in respect of charges against Shaw and D'Anglade some months earlier.[40]

Davis sought to blame Stenhouse for recent events. Writing to Shackleton, his former leader on the *Nimrod* expedition, he stated: 'I quite appreciate your position. Any unpleasantness that has arisen is due to the fact that Mr Stenhouse has adopted a position which made it necessary for me to replace him.'[41] Davis also wrote to his father:

Shackleton is arriving at Wellington on December 2 and I suppose will come down with us. The difficulty has been that the Governments wish to retain control . . . I thought a way out would be found for me when it was certain Shackleton was coming out but this does not now seem likely . . . I consider the matter will be adjusted between Shackleton and the governments amicably.[42]

Accompanied by Frank Worsley, former skipper of *Endurance*, Shackleton arrived in Wellington on SS *Moana* on 2 December.[43] He expected that the New Zealand-born Worsley would be part of the relief expedition.[44] Tripp greeted them from the pilot boat, and Minister of Marine McNab, Stenhouse and the mayor of Wellington, J. P. Luke, were at the wharf.

Shackleton informed McNab that because funds had been spent on reconditioning the ship without his consent, he would not be liable for this and added that both the New Zealand Solicitor-General and C. P. Skerrett, KC, a partner in Tripp's law firm, had advised that he was legally entitled to take charge of the ship.[45]

McNab's plan was for Shackleton to go down as a passenger on *Aurora*, with Stenhouse and Worsley accompanying him. Sir Ernest was, according to Tripp, 'all out for a fight' but recognised 'this is a question of saving life' and nothing must prevent the ship's leaving in the following few weeks. Shackleton said he would agree to Davis's taking *Aurora* south so long as he took charge when they got ashore, and Stenhouse and Worsley accompanied him.[46]

McNab met with Davis and pressed strongly for Stenhouse's inclusion in the party, noting that he had acted loyally to his leader throughout, but Davis would have nothing of it. Stenhouse and Worsley then withdrew from contention as members of the party after the minister promised them a first-class passage to England and that the New Zealand government would meet the wages of Stenhouse and his men who had been standing by the ship.

An Australian inquiry in May 1916 into the outfitting of *Aurora* at the Commonwealth Naval Dockyard in 1914 had found that expenditure exceeded the amount authorised by almost £3,000.[47] The manager of the dockyard explained that 'the vessel ... was found [to be] ... in a very bad condition ... it became a question of not what to do, but what not to do ... we were being squeezed by the ship's officers at every turn to do this and that, and we in our turn had to constantly choke them off ...'[48]

In 1916, the Australian government, still smarting over the *Aurora* budget blow-out, initially saw the deficit as 'a claim which it may be possible to exercise if it be necessary to do so'. Kinsey urged the Australian committee to agree to the return of the ship to Shackleton, noting that the New Zealand Solicitor-General had said 'we have to do it by law'.[49]

In order to settle the ongoing dispute, the New Zealand government pressed its British and Australian counterparts to have *Aurora* handed back to Shackleton after the relief voyage, free of any claims. On 15 December, the Australian government agreed with the proposal, as did the British three days later.[50] Shackleton thereupon signed up to sail south under Davis's command.[51]

As a further distraction for Shackleton, on his arrival in New Zealand he received a demand for £5,000 to meet wages due to the men of the Weddell Sea party. This sum was quickly raised with the assistance of Tripp. Contributors received a stuffed penguin as a memento and were to be, and in fact were, repaid on the sale of the ship.[52]

The ownership impasse had held up the loading of *Aurora*, causing a frustrated Davis to threaten to resign. With the impasse resolved through McNab's intervention, loading resumed and Davis agreed to Shackleton's request to postpone sailing until 20 December.

In finalising instructions to Davis, the Minister of Marine advised:

> The ship is placed under your command. The members of Sir Ernest Shackleton's expedition have to be relieved, and you will carry out such work with the *Aurora* as will, in your opinion, bring about the best results in the end ... Your position as Captain of the ship makes you, by Act of Parliament, censor of all news by wireless.[53]

Davis reported to his father:

> Shackleton is as far as I know coming down in the *Aurora* as a passenger. He will lead any sledge journey that may be necessary ... I shall not leave the *Aurora* ... the

Governments have declined to alter their arrangements and so I suppose that
Shackleton is not feeling too pleased about things. As however I have nothing to
do with the arrangements and should certainly not agree to accepting the responsibility unless given absolute control I do not anticipate any difficulty . . .[54]

By late December 1916, after weeks of politicking and controversy, the
relief expedition was ready to leave. McNab, in company with Worsley and
Stenhouse, escorted Shackleton in the ministerial carriage from Port Chalmers
to Dunedin, where the mayor hosted a civic reception.[55]

Back at the port, in the face of McNab's opposition and just hours before
Aurora sailed, Shackleton insisted that he 'sign on', thereby making it clear to
everyone on board that Davis was in command of the ship. However, when
Kinsey cabled the Australian committee that 'Davis will navigate the ship and
Shackleton take charge of shore operations at destination',[56] this led the Australians to fear the 'expedition had sailed under divided control in spite of the
efforts of this committee and the decision of the governments'.[57]

As officers on the relief voyage, Davis had called on old hands who had
been with him on *Aurora* during Mawson's expedition, appointing C. de la
Motte as chief officer (at £24 per month) and F. Gillies as chief engineer (£36
16s), both then serving on SS *Talawa* with the Australian Transport Service.[58]

Morton Moyes, who had also served on the Mawson expedition, was
seconded on full pay from the Royal Australian Navy, where he was a navigation instructor. He would recall over six decades later: 'I got a shock when the
signal came from the Navy Board and I was seconded to naval duties.'[59] His role
was to be navigator for any sledge journeys that might have to be undertaken.

Three men who had been on the ship during the drift of 1915–16 were
re-enlisted: James Paton as boatswain; Howard Ninnis as paymaster and
photographer (Davis described him as purser); and William ('Ginger') Kavanagh
as a seaman. Another, Lionel Hooke, having offered his services, withdrew in
protest at Stenhouse's treatment.[60]

Davis obtained the release by the Australian Transport Service of Arthur
Dakin as second engineer and Timothy Ryan as wireless operator, both having
served with Davis on SS *Boonah*. Davis regarded Ryan as 'well suited, physically
and temperamentally'.[61]

The shortage of medical personnel through war duties resulted in the
appointment of Frederick George Middleton, a fourth-year medical student
at Melbourne University, as the ship's doctor:

. . . the idea was first mooted at Dr Griffith Taylor's on Sat. Nov. 18th 1916,
Melbourne Cup Day . . . while there having afternoon tea, Capt. Davis . . . came in,
and it was jokingly suggested that I join the expedition. Nothing was again said

till Monday evening 20th inst. when Dr Taylor rang me up and offered me the position of surgeon to the party.[62]

Having sat his medical examination, Middleton travelled with other Australian members of the relief party on SS *Manuka* from Sydney to Wellington, where he met McNab and Davis, and thence to Dunedin and Port Chalmers.[63]

Arriving at Port Chalmers on 22 November, Chief Engineer Gillies, 'responsible for the general working, efficiency and cleanliness of his department', was far from happy with the condition of the ship: 'Found engine room and engines in a very dirty condition. Engines are a mass of rust.' A day later, painting began in the engine room, a new wireless engine and dynamo were soon in place and, on 1 December, the engineering firm of Stevenson and Cooke installed a reconditioned boiler.[64] When the ship was fumigated, a large number of rats were found.[65]

A load of 497 tons of 'Best Navy Westport' coal was taken on board to supplement the 30 tons there.[66] The ship's four chronometers were inspected, lighting circuit batteries were charged and the wireless equipment was test run. A full set of Antarctic clothing was issued to members of the relief expedition. This included three khaki shirts, three woollen underpants and long-sleeved singlets, six pairs of woollen socks, a woollen cap, a pair of heavy boots and another of knee-high sea boots, a woollen sweater, two pairs of woollen mitts and one of leather mitts.[67]

Although *Aurora* was due to sail at 6 a.m. on 16 December, the task of refitting and reprovisioning delayed her departure for a further four days.[68]

On 13 December, Austin Le Gros signed on as second officer.[69] Born in Jersey, he had entered the Merchant Service in 1903 and the Australian Government Service in February 1916.[70] W. Aylward, a 21-year-old from Auckland who had trained and served with the Union Steam Ship Company, was appointed *Aurora*'s third officer.

Other crew included Alexander Webster from Dunedin as chief steward, Baden Robertson (Melbourne) as second steward, Henry Voegeli (Liverpool) as cook, M. Hannan (Liverpool) as donkeyman, and William Peacock (Llangefni, Wales) as an able seaman.[71] Three of the seamen were Scots: Malcolm MacNeill from Barra in the Western Isles, and Ewen MacDonald and Alasdair Mackinnon, both from Skye.[72] Also signed up were seaman C. Brock and firemen T. Rafferty, E. Murphy and T. Smith.[73]

At 11 a.m. on 20 December, in overcast and calm weather, *Aurora* left Port Chalmers on her voyage to rescue the Ross Sea party, whose fate was still unknown to the world in general. The ship was flying the Blue Ensign with the burgee of the Royal Clyde Yacht Club, evidence that she was Shackleton's yacht, according to his first biographer.[74] McNab and local dignitaries accompanied *Aurora* down the harbour on the tug *Plucky*. Later that day, the minister cabled Tripp: 'I saw the vessel away this morning . . . Shackleton greatly pleased with news and in excellent spirits.'[75] McNab, whose assiduous work had brought about a satisfactory outcome, also issued a confident press statement:

> The *Aurora* goes south practically the best equipped Antarctic exploration vessel that has ever sailed. No money has been spared in regard to the work . . . it only remains for me to wish Captain Davis, Sir Ernest Shackleton, and the sturdy officers and men of the *Aurora* success in their mission.[76]

CHAPTER TWENTY-ONE

'Marooned on a desert island'

SOON AFTER their arrival at Cape Evans on 15 July 1916, Richards, Joyce and Wild each had 'a good bath';[1] for Wild, his first in 300 days. Other luxuries abounded. Wild wrote: 'I killed a sea-leopard last week, the first one we have seen. We ate its tongue and it was delicious. We have only to fry flippers and brains now and then we've tried the lot. It's a treat getting vegetables and sauces again . . .'[2]

Seal meat continued to be a staple item of diet, in addition to penguins and some small fish. Joyce, Wild, Richards, Gaze and Jack maintained a daily look-out for seals and hunted the animals as a morning routine. Jack made two 'blubber hooks', and dog teams were used to haul the carcasses to North Cape, where blubber was placed in a depot. With the possibility of their spending another winter in Antarctica, the men tried to procure as many seals as possible. According to Joyce, the blubber from one seal provided enough fuel for five days, though Stevens maintained that about 40 seals were required for two months in winter.[3]

The seals were concealed by the winter darkness on the open sea ice, and Gaze would recall that 'the only place we'd go, was around the tide cracks, between the sea ice and the land, often walk[ing] five or six miles before breakfast'.[4]

The men could not escape the grease and filth of their existence. Richards later wrote:

We had no soap for most of the time and no change of clothes . . . you went out in darkness, you cut their throats and the blood splattered all over you as they squirmed around and you simply couldn't keep things clean it was shocking. Unless you'd experienced it you couldn't realise it.[5]

He also described the hunting rituals, which resulted in the killing of over 140 seals in 1916:[6]

We usually worked in teams of two. In my case, it was Tubby Wild. He used the cargo hook and I the flensing knife. We became expert at ripping off blubber in double quick time – laying the slabs of blubber on the ice and coming out for it the next day – loading [it] onto a sledge in the form of planks of blubber, and then cutting it into squares with an axe . . . We weren't worried about the possibility of reducing the number of seals.[7]

Wild manufactured new canvas trousers and washed old clothes in petrol.[8] Gaze maintained the acetylene plant, and most hands shared in general duties of collecting ice for the daily supply of water from a berg stranded off Cape Evans, regular sweeping out of the hut and tidying of the galley. A wheelbarrow was made to move ice from the annex to the galley.[9]

Bags of 'oil cake', taken south by Scott's expedition in 1910 as food for the ponies, were excavated from the ice and used as fuel to supplement the blubber.[10] Coal, too, was used in this way from occasional lumps found buried under the scoria in the vicinity of the cache landed there from *Aurora* the previous season.[11]

Blubber soot and grease permeated every part of the hut and the belongings of its inhabitants. To maintain heat the men nailed sacks on the inside of the windows and boarded over the outside. Joyce and Stevens on occasions slept in a tent they erected near the meteorological screen in order to escape the pungent smoke.[12] Jack went to the trouble of stitching a sack around the backrest of his chair to obtain a small degree of comfort.

The men, often with the exception of Cope, generally ate their meals together around the galley stove. At times this glowed red hot, but the hut remained a cold place in midwinter.[13] The gramophone donated to the Ross Sea party by HMV in London was put to good use, the short-term transfer of this device from *Aurora* before it was blown away giving a degree of pleasure to the castaways.[14] Spirited arguments were conducted on subjects such as the war in Europe, and Darwin's *Origin of Species*.[15] Without a sledging programme to prepare for, there was little urgency to do anything. Some of the men made canvas clothing,[16] while others went out in search of seals.

Sugar was rationed to fourteen pounds per person, to last until January 1917, and this became a popular trading commodity.[17] Gaze would recall: 'We used to play bridge for sugar.'[18] Jack confined his daily usage to eight lumps.[19]

Moving through the soot-begrimed hut a few days after his return, Richards heard Cope calling from his cubicle: 'Thieves, murderers! Thieves, murderers!' Richards responded: 'Hello, Copey, what's wrong?' 'Oh, Richie, nothing wrong,' came the reply.[20]

Cope was, at least temporarily, deranged and had lost spirit. Gaze attributed his companion's condition to the disappearance of *Aurora*[21] and would recall many years later: 'There was only one man who gave up and I won't name him. He was in his bed and we couldn't get him out of it.'[22] What is more, he 'never took off any of his clothes the whole time down there. Anything he could get he would put on . . . He lost his bundle altogether.'[23]

Richards confirmed that Cope 'was not responsible for his behaviour'.[24] Stevens wrote: 'What he would allow, was done for him in the way of cooking and attention but he was very difficult.'[25] In more lucid moments, Cope proposed an expedition of his own, using the depots the party had laid.

Con, the Samoyed lead dog and veteran of the Mt Hope journey, was attacked by the other dogs and died ten days after the return to Cape Evans. Jack wrote a tribute: 'Con had a character all of his own. An aristocratic looking dog in appearance, white almost in colour the Samoyed. Of slight build yet he was strong and wiry and a great favourite with all and always ready for work.'[26] These sentiments were echoed by Richards, Wild and Joyce, who recognised that without the four dogs the journey to Mt Hope could have ended in complete disaster.

On 16 August, the first rays of the sun skimming Mt Erebus and the Western Mountains across McMurdo Sound heralded the end of what Jack described as 'the perpetual darkness of the dismal winter'. It was an opportunity to celebrate. Stevens and Wild, with the help of a recipe from *Encyclopaedia Britannica* and recognising the opportunities that a providential supply of yeast in the hut offered, succeeded in making a brew of beer and laced it with pure alcohol intended for scientific specimens.[27] This concoction made for a grand party. Wild, one of the ringleaders of the festivity, noted: 'We were all tight after a few drinks. I don't know how we shall get on when we get back to "Civvy".'[28] Richards recalled: 'I remember Gaze who was rather a dignified sort of bloke, about three in the morning . . . tearing up to his bunk . . . yelling, "Come to bed, Richards" . . . Joyce went to sleep on a pile of tins.'[29] On another occasion he recalled: 'We really got plastered, dogs included.'[30] A week later the men again sampled the brew. Jack remarked: 'Stronger than expected resulting in a high degree of conviviality.'[31]

Wild damaged his ankle in mid-August and was laid up for a month. Richards, his companion in the escapade that led to the injury, recalled:

> We sometimes sewed three ply to the seat of our home made canvas trousers and used this as a sort of self-contained toboggan to slide down snow slopes. This particular morning Wild and I had gone up the ramp and Wild after sliding down hit a rock and broke a bone in his foot. It was pretty cold and I did not fancy leaving him there while I got help so I carried him back to the hut. I was pretty debilitated after the scurvy of the sledging journey and collapsed shortly after . . .[32]

Wild himself reported: 'Luckily nothing was broken. I half crawled, & half walked, halfway back & Richards carried me the other half.'[33]

Cope diagnosed the damage as a sprain[34] and it did not stop Wild from hobbling outside on 25 August 'to see the sun for the first time'. He added: 'Our faces are pretty yellow. I hope this is the last winter down here.'

Wild's mishap meant there were fewer men for sealing duties. The dogs, however, assisted as hides and blubber were hauled in by sledge, the pups at first learning their role in harness alongside the old hands Gunner, Towser, and Oscar.

On 23 August, Richards, Gaze and Joyce made a return trip to Shackleton's hut at Cape Royds. Jack remarked: 'Splendid change of food tonight. Bacon, fish, chicken, plum pudding, jelly etc.'[35]

Several weeks later, on 10 September, Richards fell seriously ill while returning with Jack from a cold afternoon's sealing at Turk's Head Glacier:

> Richards taken with a heart attack yesterday. Felt it come on when out with me in afternoon. Noticed that he was much inclined to lag behind and this seemed the more strange since the temperature was very low; but he said nothing. He was complaining of the cold right up to time when he got into bed. Some little time later he was attacked by quelling and got me to call Cope who gave him NH₂Br. This morn[ing] Cope sounded him with a stethoscope and according to Richards his heart gives 5 or 6 regular beats and then an irregular feeble one.[36]

Cope, however, was to make no mention of such a condition in his medical report on the party.

Within a week Richards had recovered sufficiently to accompany the others with a seven-dog team to bring in ice and blubber, but he 'did not attempt to do anything'.[37] On 22 September, he suffered a further attack and was moved into 'Scott's old bunk'. Cope tended to him assiduously and Richards' illness re-established his colleague to some degree as a functioning member of the party:

> [Cope] refused to eat with them. I don't know why and he used to get up in the middle of the night and make Trumilk . . . he was absolutely marvellous to me. You see for one thing they used to send up food – I was in Scott's bunk, I didn't eat and I'd say to Cope – 'Look Copey will you take it and will you eat it, because I don't want to send it back to those chaps and not have eaten it.' I thought I might be doing a good turn to Copey because he was like a rake. He hadn't been eating and from then on he recovered.[38]

When Richards' health deteriorated further on 8 October, Cope repositioned his bed adjacent to the patient's bunk to monitor him more closely. He administered digitalis and strychnine, standard medicines held by the party for the treatment of heart conditions. Gaze wrote in his diary: 'Digitalis increases force and regularity of heart beat, but lessens rate. Strychnine sulphate. Heart failure.'[39]

Jack reflected the party's concern: 'Richards has been in a state of utter frustration all afternoon and remains so this evening . . . sincerely hope nothing serious eventuates from this . . .'[40]

Richards was now at his lowest and his illness showed itself increasingly as an emotional nervous disorder. It was as if he were suffering from the affliction of First World War soldiers that became known as shell shock. 'Poor chap is very nervous of himself. No place for a man to be laid up,' wrote Jack,[41] indicating that the illness was something more than physical.

According to Gaze, Richards 'had to watch what he did very carefully. [He] couldn't take [any] risk of undue exertion.'[42] Cope spent many hours sitting by his friend's bed holding his wrist and checking him with a stethoscope.[43] Later, Richards readily acknowledged a debt of gratitude for the 'unremitting care [Cope] gave me when I was seriously ill'.[44]

He slowly improved, however, and got up for the first time on 7 October, walking with the aid of a stick. Jack wrote: 'Was surprised to see him come out to me at [the] hole in the ice about 100 yards from the hut. He is very weak and walks with great care.'[45] By mid-November, in addition to assisting Jack and Stevens in light scientific duties, Richards was taking some light exercise. There had been some talk of his joining Wild and Joyce on a sledge journey to explore the ranges around Shackleton Inlet, but Richards' illness ruled that out.[46] In any case, given the distance contemplated (in excess of 500 miles) and the expectation that a rescue ship would appear, it seems most unlikely that this trip would have eventuated.

At Joyce's suggestion, the recuperating Richards copied out his companion's sledging diary. He later recalled: 'When I first read [Joyce's] diary at Cape Evans, I at times used to blink and wonder whether I was there or not.'[47] Richards fondly remembered Joyce as an endearing yet larger-than-life character, who 'should have lived at the time of Drake. He was a bit of a buccaneer.'[48]

The *Nimrod* expedition hut at Cape Royds, five miles from Cape Evans, had been visited only occasionally during Scott's second expedition.[49] Scott himself had seemed rather disdainful of the place, writing on 23 May 1911: 'It seemed to me much less inviting than our old Discovery hut at C. Armitage. There was nothing to detain us and we started back, the only useful articles added to our weights being a scrap or two of leather and five hymn books.'[50]

Norwegian Tryggve Gran had a different view. On 30 July, he made a solo return trip on ski and recorded: 'I have set foot on historic ground; I have today been on a skiing trip to Cape Royds . . .' In the latter days of the Scott expedition, Cape Royds became a 'sort of place for outings', according to Gran.[51]

In the spring of 1916, with some of the survivors of the Ross Sea party looking for a change of scene and desiring home comforts, Shackleton's old hut became a second base. Situated beside the world's southernmost Adélie penguin rookery, it provided a valuable source of food.

On 7 October, Gaze, Wild, Joyce and Stevens travelled to the hut, Joyce staying there until 11 December. Over this period Gaze made several return trips, ferrying to Cape Evans at least six loads of stores, including soap and matches. Stevens returned by himself to Cape Evans on 9 October. Over a month later, on 12 November, he accompanied Wild back to Cape Royds to collect penguin embryos 'for a friend in Scotland'.[52] While there, he experimented with the late Padre's cinematograph. Stevens and Wild returned to Cape Evans on 30 November.

Jack had a change of scene, too, travelling to Cape Royds with Gaze on 23 October and returning with Wild on 5 November. While there he attempted to locate a 'grooved boulder mentioned by [Professor Edgeworth] David indicating direction of ice movement'. Three days later he was hunting for 'a granite rock described by [Raymond] Priestley and David at head of Backdoor Bay'. The following day he found the 'raised beach described by Priestley and David at head of Backdoor Bay'. During this sojourn he was troubled with neuralgia and a tooth abscess, to which he applied 'three mustard plasters'.[53]

Adélie penguins started to arrive at Cape Royds rookery on 16 October,[54] and Joyce and Wild began plundering the eggs on 9 November. Wild noted that over the next month they collected 3,150 eggs. 'Everybody likes them very much. 348 was the most we got in one day.'[55] The eggs were fried in butter and were much appreciated by Jack:

> Tonight we had what to me is the most civilised dinner for nearly two years namely, fresh-boiled penguin eggs and bacon – I caused three eggs to disappear rapidly – a thing I have never in my life accomplished before, and others managed as many as four . . .[56]

Gaze took about 30 dozen eggs back to Cape Evans for the recuperating Richards and Cope on 17 November, and returned to Cape Royds the following day.

Skua eggs were also welcome. Wild wrote: 'I got the first skua's egg on the 3rd December. They are very good too (when they are fresh).'[57] Nor were emperor penguins spared, with some 50 birds being taken over the two-month period, including nineteen on one day alone.[58]

The Cape Royds hut, designed as a temporary shelter and draughty and cold at the best of times, nevertheless represented something of an oasis of Edwardian civilisation. A portrait of the late King Edward VII and Queen Alexandra adorned the wall, boxes of food and provisions lay about, and there was a refreshing cleanness to the place. Unlike the two bases to the south, the grime of soot from seal-blubber fires was absent.

The men repositioned roughly constructed beds from Shackleton's day in front of the Mrs Sam coal range, which they fuelled with wood from packing cases and also blubber. A canvas screen created a semblance of confinement and comfort in the large room, despite the absence of an outer door.

Joyce, who had had some experience in taxidermy before the *Nimrod* expedition, skinned a large number of penguins and seals. To advertise his trade, he used ink left over from the printing of *Aurora Australis* (the first Antarctic-produced book, published at Cape Royds in 1908) to daub on an inside wall of the hut the words: 'Joyce's Skining [*sic*] Academy Free.'[59]

On 11 December, Joyce, Gaze and Wild left Cape Royds for what would be the last time, leaving boxes of specimens in the hope that they could be retrieved when a relief ship arrived.

As daylight returned to Cape Evans in the latter months of 1916, Stevens and Jack undertook scientific work.

> The day is fully occupied from breakfast up till eleven and twelve at night, there are hourly readings to be attended to during this period, in addition to the usual four hourly observations day and night.[60]

They observed the aurora australis and the drift of the plume from the crater of Mt Erebus, and studied ice phenomena, soil temperatures, the tidal range, sea currents and marine life. Jack's improvised equipment included a tripod from which blocks of ice were suspended and weighed at intervals, stakes for lake-ice ablation measurements, an evaporimeter for use 'when the lake ice thaws out', a self-recording tide gauge and a sea-current indicator. In addition, the anemograph and the lighting circuit required constant attention.[61] Gaze would recall: '[Jack] was always making things – it was marvellous what he could do.'[62]

Richards was of the opinion that 'Cope mucked around with a microscope and beasties he got out of the soil and lake but did not do much. As things turned out we dropped most things but Jack carried on with a few projects.'[63]

Jack's ablation studies indicated that daily evaporation from the lake surface in winter was about 0.1 millimetre, and that the spring-tide range of about 125 centimetres was in agreement with observations from the *Discovery*, *Nimrod* and *Terra Nova* expeditions.[64]

The men at Cape Evans had a further sledging mission – to visit the Padre's grave, a journey especially important for his cousin Irvine Gaze. Jack, 'with a little help' from Gaze made a cross from timber found around the hut to put on the grave.[65]

Gazee also set about making a second, larger cross for Wind Vane Hill to commemorate the loss of Mackintosh and Hayward, and Jack designed an inscription intended to be carved on this.[66]

Joyce, Wild and Gaze, with six dogs, set out on a short sledge journey on 17 December. Wild wrote:

> We are bringing out a cross to put over Smithy's grave, then we are going on to the depot where we left all our spare gear and Mt Hope stones. After that to Cape Crozier to see what there is to see and then back. We don't want to be left at H[u]t P[oin]t again for another winter. We shall search between Ht Pt [and] Cape Evans for traces of Mackintosh and Haywood [*sic*] . . .[67]

The dog team included two veterans of the journey to Mt Hope – Oscar and Gunboat – plus the younger Blackie, Peddlar, Pup and The Bitch. All the old problems recurred. The sledge was 'far heavier than anticipated' on a poor surface with the dogs not co-operating. The party had to camp the first night four miles short of Hut Point, which they reached the next morning and retrieved a shovel. A considerable quantity of snow had found its way into the hut, and Gaze, noting that there was blubber everywhere, mused: 'Pity the poor blighters who have to spend another winter there.'[68]

Once on the Barrier, the dogs gradually settled down, with Joyce going ahead to break the trail. At Safety Camp an unsuccessful search was made for sugar. Gaze noted: 'There should be 2 boxes I believe – suppose they're buried under the snow.'

In contrast to the sledging journeys of the previous season, on this occasion each man had a pair of skis, but they discarded two pairs at Safety Camp, leaving one set only for the lead person. Within a day Wild was regretting the decision. 'I now wish we had brought them. They would have been all right on this surface.'[69] That night, because of the poor conditions, the party camped just two and a half miles past Safety Camp.

Joyce, Wild and Gaze had expected to reach the Padre's grave within a further half-day, but they missed it in thick weather and instead came upon the more southerly Cope's No. 2 depot, established in the first season. This was just six miles short of the depot of gear jettisoned by the Mt Hope party in their desperate retreat the previous season. This they reached at lunchtime on 22 December. Joyce went down a crevasse to his waist, and Gaze observed that 'the dogs didn't like the look of things at all; specially Oscar and the Pups'.

The party was in the vicinity of where Mackintosh had been left alone before being rescued in heroic circumstances nine months earlier. Wild noted with understated pride: 'That makes it 40 miles from H[u]t P[oin]t to where we left the Skipper last March and we brought him in, in 4 days and a bit. Not bad going that.'[70]

The depots could now be raided with impunity, as Shackleton's party had failed to arrive from the south. Gaze wrote:

> Did our trip to Joyce's depot (lunched there) and are now camped at No. 2 depot again. Only saw one crevasse; it's remarkable how the place changes, the last time I passed here it was riddled with the rotters. Beautiful day – rather too warm in afternoon. Am . . . picking up 30 lbs sugar . . . this depletes the depot bar for one bag of pemmican and 3 bags of salt.[71]

The party reached the Padre's grave in beautiful weather in midmorning, 23 December. They found a note, apparently left by Hayward, containing a simple and poetic message: 'Beneath this cross lies the Rev. A. P. Spencer-Smith who died here Mar. 9 1916 on the return journey from Mt Hope.'

Gaze remarked upon the irony of this:

> I don't suppose poor old Hayward thought he himself was going to 'peg out' within a couple of months when he wrote this little note. It seems very hard to me that poor old AP should have got so close to home, and then to just miss it – anyway, everyone spoke in the highest praise as to how he stuck it; was always cheerful in spite of the fact he'd been on his back for a month . . .[72]

Wild wrote:

> We got to Smith's grave at 10.40 a.m. Joyce had a dish up with the cooking gear, while Gaze and I built a large cairn and put the cross on top. It is 4 miles 1210 yards from No 2 Depot. We are on our way to Crozier now. Gaze and Joyce both took a couple of photos.[73]

It was the last time the grave was to be seen. A clue as to how quickly it would have been buried in snow is contained in Gaze's diary of 27 December 1916:

> We came upon our old Corner Camp that Joyce, Keith [Jack] and self laid last Jan[uar]y 12 months – this is the first time we've seen it since then having used

a course closer to W[hite] Island. There must have been a lot of snow, as only the pole is visible; the big cairn long gone.

The party had also intended to travel to Cape Crozier, but they were held up because of bad weather until Christmas Day. Gaze recorded: 'The going was so heavy ... all three of us were pulling ... [but] we only managed just 4 miles for the afternoon (3 hours).'[74]

Progress was worse on Boxing Day and, after a half-mile of travel, the men decided to head back to base. Gaze expressed their sentiments:

> None of us liked to abandon the trip, but it would have meant at least 8 or 9 days of heartbreaking pulling and we are out for pleasure not graft ... I wonder if Father and Mother have been to the races today? I hope they've had good luck if they have.[75]

After little progress the next day, a south-west wind enabled them to erect a sail. They reached Safety Camp on 29 December and Hut Point the following day, where they spent time collecting rocks and taking photographs.

Leaving Hut Point for what would be the last time, they spent New Year's Eve camped beside Glacier Tongue, near hundreds of seals, but it was to be another two days before they could continue. They made a circuit of Tent Island in case some trace of Mackintosh or Hayward could be found, and on 3 January the party arrived back at Cape Evans, where Gaze recorded: 'I was very glad to be back.'[76]

This journey of some 147 miles over a period of three weeks, although little more than a midsummer jaunt, was to be the last on the Barrier during the expedition.

Those who had remained at Cape Evans had continued a daily routine of science, sealing and watching for a relief ship. They had celebrated Christmas with a dinner, made by Stevens, of soup, roast skua and vegetables, plum pudding, tinned pears and jelly.[77]

Soon after breakfast on 10 January, Richards, who was slowly regaining his health, took the binoculars and went for a walk to look for seals. To the north-west he observed icebergs and patches of open water.

CHAPTER TWENTY-TWO

'Like wild men'

ONE DAY OUT from port on the relief voyage, Shackleton wrote: 'After all the rush and worry of the last months it is peaceful on board here and I had a good night's sleep.' Yet he could not feel at ease. 'I am anxious more and more to see our ten men safe and well, then I will rest.'[1]

According to Ninnis, *Aurora* looked 'quite her old self again after the big overhaul'.[2] Entries in the ship's logbook paint a picture of the voyage south:

December 20th 1916. 5.30 a.m. Called all hands and prepared to get under weigh . . .

December 21st 1916. 4 p.m. Gentle breeze and moderate south-west swell, cloudy sky and fine weather. 4.50 Lowered and furled upper Topsail. 6.40 Large flock of birds, petrels sooty albatross etc. a school of killer whales . . .

December 25th 1916. 4 p.m. fresh following breeze and big westerly swell, vessel rolling and shipping waters . . .

December 27th 1916. 2.30 a.m. Wireless aerial carried away . . .

December 28th 1916. 4 p.m. Snowing throughout watch. 4.40 Sighted small rugged berg out on port bow . . .

December 30th 1916. 4 p.m. Long line of pack ice off port beam . . . 10.30 Ice becoming thicker. Midday. Passing through loose drift at full speed. Ice extending from horizon to horizon. Constant alteration of course necessary.

December 31st 4 p.m. Fine clear weather, light airs and smooth sea. Pack thinning. Steaming at half speed in scattered pack ice. 8.00 Passing through loose pack at full speed . . . 10.30 Ice getting heavier, reduced speed.

January 1st 1917. Steaming full through broken pack . . .[3]

The ship consumed five tons of coal a day as she pushed into the high swell. Moyes wrote on 26 December:

We managed to keep the fore sail & lower foretopsail set most of the time, and with steam at economical, have managed to average about 6 knots . . . We are going much further E[ast] than we want, but cannot help it, as the wind is so strong. We do a fair amount of reading and Shackleton, Gillies, Dr [Middleton] & myself have a little Bridge at night.[4]

Aurora displayed all the rolling characteristics demonstrated on the voyage south two years earlier. Several men, including the wireless operator Tim Ryan and the acting medical man Freddie Middleton, were seasick.

> . . . the ship at present rolls 75 to 80 degrees, with an occasional 84 degrees. There is very little pitching – more a corkscrew when she wants to pitch. This has been going on continuously for 7 days . . . It is considered no disgrace to be ill on a 300 ton boat . . . As the ship rolls on both sides she ships a sea at the waist of the ship, and this sea rushes to and fro across the ship until it gets rid of itself through the openings and then is ready to ship another decent sized one . . . a wave caught me from behind and gave me a good ducking, and filled my sea boots . . .[5]

Each man received a week's supply of tobacco. Ryan, with a flute, and Middleton, on the piano, entertained in the saloon in the evening. Henry Voegli the cook ('a great improvement on the last one', according to Ninnis), assisted by stewards Alexander Webster and Baden Robertson, performed minor miracles in fierce seas, serving roast beef and pork for Christmas dinner. Davis recorded his gratitude: 'The cook gave us an excellent dinner in spite of the weather.'[6] By contrast, in the forecastle 'there was nothing to mark the difference between Xmas and another day excepting that a case of apples and some chocolates were sent forward. We are a happy crew however, and the day was terminated pleasantly playing 500 which has become a popular game on board.'[7]

Middleton reported that it was 'light almost all night – darkest at 11.30'. Ryan sent and received several wireless messages over a distance of almost a thousand miles, 'so beating our last trip's record', according to Ninnis.

The medical, officer treated minor injuries under trying conditions: 'The sea was rolling its best and it was surgery under difficulties . . . we can't get hot water as at home . . .' He noted that wounds healed in the Antarctic environment despite the absence of 'aseptic precautions', and would later observe: 'It seems extraordinary that a man who will crawl up ropes in a storm and climb along ropes from an ice floe to a ship, looks terrified at the thought of having a stitch put in or taken out.'[8]

When not assisting in navigating duties, Moyes would often seek the warmth of the engine room, where he would sometimes be joined by Shackleton:

> We all hope we pick up the 10 men and can come straight back. Sir E[rnest] often speaks of it, and no wonder, as he must want a rest after 2½ years of it. He looks much better today than when he came aboard, as it is really his first spell. His stories of the life on the ice after the wreck of the *Endurance* are very good, and it is really wonderful how they all pulled through.[9]

Over six decades later, Moyes would recount:

> On the way down I shared a cabin with [Shackleton]. He was very nervy . . . he had
> the lower bunk. A blanket would slip off my top bunk and he pulled hold of the
> blanket and said, 'You awake, Moyes, you awake?' Of course, by the time he pulled
> the blanket off, I was awake. I was freezing with cold! So then we'd talk and we'd
> talk and we would go out into the saloon and sit down and talk for an hour or two
> and he wondered where everyone was, and he also told me about all his future
> hopes . . . he was a great man . . . he was rather worried that his expedition had
> failed.[10]

Middleton, too, in the context of examining Shackleton's teeth, said: 'He is
so jolly nervy, and can't bear to think of pain, let alone bear any.'[11]

Later in the voyage, Shackleton relaxed a little. 'Played poker patience with
Sir E[rnest] most of the evening. We have a bet of a dinner for the biggest score
before we get back.'[12]

Seaman Alasdair MacKinnon, one of three seamen on the relief voyage from
the Isle of Skye, recorded a significant milestone:

> Dec 30th 4 a.m. sea smooth, clear and cold . . . 5.30 a.m. Entered Antarctic Circle
> 64° 33' S. Occasional berg and drift ice. 7 p.m. Entered a sea of pack ice that makes
> the old *Aurora* tremble fore and aft. 68° S still 600 [miles] from the base.[13]

At midnight on 31 December, the crew gave New Year greetings to the
captain and officers. Paton said: 'We turned Sir Ernest out, and he apologised
for not having anything on board with him, we then sang Auld Lang Syne and
retired to our beds, those who were off duty.'[14] Davis reciprocated by presenting
the crew with two bottles of whisky. They might have got hold of another, as
Ninnis noted that a bottle intended to celebrate the occasion had disappeared
from the wardroom.[15] New Year's Day dinner featured fresh mutton, the cook
having slaughtered two of a number of sheep on board for that purpose several
days previously.

With *Aurora* steaming in loose pack ice at 70° South, Middleton wrote:
'Captain Davis has hardly been to bed since we entered the pack. He lives on
the bridge and up in the crow's nest. He must be very wiry and is a very able
skipper and very conscientious.'[16]

Moyes, doubtless also drawing on his Mawson expedition knowledge, would
recount:

> He was a dual-purpose man. There were two men, two J. K. Davises, one ashore
> and one afloat. Ashore he was a quite nice, bright, chatty man . . . but afloat he was
> just a hard man, he just thought of nothing else but the ship, that's all very diffi-
> cult, a very hard captain but a wonderful skipper, my word he was . . . not so hard
> on the men, but he stuck to rules you might say, and he saw that other people stuck

to rules, but he took so much on himself, he took too much on himself really, I don't think he trusted his officers enough, not that I blame him, because none of them had had any Antarctic experience before, whenever we got into troubled waters very heavy blizzard and so on, he stayed on the bridge, I've seen him stay on the bridge for 30 hours without coming off, and then when we were cleaning out again, the engines would stop and we would drift and he would have a good sleep.[17]

On 3 January, Davis made *Aurora* fast alongside an ice floe and all hands 'iced ship', obtaining enough ice to give 25 tons of fresh water. In the evening the crew all had a break, the ship's log recording: '8 p.m. Engines stopped and vessel drifting about.' That night Ninnis had a disturbing dream: 'I met four of them in the hut. The others were said to be missing. It is to be hoped that dreams are *not* always true.'

After five days of little progress, *Aurora* cleared the pack ice on 7 January but was temporarily held up the following day, 180 miles from her destination. Middleton made a medicine chest and familiarised himself with amputation and haemorrhage techniques.[18] Moyes, designated as the sledging navigator, smoothed the runners of a sledge and helped load it ready for use. His diary entry summed up the atmosphere on board the ship: 'Everyone is under rather a tension, as tomorrow may mean so much – 5 weeks sledging & looking for dead men or return to Aust[ralia] at once.'[19] Although Tripp was to report that Davis was convinced the shore party would all be dead,[20] his main concern was for Mackintosh, Joyce, Wild, Cope, Hayward and Jack, who had been overdue at Cape Evans when *Aurora* was carried away.

Mounts Erebus and Terror came into view on 9 January as final preparations were made for landing at Cape Evans. Ten bags of coal were made up for taking ashore, and Ninnis repaired rat-damaged sleeping bags.

Davis sent a wireless message in the hope those at the base might be listening: 'Ross Sea Party, Cape Evans. Aurora is now within 100 miles of Cape Evans. Hope you are all well and that ice will allow us to communicate with you shortly. Davis.'[21]

Because the ship's progress was largely unimpeded by ice, events unfolded rapidly. The log for 9 January recorded: 'Steaming full towards Ross Island. Skirting some scattered bay ice.'[22] On the following day, Davis wrote:

Passed Beaufort Island in beautiful, fine weather about 6 miles and proceeded round Ross Island (Cape Bird). The Sound was clear and at 10.20 we were off Cape Royds and met the fast ice which extends southward from Cape Royds. To the southward Cape Evans is visible but there is no sign of life. We fired a rocket distress signal hoping to rouse someone out of Shackleton's old hut.[23]

From the crow's nest Ninnis had a view of the Cape Evans hut just past the

Barne Glacier. 'I picked up 3 objects. The weather screen and anemometer I knew. What was the 3rd? We tried to decide that it was not a cross and yet feared it was one. No smoke rising from the hut and no life visible. We felt vaguely uneasy.' He thought the party might either be at Cape Royds or out sledging looking for Shackleton.[24]

On shore, Richards was looking north towards the Barne Glacier for seals with the aid of binoculars when he thought he saw an iceberg, but suddenly a puff of smoke appeared. When he returned to the hut, shouting as he entered the door, 'Come on, she's here!' the other six men thought he was joking: too often in the past they had been fooled by ghost ships appearing and then vanishing. However, Richards insisted, 'Yes, come on she's here, the ship's here!' Jack's dairy, the only contemporaneous record, recounts the events that followed:

> With this, all hands made a bolt for the door. The eyes took a moment to accustom themselves to the glare after the gloom of the hut, but sure enough there was a ship lying off the Barne Glacier away to the NW, looking at first very much like a berg of which there were many in the sound at the time. I can't describe our feelings, they were too deep. It was not a time for words, our hearts were too full for this and I am not ashamed to say that tears of joy forced their way into my eyes in spite of myself. To think that our long time of waiting was over at last and the relief had come – no more hunting for seals, no more blizzards and frost-scarred feet and hands. It was too good to be true. Was it to be wondered that anyone should be overcome at a time like this.[25]

Joyce later wrote a slightly different account of this famous moment:

> On January 10th, after breakfast, Richy went out of the hut. Shortly afterwards, he walked in quietly and whispered in my ear: 'Joycey, the b— ship.'[26]

This account seems authentic and the utterance would be typical of Richards. It probably occurred after an indifferent response to his initial announcement. Richards later stated:

> I went back to the hut and I said the ship is here and they called me a bloody liar and a few other choice terms, but one of them got up to a window . . . and looked through and said I believe there is something there. It was all hurry and bustle.[27]

Jack climbed a snow slope south-east of the hut, hoping that 'someone on ship would see the black object moving against white background and thereby know we were at the hut'. It is possible that he was the mysterious third object that Ninnis had seen from the crow's nest, although Jack later considered that no one had seen him.

The Ross Island castaways hastily prepared to leave the base that had sheltered them through months of tedium and anxiety. *Aurora*'s anchors were still embedded in the beach nearby, and the Girling motor sledge, which had promised a new era in polar travel, lay abandoned amidst debris jettisoned by men who had been reduced to a desperate existence. There was still a further journey to be made, across several miles of sea ice that was thawing in summer conditions, to the ship.

Wild, Gaze, Richards, Cope, Stevens and Joyce, together with dogs and two sledge-loads of gear, left the hut at midmorning. Jack, ever the scientist and perhaps by now the recluse, remained at the base to take observations and clean up Davis reported that he 'actually refused to credit his senses, and remained behind in the hut'.[28]

A landing party comprising Shackleton, Middleton, Moyes and Ninnis reached the *Nimrod* expedition hut at Cape Royds a few minutes after leaving *Aurora* at 11 a.m. Shackleton recorded:

> No sign of life at my old hut . . . there was a note unsigned dated Dec. 15 1915 stating that the party was housed at Cape Evans. There was no statement as to the safety of all hands but the very absence of this augured well especially as on looking round, I noticed Wild's name and Jack's in paint that was still wet. As the two men were on the Barrier party they were the ones we were most anxious about.[29]

The first sign that members of the Ross Sea shore party had survived was reported by Davis in his diary:

> Just before [the Cape Royds party's] arrival on board a black patch was seen southward which was later on made out to be a party of six approaching us from C. Evans with a sledge and dog team.[30]

Moyes would recall that the ship's lookout reported that there were objects on the ice ahead and thought these must be men because they were too big to be penguins.

> And so Captain Davis called out to me, 'If they are those men go and lie down, up and down, tell me how many there are.' So we went straight out, instead of going aboard we went straight down and we saw this group of people in the distance . . .[31]

Those on board *Aurora* watched proceedings through binoculars and a telescope. Middleton recorded the historic sighting:

> Just as we got back to the ship a sledge party was reported coming from C. Evans, and consequently all glasses were turned on these, and there were all sorts of guesses

as to the number. We distinctly counted 5 and thought there was one on the sledge making six out of ten. There were others who counted nine and others seven. We were then satisfied, or rather, sure that the party of the six of whom we had doubts, had probably returned from their trip south.[32]

Davis continued in his diary:

Sir E. Shackleton, Moyes and Middleton went out to meet the party and it was arranged before they left that they should signal to us whether all hands were there, when they met.

The six men and five dogs moved at varying speeds across the sea ice north of Cape Evans as the ship was repositioned at the edge of the fixed ice, some six miles away. Davis noted that, as the Shackleton trio moved forward 'in a compact body', the approaching figures 'struggled towards them in a ragged procession'.[33]

The survivors had a sweepstake on the distance to the ship, which Gaze would win 'and actually be paid'.[34] Almost 50 years later, Stevens recalled:

. . . there was a proper stampede across the ice. And we hadn't gone very far when [*Aurora*] seemed to turn and go north. We were scared we were going to be left. So we hurried faster and eventually saw three men coming ashore and we knew it was true we were relieved.[35]

They had often rehearsed this moment. Stevens said:

We used to say – we knew the war was on, of course – 'What's the first thing you'll say when you see civilised beings again?' We'd say: 'Ah well, we'll ask them first who won the war.' We knew it would be finished. Then we'll say: 'Have you got such a thing as a fag about you?'[36]

Middleton, approaching from the ship with Shackleton and Moyes, recorded the historic encounter in his diary:

We walked about 1½ miles along this sea ice and when they saw us coming, one of them came forward to meet us, leaving the team and men waiting. This one was Joyce. Sir E.H.S. recognised him and spoke to him when about 40 yards off. The latter was very glad and surprised to see Sir E.H.S. As the men came up, Joyce called for 3 cheers for Sir E.H.S. The next question was how many alive, the answer seven, and then the names of those who had died – Mackintosh, Smith, and Heywood [*sic*] . . .

To the ragged and weary remnants of Mackintosh's men, Shackleton's appearance from the north, when for the last two years their very existence had been predicated by his planned appearance from the south, was a poignant experience. That it heralded the release from their horrific circumstances was an overwhelming emotion, but it also underlined the futility of their endeavours and what a colossal fiasco the Imperial Trans-Antarctic Expedition had been. It was profound and shocking for Shackleton to learn that three of his men were dead, and to be confronted by these battered castaways who looked scarcely of this world.

Joyce quoted Sir Ernest as greeting him with the words: 'Joyce old man, more than pleased to see you; how many of the party are alive?'[37] When the response was given in a few short words, Shackleton, Moyes and Middleton lay down on the ice as a pre-arranged signal to those on *Aurora* to show how many of the party had died.[38]

From the ship Davis observed:

The parties rapidly approached each other and we anxiously watched for this signal when they met. The news they received was apparently that 3 of the party had not survived. We were able to see something serious had occurred.[39]

In another account he wrote:

We watched the little groups through telescopes approaching one another, sharply silhouetted against the glistening snow. Three men with a small dog-sledge were in the lead, and three others were strung out across the landscape. Presently the leaders met, and by and by the laggards caught up. There was a short conference, then one figure detached itself from the group, walked off a little distance, and lay down; another followed, and another. Then we knew that three members of the party had perished.[40]

Stevens noted that 'Two of the fellows had never seen Shackleton before, and behaved like perfect strangers.'[41]

Middleton wrote:

They looked very fit physically, but very unkempt and their clothes were about on their last legs . . . We talked straightaway about war. They were surprised it was still on. We then talked on many things, and they plied many questions one on top of the other, and then they had their first smoke of tobacco for close on two years. After a spell and a talk and reply to questions, we moved towards the ship.[42]

Moyes commented that the six men 'looked awful wrecks', and later recalled:

They could not possibly be more filthy and untidy as their fuel had been blubber which gives off a filthy sticky smoke, and as they each had only one set of clothes and no soap, all were a dirty brown . . . on the walk back to the *Aurora* they smoked the first cigarettes they seen for 18 months and asked questions innumerable.[43]

In another recollection, he described the survivors as 'a dreadful looking lot'.[44]

Despite the harrowing circumstances, the greeting between fellow Australians Middleton and Richards was as if they had met while strolling in the park. 'The first I shook hands with after Joyce, was one Richards who was at the Ballarat

Technical school – School of Mines – and [he] asked me if I was related to Les (my brother) – "Not Middleton of Ballarat?" [45]

Davis also joined the welcoming party:

> Bringing the ship to the edge of the floe again we put out an anchor and I went over the ice to meet the party, who were now close at hand. They looked very unkempt and dishevelled and smelt strongly of blubber. In a few seconds we learnt [their story]. [46]

Their arrival on board was recorded by 'Mr Ninnis taking cinema photos'. [47] Middleton also took photographs and the crew gave the rescued men 'three hearty cheers'. [48]

Davis hinted at the state of mind of the rescued men: 'Naturally the party we had relieved are labouring under considerable excitement and it is just a little difficult to obtain a coherent statement other than to the effect that they had given these people [Mackintosh and Hayward] up long ago.' [49]

Four years later, Davis wrote:

> Shackleton told me afterwards that the men were so excited and hysterical over the rescue they could not talk coherently, and it was some little time before he could obtain any intelligible account of what had happened . . . They were literally blots on the virgin landscape. Anything more remote from normal civilised human beings would be hard to imagine. With their haggard, lined faces from which smoke-bleared eyes looked out above their unkempt beards, their jerky, hysterical speech – they were strange objects. And, to put it baldly, they reeked to heavens – but not, considerate Mother Nature be praised – not to each other.
>
> But when the rescued seven had been got aboard, when their inner men had been regaled with the food of civilised countries, and their outer men had been sloughed of their dilapidated garments and hosed down, they gradually became normal, and were able to recount their experiences. These comprised a tale of adventure, hardship, courage, and endurance that has rarely been surpassed. [50]

His shock at what he saw was undiminished over 40 years later when he published an account of his Antarctic experiences.

> I . . . had not fully anticipated what a profound effect such a long period of isolation would have on their personal appearance. They were just about the wildest looking gang of men that I have ever seen in my life. [51]

Another graphic account is found in Ninnis's diary:

> We smelt their approach before we could distinguish their faces . . . I had to light one man's pipe for him, he seemed unable to do it. Forgotten the knack I think. How they talked, a good deal of emotion present and torrents of excited talk. Questions that one did not wait to have answered before another sprang up. War details and amazement at the hugeness of it all. Several seemed semi hysterical. Fearfully

unkempt but not semi naked, they wore mostly the gear we left them in and old gear found in the huts. No skin garments. Hair and beards! Like wild men several of them . . . I took official photos of each and of all and a cinema film of the approach with dogs and the stop at ship . . . One or two had managed to keep quite respectable in appearance. All very sun tanned. First meal on board was ravenously eaten . . . Little did they expect to see the *Aurora*. They thought us smashed and all lost and were amazed to hear *Endurance* was the ship really lost, and expecting her to relieve them.[52]

According to Bosun Paton: 'The sad fate of the other three men we are not allowed to know but that Captain McIntosh, Revd Spencer Smith and Hayward are dead and that it happened last May.'[53]

Richards noted how the survivors 'felt acutely embarrassed alongside the white faces and clean garments of the ship party'.[54] Their smell was such that the others could not stay in the wardroom with them.[55] Some of the rescued men were seen to cower and protect the food served to them.[56]

Remarkably, within an hour or two of coming on board, most of the erstwhile castaways were back into action. However, neither Richards, who later said he was 'non compos mentis' when he went on board,[57] nor Cope were in a psychological or emotional state to leave the ship before it got back to port.

Gaze, Wild and Stevens, together with Moyes, Ninnis and the dogs, returned to Cape Evans 'with orders to bring instruments etc. off. Mr Moyes in charge.'[58] Moyes wrote: 'It was a hard march for 6 miles over smooth sea ice, I went on as a forerunner for the dogs, and got very sore. We got two large sledge loads and as we had to help the dogs, I have never found 6 miles so long.'[59] Jack, who had stayed at the hut and had 'got cleaned up', saw the approaching men and was greeted with the news, 'Shackleton on board' and '*Endurance* crushed'.[60]

Returning to Cape Evans for the first time since the ship had blown out in May 1915, Ninnis found:

> Hut very dirty with blubber smoke, everything black and greasy . . . the general disorder of things . . . around the hut lies various wreckage and empty tins, odd gear etc of little further use. My old motor is among the items.
>
> Had to destroy one of the old sick dogs, useless to take him away. The remaining dogs look fine and fit. Towser, Oscar, Gunboat (now Gunner) and my old friend Beechie are the only dogs of the original 26.[61]

The party, including Jack, evacuated the remainder of the dogs to *Aurora*, then off Cape Barne, by late evening. In the late afternoon, de la Motte led Middleton, Ryan and the redoubtable Joyce to Shackleton's old headquarters at Cape Royds, from which they retrieved 'a load of gear'.

Jack's arrival at the ship brought him profound relief:

How good it was to get aboard! First thing a real, hot bath, plenty of hot water ready and wonderfully white woollens. Everything seemed so strange. Then came my first meal on board – real fresh mutton. I ate and ate and wished I could eat more – oranges too and fresh potatoes. Devoured home mail with my meal and thankful to hear all well . . . Then came bed and real, clean blankets . . . I feel as if I want to sleep and sleep and dream. Everything seems so strange.[62]

Paton recorded that each of the rescued men was 'allowed three buckets of warm water', and by next day, 'after getting on clean clothing and having a haircut and their whiskers trimmed they were scarcely recognisable'.[63] All seven were outfitted in ready-made suits from Dunedin.

Middleton disclosed over 50 years later:

When we eventually got them on board . . . two fellows would get over there in that corner and have nothing to do with the fellows over here, it was only for a few days though. I used to spend my time going around and talking to their little groups . . . I suppose they hated the sight of each other, two years down there and six months of dark it's a wonder they didn't, oh, they did go a bit queer.[64]

Ninnis wrote on 11 January:

The men mostly look well . . . and look far from distressed now that they are clean and in clothes we brought for them . . . Listening to various versions of the shore party's story one soon gathers a lot of unspoken items and it is quite a normal thing to find that some of the loud talk at this time covers the confession of a far different mental attitude before rescue was assured. Several members clearly show the effect of mental strain (J, S & C especially) in their speech or lack of speech. Despondency hardly yet overcome and hysteria hardly yet suppressed indicate all too clearly where the effect has been most felt. Quite naturally little things pop out unawares and we learn that one of the cheerful ones of present time was only able to keep to his bunk and lost all interest in his share [of] work for weeks. Another had a depressing influence by harping on his fears that no ship would arrive to pick them up. He even set a date to the limit of his expectations of relief.[65]

As some kind of melancholic record in case the whole party should perish, Richards had, in the depths of winter, inscribed the following record on the wall by his bunk in the Cape Evans hut:

R W Richards
August 14 1916
Losses to date
Hayward
Mack
Smyth [*sic*]
ship?[66]

Alongside the reference to 'ship' is the numeral '7', perhaps indicating the number of survivors.

A startling improvement was observed in Cope's condition after the rescue as something of the former man returned. Gaze would recall over 60 years later:

> He was a remarkable chap in many ways. He was a comedian. He could tell funny stories without repeating himself for months and months. He was the life and soul of the party at the beginning in that way. He used to amuse us tremendously when we first went down. [When the ship went out] he lost his bundle all together. He was a different fellow. You couldn't get him out of his bunk. He stayed there for over a month. It all came back when he got back to Wellington . . . it was remarkable as soon as we got on board the *Aurora* the change in him. I can remember him never taking off any of his clothes the whole time down there. Anything he could get he would put on. I'm not libelling him, but when he got on *Aurora* and was stripped of his clothes and threw them into the water, it was just like a pool of grease being thrown out.[67]

Middleton trimmed Cope's beard and cut his hair. 'I weep when I see the ladders at the back of his head – he can't see that but everyone else does . . . Cope is an awfully decent chap and it is quite decent to be able to talk shop once again.'[68]

The medical officer examined the party and found surprisingly few physical problems:

> Mr Stevens was suffering from an axillary abscess, which has been under Dr [*sic*] Cope's treatment for some weeks . . . Dr Cope reported that Mr Richards was recovering from strain, contracted while sledging early in 1916. On examination, his heart was normal and his general condition was very good. The whole of the relieved party were more or less sunburnt.[69]

He also noted that Shackleton was greatly affected by the events of the day: 'Sir EHS is not at all well and I don't think he is in too fit a condition. He is of course very much disturbed at the death of his three comrades.'[70]

CHAPTER TWENTY-THREE

Inquiry

IMMEDIATELY AFTER learning of the fate of Mackintosh and Hayward, Captain Davis condemned the Ross Sea party leader's decision of 8 May 1916 to travel from Hut Point to Cape Evans: 'The crossing of the sea ice, during the darkness of winter, is a terribly risky undertaking and ... the ice [being] only 4 inches thick, makes it difficult to understand why they should have attempted it at all.'[1] The two men perished, he said, 'some time after their work may fairly be said to have been accomplished'.[2]

Middleton, an Antarctica novice, probably reflected the views of all on the ship: 'It is annoying to think that with the exception of Smith, who died naturally from scurvy, the other two just practically threw their lives away ... it is terribly hard and one of the things that should not have been.'

On the same day that the Ross Sea survivors came aboard *Aurora*, Davis directed Shackleton to carry out an inquiry into the loss of the two men on the ice. Joyce, Richards and Wild each wrote a statement outlining the events of 7–10 May 1916 and the subsequent searches, and Richards spent some time with Shackleton in his cabin. 'He was cross-questioning me. He wanted to know exactly what went on. He'd get me in and then Joyce and compare stories.'[3]

Shackleton reported to Davis on 11 January 1917:

> ... I am forced to a definite conclusion ... that both men lost their lives on the afternoon of May 9th 1916 through venturing on thin sea ice and being caught in a blizzard which drove this ice out of the sound. As neither man had any equipment I consider it impossible for them to have survived more than a few hours ... a search should be made for their bodies in two directions; the area North of Glacier Tongue and at the depot at Butter Point; as Joyce and party have searched the South side of the Tongue nothing more can be done.[4]

Ninnis wrote that had Mackintosh and Hayward reached the western shore of McMurdo Sound on drift ice, they 'would have been forced' to go to the Butter Point depot for food.

In Davis's words:

Although there did not appear to be the faintest hope of finding that anyone had visited this depot . . . as it was the only place where food could be found, supposing that the party of missing men had reached the western shore of the Sound, it was deemed advisable to examine this vicinity.[5]

The search for the remains of these two men was delayed while Davis allowed *Aurora* to slowly drift west as the engineers repaired the engines and tested the wireless.[6] The captain wrote: 'It is a beautiful clear day and one is able to see a great distance, but there is no sign of life visible anywhere to the West.' The rescued men and the ship party welcomed an opportunity to relax. Middleton wrote:

So we all have been sitting on the ship's rail, while the ship drifted. By jingo it was A1 and the sun was shining beautifully. We talked war and the trips of these fellows . . . Nobody is sleepy and we are all here eating ham sandwiches, and talking and laughing.[7]

Shortly after midnight on 12 January, *Aurora* was six miles away from Butter Point, with fast sea ice preventing further passage. The ship's log tells the story of the attempted search that began in the early hours of the morning:

Jan. 12th. 12.40 a.m. Party consisting of Sir E. Shackleton, Joyce and Wild left ship with sledge and dogs but found it unfit for dogs and sledge and brought same back and proceeded over sea ice without them . . . 5.35 a.m. party returned to ship. Sir E. Shackleton reported that after crossing 5H miles of rubbly and waterlogged ice, they reached within 30 yards of the [piedmont] ice but owing to cliff being too high with moving slush intervening they could not land . . . There was no sign of the depot or of anyone having visited the vicinity.[8]

Paton reported that he had 'heard' the party failed to find the Butter Point depot because the glacier had shifted four miles since supplies had been placed there.[9] Ninnis commented that 'the ice breaking away from the edge of the field . . . shows what probably happened to Captain and Hayward'.[10]

Aurora then steamed to Cape Barne in the east of the Sound. After lunch on 13 January, Shackleton, Wild, and Joyce with five dogs and sledging equipment disembarked on the fast ice to complete the search for the remains of Mackintosh and Hayward.[11] Ninnis noted: 'Food unusual for a sledging party – roast mutton, ham, bread, and a lot of luxuries.'[12] This would be the last sledging foray of the heroic age of Antarctic exploration.

Jack accompanied the party to the Cape Evans hut to complete the task of erecting a memorial to the three lost men, a task that had been interrupted by the arrival of the relief party. Before leaving the ship, Shackleton wrote an epitaph for that memorial – a cross to be erected at Cape Evans.

A brass cross had been made 'to put on Revd. Spencer-Smith's grave at Cape Crozier [*sic*] where he lies buried'.[13] Curiously, this memorial also included the names of Mackintosh and Hayward. However, Davis did not have any plans to sledge to the Padre's grave. His priority was to look for the remains of Mackintosh and Hayward, and then evacuate the party as quickly as he could.

Shackleton and Joyce searched in the vicinity of the Razorback Islands, south of Cape Evans, returning to the hut in the evening of 13 January. Their attempts the following morning to search the north side of Glacier Tongue were curtailed when increasing south-easterly winds created dangerous conditions. Shackleton wrote: 'The ice was moving rapidly at the end of Cape Evans and the pool between Hut and Inaccessible island [was] growing larger.'[14] The two men were confined to the hut in blizzard conditions the following day, but set out 'at greatest possible speed' at 4.20 a.m. on 16 January in fine, calm conditions. Shackleton reported to Davis:

> We arrived [at Glacier Tongue] about 7 a.m.; from the top we searched with glasses. There was nothing to be seen but blue ice crevassed showing no protuberances. We came down and half running, half walking, worked about 3 miles towards root of glacier; but I could see there was not the slightest chance of finding any remains owing to the enormous snow drifts . . .[15]

Meanwhile, Wild and Jack erected the memorial cross on Wind Vane Hill. The men had insufficient time to inscribe any words on the cross. Instead, they left a corked copper cylinder containing a sheet of paper on which was written:

I.T.A.E.

1914–1917

Sacred to the Memory

of

Lieut. Aeneas Lionel A. Mackintosh, RNR,

V. G. Hayward

and

The Rev. A. P. Spencer-Smith, BA,

Who perished in the service of the Expedition.

'Things done for gain are nought
But great things done endure.'

'I was ever a fighter so one fight more
The best and the last
I should hate that death bandaged
my eyes and bid me creep past.
Let me pay in a minute Life's glad
arrears of pain darkness & cold.'[16]

From *Aurora*, Davis observed: 'Cape Evans hut plainly visible. The cross to those who perished having just been erected, is clearly defined against the snow ...' At midmorning on 16 January, Joyce, Wild, Jack and Shackleton had a hasty meal at the hut, closed the building and returned to the ship.

Davis had been watching anxiously for the returning party. After dropping the men off at Cape Evans on 13 January, he had continued to Cape Royds, where ice was obtained from a stranded berg. Late in the afternoon, the captain had briefly left the ship and, accompanied by Moyes, Aylward (the third officer) and Webster (the chief steward) to revisit his old *Nimrod* expedition haunts, collect boxes of specimens and leave a record of the relief expedition.

Aurora spent the next two days near Cape Evans, head to wind, riding out the gale with engines often at half-speed. Davis recorded on 16 January: '9.45 Party reported coming off. Stood back to the fast ice and embarked party.' Conditions held the ship there until the following day, when Davis wrote: '11.50. We got under way and proceeded toward the western side of the Sound, wind freshening, occasional snow squalls.' After *Aurora* steamed away from Cape Evans for the last time, pack ice soon blocked the route northwards. Late on 18 January, the ship was in the vicinity of Cape Roberts, but no sign could be seen from on board of the old *Terra Nova* depot there. The following day *Aurora* briefly entered Granite Harbour.

Davis had second thoughts about the adequacy of the searches for the missing men and decided on a further one to 'relieve his mind'. On 22 January, after the main pack was again met, he turned south, reaching Beaufort Island on 25 January. Middleton commented: 'The relieved party are naturally very hurt over having turned back...'[17] However, ice prevented a return to McMurdo Sound so Davis abandoned his plans. *Aurora* turned northwards on 26 January and passed Cape Adare in rough weather. Middleton recorded: 'I think we are for home and beauty – for good now. The relieved party are very relieved and Sir E.H.S. is very pleased. His trip on shore and everything else has bucked him up tremendously and he is a very different man.'[18] The next day, in a 'remarkably steep and confused sea', Beechie gave birth to 11 pups. With other progeny, there were now 29 pups all told.[19]

Aurora left the pack on 31 January and, the following day, crossed the Antarctic Circle. Davis noted: 'We have been extraordinarily fortunate in getting out as easily as we have done...'[20]

As the ship made rapid progress into more northern latitudes, Moyes wrote: 'It gets dark for a while at night now, about 10 minutes, quite a change after six weeks of daylight'.[21] Even before leaving the pack there had been a noticeable swell that 'upset the equilibrium of the relieved party'. Middleton observed 'plenty of whales on the horizon and in the distance and a good many seals on the floes as we passed through the pack'. Mollymawks, petrels, Cape pigeons and albatrosses were plentiful. Some of the men spent spare hours playing various gambling games such as vingt-et-un, Uncle Sam and poker.

After an attempt to send his first wireless message on 2 February, Ryan was able to hear Awarua station, near Bluff, without difficulty on the following evening. News of the war was received, and Ninnis noted: 'So war is not over. Hardly to be expected, yet we hoped.' On 4 February, when Bluff and Hobart stations were also heard, Ryan was able to transmit a coded message to the New Zealand government reporting on the outcome of the relief expedition. John Mill of Port Chalmers sent a message to the ship advising of the death of McNab, the Minister of Marine.

With all sails set, *Aurora* achieved her best daily run of the voyage, 216.2 miles on 6 February.[22] Middleton noted how huge waves 'rise and rush past the ship'. Stevens used a typewriter lashed to the wardroom table to type his report on the expedition, which, he explained, 'leaves aside, besides what was in the ordinary course, most of the unpleasantness which cannot be blamed anymore than it can be righted'.[23] There was a poignant moment during the return voyage when a cake, taken south for the now-deceased Mackintosh, was cut.

Shackleton presented mementos to members of the Ross Sea party. Joyce and Richards each received a prismatic compass, on the back of which Sir Ernest had engraved an inscription by means of a diamond in a ring. Richards would later say that the compass given by Shackleton 'had very emotional associations for me, as in a difficult six days in 1916 [referring to the return journey from Mt Hope], our lives very definitely depended on [the use of a compass]'.[24] The survivors presented Davis with the set of *Encyclopaedia Britannica* that he had donated to the expedition in 1914, and added an inscription of gratitude.

The ship's company readied themselves for arrival in New Zealand. Middleton noted: 'Sir E.H.S. had a clean shave today. It has made a tremendous difference to him. He looks 15 years younger. Everyone else is shaving and looking more like shore people.'

Richards would later recall that, as *Aurora* moved along the coast of the South Island of New Zealand, 'there was a wind off-shore and the smoke and the smell of burning foliage was very nostalgic, after nothing of that sort of thing for so long'.[25]

In the early evening of 9 February 1917, the ship, assisted by the tug *Karaka*, arrived at the wool wharf in Wellington. The *New Zealand Times* reported:

> As the vessels drew near, three lusty cheers were given (called for by the Mayor) then three more for Sir Ernest Shackleton and Captain Davis. The bronzed faces of those intrepid explorers could be discerned on the bridge, and hearty welcomes were shouted.[26]

CHAPTER TWENTY-FOUR

Fêted, honoured and forgotten

T HE ARRIVAL OF *Aurora* in Wellington heralded not only the conclusion of the successful Ross Sea relief voyage, but also the end of the Imperial Trans-Antarctic Expedition. The rescued men and their rescuers were briefly fêted and honoured in New Zealand. Leaving the ship after the voyage from the ice, Jack noted: 'Had to run the gauntlet to reach motors, which were to whisk us off to the Grand Hotel. Had a great supper – chicken, pork and fresh vegetables, the first for two years.'[1] The Commercial Travellers' Club provided hospitality and members drove Jack and others to the Trentham military camp. The rescued men received new clothing, supplied by the Wellington department store of Kirkcaldie and Stains, and free train and tram passes.[2]

Richards was always to be grateful for the New Zealand welcome. Writing in 1984, he said that the tug that greeted *Aurora*

> was fairly crowded with notabilities [*sic*] and the welcome at the wharf was a warm one as indeed was the whole of the attitude of those people we met during our stay. That experience has coloured my feeling for New Zealanders who took us in as derelicts and in spite of the seriousness of the war at the time made us feel more than at home. I have never forgotten it.[3]

In contrast, he maintained that 'back in Australia they couldn't care less'.[4]

The mayor of Wellington hosted a civic reception, providing an opportunity for Davis and Shackleton to share the same stage. Despite Shackleton's initial grievance concerning the leadership of the relief expedition, he had come to accept the situation. Davis wrote to his father: '[Shackleton] gave us no trouble and although a great many people predicted that we should quarrel, we did not do so.'[5]

While Ninnis, established in an office of the Marine Department in Wellington, assisted Shackleton with winding up the expedition's affairs, Sir Ernest gave a series of public lectures, the proceeds of which were divided between 'Captain Mackintosh's widow', who received £538, and the Red Cross Society.[6] He told one audience: 'You may write down this expedition as a geographical failure, but . . . there is always time to go again, and when . . . peace comes again, we may make another attempt.'[7]

On 18 February 1917, *Aurora*, with her engines and boiler cleaned, batteries recharged, funnel repainted and generally spruced up as well as Gillies and other crew members could achieve, was returned to Shackleton,[8] who had been impatient to sell the ship, get back to England and offer his services to the war effort. Moyes recalled taking 'a couple of girls' down to have a look at the ship. 'As they ran down the pier to the gangway leading to the *Aurora*, Shackleton was coming up. I'll never forget it. He came up and stood there and looked at us, looked at the girls and said: 'You know, I'm always too late!''[9]

Within a fortnight, Shackleton was able to report to Leonard Tripp that the ship had been sold. The solicitor replied: 'There is no doubt that [shipping agents] Scales & Co have done a great deal for you.'[10] Total receipts for ship, stores and equipment amounted to £15,867 and, after discharging a ship's mortgage, repaying Tripp the monies he had raised to meet the *Endurance* party's wages (some £5,000), with interest, and the New Zealand government £1,500 for crew wages, there was a surplus of £1,354.[11] Shackleton could indulge in a rare financial gesture to his wife, sending her £200. He also sent a 'gift' to the three Australians of Mackintosh's party: Jack, Gaze (£20 each) and Richards (£25).[12] Richards would express gratitude at the '70 quid', his salary plus the bonus, he was paid for his 26 months' service to the expedition.[13]

Stenhouse was still in New Zealand when the relief expedition returned and met the rescued men.[14] On 20 February, he wrote to Tripp from Auckland: 'We (Worsley, Cope and I) sail [on RMS *Makura*] at noon today . . . I thank you again for all your kindness to me during my stay in New Zealand.'[15] Three days later, Worsley reported that the three men were 'having a splendid time on board here'.[16] This was a happy finale to Stenhouse's New Zealand stay, and he and Worsley, the former skippers of the two expedition ships that had been simultaneously adrift in unique circumstances, doubtless felt that they had much in common. Cope was apparently restored to former spirits.

Captain J. K. Davis, accompanied by de la Motte, chief officer on *Aurora*'s relief expedition, sailed for Sydney on 22 February.[17] Davis summed up his feelings to his father: 'The last voyage in the *Aurora* was a very fine one . . .' and added that it was also 'a very sad one. Mackintosh and Hayward were lost after their work was completed.'[18]

Shackleton left New Zealand for Australia on 8 March. Richards was at the Spencer Street railway station in Melbourne to greet him and was to recall: 'The first words he said to me were "Where's [Minister for Navy] Jensen?"'[19] Sir Ernest felt he had some unfinished business to settle with the Australian

Advisory Committee, and a stormy meeting soon took place. A member of the committee, Professor Orme Masson, reported to Davis on the outcome:

> Our committee, anxious to avoid any appearance of discord, turned up in force at the station to meet Shackleton, but he at once made it apparent that he was boiling over with a grievance and he demanded to meet the committee and have it out ... he challenged me personally with thwarting his schemes and spoiling his reputation. Afterwards at the Navy Office, we went at it hammer and tongs for about an hour and there was plain speaking on both sides. Finally the position was made clear – that he thought he was the best man to command the rescue expedition while we preferred you and were determined that you should have undivided control. So we agreed to differ and shook hands over it.[20]

Shackleton gave a public lecture in Melbourne at which he introduced the three Australians of the rescued party – Richards, Gaze and Jack – to the audience. Richards recalled: 'It was amazing to see [Shackleton] before an audience without any visual aids holding them enthralled.'[21] Writing from Bendigo, he reported to Tripp that, while in Melbourne for two days, he had had 'a long talk to the Lord Mayor (Sir D. Hennessy) and met the [Australian] committee ... I think the feeling here is very sympathetic to [Shackleton].'[22]

Tripp, aware of the anti-Shackleton sentiment that had preceded the relief expedition, was keen to promote a sympathetic attitude to him. In his response to Richards, he wrote: '[Shackleton] will arrive in England debt free. Considering he has lost the *Endurance*, this is a great performance.'[23] Tripp was glossing over the fact that any satisfactory financial outcome for Shackleton was because of the forbearance, following McNab's negotiations, of the three governments that had financed the relief expedition and the refitting of the ship in 1914 and 1917 to press for any repayment. The total cost of the relief expedition was assessed at £20,312.[24]

Davis's reservations about his former leader would remain. In June 1917, he wrote: '... [Shackleton] has had a triumph ... by his fine boat journey but certainly not by his organisation ... he has monopolised all of [the credit for the relief expedition] ... [I] speculate ... how much of the blame he would have accepted had I made a mess of it.'[25]

This followed a letter from Sir Douglas Mawson, suggesting that

> the whole Ross Sea business has been smothered by the press acting under instructions from the Daily Chronicle ... Shackleton is anxious, as his Weddell Sea side came to grief, not to be coupled with any further disasters ... it was arranged that on no account would you get any credit for the work ... However don't bother about them – Shackleton's sun has really set – it certainly has amongst the better people here.[26]

❖

The survivors of the Ross Sea party returned to a world that showed only a momentary interest in their story before it was largely forgotten amidst the closing stages of the First World War. They soon went their separate ways.

Ernest Wild returned to the Royal Navy but within a year was dead, the victim of typhoid. Keith Jack volunteered for the Australian Expeditionary Force, then was seconded to a munitions factory. The officers of *Aurora* during the drift, Joseph Stenhouse and Leslie Thomson, both had active service in the Royal Navy. Wireless operator Lionel Hooke served on minesweepers in the North Sea and flew airships.

Howard Ninnis, something of a 'mystery man' to others on *Aurora*, accompanied Shackleton to England after the conclusion of the relief expedition. The former Admiralty man served in the latter days of the war in eastern waters 'in a special capacity'.[27] Alfred Larkman worked for the Admiralty, surveying and fitting out warships.

Many of the crew from the engine room and decks of *Aurora* enlisted in the army and fought at the front line. 'Chippie' Mauger was wounded at Passchendaele while serving with the Otago Rifles.

Irvine Gaze joined the Royal Flying Corps,[28] flew two-seater Bristol fighters and was shot down twice behind enemy lines. He would recall in a 1977 interview:

> Eleven days before the armistice I was flying at 18,000 feet without oxygen and without parachutes. The aircraft was very sloppy. It was a Bristol Fighter, a two-seater, and I had an observer, but one of the [German] Fokkers came up underneath and luckily only shot the engine. I went down as quickly as I could and [the German pilot] was shooting most of the time. But when he saw what was going to happen – that I hadn't a chance – he desisted and I landed the aircraft in a vegetable garden next to the German Headquarters. As happened 10 days earlier when I crashed and got thrown over, I wasn't seriously hurt, except that during the dive I got a terrific headache, and so did the observer. I had it for about three weeks. The observer was slightly wounded and was taken to hospital straight away. The German pilot landed afterwards and came and told me I was his 31st victim. The guard took me prisoner and took me in to the adjutant. He saw I had the [Polar Medal] white ribbon and asked me with whom I had been there. I told him 'Shackleton'. He said, 'Oh, I was at school with Shackleton at Dulwich College.' He asked me if I had any money and said, 'We'll take that but I'll give you the equivalent in marks.' He said, 'We would like you to dine with us tonight', which I did, and they all talked English and were quite friendly with the exception of one, and that was [Herman] Goering. A little later I was tapped on the shoulder and taken prisoner, taken to the prison camp. After the Armistice, I started to walk to the German border through Belgium and we got to the border and I saw the whole passing of the German northern army over the bridge. They piled their arms on

the other side. The three of us, including another Australian, must have walked over the whole of Belgium and eventually arrived back in Brussels, where we made contact with the British Embassy that had just been established. They arranged for us to get back to Foxton and get across to England again.[29]

Boatswain James Paton stayed with *Aurora* and was lost with all hands after the old vessel (veteran of five voyages to the Antarctic continent), laden with coal, disappeared on a voyage from Newcastle, Australia, to Chile in June 1917. A bottle and a lifebuoy from the ship were found on Australian beaches, and Morton Moyes, a former Mawson man and a veteran of the relief expedition, later speculated that *Aurora*

> struck a storm and was overloaded with coal . . . I think she had got strained and sank. When she came back from leaving the men down there at Ross Island, she must have had a terrible lot of straining in the ice and although they overhauled her at Port Chalmers, you can't find out that kind of thing from a ship in dock. When Mawson left Hobart [in December 1911] to go to the Antarctic, she was heavily loaded and she struck a bit of a storm and became pretty well unmanageable. I don't know too many people know that. She was nearly rushed up into Bass Strait instead of going to Macquarie Island. The wind would catch her and move her along and the wheel wouldn't bring her back.[30]

On the voyage south in 1915, Stenhouse had observed: 'Old ship is beginning to take seas on board and as she occasionally stands on her head and threatens to somersault, life is rather uncomfortable.'[31]

'Richie' Richards was badly affected by his Ross Sea experiences, and ill health prevented his going to war:

> Prior to going to Antarctica I had been a very active person and rowing and football – when I came back I had to live like an old man – I still had the key to the rowing sheds, but I never once entered the door because I felt I just couldn't . . . I broke down in health at one time about three months and another about one month. I was about the age of 40.[32]

> I never recovered . . . I had quite a number of quacks including a specialist in Melbourne. None could find anything wrong. The symptoms were physical weakness and the breakdown after physical strain either or mental. Terrific migraine up to about 40 when it ceased for no apparent reason . . . my beloved football and rowing were cut out.[33]

On his return from Antarctica in 1917, he would receive a white feather from an anonymous sender,[34] an insidious and ill-informed suggestion of cowardice to a man who was to receive the highest award for gallantry in saving life. Richards later resumed teaching and eventually became principal of the Ballarat School of Mines. In retirement, he maintained occasional contact with surviving members of the Ross Sea party and the relief expedition, including Gaze, Jack, Larkman, Stevens, Joyce and Davis.[35] He and Dr Fred Middleton, however, had little contact. In 1961, Stevens described Richards as 'a grand lad'.[36] Perhaps one of the finest tributes came years earlier from Mackintosh in a testimonial dated 29 September 1915, prophetically given before the Mt Hope journey. 'His services have been such as no money could buy, [n]or could I speak of [him] too highly.'[37]

The last of the Shackleton men, Richards died in 1985. Not forgetting his gratitude to New Zealanders after the relief of the party in 1917, he donated immensely valuable artefacts from the expedition, including his diary and medals, to the Canterbury Museum, Christchurch.

Ernest Joyce, who married a New Zealand woman, fell upon hard times after his Antarctic experience. In 1929, he published *The South Polar Trail,* an account of the Ross Sea expedition that has since distorted historical perspective, and which this book seeks to remedy. Numerous passages in Joyce's book imply his taking a leadership role that did not occur other than his shared leadership on the return from Mt Hope following Mackintosh's enfeeblement through scurvy. Some sections imply a challenge to Mackintosh that is inconsistent with Joyce's deference to authority, instilled in him during his time in the Royal Navy.

In his book, Joyce reproduced a letter of appointment purportedly written by Shackleton but differing in significant respects from that printed fifteen years earlier in the *Sydney Morning Herald.* Contrary to the book version, the letter in the newspaper made no reference (or indeed inference) to Joyce as a leader. It is clear that he was to be responsible to an officer in charge of the shore party. This is omitted from the book version, which also suggests that the depot-laying party to the Beardmore Glacier would proceed under Joyce's direction.

Richards was to later explain:

Joyce and I were pretty close. I knew his good qualities and his weaknesses . . . I think he really believed things that at times were just not true, e.g. we saw Scott's grave. It was partly this – perhaps entirely this – that impelled me to write that diary from February to March 1916 when it was a distinct possibility we would not get back. I wanted my version of what had taken place to go on record . . . He saw himself larger than life. This comes out in his book . . . He says many times 'I did this or that.' Not so. From 82° S when Mac proved incapable of seeing it through, what was done was a consensus of the three in our tent – Hayward, Joyce and myself. I was only young but I flatter myself I could always handle Joyce.[38]

Unfortunately, Joyce's falsification of key elements of the letter of appointment, now exposed for the first time, goes beyond the characteristics described by Richards.

In December 1928, Stevens wrote to H. R. Mill, Shackleton's first biographer, who also contributed a very guarded introduction to Joyce's book:

> I am sorry if Joyce gave himself away in his book . . . a good fellow in his own sphere, it is not fair to expect more of him than his fortune in life warrants . . . As much as the rest of us, he is entitled to his 'foibles' and the critic ought to have some background to give perspective to views of him. I came across traces of his lecture tour which were not creditable to him perhaps . . .[39]

Following publication of his book, Joyce wrote:

> This expedition was no doubt the most extraordinary that ever left the shores of civilisation. The playing of chances in equipping the ship in Australia, the sending out of men to join who were only fit for drawing room tea parties. Shackleton's letter of my appointment was practically annulled by giving Captain Mackintosh discretionary powers, unfortunately he did not show this to me until we left, when I was arguing the point with him about taking the dogs south on the first trip . . .[40]

As is indicated by the letter of appointment published in the *Sydney Morning Herald* in 1914, Joyce had no valid complaint as regards the leadership issue.

Before his death in 1940 at the Ecclestone Hotel, London, where he worked as a doorman, Joyce had proposed his own Antarctic expedition in 1930, a trade exhibition in 1931–32, an air expedition to the North Pole in 1934 and had attempted, on behalf of Russia, to purchase Scott's old ship, *Discovery*.[41]

In a letter written in the early 1960s, Gaze compared the characters of Joyce and Mackintosh:

> They had two different natures and temperaments. The skipper was a bit jealous of Joyce's experience – very impatient to get on with things even if it meant taking silly risks. In other words, not the ideal man to have the 'say so'. [Joyce] was patient and unwilling to take unnecessary risks. He was much more knowledgeable as to the land and the barrier conditions.[42]

Alexander Stevens, who felt the Shackleton escapade had wasted two years of his life, had little wish to recall it. He wrote in 1920: 'I went out as a geologist, with, I think, a keen interest and a desire to make good. All the way out I found my attempts to study Antarctic geology more thoroughly thwarted in absurd ways.'[43] In his 1928 letter to Mill, he wrote: 'I do not know just how familiar you are with the circumstances of the whole thing. In my confidential opinion they are disgraceful, and the less said about them the better.'[44]

Stevens later became professor of geography at the University of Glasgow, and in later years suffered from blindness and emphysema. He died in 1965. A student would remember with affection field trips that the professor led to

Europe,[46] and an obituary in the *Glasgow Herald* stated that he was a 'legend in geographical circles for his independence of judgement and his fighting qualities in support of it, and he was formidable in debate'.[46]

Irvine Gaze ran a family boot-making business in Victoria, Australia. As an instructor with the Royal Australian Air Force during the Second World War, he trained nearly 10,000 air crew. Gaze died in 1978, a year after being a guest of honour of the New Zealand Antarctic Society at the opening of Canterbury Museum's Antarctic Centre.[47]

Keith Jack was, until his retirement in 1950, secretary of the Operational Safety Committee of the Department of Munitions and Supply in Australia. At the time of his death at the age of 81 in 1966, he was still using a watch given to him by Shackleton after the ITAE.[48] His diary and significant expedition clothing, lantern slides and equipment are held at the La Trobe Library, Museum of Victoria.

John Cope was responsible for an expedition to Graham Land in 1920, where he abandoned two men (Thomas Bagshawe and Charles Lester), who, quite cheerfully as it turned out, passed a winter in a makeshift shelter on the Antarctic Peninsula. Cope's actions were widely condemned. One of the four expedition members, Australian Hubert Wilkins, described it as 'perhaps the most mismanaged Antarctic expedition in history'.[49] Cope died in 1947.

Joseph Stenhouse married Mackintosh's widow, Gladys, in 1923. He returned to Antarctica as co-commander of Scott's *Discovery* on whaling research in 1925–27 and 1928. In the Second World War, he was one of twelve survivors when his ship *Sheba* struck a mine and sank in October 1940. Stenhouse was posted missing while on active service in the Red Sea in September 1941. Among other awards he received the Distinguished Service Order, Distinguished Service Cross, and the Croix de Guerre (with palm).[50]

Leslie Thomson served in the Royal Navy from 1917 to 1919, but poor health prevented his enlisting in the Royal Australian Navy on the outbreak of the Second World War. At the time of his retirement from the sea in February 1942, he was a third officer on a merchant vessel. In the words of Stenhouse, he had proved himself to be 'a thorough seaman, first class navigator and an officer of outstanding ability'.[51] Thomson died in 1946, aged 59.

Lionel Hooke was knighted for his services to the radio industry in Australia and died in 1984. Alf Larkman taught engineering at technical colleges in Hawera and Wanganui in New Zealand, and died in 1962. Clarence Mauger spent his working life as a shipwright and carpenter, and died in Dunedin in 1963. Howard Ninnis became a radio announcer and station manager in the 1940s in Dunedin, where he died in 1956.

After the relief expedition, Morton Moyes returned to his former position of navigation instructor with the Royal Australian Navy before undertaking a significant post-war task as Chief Rehabilitation Officer. Shackleton showed his gratitude to him by presenting him with a theodolite.[52] He lived to the age of 95 and died in 1981.[53]

Frederick Middleton resumed his studies, became a resident medical officer at Melbourne Hospital and practised medicine in Australia until retirement. He died in 1972.[54]

Captain John King Davis was awarded the OBE in 1964 and died three years later after a distinguished maritime career.

Sir Ernest Shackleton's death from cardiac causes in 1921 at South Georgia throws into question his physical fitness for the transcontinental crossing, had he succeeded in landing on the Weddell Sea coast. Richards said in 1973: '[We] all thought at the time he would get through. Since my return I believe he would have collapsed on the journey . . . the atheroma that finally killed him was in evidence when we met in 1917.'[55]

The question arises as to Shackleton's part in the deaths of three men of the Ross Sea party. He underestimated the task of the Ross Sea party, as evidenced by his comments to the Royal Geographical Society in 1913. His choice of scientific staff in England took no account of their prowess for sledging duties, as did the appointment of a clergyman, no matter his other qualities. With Shackleton's geographical remoteness from the party, much rested on his appointed leader, Æneas Mackintosh, no leader of men and who had demonstrated flawed judgement that almost cost two lives on the *Nimrod* expedition. Mackintosh's considerable achievements in the course of the ITAE are overshadowed by the circumstances of his death and that of a subordinate, the direct consequence of flawed decision-making, as was the inclusion of the Reverend Arnold Spencer-Smith in the Mt Hope party, a decision that cost a further life. Shackleton's expectations as to the timing of his transcontinental journey played an important part in Mackintosh's decision-making, and were inadequately conveyed to Mackintosh, especially after Shackleton learnt of ice conditions in the Weddell Sea late in 1914. All of these factors compounded and resulted in Shackleton's bearing at least indirect responsibility for the loss of three of his men, as well as his ultimate responsibility as leader of the ITAE. It was a loss he keenly felt when he learnt the news from the survivors.

Relief expedition personnel Le Gros, Gillies, de la Motte and Dakin all returned to their former positions in Australia. Le Gros continued his career at sea and in 1924 was serving on SS *Goulburn*. Of the AB's, MacNeill emigrated to Canada in the 1930s and served for 22 years with the Canadian Steamship

Company; MacDonald served for ten years on ships in New Zealand waters; and Hannan and Murphy settled in New Zealand.[56] Wireless operator Tim Ryan went to the Arctic for nine months before returning to Sydney as a telegraphist. He died in 1946.[57]

The former lead dog Oscar is reputed to have spent his final days in the Wellington Zoo. Joyce retained Gunner and the skinned coat of this dog later became a mat in his home. Gunner's collar, with other items of Joyce's memorabilia, including an inscribed compass given to him by Shackleton in February 1917, was held by the family of Joyce's widow until being sold in 1987.[58]

In 1923, Victor Hayward (deceased), Ernest Edward Mills Joyce, Richard Walter Richards and Ernest Henry Wild were each awarded the Albert Medal for gallantry in saving life on land, the civilian equivalent of the Victoria Cross. The award to Hayward was for saving the life of Mackintosh, and to Joyce, Richards and Wild for saving the lives of Mackintosh and Hayward.[59]

In February 1918, nine members of the shore party were awarded the silver polar medal with clasp, inscribed 'Antarctic 1914–16'. The tenth member, Joyce, received the clasp only, as he was already the holder of the silver medal. Mackintosh, too, already had the silver polar medal, but through a clerical error he received (posthumously) a second silver medal. Of those on *Aurora*'s drift, Stenhouse, Thomson, Larkman, Donnelly, Mauger, Hooke and Ninnis likewise received the silver medal with clasp, and Paton the silver clasp. The rest of the ship's crew during the main voyage and drift, with two exceptions, received the bronze polar medal with clasp, similarly inscribed. The exceptions were D'Anglade and Shaw, on the recommendation of Shackleton, doubtless because of their refusal of duty in the closing days of *Aurora*'s drift and voyage.

In May 1921, after some fuss with the Admiralty as to the issuing of any polar awards to members of the relief expedition, the award of the bronze polar medal without clasp was made to 21 members of 'the *Aurora* Relief Expedition of 1916–17'. The award of a special bronze clasp 'Antarctic 1917' was made to three previous recipients of the bronze medal – Davis, Paton and Kavanagh.[60]

The only person on the relief expedition to miss out on a medal or clasp was Shackleton. Some have suggested this resulted from his supernumerary status on the relief expedition. Shackleton died in January 1921, just months before the announcement. The controversy of his participation in the relief expedition is likely to have tainted the decision resulting in this apparent slight.

To cover the extended period of the Ross Sea component of the ITAE, the

1917 clasp in silver was awarded to the ten men 'of the original *Aurora* party who were in the Antarctic in 1917', including, curiously, the three who had died in 1916.

Despite the award of the Albert Medals in 1923 to four of the men who toiled to Mt Hope and back, there was little recognition or acknowledgement of the achievements of the men and dogs who laid the depots required by Shackleton, or of the men who nursed the near-stricken vessel back to port.

After the departure of the relief expedition in 1917, no human visited the wooden huts on Ross Island for 30 years. Unlike the northern outpost at Cape Royds, the buildings at Cape Evans and Hut Point became substantially filled with ice. A Norwegian whaler, *Star 1* of the Ross Sea Whaling Expedition, penetrated McMurdo Sound in January 1924, but from a distance 'nothing was to be seen [at Cape Evans] except ice and snow'.[61]

In 1947, 'task force personnel' of Operation Highjump from the United States icebreaker *Burton Island* visited Cape Evans. An article in *National Geographic* described the state of the hut:

> It appeared somewhat disorderly after the buffetings of 35 winters. Snow had drifted through cracks in the planks of the sealed cabin. Straw and debris were strewn over the nearly ice-frozen volcanic ash.

The frozen carcass of a dog stood on four legs as if it were alive. Seal carcasses from which fresh steaks might have been cut lay about. Scattered around the cabin were cartons of provisions, still good to eat. A box of matches ignited easily.[62]

In December 1955, a *National Geographic* photographer, John E. Fletcher, travelled south with the American Operation Deepfreeze I, whose personnel were forbidden to enter the historic Cape Evans hut. He aimed a camera and flash through a window in its north-west corner into the dark interior.[63] The result was a ghostly scene set in silence – a half-completed meal, abandoned by Joyce, Wild, Jack and Shackleton 39 years before, frozen in time.

Although the visitors 'sealed the cabin as a memorial to Scott and Shackleton', it did not remain secure for long. In December 1956, apparently against orders (and probably enticed by the recently published *National Geographic* photo), men from USS *Glacier* entered the hut through a blown-out window over the pony stables at the kitchen (west) end of the hut. They interferred with the historic scene and broke open some of the food-supply cases to see what was in them.[64]

Two months later, Dr R. A. Falla, then Director of the Dominion Museum, Wellington, inspected the hut and reported: '[It] is filled with ice except for the kitchen section, to which access may be gained by a leadlight [*sic*] window. Stores and equipment still reasonably well preserved are scattered about, both inside and outside the building . . . although most of them are embedded in the ice.'[65]

In March 1957, some members of the New Zealand party of the Trans-Antarctic Expedition who entered the hut were unimpressed. The official account records: '[T]he inside was a shambles. Either the last party had left in a hurry or had been very slack in their habits. Much of the hut was drifted up with snow and ice, and the interior was badly sooted up.'[66] The account seems to have been written without knowledge of the circumstances of the last inhabitants of the precincts, as was another concerning a 'pilgrimage' by New Zealanders to Cape Evans a month later:

> It was a saddening disappointment to all of us! The ground around the hut was a complete shambles, with rubbish, empty tins and the ancient carcasses of seals strewn in every direction. The bottom floor of the hut was filled with ice and only the top floor was accessible, but this too was an unpleasant mixture of disorder and dirt. Obviously no attempt had been made . . . to keep it in the least bit tidy. [A]s there was little we could do, we were glad to go.[67]

R. W. Richards, a veteran of the Ross Sea party, reacted strongly to such statements:

> It's a pity they did not have a little more imagination. We were only five effectives left towards the end, Cope was not responsible for his behaviour and I was very ill and it was a desperate fight for survival. We had just done 1500 miles man-hauling and had lost three of our men. One who did not live through 1916 would have difficulty in appreciating [the] conditions. It took all we knew to just survive and I guess orderly disposal of unused stuff took a very minor place in our scheme of things . . . I am not very impressed with the holier than thou attitude of some of the moderns. Anyhow the British government thought the effort worth the award of three Albert Medals to us – and during the last few months we have been given the George Cross as the equivalent to the now discarded Albert Medal.[68]

The motorised tractors and sledges, backed by air support and radio, of the Commonwealth Trans-Antarctic expedition of 1955–57 fulfilled Ernest Shackleton's dream of a transcontinental crossing. This has been followed by an international effort to protect the heritage of the historic sites (notably through the work of the Antarctic Heritage Trust), none of which is more important than the huts used by the men of Shackleton's 1914–17 expedition.

In the early 1960s, a British glaciologist scrutinised the snow surface in the Gap near the bottom of the Beardmore Glacier. Dr Charles Swithinbank reported in a letter to Richards:

> I can say with considerable assurance that the depot is lost, since we sledged right through The Gap and saw no sign. There were large sastrugi on the highest part of The Gap and this means that it is an area of snow accumulation. We left a sledge on the southern slope and found it under a foot of snow when we dug it out a year later. I would only expect the depot to survive 45 years if it had been placed on bare ice that is quite extensive on the southern slopes a mile or more from the highest part of The Gap. We searched very carefully towards the Granite Pillars with binoculars, and though there was many a boulder lying about on the ice, we saw no artefacts.[69]

The depots on the Barrier and at Mt Hope, laid at such a cost by the Ross Sea party, have been lost to the eternal elements of Antarctica.

NOTES

Abbreviations

AA   Australian Archives, Canberra
CM   Canterbury Museum, Chrictchurch
HL   Hocken Library, Dunedin
ML   Mitchell Library, State Library of New
            South Wales, Sydney
PRO   Public Record Office, London
RGS   Royal Geographical Society, London
SLV   State Library of Victoria, Melbourne
SPRI   Scott Polar Research Institute,
            Cambridge

1   *An expedition to cross Antartica*

1. Shackleton was knighted 14 December 1909.
2. Scott 1905, ii, p. 172.
3. Shackleton 1909, ii, pp. 348–49.
4. See e.g. Jones 1982.
5. See e.g. Ross 1982.
6. See e.g. *Reader's Digest* 1985.
7. Bruce 1911, p. 19.
8. Mill 1923, p. 184.
9. Quartermain 1981, p. 18, quoting *Scottish Geographical Magazine*, April 1910, pp. 192–95.
10. Headland 1989, entry 1317; *Reader's Digest* 1985, pp. 160–63; Mill 1905, pp. 427–31.
11. Shackleton 1919, pp. 23–27.
12. Headland 1989, entry 1451; Hayes 1932, pp. 129–37; *Reader's Digest* 1985, pp. 202–05.
13. Quartermain 1981, p. 19, quoting W. S. Bruce in *Nature*, January 1914, p. 533.
14. See e.g. Mill 1923, p. 201; Fisher 1957, pp. 297–99.
15. Prospectus 1913, SPRI.
16. Markham to RGS, February 1914, Colbeck papers, CM.
17. Report 4 March 1914, RGS.
18. Shackleton to Bruce, 20 August 1913, SPRI.
19. In fact, 1,740 nautical miles, including the proposed deviation westwards along the Queen Maud Range.
20. Headland 1989, entry 1438.
21. Cottesloe, 'The Story of the Battersea Dogs'.
22. Admiralty memo, 7 February 1914, PRO.
23. Ibid., 27 February 1914.
24. Admiralty minute, 31 July 1917, PRO.
25. Shackleton to Admiralty, 2 February 1914, PRO.
26. Ibid.
27. Shackleton to Churchill, 27 February 1914, PRO.
28. Minute, W. S. Churchill, 28 February 1914, PRO.
29. Admiralty to Shackleton, 14 March 1914; Memo to First Lord, January 1914, PRO.
30. Shackleton to Commonwealth Government of Australia, AA.
31. Shackleton to W. Mather, 30 June 1914, SPRI.
32. *The Times*, 16 January 1914.
33. Naval Secretary to Shackleton, 27 August 1914, AA.
34. See e.g. Mill 1923, p. 202.
35. Shackleton 1919, p. xiv.
36. Davis 1962, p. 258.
37. Prospectus 1913, SPRI.
38. Report of meeting, 4 March 1914, RGS.
39. Baptism certificate, courtesy E. Dowler.
40. Davis 1962, p. 63.
41. Mackintosh 1990, pp. 105–21, has his own account of this journey.
42. Dr Marshall, assisted by Drs Michell and Mackay; Mackintosh 1990, p. 44.
43. Davis 1962, p. 138; Ayres 1999, p. 37.
44. *Bedfordshire Times*, courtesy E. Dowler; Mackintosh 1990, p. 134.
45. Mackintosh 1990, pp. 99–104; Shackleton 1909, ii, pp. 42–51. Spelling of McGillon from Agreement and account of crew, *Nimrod*. Referred to as a New Zealander in Mackintosh's diary, 9 January 1914.
46. Bull diary, 3 January 1909.
47. Harbord dairy, 3 January 1909.
48. Mackintosh 1990, p. 101.

49. Shackleton 1909, ii, p. 48, referring to Bernard Day, motor expert on the *Nimrod* expedition.
50. Prospectus 1913, SPRI.
51. Scott 1905, ii, pp. 210–11; Yelverton 2000, pp. 259, 270.
52. Joyce 1929, p. 21.
53. M. Barne, November 1905, Admiralty, PRO.
54. Joyce 1929, p. 22.
55. Shackleton to Marshall, 21 October 1908, CM.
56. Marshall diary, 12, 13 July, 3 October 1908.
57. Mawson 1914, i, p. 26.
58. *The Times*, 12 October 1911, courtesy S. P. McElrea.
59. Mawson 1914, i, p.17.
60. Sydney Harbour Trust Office to Joyce, 16 July 1918, Curlett correspondence.
61. *Sydney Morning Herald*, 29 June 1914.

2   *The* Ionic *contingent*

1. *Hobart Mercury*, 2 November 1914, courtesy R. F. Perachie. The eleven were Stenhouse, Hayward, Spencer-Smith, Wild, Stevens, Cope, Larkman, Ninnis, Mauger, Leonard and Mason.
2. *El Liberal,* Madrid, 30 September 1914, courtesy R. F. Perachie.
3. *Sydney Morning Herald*, 9 October 1914; Fisher 1957, p. 312.
4. Deaconess Spencer-Smith to the Rev. Mr Fraser, 9 December 1953; H. Skelton to Fraser, 15 December 1953; Dr Venn to Fraser, 15 December 1953,Spencer-Smith papers; Spencer-Smith diary, 7 March 1915.
5. A. J. T. Fraser, Antarctic Padre.
6. *Scottish Chronicle*, 18 September 1914, Spencer-Smith papers.
7. Richards to Harrowfield, 25 September 1981, 10 June 1982.
8. A. G. E. Jones to R. W. Richards and Harrowfield, 21 February 1982.
9. John Stevens to McElrea, 27 November 1982.
10. *Polar Record*, vol. 3, no. 42; *The Times,* 19 March 1942, Stenhouse papers.
11. Report of meeting 4 March 1914, RGS; B. A. Simpson to Harrowfield, 26 May 1983; Richards, interview with McElrea.
12. A. G. E. Jones, 'Tubby'.
13. Davis 1961, p. 260.
14. *Antarctic*, vol. 1, p. 79.
15. Ninnis diary.
16. *The Motor*, vol. 26, no. 259 1914, Ninnis papers. Also termed a motor tractor.
17. *Daily Graphic*, 24 May 1914, courtesy R. F. Perachie.
18. Shackleton library, RGS.
19. *Antarctic*, vol. 3, p. 414.
20. C. C. Mauger, Intentions Hopeful.
21. The account of the voyage to Australia is substantially taken from the Ninnis and Stenhouse diaries.
22. Larkman diary, 11 October 1914.
23. *Wanganui Chronicle*, 4 June 1962, courtesy Margaret Grayson.
24. Ninnis diary, 18 September 1914.
25. Stenhouse diary, 21 September 1914.
26. Ninnis diary, 22 September 1914.
27. *Sydney Morning Herald,* 9 October 1914.
28. Davis to Shackleton, 16 March 1914, SPRI.
29. Davis to Kinsey, 16 March 1914, CM.
30. Davis 1962, p. 245; Stenhouse diary, 5 November 1914.
31. Stenhouse diary, 5, 6 November, 4 December 1914.
32. Shackleton to Mackintosh, 18 September 1914, quoted Fisher 1957.
33. David to Fisher, 13 October 1914, AA.
34. Memo (PM's Office), 21 December 1915, AA. There was no budgeting limitation conveyed to the manager of the Naval Dockyard at Cockatoo Island, who considered he was 'practically given carte blanche' in the matter. The actual cost of repairs was £3,281 4s 1d. (Report from the Joint Committee of Public Accounts, AA.)
35. Stenhouse diary, 9 November 1914.
36. Paton to Mackintosh, 20 October 1914; Mackintosh to Paton, 20 October 1914; Stenhouse papers.
37. Crew list, ATL.
38. Stenhouse diary, 5 November 1914.
39. Stenhouse, *Aurora* logbook, 1 November 1914; Stenhouse diary, 1 November 1914.
40. Stenhouse diary, 31 October 1914.
41. Larkman diary, 30 October 1914.
42. Ninnis diary, 1 November 1914.
43. Ibid.
44. Spencer-Smith to mother, 8 November 1914, Spencer-Smith papers.
45. Stenhouse diary, 2 November 1914.
46. Wild diary, 3 November 1914.
47. Ninnis diary, 1 November 1914.
48. Ibid., 3 November 1914.

49. Ibid., 7 November 1914.
50. Ibid., 23 December 1914.
51. Wild diary, 24 November 1914; Ninnis diary, 30 November 1914.
52. Hayward diary, 5, 6 November 1914; Stenhouse diary, 5 November 1914.
53. Spencer-Smith to mother, 8 November 1914, Spencer-Smith papers.
54. Stenhouse diary, 6 November 1914. A ticket for this ferry crossing was found at Cape Evans in 1999, along with photos that identified it as belonging to Spencer-Smith.
55. Spencer-Smith to mother, 8 November 1914, Spencer-Smith papers.
56. Stenhouse diary, 6 November 1914.
57. Stenhouse diary and work diary, various dates.
58. Larkman, 'An Engineer's Antarctic Logbook'.
59. Ninnis diary, 5 December 1914; General Manager Dockyard to Navy Office, 7 December 1914, AA.
60. John Hooke to Harrowfield, 1 November 1983; *Antarctic*, vol. 7, p. 29.
61. Stenhouse papers.
62. Spencer Smith to mother, 18 November 1914, Spencer-Smith papers.
63. Stenhouse diary, 8, 22 November 1914.
64. Stenhouse diary, various entries 14–29 November 1914; Larkman diary 1–10 December 1914. Two of the plays were Y*eoman of the Guard* and *HMS Pinafore*.
65. Stenhouse diary, 14 November 1914.
66. Ibid., 16 November 1914.
67. Mauger, Intentions Hopeful.
68. Ibid.
69. Larkman, 'An Engineer's Antarctic Logbook'.
70. Crew list, ATL.
71. Doreen Smith to Harrowfield, February 1984.
72. Stenhouse diary, 10 December 1914.

3   *'God-speed and a safe return'*

1. Stevens report.
2. *The Times*, 16 July 1914, quoted in Fisher 1957, p. 314.
3. Mackintosh to Andrews, 3 December 1914, Stenhouse papers.
4. B. A. Carson, Record Office, University of Cambridge, to McElrea, 22 June 1984.
5. *Sydney Morning Herald*, 11 December 1914.
6. Stevens report.
7. Richards to Mackintosh, 21 November, 1 December 1914, Stenhouse papers.
8. Richards, interview with Lathlean.
9. Richards to McElrea, 25 January 1985.
10. Gaze, Radio NZ interview.
11. Gaze to Mackintosh undated, Stenhouse papers.
12. Stevens report.
13. Stenhouse papers.
14. Jack to Mackintosh, 7 December 1914, Stenhouse papers.
15. Stevens report.
16. Mackintosh to Hutchison & Cuff, 28 November 1914, Stenhouse papers.
17. Mawson to Hutchinson & Cuff, 23 December 1914, Tripp papers. Knighthood details: Ayres 1999, p. 102.
18. Mackintosh to White, 10 December 1914, Stenhouse papers.
19. Tripp to Mackintosh, 14 December 1914, Tripp papers. Tripp appears to include the £700 raised by the Sydney committee in his total of £2,400.
20. Stenhouse, *Aurora* logbook, 11 December 1914; Stevens report.
21. Stevens report.
22. Clifford Love to J. T. Isles, and reply, 3 December 1914, Stenhouse papers.
23. Stenhouse papers.
24. Stevens report.
25. Stenhouse diary, 26 November 1914, *Sydney Morning Herald*, *Sydney Daily Telegraph*, 5 December 1914, Stenhouse papers.
26. Larkman diary, 10 December 1914.
27. Agreement and account of crew, ATL.
28. Stevens report; Agreement and account of crew, *Aurora*.
29. Stenhouse papers.
30. Stenhouse, *Aurora* logbook, 11 December 1914. Why sails were being measured up at this late stage is not clear.
31. Stenhouse, *Aurora* logbook, 10, 12 December 1914.
32. Stevens report. Jack diary, 15 December 1915.
33. *Sydney Morning Herald*, 16 December 1914.
34. Stenhouse, *Aurora* logbook, 19 December 1914. Spencer-Smith to mother, 30 December 1914. , Spencer-Smith papers. A fuller description of *Aurora*, 'a three-mast vessel, square-rigged on the foremast, and schooner-rigged on the main and mizzen mast', is in Mawson 1914, i, p.14.

35. Stenhouse diary, 19 December 1914.
36. Spencer-Smith to mother, 20 December 1914, Spencer-Smith papers.
37. Stenhouse diary, 19 December 1914.
38. Stenhouse, *Aurora* logbook, 20 December 1914.
39. Thomson diary, 23 December 1914. A temporary appointment as second mate, R. B. Roberts, left the ship in Sydney, Stenhouse diary, 21 December 1914.
40. Malcolm Thomson to Harrowfield, 27 November 1985.
41. Lance Grubham to Mackintosh, 21 December 1914, Stenhouse papers.
42. 1912–14 French expedition, Headland 1989, entry 1479.
43. Stevens report.
44. Ninnis diary, 20 December 1914.
45. Hayward diary, 20 December 1914.
46. Paton diary, 23 December 1914; Stevens report.
47. Stenhouse diary, 21 December 1914.
48. Stenhouse, *Aurora* logbook, 22 December 1914.
49. Private Secretary to His Excellency and Lady Macartney to Stenhouse, 2 November 1914, Stenhouse papers.
50. Stenhouse diary, 22 December 1914.
51. Ninnis diary, 22, 23 December 1914. Stenhouse diary, 25 December 1914.
52. Shackleton 1919, p. 2.
53. Mill 1923, pp. 204–05. Fisher 1957, p. 400, points to the inconsistency of Mill's claim with Mackintosh's acute anxiety to lay the depot in the first year.
54. Shackleton 1919, p. 243.
55. Macnish diary, 24 December 1914. Spelling of name in accordance with signature on a photograph reproduced in Piggott (ed.) 2000.
56. Royal Society of New South Wales to Mackintosh, 3 December 1914, Stenhouse papers.
57. Stenhouse diary, 23 December 1914.

4 Voyage to the ice

1. Thomson diary, 25 December 1914.
2. Mackintosh to his wife, reproduced in the *Evening News*, 31 March 1916, Ninnis papers.
3. Thomson diary, 25–31 December 1914.
4. Richards to McElrea, 4 August 1980.
5. Ninnis diary, 21 January 1915.
6. Stenhouse diary, 2 January 1915.
7. Ninnis diary, 5 January 1915.
8. Ibid., 28 December 1914.
9. Stenhouse diary, 30 December 1914. He refers to these features as the Judge and Clerk Rocks.
10. Cumpston 1968, p. 269; Stenhouse diary, 30 December 1914. The third man was A. C. Tulloch, meteorologist.
11. Cumpston 1968, pp. 275ff.
12. Stenhouse diary, 31 December 1914.
13. Mackintosh to Knox, 31 December 1914, Stenhouse papers.
14. Robson to Mackintosh, 21 December 1914.
15. Paton diary, 31 December 1914.
16. Thomson diary, 1 January 1915.
17. Paton diary, 1 January 1915.
18. Ibid., 5 January 1915.
19. Mackintosh diary, 2 January 1915.
20. Paton and Hayward diaries, 1 January 1915 and following; Mackintosh diary, 4 and 6 January 1915.
21. Thomson diary, 2–8 January 1915.
22. Ibid., 2 January 1915.
23. Mackintosh diary, 3 January 1915.
24. Ibid., 1, 8 January 1915; Ninnis diary, 3 January 1915.
25. Thomson diary, 3–4 January 1915.
26. Mackintosh diary, 6 January 1915.
27. Stenhouse diary, 7 January 1915.
28. Mackintosh diary, 8 January 1915.
29. Ninnis diary, 6 January 1915.
30. Thomson diary, 8 January 1915.
31. Ninnis diary, 10 January 1915.
32. Mackintosh diary, 9 January 1915. This is now known as the west colony, the larger of two significant colonies at Cape Crozier. Mackintosh noted in his diary: 'There must have been millions of birds.' In 1966, a total of 84,934 breeding pairs were recorded there, and 150,432 in 1987. The east colony had 12,970 breeding pairs in 1966, and 26,651 in 1987. Sources: 1966, G. J. Wilson and R. S. Taylor, *New Zealand Antarctic Record*, vol. 16, no. 1; 1987, R. H. Taylor, P. R. Wilson and B. W. Thomas, *Polar Record*, vol. 26, no. 42.
33. Thomson diary, 9 January 1915.
34. Ninnis diary, 9 January 1915. Stenhouse recorded the quantum as 'hundreds of tons of weight', diary, 9 January 1915.
35. Thomson diary, 9 January 1915.

36. Jack diary, 9 January 1915.
37. Richards 1962, p. 8.
38. Mackintosh diary, 10 January 1915.
39. Thomson diary, 11 January 1915
40. Mackintosh diary, 11 January 1915.
41. Thomson diary, 13 January 1915.
42. Although destinations varied slightly, as did starting and end points, *Aurora* had the fastest southwards voyage by some eight days. *Discovery* (1901–02) took 46 days, *Morning* (1902–03) 48 days, *Morning* and *Terra Nova* (1903–04) 31 days, *Nimrod* (1908), 34 days, (1908–09) 34 days, *Terra Nova* (1910–11) 37 days, (1911–12) 51 days, (1912–13) 35 days, *Aurora* (1914–15, current voyage) 23 days, including a two-day stop-over at Macquarie Island. *Nimrod*'s northern voyage (Cape Royds to Stewart Island) at the conclusion of the BAE took 18 days.
43. Fisher 1957, p. 338.
44. Paton diary, 16 January 1915.
45. Mackintosh and other diaries, 17 January 1915.
46. Scott 1913, i, p. 135.
47. Paton diary, 17 January 1915. Stevens said it was stacked 'perhaps 30 yards from the ice-foot', Stevens report. Thomson diary, 2 March 1915, records 43 bags. At 170 lb per bag, the quantity would be 3.26 tons.
48. Larkman diary, 17 January 1915.
49. Mackintosh diary, 18 January 1915. The cinematograph is now held by CM.
50. Gaze interview with McElrea; also reference to stalactites of ice.
51. Stenhouse diary, 19–21 January 1915.
52. Spencer-Smith diary, 22 January 1915.
53. Hayward diary, 20 January 1915.
54. Located in 1986.
55. Thomson diary, 21 January 1915.
56. Hayward diary, 21 January 1915.
57. Shackleton 1919, p. 243.
58. Joyce diary, 24 January 1915.
59. Ninnis diary, 21 January 1915.
60. Ibid., 24 January 1915.
61. Larkman diary, 22 January 1915. A full set is held by Museum of Victoria (Jack bequest).
62. Stenhouse papers.
63. Ninnis diary, 10 January 1915; Hayward diary, 20 January 1915.
64. Scott 1913, i, p. 145; Spencer-Smith diary, 23 January 1915.
66. Spencer-Smith diary, 25 January 1915.
67. Mackintosh diary, 23 January 1915.

5 *Laying the Bluff depot*

1. Mackintosh, Joyce, Gaze, Jack and other diaries, 24 January 1915.
2. Mackintosh diary, 24 January 1915.
3. Larkman diary, 25 January 1915.
4. Gaze diary, 24 January 1914.
5. Ibid., 25 January 1915.
6. Jack and Gaze diaries, 25 January 1915. Joyce implies in his diary, and repeats in his book, that he went out in the night when he heard dogs barking, and was on hand when one was killed. The respective accounts of Jack and Gaze are preferred to Joyce's.
7. Jack diary, 25 January 1915.
8. Mackintosh diary, 28 January 1915.
9. Gaze diary, 27 January 1915.
10. Joyce diary, 27 January 1915. (Not included in his 1929 book.) Their tent was a cone-shaped pole model of green canvas, from the *Terra Nova* expedition and scavenged for the use of the Ross Sea party from the Cape Evans Hut.
11. Gaze diary, 26 January 1915.
12. Mackintosh diary, 25 January 1915.
13. Stenhouse diary, 25 January 1915.
14. Ibid.
15. Ibid., 26 January 1915
16. Spencer-Smith diary, 25 January 1915.
17. Spencer-Smith and Mackintosh diaries, 26 January 1915.
18. Wild diary, 26 January 1915. Mackintosh's party had a tent specially designed by George Marston, artist on the *Nimrod* expedition and with Shackleton on *Endurance*.
19. Spencer-Smith diary, 25 January 1915.
20. Ibid., 26 January 1915.
21. Ibid., 27 January 1915.
22. Ibid., 28 January 1915.
23. Mackintosh to Stenhouse, 26 January 1915, Stenhouse papers. Mackintosh did not reach the hut until 27 January.
24. Jack diary, 26 January 1915.
25. The account of who returned to the hut is as recorded by Spencer-Smith, Jack and Mackintosh. Curiously, Joyce records that it was Jack who was sent back.
26. Gaze diary, 28 January 1915.

27. Spencer-Smith diary, 28 January 1915.
28. Mackintosh diary, 28 January 1915.
29. Amundsen 1912, i, pp. 209, 349.
30. Wild diary, 28 January 1915.
31. Gaze diary, 28 January 1915.
32. Spencer-Smith diary, 28 January 1915.
33. Mackintosh diary, 29 January 1915.
34. Spencer-Smith diary, 29 January 1915.
35. Ibid., 30 January 1915.
36. Ibid., 25, 30 January 1915.
37. Wild diary, 30 January 1915.
38. Jack diary, 30 January 1915.
39. Ibid.
40. Gaze diary, 30 January 1915.
41. Mackintosh diary, 30 January 1915.
42. Spencer-Smith diary, 31 January 1915.
43. Wild diary, 30 January 1915.
44. Ibid., 31 January 1915.
45. Another had been abandoned two days later. See e.g. Ellis 1969, pp. 120–21.
46. Jack diary, 1 February 1915.
47. Paton diary, 2 February 1915.
48. Gaze diary, 1 February 1915.
49. Wild diary, 31 January 1915.
50. Gaze diary, 1 February 1915.
51. Ibid.
52. Spencer-Smith diary, 1 February 1915.
53. Mackintosh diary, 1 February 1915.
54. Spencer-Smith diary, 31 January, 1 February 1915.
55. Spencer-Smith diary, 2 February 1915.
56. Gaze diary, 3 February 1915.
57. Mackintosh diary, 2 February 1915.
58. Spencer-Smith diary, 3 February 1915.
59. Jack diary, 4 February 1915.
60. Ibid.
61. Spencer-Smith diary, 4 February 1915.
62. Ibid., 3 February 1915.
63. Ibid., 4 February 1915.
64. Wild diary, 5 February 1915.
65. Ibid., 6 February 1915.
66. Scott 1905 ii, chapter XIII.
67. Cherry-Garrard (1922).
68. Jack diary, 5 February 1915.
69. Gaze diary, 5 February 1915.
70. Spencer-Smith diary, 4 February 1915.
71. Gaze diary, 5 February 1915.
72. Spencer-Smith diary, 4 February 1915.
73. Gaze diary, 3 February 1915.
74. Ibid., 5 February 1915.
75. Mackintosh diary, 6 February 1915.
76. Spencer-Smith diary, 6 February 1915.
77. Wild diary, 2 February 1915.
78. Gaze diary, 6 February 1915.
79. Jack diary, 6 February 1915.
80. Mackintosh diary, 10 February 1915.
81. Spencer-Smith diary, 5 February 1915.
82. Wild diary, 4 February 1915.
83. Spencer-Smith diary, 4 February 1915.
84. Ibid., 7 February. Other distances compiled from Mackintosh diary, and vary slightly with Spencer-Smith diary.
85. Gaze diary, 9 February 1915.
86. Mackintosh diary, 9 February 1915.
87. Ibid.
88. As spelt by Spencer-Smith. Mackintosh refers to Canook.
89. Mackintosh diary, 8 February 1915.
90. Spencer-Smith diary, 10 February 1915.
91. Ibid., 11 February 1915.
92. Mackintosh diary, 8 February 1915.
93. Spencer-Smith diary, 9 February 1915. 'Let God's will be done'. The Padre had hoped to reach the cairn marking the position of Scott's last camp, where the bodies of Scott, Wilson and Bowers lay.
94. Jack diary, 11 February 1915.
95. Gaze diary, 11 February 1915.
96. Mackintosh diary, 11 February 1915.
97. Spencer-Smith diary, 11 February 1915.
98. Jack diary, 4 February 1915.
99. Joyce's claim in his book (p. 60) that he had laid the depot on 9 February is inconsistent with accounts of the rest of the party. His diary is ambiguous as to when it was laid.

6 *Farthest south – 1915*

1. Ninnis diary, 23, 24 January 1915.
2. Ibid., 24 January 1915.
3. *The Motor*, vol. 26, no. 259, 1914, Ninnis papers.
4. Thomson diary, 26 January 1915.
5. Stenhouse diary, 28 January 1915.
6. Mackintosh to Stenhouse, 24 January 1915, Stenhouse papers. The appointment would prove to be ineffective, as Stenhouse would be separated from the shore party when Mackintosh met his death in May 1916, leaving the survivors with no designated leader.
7. Mackintosh diary, 13 January 1915.
8. Stenhouse diary, 28, 29 January 1915.
9. Thomson diary, 27 January 1915.

10. Ibid., 29 January 1915.
11. Stenhouse diary, 28 January 1915.
12. Thomson diary, 31 January 1915.
13. Ninnis diary, 2 February 1915.
14. Hayward diary, 31 January 1915.
15. Richards diary, 31 January 1915; Richards, interview with Harrowfield; Richards to Harrowfield, 17 March 1981. This reference to the 'front crawl wheel', together with Ninnis's mention of his standing on the rear side runners, and a photo of the machine in use, indicates that it was designed and operated with the crawl wheel at the front.
16. Ninnis diary, 30 January 1915
17. Ibid., 6 February 1915.
18. Thomson diary, 1 February 1915.
19. Stenhouse diary, 1 February 1915.
20. Thomson diary, 2 February 1915.
21. Ibid.
22. Ninnis diary, 1 February 1915. Richards, in his introduction to his 1915 diary, stated they camped the night on the ice, but this does not tally with his contemporary but brief diary, nor with the accounts of Hayward and Ninnis.
23. Hayward diary, 31 January 1915.
24. Ninnis diary, 1 February 1915.
25. Hayward diary, 2 February 1915.
26. Thomson diary, 2 February 1915.
27. Stenhouse diary, 2 February 1915.
28. Paton diary, 1 February 1915.
29. Thomson diary, 3 February 1915.
30. Stenhouse, *Aurora* logbook, 3 February 1915.
31. Stenhouse diary, 3 February 1915.
32. Hayward diary, 4 February 1915.
33. Larkman diary, 4 February 1915. The ship's logbook records that they were picked up by 10.20 p.m.
34. Larkman diary, 2 February 1915.
35. Thomson diary, 31 January 1915.
36. Ninnis diary, 7 February 1915. This is the only account of the sledge journey to the hut.
37. Ninnis diary, 6 February 1915.
38. Stevens to Stenhouse, 7 February 1915, Stenhouse papers. This is one of the few contemporary items written by Stevens that has survived. Unlike this letter, his report written on *Aurora* on the relief voyage was very critical of Mackintosh's appointment of Cope as leader of the sledging party.

39. Richards diary, 12 February 1915.
40. Richards, commentary on 1916 diary.
41. Ibid., introduction, 11 February 1915.
42. Ninnis diary, 11 February 1915.
43. Ibid.
44. Richards diary, 12 February 1915.
45. Ninnis diary, 11 February 1915.
46. Richards diary, 14–17 February 1915.
47. Recorded in Spencer-Smith diary, 11 February 1915.
48. Mackintosh diary, 11 February 1915.
49. Wild diary, 14 February 1915.
50. Mackintosh diary, 14 February 1915.
51. Ibid., 13 February 1915.
52. Wild diary, 15 February 1915.
53. Mackintosh diary, 15 February 1915.
54. Ibid., 18 February 1915; Wild diary, 19 February 1915.
55. Mackintosh diary, 20 February 1915.
56. Wild diary, 19, 20 February 1915.
57. Mackintosh diary, 18 February 1915.
58. Ibid., 14 February 1915.
59. Ibid., 20 February 1915.
60. Stenhouse papers; Mackintosh diary, 20 February 1915.
61. The position of the depot, until now considered to have been laid at 80° South, is calculated from information in the various diaries and verified by Bruce S. Alexander, a registered surveyor and member of the New Zealand Geological and Survey Expedition of 1958–59.
62. Mackintosh diary, 20 February 1915.
63. Ibid., 15 February 1915.
64. Amundsen 1912 ii, pp. 22, 25, 230–31.
65. Mackintosh, Wild and Joyce diaries, 21 February 1915.
66. Mackintosh diary, 21 February 1915. Joyce 1929, p. 61, mentions a tin.
67. Mackintosh diary, 21 February 1915.
68. Joyce diary, 21 February 1915.
69. Shackleton 1919, p. 35.
70. It would be exceeded by Mackintosh's men the following year.

7   *Support parties – autumn 1915*

1. Spencer-Smith diary, 12 February 1915.
2. Jack diary, 11 February 1915. This is a reference to Mackintosh's plans, announced on the ship, that Joyce's party would make a second return trip to the Bluff.
3. Gaze diary, 11, 12 February 1915.

4. Ibid., 14, 15 February 1915.
5. Ibid., 12 February 1915.
6. Spencer-Smith diary, 14 February 1915.
7. Ibid., 17 February 1915.
8. Gaze diary, 16 February 1915. In contrast, the prodigious Arctic explorer Dr John Rae (1813–93), a Scot, would travel non-stop, occasionally munching on pemmican. (McGoogan 2002, pp. 183–83.)
9. Gaze diary, 17 February 1915.
10. Jack diary, 11 February 1915.
11. Ibid., 14 February 1915.
12. Spencer-Smith diary, 14 February 1915.
13. Gaze diary, 18 February 1915.
14. Ibid., 18 February 1915.
15. Ibid., 19 February 1915.
16. Jack diary, 18 February 1915. 'Copenhagen pemican' is Jack's terminology for that made by J. D. Beauvais of Denmark. At least one container remains at Cape Evans.
17. Spencer-Smith diary, 20 February 1915.
18. Gaze diary, 19 February 1915.
19. The description of the journey of 18–22 February is taken from Spencer-Smith and Gaze diaries.
20. Spelling from Spencer-Smith diary.
21. Spencer-Smith diary, 22 February 1915, referring to George Thomas Vince of the *Discovery* expedition, who died in the vicinity on 11 March 1902.
22. Gaze diary, 22 February 1915.
23. Spencer-Smith diary, 23 February 1915.
24. Ibid., 25, 26 February 1915.
25. Jack diary, 19 February 1915.
26. Ibid., 20 February 1915. Richards' figures differ slightly from Jack's.
27. Ibid., 23 February 1915.
28. Richards diary, 24 February 1915.
29. Jack diary, 23 February 1915. 'Uncorrected bearings by prismatic compass from this blue flagged depot peak second from S & White Island & Mt Discovery in transit 98°, Pyramided Peak in centre of White Island 107° Mt Erebus 173.5°.'
30. Richards diary, being a comment added by the diarist in later years at entry for 27 February 1915.
31. Richards diary, 1, 2 March 1915. The matter-of-fact approach is vintage Richards.
32. Ibid., 28 February 1915.
33. Ibid., 2–3 March 1915.
34. Spencer-Smith diary, 2 March 1915.
35. Richards diary, 2, 3 March 1915.
36. Ibid., 3 March 1915. This virtually ends the diary, which Richards in later years prefaced by saying it 'had no particular interest'. He evidently destroyed the original; the authors know of only a typed copy.
37. Spencer-Smith diary, 3 March 1915.
38. Shackleton 1919, p. 366.
39. Richards diary, 8 March 1915, shown as 'Monday 10 March 1915'; Spencer-Smith diary, 8 March 1915. The reference to sighting the crow's nest [of *Aurora*] was a later addition to the diary by Richards. Reference to lighting a fire as a signal was a still later comment, Richards 1962, p. 11. Scott and Wilson considered the inland route to Cape Evans on 9 March 1911, but no attempt eventuated. (Scott 1913, i. p. 201.)
40. Larkman diary, 4 March 1915.
41. Gaze diary, 11 March 1915.
42. Stenhouse, *Aurora* logbook, 1 March 1915. Stenhouse later wrote 'in my opinion ample for 12 men for 3 months', Stenhouse to Shackleton, 14 February 1920, RGS. Thomson diary, 11 March 1915, recorded 'about 2 months provisions for 6 men'.
43. Thomson diary, 11 March 1915.
44. Spencer-Smith diary, 11 March 1915.
45. Gaze diary, 11 March 1915.
46. Mackintosh to Stenhouse, 24 January 1915.
47. Thomson diary, 7 February 1915.
48. Ibid., 11 February 1915.
49. Thomson diary, 13 February 1915.
50. Stenhouse, *Aurora* logbook, 18 February 1915.
51. Thomson diary, 18 February 1915.
52. Ibid., 20 February 1915.
53. Paton diary, 14 February 1915.
54. Ibid., 21 February 1915.
55. Thomson diary, 24 February 1915.
56. Paton diary, 25 February 1915.
57. Thomson diary, 24 February 1915.
58. Ninnis diary, 28 July 1915.
59. Larkman diary, 24 February 1915.
60. Paton diary, 2 March 1915.
61. Davis 1962, p. 252.
62. *Sydney Morning Herald*, 9 October 1914.
63. Paton diary, 13 February 1915.
64. Thomson diary, 25 February 1915.
65. Stevens report, p. 24.
66. *Otago Daily Times*, c. 6 April 1916.

67. Thomson diary, 2 March 1915.
68. Ninnis diary, 7 April 1915.
69. Paton diary, 5 May 1915.
70. Stevens report, p. 20.
71. Richards 1962, p. 11.
72. Richards to McElrea, 13 October 1977. The remains of this cache are still visible at Cape Evans.
73. Stenhouse, *Aurora* logbook, 24 February 1915.
74. Thomson diary, 26 February 1915.
75. Paton diary, 1 March 1915; Stenhouse, *Aurora* logbook; Thomson diary, 28 February 1915.
76. Larkman diary, 5 March 1915.
77. Stenhouse, *Aurora* logbook, 24 February 1915.
78. Paton diary, 2 March 1915.
79. Thomson and Paton diaries, 2 March 1915.
80. Thomson diary, 3 March 1915.
81. Ibid., 4 March 1915.
82. Ibid., 7 March 1915.
83. Ibid., 8 March 1915. The anchors, rare remnants from *Aurora*, are still in position on the beach.
84. Thomson diary, 8 March 1915.
85. Stenhouse, *Aurora* logbook, 9 March 1915.
86. Thomson diary, 10 March 1915.
87. Ibid., 10 March 1915.
88. Ibid., 11 March 1915.
89. *Otago Daily Times*, c. 6 April 1916, reporting Stenhouse's copyright report to the *Daily Telegraph*.
90. Jack diary, 11 March 1915.
91. Thomson diary, 10 March 1915.
92. Ninnis diary, 15 January 1917.
93. As would happen on 23 March 1915, when Hayward and Jack saw Mackintosh's party.
94. Jack diary, 14 March 1915.
95. Ibid., 25 February 1915.
96. Ibid., 24 February 1915.
97. Ibid., 3 March 1915.
98. Ibid., 5 March 1915.
99. Shackleton to R. Hinks, secretary of the Royal Geographic Society, under covering letter of 4 February 1920, at RGS.
100. Jack diary, 7 March 1915.
101. Ibid., 9 March 1915.
102. Ibid., 11 March 1915.
103. Ibid., 13 March 1915.
104. Ibid., 13 March 1915.
105. Ibid., 14 March 1915.
106. Ibid.
107. Ibid., 24 March 1915. This diary is the only account of the Cope party from 24 February until it was joined by the Skipper's party on 24 March.

8 'The dead dog trail'

1. Mackintosh diary, 23 February 1915. Joyce records three tins of biscuits.
2. Ibid.
3. David Marshall, discussion with Harrowfield, 10 February 1986. Marshall, then veterinary surgeon to the Scott Base dog team, confirmed that dogs need 1½ lb of pemmican per day on a short field trip and 4 lb of seal meat per day when at base.
4. Mackintosh diary, 25 February 1915.
5. Joyce diary, 27 February 1915.
6. Mackintosh diary, 28 February 1915.
7. Ibid., 1 March 1915.
8. Ibid., 3 March 1915.
9. Ibid., 1 March 1915.
10. Wild diary, 1 March 1915.
11. Mackintosh diary, 2 March 1915. Joyce's implication in his book (p. 66) that he put the dogs down is inconsistent with his diary.
12. Wild diary, 2 March 1915. The diary refers to Tuesday 1 March, apparently in error.
13. Mackintosh diary, 2 March 1915.
14. Wild diary, 3 March 1915.
15. Mackintosh diary, 3, 5 March 1915.
16. Joyce diary, 3–6 March 1915.
17. Mackintosh diary, 6 March 1915.
18. Joyce diary, 3–6 March 1915.
19. Mackintosh diary, 3 March 1915.
20. Ibid., 12 March 1915.
21. Ibid., 10 March 1915.
22. In his book (p. 67), Joyce was to claim: 'Found the depot I laid on our outward course was four miles to the east of the intended position, through being unable to sight White Island bearings and land in thick weather.' In his diary he merely says, 'Took the bearing and found the depot we laid going south not in line.' There is no other suggestion that the depot was east of its true position, but on all accounts was north of it. Mackintosh records that the time taken from the true position to the depot and back to the tent was four hours out and four and a half back. It is most

unlikely that the distance travelled in this time, given the circumstances, was only four miles in each direction.

23. As calculated by the authors based on the men's diaries, with assistance from Bruce Alexander and the late Cas Roper.
24. Mackintosh diary, 10 March 1915.
25. Wild diary (date unclear).
26. Joyce diary, 8–12 March 1915.
27. Mackintosh diary, 12 March 1915.
28. Joyce diary, 8–12 March 1915.
29. Ibid.
30. Mackintosh diary, 12 March 1915.
31. Ibid., 14 March 1915.
32. Joyce diary, 13 March 1915
33. Mackintosh diary, 12 March 1915.
34. Gaze interview with McElrea.
35. Joyce diary, 3–6 March 1915.
36. Mackintosh diary, 13 March 1915.
37. Ibid.
38. Distances from the Bluff are based on general descriptions from the diaries.
39. Joyce diary, 15 March 1915. Mackintosh diary, 16 March 1915, records 53° of frost.
40. Mackintosh diary, 12 March 1915.
41. Joyce diary, 14 March 1915.
42. Mackintosh diary, 19 March 1915.
43. Position of Cope depot calculated by authors on basis of Jack diary.
44. Mackintosh diary, 21 March 1915.
45. Ibid., 16 March 1915.
46. Ibid., 18 March 1915.
47. Ibid., 15, 18 March 1915.
48. Ibid., 23 March 1915.
49. Joyce diary, 24 March 1915.
50. Mackintosh diary, 24 March 1915.
51. Ibid., 25 March 1915. These are the pressure ridges off Pram Point, where Scott Base is now situated. It is rare for sea ice to break out south of Pram Point. The pram would also be noted by Jack on 8 October 1915.
52. Joyce diary, 25 March 1915
53. Ibid.

9   Sanctuary reached

1. Mackintosh diary, 25 March 1915.
2. Joyce diary, 25 March 1915.
3. Jack diary, 24 March 1915. There is a day's difference in the dates.
4. Joyce diary, 25 March 1915.
5. Jack diary, 22 April 1915.

6. Ibid., 5 April 1915.
7. Mackintosh diary, 15 April 1915; Jack diary, 12 May 1915.
8. Mackintosh diary, 29 March 1915.
9. Ibid., 28 March 1915.
10. Ibid., 31 March, 2 April 1915.
11. Ibid., 3, 8 April 1915.
12. Joyce diary, written at Cape Evans some months later.
13. Jack diary, 9, 29 April 1915; Mackintosh diary, 11 April 1915. There is a discrepancy of two days in the diaries at this point.
14. Jack diary, 25 May 1915. This entry is a chilling precursor of events that occurred almost a year later.
15. Mackintosh diary, 13 April 1915.
16. Ibid., 15 April 1915. This is the last day's entry in Mackintosh's diary, which began early in the expedition in Australia. If Mackintosh kept other diaries, none is known to have survived.
17. Jack diary, 3, 7 May 1915.
18. Ibid., 6 May 1915.
19. Wild diary, about 27 May 1915.
20. Jack diary, 8, 17 May 1915.
21. Ibid., 8 April 1915.
22. Joyce diary, written at Cape Evans some months later.
23. Paton diary, 12 March 1915.
24. Thomson diary, 12 March 1915.
25. Stenhouse, *Aurora* logbook, 12 March 1915.
26. Thomson diary, 13 March 1915.
27. Ibid.
28. Spencer-Smith diary, 12 March 1915.
29. Ibid., 14 March 1915.
30. Larkman diary, 20 March 1915.
31. Ibid.
32. Thomson diary, 26 March 1915.
33. Paton diary, 15 March 1915.
34. Thomson diary, 27 March 1915.
35. Ibid., 10 April 1915.
36. Thomson diary, 25 March 1915.
37. Ninnis diary, 25 April 1915. Confirmed in Stenhouse diary, 12 May 1915.
38. Ninnis diary, 23 April 1915.
39. Spencer-Smith diary, 23 March 1915.
40. Ninnis diary, 19 April 1915.
41. Thomson, stores book.
42. Stenhouse diary, 1 May 1915 and Ninnis diary, 21 April 1915.
43. Stevens report; Spencer-Smith diary, 29 April 1915.

44. Thomson diary, 21 April 1915.
45. Ninnis diary, 26 March 1915.
46. Thomson, stores book.
47. Stevens report.
48. Stenhouse, *Aurora* logbook, 16, 21 April 1915; Spencer-Smith diary, 16 April 1915; Ninnis diary, 24 April 1915.
49. Spencer-Smith diary, 14 April 1915.
50. Ibid., 15 April 1915.
51. Ibid., 2 May 1915.
52. Paton diary; Stenhouse, *Aurora* logbook, 3 May 1915; Spencer-Smith diary, 3, 4 May 1915. In December 1977, Harrowfield located a dipole radio aerial from this equipment in the annex of the hut.
53. Ninnis diary, 31 May 1915.
54. Ibid., 17 March 1915; Paton diary, 20, 21, 26 April 1915.
55. Ninnis diary, 7 April 1915; Paton diary, 21 April 1915; Stenhouse, *Aurora* logbook, 4, 5 May 1915.
56. Paton diary, 21 April 1915. Thomson observed an apparently similar phenomenon two months later, 120 miles north of Cape Evans, Thomson diary, 18 June 1915.
57. Stenhouse, *Aurora* logbook, 5 May 1915.

10 *'A glimpse of hell'*

1. Stenhouse, *Aurora* logbook, 6 May 1915.
2. Mauger, Intentions Hopeful.
3. Thomson diary, 6 May 1915.
4. Hooke diary, 6 May 1916.
5. Stenhouse diary, 6 May 1915, written up 11 May.
6. Stenhouse, *Aurora* logbook, 7 May 1915 (records Force 8 ESE).
7. Ibid., 6 May 1915; Thomson diary, 6 May 1915; Mauger, Intentions Hopeful.
8. Stenhouse diary, 5 July 1915.
9. Paton diary, 7 May 1915.
10. Thomson diary, 7 May 1915.
11. Stenhouse diary, 7 May 1915.
12. Ibid.
13. Larkman diary, 7 May 1915.
14. Stenhouse diary, 7 May 1915.
15. Paton diary, 7 May 1915.
16. Spencer-Smith diary, 7 May 1915.
17. Richards, interview with Lathlean.
18. Gaze, interview with McElrea.
19. Stevens report; Spencer-Smith diary, 7 May 1915.
20. Thomson diary, 8, 11 May 1915; Stenhouse diary, 9 May 1915.
21. Stenhouse diary, various dates in May 1915.
22. Richards to McElrea, 16 March 1972.
23. Ninnis diary, 9–11 June 1915; Hooke diary, 9, 10 June 1915.
24. Paton diary, 10 May 1915.
25. Stenhouse, *Aurora* logbook, 10, 11 May 1915; Ninnis diary, 9 May 1915.
26. Stenhouse, *Aurora* logbook, 10 May 1915.
27. Thomson diary, 11 May 1915.
28. Ibid., 16 May, 4 June 1915; Stenhouse diary, 4 June 1915.
29. Paton and Stenhouse diaries, 11–13 May 1915.
30. Thomson diary, 14 May 1915.
31. Larkman diary, 17 May 1915.
32. Thomson diary, 17 May 1915.
33. Quoted in Shackleton 1919, p. 47.
34. Ninnis and Thomson diaries, 13 May 1915.
35. Larkman, 'An Engineer's Antarctic Log'.
36. Thomson, Stenhouse and Ninnis diaries, 15 May 1915.
37. Stenhouse diary, 19 May 1915; Thomson diary, 23 May 1915; Ninnis diary, 18, 27 May 1915.
38. Thomson diary, 7 June 1915.
39. Stenhouse diary, 18, 20 May, 3 June 1915.
40. Thomson diary, 19 June 1915.
41. Ibid., 16, 17 May, 19 June 1915.
42. Stenhouse diary, 21, 24 May 1915.
43. Thomson diary, 17 May, 19 June 1915.
44. Stenhouse diary, 26 May, 1915.
45. Thomson diary, 25 May 1915.
46. Ninnis diary, 6 June 1915.
47. Ibid., 6, 10 June 1915.
48. Thomson diary, 3 June 1915.
49. Stenhouse diary, 3 June 1915.
50. Thomson diary, 7 June 1915.
51. Larkman, 'An Engineer's Antarctic Log'.
52. Hooke diary, 22 June 1915.
53. Paton diary, 22 June 1915; Ninnis diary, 22 June 1915.
54. Thomson diary, 22 June 1915.
55. Ibid., 26 July 1915.
56. Ibid., 9 July 1915.
57. Ninnis diary, 22 July 1915.
58. Thomson diary, 6 July 1915.
59. Larkman diary, 16–18 July 1915; Thomson and Paton diaries, 7 July 1915.
60. Thomson diary, 16 July 1915.
61. Ibid., 19 July 1915.

62. Stenhouse diary, 21 July 1915; Thomson diary, 21 July 1915.
63. Ninnis diary, 21 July 1915.
64. Hooke diary, 21 July 1915.
65. Larkman diary, 15–18 July 1915.
66. Larkman diary, 26 July–1 August 1915.
67. Hooke diary 22, 23 July 1915. His next and last entry was 1 December.
68. Stenhouse, Ninnis and Thomson diaries, 22 July 1915.
69. Stenhouse diary, 22 July 1915.
70. Ninnis diary, 23 July 1915.
71. Hooke report, 21 June 1915.
72. Thomson diary, 24 June 1915.
73. Hooke, report to Stenhouse, 21 June 1915; Stenhouse diary, 24, 25 June 1915.

11 *Crossing to Cape Evans*

1. Jack diary, various dates.
2. Ibid., 19 May 1915.
3. Ibid., 18 May 1915.
4. Ibid., 23 May 1915.
5. Ibid., 27, 30 May 1915.
6. Ibid., 30, 31 May 1915.
7. Ibid., 2 June 1915.
8. Ibid.
9. These observations included: pressure (mercury barometer and barograph), temperature (dry bulb, maximum, minimum, solar minimum) and terrestrial with thermometers and thermograph, humidity with hair hygrometer and wet-bulb readings, wind direction and strength from recording anemometer, cloudiness, frequency of precipitation and snowdrift, direction of smoke plume from Mt Erebus and observations of sky cover and weather conditions. (Loewe 1963; Jack meteorological records; Stevens report.)
10. Spencer-Smith diary, 8, 25 May 1915.
11. Ibid., 9 May 1915 and following.
12. Stevens report, p. 27.
13. Spencer-Smith diary, 25 May 1915.
14. Wild diary, 2 June 1915.
15. Stevens report, p. 28.
16. Spencer-Smith diary, 14, 15 May 1915.
17. Ibid., 9 May 1915.
18. Ibid., 30 May 1915.
19. Richards 1962, p. 15.
20. Spencer-Smith diary, 2 June 1915.
21. Joyce diary, 2 June 1915.
22. Stevens report.
23. Wild diary, 28 December 1915.
24. Spencer-Smith diary, 3 June 1915; Stevens report; Wild diary and others.
25. Spencer-Smith diary, 14 May, 7 June 1915; Wild diary, written up 28 December 1915; Stevens report.
26. Jack diary, 21, 24 June 1915.
27. Stevens report, p. 29; Jack diary, 18, 19 June 1915.
28. Jack diary, 4 June 1915.
29. Richards to Harrowfield, 10 June 1981; Richards to McElrea, 15 November 1971, 5 November 1982.
30. Stevens report. Stevens does not elaborate and the diaries and other records do not disclose further details.
31. Spencer-Smith diary, various dates 25 June – 8 August 1915.
32. Ibid., 28 March – 20 June 1915. Archdeacon Michael Brown (later Dean of Wellington, New Zealand) celebrated the Eucharist on the same altar using the same Communion vessels in December 1983, *Anglican* (1984). Spencer-Smith's rosary beads and sanctuary lamp are held by the Antarctic Heritage Trust, pending conservation. The Padre's silver wafer box has disappeared in recent years, highlighting issues of security at these historic sites.
33. Spencer-Smith diary, 22 June 1915; further account in Wild diary.
34. Spencer-Smith diary, 22 June 1915.
35. Hurley 1948, pp. 47–48.
36. Spencer-Smith diary, 25, 26 June, 14 July 1915.
37. Ibid.
38. Ibid., 14 July, 19, 29 August 1915.
39. Ibid., 17 July, 4 August 1915. One such menu card was offered for sale by auction in New Zealand in 2003.
40. Richards interview with Harrowfield.

12 Aurora *under siege*

1. Paton diary, 23 July 1915.
2. Thomson diary, 24 July 1915.
3. Ibid.
4. Stenhouse diary, 1 July 1915, but omitted from published account in Shackleton 1919.
5. Stenhouse diary, 2 July 1915; Larkman diary, 6–13 July 1915.
6. Stenhouse diary, 19 June 1915; Thomson

diary, 27, 29 June, 12 July 1915.
7. Ninnis diary, 1 August 1915.
8. Ibid., 29 July 1915.
9. Thomson workbook.
10. Mauger workbook.
11. Thomson diary, 28 July 1915; Paton diary, 30 July 1915.
12. Ninnis diary, 13 August 1915.
13. Stenhouse notebook.
14. Paton diary, 30 July 1915.
15. Larkman, 'An Engineer's Antarctic Log'.
16. Stenhouse diary, 4 August 1915.
17. Thomson workbook; Thomson diary, 13 August 1915.
18. Thomson diary, 26 August, 14 September 1915; Stenhouse, *Aurora* logbook.
19. Quoted in Hurley 1948, p. 63.
20. Thomson diary, 26 July 1915.
21. Paton diary, 9 August 1915.
22. Thomson diary, 7–8 August 1915.
23. Stenhouse diary, 10 August 1915.
24. Paton diary, 10 August 1915.
25. Thomson diary, 19 August 1915.
26. Paton diary, 3 August 1915; Thomson diary, 17 August 1915; Stenhouse diary, 25 August 1915.
27. Paton diary, 27 August 1915; Ninnis diary, 29 August 1915.
28. Thomson diary, 12 August 1915. The Cloudmaker is a conspicuous landmark along the west side of the Beardmore Glacier.
29. Ibid., 2 September 1915.
30. Ibid., 5 September 1915.
31. Paton diary, 5 September 1915.
32. Stenhouse diary, 7 September 1915.
33. Thomson diary, 6 September 1915.
34. Ibid., 7 September 1915.
35. Larkman diary, '27 September to 3rd October'.
36. Stenhouse diary, 5 October 1915. *Aurora* had four stoves: in the forecastle, galley, master's cabin and wardroom – Thomson diary, 13 November 1915. Carbon monoxide poisoning is a well-documented cause of accidental death in such circumstances and may well have resulted in Stenhouse losing consciousness.
37. Stenhouse diary, 16 February 1916.
38. Ibid., 9 September 1915.
39. Thomson diary, 9 September, 1915.
40. Stenhouse diary, 8 September 1915.

Larkman diary, 13–19 September 1915.
41. Stenhouse diary, 7 November 1915.
42. Thomson diary, 25 January 1916; Stenhouse diary, 28 January 1916.
43. Thomson diary, 14 January 1916.
44. Ninnis diary, 10 November 1915; Stenhouse, *Aurora* logbook; Mauger workbook, 18, 20 October 1915.
45. Thomson diary, 22 November 1915.
46. Ninnis diary, 22 November 1915.
47. Stenhouse diary, 8 December 1915.
48. Stenhouse papers, including Ninnis report, 8 December 1915, and statements of Atkin, Paton, Grady and Shaw.
49. Thomson diary, 8 December 1915.
50. Stenhouse diary, 8 December 1915.
51. Ibid., 9 December 1915.
52. Ibid., 27 November 1915.
53. Thomson diary, 13 December 1915.
54. Ibid., 8, 9 December 1915.
55. Stenhouse diary, 16 November 1915.
56. Ninnis, Bird and Animal Life.
57. Stenhouse diary, 10 December 1915.
58. Paton diary, 25 December 1915.
59. Ninnis, Bird and Animal Life.
60. Stenhouse diary, 19 January 1916.
61. Thomson diary, 23 October 1915; Ninnis, Bird and Animal Life.
62. Stenhouse diary, 25 October 1915.
63. Thomson diary, 2 November 1915.
64. Ibid., 18 November 1915.
65. Ibid., 7 December 1915.
66. Stenhouse diary, 11 November 1915.
67. Ninnis, Bird and Animal Life.
68. Thomson diary, 30 November 1915.
69. Ninnis diary, 10 December 1915.
70. Stenhouse diary, 14 December 1915.
71. Thomson and Ninnis diaries, 24 December 1915.
72. Mauger workbook.
73. Paton diary, 29 December 1915.
74. Estimate based on latitude of 31 August (69° 33' S) and position of 29 December (69° 12' S, 164° 32' E).
75. Thomson, Stenhouse, Ninnis and Paton diaries, 22 September 1915.
76. Thomson, Stenhouse and Paton diaries, 23 November 1915.
77. Now known as Cape Freshfield, at 68° 20' S, 151° 00' E, *Geographic Names of the Antarctic.*
78. Paton diary, 3 September 1915.

79. Stenhouse diary, 30 December 1915.
80. Ibid., 17 December 1915.
81. Thomson diary, 1 December 1915.
82. Ibid., 19 September 1915.
83. Thomson diary, 19 September, 1, 12 December 1915.
84. Stenhouse diary, 31 December 1915.

13 '*A new heaven and a new earth*'

The chapter title is from Revelations 21:1 and was quoted by Spencer-Smith in his diary, 1 September 1915. Principal references for this chapter are taken from this diary, 1–30 September 1915.

1. Gaze, interview with McElrea.
2. Richards to McElrea, 11 April 1972; Richards to Harrowfield, 24 August 1976.
3. Spencer-Smith diary, 21 September 1915.
4. Stevens report, p. 32. The motor sledge is now at CM.
5. Spencer-Smith papers, CM.
6. Joyce diary, 1, 4 October 1915. In his rewritten diary and book, Joyce mentions dropping two sledges.
7. Spencer-Smith diary, 3, 4 October 1915; Joyce diary, 6 October 1915.
8. Jack diary, 5–8 October 1915.
9. Spencer-Smith diary, 3 October 1915.
10. Joyce diary, 11 October 1915.
11. Ibid.
12. Spencer-Smith diary, 10 October 1915.
13. Joyce diary, 12 October 1915.
14. Jack diary, 11 October 1915.
15. Ibid., 11, 12 October 1915.
16. Joyce diary, 14 October 1915.
17. Spencer-Smith diary, 15 October 1915.
18. Wild diary, 14, 16 October 1915.
19. Jack diary, 22 October 1915.
20. Ibid., 21 October 1915.
21. Joyce diary, 22 October 1915. His rewritten diary records 313 lb, and his book 373 lb. Stevens would not return to this latitude.
22. Joyce diary, 26 October 1915.
23. Ibid. Joyce's book suggests they found eight cases of dog biscuits. Jack diary, 26 October 1915, mentions 'a box of dog biscuits . . . a case of sledging biscuits (stale), one of dog biscuits, and two tins of rubber solvent'.
24. Jack diary, 26 October 1915. This note, in fact dated 16 March, was retrieved from under a pillow by a restoration party led by the late L. B. Quartermain during the period December 1960 – January 1961. (Quartermain 1963, p. 72.)
25. Jack diary, 20 October 1915.
26. Joyce diary, 20 October 1915.
27. Jack diary, 27 October 1915.
28. Joyce diary, 27 October 1915. This piece was omitted from his rewritten diary.
29. Jack diary, 27 October 1915.
30. Gaze diary, c. 27 October 1915.
31. Gaze, interview with McElrea.
32. Gaze, c. 27 October 1915.
33. Mackintosh to Stenhouse, 27 October 1915, part illegible, CM. Transcript refers to A. Ernest Mackintosh. This letter was located in 1964 during restoration of the *Discovery* hut.
34. Spencer-Smith diary, 29 October, 1 November 1915. 'Biscuits 86 lbs., Streimer 16 lbs. 14 oz, Milk 5 lbs. 4 oz, Ration 132 lbs. 12 oz, Oil and spirit 50 lbs., Cocoa 5 lbs. 14 oz, Sugar 28 lbs., Bov[ril] cubes 4 lbs. 4 oz.'
35. Wild diary, 12 November 1915.
36. Ibid.
37. Spencer-Smith diary, 18, 21 November 1915; Wild diary, 21 November 1915. The trans-continental party would not have required seven weeks' supply at this point. It was intended that the supplies be taken further south.
38. Although Mackintosh had requested Joyce to deliver some cooked seal meat to Safety Camp (a request apparently ignored), it is clear he underestimated the benefit of fresh seal meat in combating scurvy.
39. Shackleton diary, 21 November 1915, Fisher papers. The identity of the person referred to as 'H' is not clear.
40. Copy of the letter is in Jack diary, 29 October 1915.
41. Joyce diary, 30 October 1915. Jack diary mentions only Hayward and Stevens.
42. Joyce diary, 1 November 1915.
43. Ibid., 29 October 1915.
44. Gaze diary, 5 November 1915.
45. Ibid., 7 November 1915.
46. Ibid., 8 November 1915.
47. Ibid., 15 November 1915.
48. Joyce to Mackintosh, 15 November 1915. The letter was located in 1964 during restoration of the *Discovery* hut and is now at CM.
49. Joyce diary, 17 November 1915. Joyce

would rewrite this account, first in his reworked log written after main journey: '. . . if the Skipper goes against this I shall still carry it out there has been enough bungling.' In his book he would go even further, making out that he had taken over control of the party. 'I am leaving a note to this effect for the Skipper.' However, the mild letter he wrote to Mackintosh on 15 November, together with the Skipper's letter of 29 October, clearly indicates that their respective roles were those of leader and subordinate.

50. Ibid., 20 November 1915.
51. Jack diary, 20–25 November 1915.
52. Gaze diary, 25 November 1915.
53. Joyce diary, 28 November 1915. It is likely that this account, even in Joyce's less sensational diary, is unreliable. His subsequently rewritten log would further enhance certain aspects of the discussion in his own favour. The criticism of Mackintosh was omitted from his 1929 book.
54. Joyce diary, 30 November, 3 December 1915; Jack diary, 3 December 1915.
55. The letter was found in the Cape Evans hut in January 1958 and was then held by the Museum of New Zealand, Wellington. The copy quoted is based on a copy, apparently incorrectly dated 2 October, ex R. A. Falla estate, private collection, Richard McElrea. A typed copy held by SPRI, dated Oct 21st, and a copy at ATL, dated Oct 2, differ slightly from above. It might better reflect the true Joyce rather than the opinionated and distorted views in other writings. Although Joyce was at the Bluff depot on 21 October, his reference to taking out 'the last load' is inconsistent with that date. The letter may have been written or completed on 2 December.
56. Gaze diary, 5 December 1915.
57. Jack diary, 4 December 1915.
58. Ibid.
59. Mackintosh found letters at Cope's No. 2 depot from Stenhouse, Cope and Ninnis, left there earlier in the year. – Spencer-Smith diary, 30 November 1915.
60. Spencer-Smith diary, 15 December 1915. Wild diary has 180 lb.
61. Wild diary, 20 December 1915.
62. Spencer-Smith diary, 25 December 1915.
63. Wild diary, 25 December 1915.

64. Gaze diary, 28 December 1915.
65. Wild diary, 29 December 1915.
66. Joyce diary, 31 December 1915.

14 *Journey to Mt Hope*

1. Place names as at 1916 are taken from the map contained in Scott 1913.
2. Now known as the Polar Plateau.
3. Joyce diary, 3 January 1916.
4. Gaze diary, 3 January 1916.
5. Jack diary, 5 January 1916.
6. Gaze diary, 6 January 1916.
7. Jack diary, 6 January 1916.
8. Joyce diary, 5 January 1916.
9. Richards, interview with McElrea; Richards to Harrowfield, 19 September 1982; Richards to McElrea, 19 September 1984.
10. Jack diary, 6 January 1916.
11. Gaze diary, 6 January 1916.
12. Ibid.
13. Jack diary, 6 January 1916.
14. Spencer-Smith diary, 7 January 1916.
15. Jack diary, 7 January 1916.
16. Gaze diary, 14 January 1916; Jack diary, 14 January 1916.
17. Jack diary, 13 January 1916.
18. Ibid., 14 January 1916.
19. Gaze diary, 15 January 1916.
20. Spencer-Smith diary, 12 January 1916.
21. Ibid., 8, 9 January 1916.
22. Joyce diary, 9–16 January 1916. The accounts in his rewritten version and his book both vary from his diary.
23. Spencer-Smith diary, 8 January 1916.
24. Richards, correspondence with authors.
25. Spencer-Smith diary, 16 January 1916.
26. Joyce diary, 13 January 1916.
27. Spencer-Smith diary, 11 January 1916.
28. Wild diary, 21 January 1916. Also recorded by Spencer-Smith.
29. Spencer-Smith diary, 18, 19 January 1916.
30. Memorandum signed by Richards on 3 February 1956 and attached to the original agreement, now held at CM.
31. Richards, interview with Lathlean.
32. Richards, interview with Harrowfield.
33. Mackintosh/Richards agreement at latitiude 82° South, 18 January 1916, CM. The amount of annual payment is not specified in the signed agreement.
34. Spencer-Smith diary, 18 January 1916.
35. Wild diary, 18 January 1916.

36. Richards 1962, p. 24.
37. Richards to McElrea, 16 March 1972.
38. Joyce diary, 19 January 1916. This varies slightly from his rewritten version and his book.
39. Ibid., 20, 21 January 1916. Again, Joyce's other accounts vary.
40. Spencer-Smith diary, 21 January 1916.
41. Ibid., 21, 22 January 1916.
42. Wild diary, 22 January 1916.
43. Joyce diary, 22 January 1916. His claims in his book that he examined Mackintosh's knee ('it is blue . . .') is not in his diary.
44. Joyce diary, 21 January 1916.
45. Wild diary, 23 January 1916.
46. Ibid., 25 January 1916. Joyce's references in his book to rubbing down the Skipper with methylated spirits is not in his diary.
47. Shackleton 1909, i, p. 310. Scott's expedition termed this feature 'the Gateway', Scott 1913 i, p. 628.
48. Joyce diary, 26 January 1916.
49. Ibid., 26 January 1916. This differs from the description in Joyce's book.
50. Recounted by Richards on several occasions, including interview with Lathlean.
51. Joyce diary, 26 January 1916. Joyce confuses the portrayal of events by writing in his book: 'I decided to take the depot up Mt Hope . . . Arrived at the summit.' This, like many entries quoted as verbatim diary entries in his book, does not appear in his diary. No photographs of the Mt Hope depot are known to exist.
52. Wild diary, 26 January 1916.

15   Aurora *breaks free*

1. Paton diary, 30, 31 January 1916.
2. Stenhouse diary, 27 January 1916.
3. Thomson diary, 8 January 1916.
4. Ibid., 5 January 1916.
5. Stenhouse diary, 19 January 1916.
6. Thomson diary, 19 January 1916. This is from the end page of his diary. No such further record has survived; M. Thomson to McElrea, 10 September 1985. Given his meticulous observations throughout the voyage, it is likely that Thompson continued his diary entries in another notebook.
7. Thomson diary, 28 September 1915 and subsequent entries.

8. Stenhouse diary, various dates.
9. Ninnis diary, 2 February 1916.
10. Stenhouse diary, 2 February 1916.
11. Cumpston 1968, p. 269.
12. Paton diary, 12 February 1916.
13. Ninnis diary, 12 February 1916.
14. Stenhouse diary, 13 February 1916. This is explained by Stenhouse – 'Turn out when called'.
15. Paton diary, 14 February 1916.
16. Stenhouse diary, 14 February 1916.
17. Ninnis, Bird and Animal Life.
18. Larkman diary, 18 February 1916.
19. Ibid., 13 February 1916.
20. Stenhouse diary, 16 February 1916.
21. Stenhouse, *Aurora* logbook, 15 February 1916.
22. Ibid., various dates.
23. Ibid., 20 February 1916.
24. Paton diary, 29 February 1916.
25. Ninnis diary, 29 February 1916.
26. Stenhouse, *Aurora* logbook, 29 February, 1 March 1916.
27. Stenhouse diary and *Aurora* logbook, 1 March 1916.
28. Larkman diary and Stenhouse, *Aurora* logbook, 2 March 1916.
29. Paton diary, 21 February 1916.
30. Stenhouse diary and *Aurora* logbook, 2 March 1916.
31. Paton diary, 4 March 1916.
33. Ibid., 6 March 1916.
33. Stenhouse, *Aurora* logbook, 6–9 March 1916.
34. Paton diary, 9 March 1916.
35. Stenhouse diary, 9 March 1916.
36. Ninnis diary, 10 March 1916.
37. Paton diary, 10 March 1916. Larkman's diary appears to be substantially the same as that of Paton.
38. Stenhouse diary, 10 March 1916.
39. Paton diary, 10 March 1916.
40. Stenhouse diary, 10 March 1916.
41. Paton diary, 11 March 1916.
42. Ibid., 12 March 1916.
43. Ninnis diary, 12 March 1916.
44. Paton diary, 13 March 1916.
45. Ninnis diary, 13 March 1916.
46. Paton diary, 14 March 1916.
47. Shackleton 1919 refers to *Aurora* clearing the main pack at 4.50 p.m. on 13 March. This would appear to be in error.

A diagram in Stenhouse diary of 13 March is helpful. On the night of 12 March the ship had worked its way back into the pack from the large enclosed lane (Paton called it a bay) it had been in during that day. At 4.50 p.m. the ship cleared the pack back into the lane it had been in on 12 March. The diagram in Stenhouse's diary for 14 March shows what then happened and how the ship then pushed through a 'narrow pack belt'. Stenhouse heads his diary for 14 March: 'Left pack ice.'

48. Stenhouse diary, 14 March 1916. This is the entry for 15 March, as Stenhouse used a 1915 diary and did not apparently take into account that 1916 was a leap year. His diary ceases at this date and his entries in the ship's log continue the record.
49. Ninnis diary, 15 March 1916
50. Ibid.; Stenhouse, *Aurora* logbook, 17 March 1916.
51. Ninnis, Bird and Animal Life.
52. Paton diary, 15 March 1916. Larkman's diary has a similar passage.
53. Stenhouse, *Aurora* logbook, 16–20 March 1916; Ninnis diary, 15–20 March 1916.
54. Stenhouse, *Aurora* logbook, 21 March 1916.
55. Stenhouse diary, 3 March 1916.
56. Ninnis diary, 21 March 1916.
57. Ninnis diary, Paton diary and Stenhouse, *Aurora* logbook, 25 March 1916.
58. Paton diary, 25 March 1916.
59. Stenhouse, *Aurora* logbook, 20 March 1916.
60. Ibid., 1 January 1916.
61. Larkman diary, 21 March 1916. D'Anglade and Shaw were duly charged in the Magistrates' Court at Port Chalmers for disobeying lawful commands at sea and refusing duty on the high seas. Prominent Dunedin lawyer Mr A. C Hanlon appeared for Stenhouse, Mr Irwin appeared for the accused Shaw and d'Anglade. Mr J. R. Bartholomew, SM, presided in a crowded courtroom. Mr Hanlon stated that the circumstances were not so serious in the case of d'Anglade, who was merely a steward, and the captain was prepared to overlook his offence. Shaw had been examined by two medical men who had given a certificate regarding the state of mind that would make the proceedings look like persecution if the case went on.

The court acquiesced in counsel's request and the charges were withdrawn. (*Otago Daily Times*, 8 April 1916.)
62. Ninnis diary, 22 March 1916.
63. Stenhouse, *Aurora* logbook, 23 March 1916.
64. *New Zealand Official Year Book*, 1915.
65. *Daily Mail*, 25 March 1916, courtesy R. F. Perachie.
66. Paton diary, 25 March 1916.
67. Ibid., 26 March 1916.
68. *Otago Daily Times*, 4 April 1916.
69. Stenhouse, *Aurora* logbook, 26, 27 March 1916.
70. Ibid., 27 March 1916.
71. Paton diary, 26 March 1916.
72. Ninnis diary, 27 March 1916.
73. Stenhouse, *Aurora* logbook, 28 March 1916; Ninnis diary, 30 March 1916.
74. *Otago Daily Times*, 29 March 1916.
75. Ninnis diary, 30 March 1916.
76. Stenhouse, *Aurora* logbook, 30 March 1916.
77. Paton diary, 31 March 1916.
78. Ninnis diary, 2 April 1916.
79. Les Jack (a passenger on the tug), interview with authors; Otago Harbour Board records, HL.
80. Paton diary, 2 April 1916.
81. *Otago Daily Times*, 4 April 1916.
82. Ninnis diary, 3 April 1916.

16 *Return from Mt Hope*

1. Shackleton 1909, i, p. 355.
2. Generally spelt Dimitri but appears as 'Demetri' in Scott 1913.
3. But see Cherry-Garrard 1922, ii, p. 380.
4. Ibid., pp. 382–83.
5. Lashly diary, quoted in ibid., pp. 401, 404.
6. Wild and Joyce diaries, 28 January 1916.
7. Spencer-Smith diary, 25 January 1916.
8. Wild diary, 29 January 1916.
9. Joyce diary, 29 January 1916. In his book this is changed to read: 'Gums slightly swollen. Every indication of scurvy.'
10. Ibid., 31 January 1916.
11. Richards, Four Dogs.
12. Richards, interview with McElrea.
13. Richards 1962, p. 27; Wild diary, 12 February 1916.
14. Wild diary, 3 February 1916.
15. Joyce diary, 3 February 1916.
16. Wild diary, 7, 11 February 1916. Distances taken from Spencer-Smith and Joyce diaries.

17. Richards, interview with Lathlean.
18. Wild diary, 4 February 1916.
19. Richards, interview with Lathlean.
20. Spencer-Smith diary, 9, 14 February 1916.
21. Wild diary, 17 February 1916.
22. Joyce diary, various dates.
23. Richards to McElrea, 19 September 1984.
24. Richards diary, 23, 24 February 1916.
25. Richards to McElrea, 24 November 1982.
26. Spencer-Smith diary, 8 February 1916;
    Joyce diary, 8, 16 February 1916.
27. Richards diary, 24 February 1916. Richards
    wrote his diary retrospectively for events to
    24 February.
28. Wild diary, 12 February 1916.
29. Spencer-Smith diary, 14 February 1916;
    Richards, Four Dogs.
30. Spencer-Smith diary, 15, 17 February 1916.
31. Joyce diary, 17 February 1916; Richards,
    interview with Lathlean; Richards diary,
    23 February 1916.
32. Spencer-Smith diary, 18 February 1916.
33. Richards to Harrowfield, 2 August 1982.
34. Spencer-Smith diary, 19, 20, 22 February
    1916; Wild diary, 19, 21 February 1916;
    Richards, interview with Lathlean; Joyce
    diary, 21, 22 February 1916.
35. Joyce diary, 22 February 1916.
36. Richards to McElrea, 13, 19 September 1984.
37. Joyce diary, 22, 23 February 1916; Spencer-
    Smith diary, 23 February 1916.
38. Richards diary, 28 February 1916, writing
    of events of 23 February.
39. Joyce diary, 23 February 1916. Later
    changed in his rewritten diary to 'wrap me
    in a snowcloth and leave me in the snow'.
    In Joyce 1929 (p. 151), there is reference to
    a magnum of champagne that does not
    appear in either his field diary or rewritten
    diary.
40. Richards, interview with Lathlean.
41. Richards diary, 28 February 1916.
42. Wild diary, 23 February 1916; Spencer-
    Smith diary, 23 February 1916.
43. Richards diary, annotated by Richards in
    February 1976: 'Copied at C. Evans,
    October 1916. I do not know what became
    of this letter. Joyce gave it to me to copy
    and after which I returned it to him.' Gaze
    also copied a version into his diary.
44. Spencer-Smith diary, 23–28 February 1916.
45. Richards, interview with McElrea. Another

example of steering by compass in zero
visibility through violent snow storms was
that of the Arctic explorer Dr John Rae.
(McGoogan 2000, pp. 183–84.)
46. Richards diary, 23 February 1916; Richards
    to McElrea, 20 June 1980.
47. Richards diary, 24 February 1916.
48. Ibid.
49. Ibid., 25 February 1916.
50. Joyce diary, 25 February 1916.
51. Richards 1976, Four Dogs.
52. Richards, McElrea interview.
53. Richards diary, 25 February 1916.
54. Richards, interview with Lathlean.
55. Richards, interview with McElrea.
56. Richards diary, 26 February 1916.
57. Richards to Harrowfield, 14 May 1981
58. Joyce diary, 26 February 1916. Joyce 1929,
    p. 156, states that Hayward collapsed after
    Richards sighted the depot and had to be
    bought in on the sledge. This is not in his
    diary ot the later versions of his diary.
59. Richards diary, 27 February 1916.
60. Richards 1962, p. 30.
61. Richards diary, 27 February 1916.
62. Ibid., 28 February 1916.
63. Ibid., 27 February 1916
64. Joyce diary, 27 February 1916.
65. Richards diary, 28 February 1916; Joyce
    diary, 28 February 1916.
66. Richards diary, 7 p.m. 28 February 1916.
    'Waiting, waiting, waiting' also occurs in
    Shackleton's diary for 26 January 1916,
    at Patience Camp. (Shackleton diary,
    SPRI.)
67. Wild diary, 24 February 1916.
68. Richards diary, 29 February 1916.

17 *Death of the Padre*

1. Joyce diary, 29 February 1916. In his book
   the description is: 'Poor old Mack crawled
   out of the tent, very weak, could just
   stagger, and thanked us.'
2. Spencer-Smith diary, 29 February 1916.
3. Wild diary, 29 February 1916.
4. Joyce diary, 29 February 1916.
5. Richards, commentary on diary to
   McElrea, 22 June 1980.
6. Wild diary, 29 February 1916.
7. Richards 1962, p. 31.
8. Richards diary, 1 March 1916.
9. Richards, interview with Lathlean.

10. Richards to Harrowfield, 14 May 1981, and other references.
11. Richards diary, 2 March 1916.
12. Wild diary, 4 March 1916.
13. Joyce diary, 4 March 1916.
14. Ibid.
15. Richards, commentary on diary, to McElrea, 22 June 1980.
16. Wild diary, 6 March 1916; Joyce diary, 4 March 1916.
17. Spencer-Smith diary, 5 March 1916.
18. Ibid., 7 March 1916.
19. Jack diary 7, 8 March 1916; Stevens report.
20. Wild diary, 7 March 1916.
21. Richards, interview with McElrea.
22. Joyce diary, 7, 8 March 1916.
23. Richards diary, 7 March 1916.
24. Ibid., 8 March 1916; Joyce diary, 8 March 1916.
25. Richards and other diaries, 9 March 1916.
26. Cope, medical report, SPRI. As Cope was not present when Spencer-Smith died, he must have learnt these details from a member of the sledging party.
27. Richards 1962, p. 32.
28. Wild diary, 10 March 1916.
29. Richards diary, 9 March 1916. 'Tabloids' was a term registered by Burroughs, Wellcome & Co. In later years, Richards reviewed his assessment of how many opium tablets Spencer-Smith had taken. 'Say 4 tablets found from examination of the tube containing the opium. This is now in the Canterbury Museum and no more than 4 small tablets are missing . . .' Richards objected to the implication in an article that Spencer-Smith died after taking opium. However, as he acknowledged, the contemporary account is very persuasive. 'I suppose one would place reliance on what was written at the time but my memory always has been that he took no tablets that night.' (Richards to McElrea, 4 September 1981.)
30. Richards to McElrea, 17 September 1981.
31. Richards, interview with Lathlean.
32. Joyce diary, 9 March 1916. In his book, (p. 170), his diary 'quotation' is: '. . . noticed to my surprise that the Padre's head lay out of his bag . . . He appeared to be asleep, the ice had formed on his beard . . .'
33. Joyce's diary, 9 March 1916. This contains a reference to his sleeping bag not included

in his book. The diary states: 'We buried him in his bag at 9 o'clock at the following position Erebus 184 – Observation Hill 149 Discovery 93. We made a cross of bamboo and we built a mound and cairn with particulars.' In his book he adds: 'We bared our heads and with a prayer, buried him at 9 o'clock.' There is no contemporary account of this.
34. Richards diary, 9 March 1916.
35. Richards to Harrowfield, 14 August 1981.
36. Spencer-Smith papers, CM.
37. Spencer-Smith diary, 29 January, 17 February 1915.
38. Spencer-Smith papers, CM.
39. *Evening Dispatch,* Edinburgh, 6 February 1917. Spencer-Smith papers, CM. Spencer-Smith's two sisters served the church: Elizabeth in India and Joan in Christchurch, New Zealand, where she founded a Deaconess Order. Two brothers, Philip and Martin, both died in the 1914–18 war. (Canon Philip Gaze to Harrowfield, 17 March 1985.)
40. Joyce diary, 18 March 1916.
41. Wild diary, 10, 11 March 1916.
42. Joyce diary, 9, 12 March 1916.
43. Ibid., 11, 12 March 1916. In his book Joyce suggests that entry to the hut was via a window, through which they passed Hayward.
44. Richards diary, 10 March 1916 (should be 11 March)
45. Wild diary, 11 March 1916.
46. Richards 1962, p. 33; Richards, interview with Lathlean.
47. Joyce diary, 11 March 1916.
48. Ibid., 13 March 1916
49. Ibid., 16 March 1916
50. Ibid. Richards verified Mackintosh's hallucinations: '[He] talked to people all the time in his tent'. (Richards, interview with Lathlean.)
51. Joyce diary, 16 March 1916.
52. Richards diary, 16 March 1916; commentary on diary to McElrea, 22 June 1980.
53. Joyce diary, 17 March 1916.
54. Ibid., 18 March 1916.
55. Ibid.
56. Richards diary, 18 March 1916.

18 *Deaths of Mackintosh and Hayward*

1. Stevens report. His journals and geological records were lost with the *Medina* through enemy action during the First World War. Because he was alone at Cape Evans from early November 1915 to 16 January 1916, there is no other reference to these journeys.
2. Ibid. Stevens says he made the trip to Hut Point on 15 January. However, he was expected there in mid-December. There is no suggestion in the diaries that he had just returned to Cape Evans the day before Cope, Gaze and Jack arrived at Cape Evans.
3. Ibid.
4. Ibid.; Jack diary, 14, 15 March 1916.
5. This dog was also called Beechy, Beechey and Maddo.
6. Jack diary, 15 March 1916.
7. Richards, interview with McElrea; Richards to Harrowfield, 5 February 1980.
8. Jack diary, various references 29 February – 8 April 1916.
9. Stevens report.
10. Jack diary, 14 March 1916.
11. Stevens report; Jack diary, 11, 12 March, 19 April 1916.
12. Jack diary, 20 March 1916.
13. Stevens report; Jack diary, 18 April 1916.
14. Jack diary, 24 April 1916.
15. Wild diary, 8 July 1916.
16. Richards, interview with Lathlean; Wild diary, 8 July 1916.
17. Wild diary, 23 April 1916; Jack, meteorological records.
18. Joyce diary, 5–12 April 1916; Richards, commentary on diary to McElrea, 22 June 1980; Wild diary, 27 April 1916.
19. Joyce diary, 20 March 1916; Richards to McElrea, 6 June 1984.
20. Richards, commentary on diary to McElrea, 22 June 1980.
21. Joyce diary, 14–21 June 1916.
22. Ibid., 22–29 March 1916, 5–12 April, 26 April – 3 May 1916; Wild diary, 23 April 1916.
23. Richards, Notes on events at Hut Point during April and May 1916, AA.
24. Richards, interview with McElrea.
25. Joyce diary, 19–26 April 1916.
26. Richards 1962, p. 36.
27. Joyce, statement to Inquiry.
28. Richards, statement to Inquiry.
29. Ibid.
30. Ibid.
31. Wild, statement to Inquiry.
32. Joyce diary, 3 –10 May 1915.
33. Joyce, statement to Inquiry.
34. Joyce to Sir Charles Royds, 7 April 1930, SPRI.
35. Wild diary, 8 May 1916.
36. Stevens, statement to Inquiry.
37. Jack, statement to Inquiry.
38. Richards 1962, p. 38.
39. Richards to McElrea, 22 November 1977.
40. Wild diary, c. 27 May 1915.
41. Joyce, statement to Inquiry.
42. Richards 1962, p. 38.
43. Richards, statement to Inquiry.
44. On 8 June 1911, Debenham and Gran crossed from Cape Evans to Hut Point in four hours with provisions on ski. On 19 October of that year, Mears and Dimitri crossed in two hours with a following wind. In view of the distance, it is likely that they travelled on ski. (Hattersley-Smith 1984, various entries.)
45. Richards, statement to Inquiry.
46. E.g. Richards, interview with Lathlean.
47. Joyce, statement to Inquiry.
48. Ibid.
49. Wild, statement to Inquiry.
50. Based on Jack's weather observations at Cape Evans.
51. Mackintosh to his mother, 28 February 1916.
52. Hattersley-Smith 1984, pp. 194–95.
53. Wild diary, 8 May 1916.
54. Joyce diary, 3–10 May 1916.
55. Wild, statement to Inquiry.
56. Joyce, statement to Inquiry.
57. Richards, statement to Inquiry.
58. Joyce diary, 14–21 May, 7–14 June 1916.
59. Wild diary, 8 July 1916.
60. Ibid., 16 July 1916.
61. Jack diary, 22 May 1916.
62. Jack, meteorological records, 8, 9 May 1916.
63. Jack diary, 1 July 1916.
64. Richards, interview with Lathlean; Richards to Quartermain, CM.
65. Jack diary, 20 May 1916.
66. Ibid., 21 June 1916.
67. Venesta boxes containing human excrement were excavated from ice in the stables by an Antarctic Heritage Trust field party in 1989.

(Ritchie, Ross Island Historic Huts, p. 10.)
68. Jack diary, 3, 8 July 1916.
69. Ibid., 15 July 1916.
70. Richards, interview with Lathlean.
71. Joyce diary, 12–17 July 1916.
72. Jack diary, 15 July 1916.
73. Stevens report.
74. Wild diary, 16 July 1916.
75. Joyce diary, 12–17 July 1916.
76. Wild diary, 16 July 1916.
77. Richards to Harrowfield, 27 August 1982.
78. Richards, interview with Lathlean.
79. Richards to Harrowfield, 3 November 1982, 7 August 1983.
80. Joyce diary, 12–17 July 1916.
81. Jack diary, 17 July 1916.

19 *Apparent treachery*

1. Mawson to Stenhouse, 28 March 1916, Stenhouse papers.
2. Mill to Stenhouse, 28 March 1916, Stenhouse papers.
3. Memo, Stenhouse to Shackleton, 18 November 1916, Stenhouse papers.
4. Stenhouse to Mabin, 7 April 1916, Mabin collection.
5. Memo, Stenhouse to Shackleton, 18 November 1916, Stenhouse papers.
6. Perris and Hutchison to Stenhouse, 18 April 1916, Stenhouse papers.
7. Ninnis to Stenhouse, 31 March 1916.
8. Ninnis diary, 19 April 1916.
9. Massey to Fenwick, 9 April 1916, Stenhouse papers.
10. Massey to Stenhouse, 5 June 1916, Stenhouse papers.
11. Davis notebook, 20 May 1916.
12. Stenhouse to Mabin, 6 June 1916, Mabin collection.
13. *Evening Star*, 27 March 1916.
14. *The Times*, 27 March 1916, courtesy R. F. Perachie.
15. Ibid.
16. Perris and Hutchison to Davis, 10 April 1916, Davis papers.
17. Davis to Hutchison and Cuff, 14 April 1916, Davis papers.
18. C. D. MacKellar to William Bruce, 4 April 1916, SPRI.
19. Bruce to MacKellar, 14 April 1916, SPRI.
20. Fisher to Secretary of State for the Colonies, 8 May 1916, AA.
21. Précis on Relief Expedition, AA.
22. Governor-General of Australia to Secretary of State for the Colonies, 2 June 1916, AA.
23. Treasury Chambers to Admiralty, 31 May 1916, Admiralty, courtesy of R. F. Perachie.
24. Lord Liverpool to Secretary of State for the Colonies, 15 June 1916; Acting Prime Minister of Australia to Prime Minister of New Zealand, 5 August 1916, AA.
25. Prime Minister of Australia to Governor-General of Australia, 5 August 1916, AA.
26. Précis on Relief Expedition, AA.
27. Stenhouse, *Aurora* logbook, 1 June 1916.
28. HMS *Avoca* to Admiralty, 1 June 1916, Admiralty, courtesy of R. F. Perachie.
29. Shackleton 1919, p. 211.
30. Perris to Stenhouse, 3 June 1916. Stenhouse papers.
31. Mawson to Fisher, 7 June 1916, AA. Mawson would be referring to the *Discovery*, *Nimrod* and *Terra Nova* expeditions.
32. Précis on Relief Expedition, AA.
33. Governor-General of New Zealand to Prime Minister of Australia, 14 June 1916, AA.
34. Ninnis to Mabin, 27 June 1916, Mabin collection.
35. Stenhouse, *Aurora* logbook, 22 June 1916.
36. *Otago Daily Times.*
37. Stenhouse, *Aurora* logbook, 15–16 June 1916.
38. Ninnis to Ethel Douglas, 10 June 1916. A 1908 popular text refers to barber's rash (or itch) being caused by a 'vegetable parasite' that develops in the hair follicles on the chin, the cure being a clean razor, etc.
39. Report, Kinsey and Mill to AAC, 1 August 1916, AA.
40. Stenhouse, *Aurora* logbook, 28–29 June 1916.
41. Les Jack to Harrowfield, 1 February 1983.
42. Report, Kinsey and Mill to AAC, 1 August 1916, AA; surveyors' reports, 28 June, 3 July and 9 August 1916, AA.
43. S.Y. Aurora, record of material used Port Chalmers 1916, Stenhouse papers.
44. Minute book, Davis papers.
45. Kinsey to J. R. Barter, 14 July 1916, Davis papers.
46. Report, Kinsey and Mill to AAC, 1 August 1916, AA; Middleton diary.
47. Admiralty to Davis, 28 May 1916, Admiralty, courtesy of R. F. Perachie.

48. Admiralty minute, 5 June 1916, Admiralty, courtesy of R. F. Perachie.
49. Secretary of State for the Colonies to Governor-General of Australia, 30 June 1916, AA.
50. Admiralty minute, 13 June 1916, Admiralty, courtesy of R. F. Perachie.
51. Secretary of State for the Colonies to Prime Minster, 10 June 1916, AA.
52. Kinsey and Mill to George Allport, Secretary of Marine, Wellington, 7 July 1916, AA. See also, Governor-General of New Zealand to Secretary of State for the Colonies, 13 July 1916, AA.
53. Governor-General of New Zealand to Prime Minster of Australia, 12 July 1916, AA.
54. Report, Kinsey and Mill to AAC, 1 August 1916, AA; Governor-General of New Zealand to Prime Minister of Australia, 12 July 1916, AA.
55. Admiralty to Dockyard, Devonport, 30 July 1916, Admiralty, courtesy of R. F. Perachie; Admiralty to Shackleton, 2 August 1916, AA.
56. Secretary of State for the Colonies to Governor-General of Australia, 19 July 1916, AA.
57. Report, Stenhouse to Shackleton, 18 November 1916, Stenhouse papers.
58. *The Press*, 28 June 1916.
59. Report, Kinsey and Mill to AAC, 1 August 1916, AA.
60. Mawson to Secretary of State for the Colonies, 14 September 1916, AA.
61. Report, Stenhouse to Shackleton, 18 November 1916, Stenhouse papers.
62. Kinsey and Mill, Report to AAC, 20 September 1916, AA.
63. Telegram, Kinsey and Mill to Allport, 7 July 1916, AA.
64. Report, Stenhouse to Shackleton, 18 November 1916, Stenhouse papers.
65. Ibid.
66. Kinsey to McNab, 19 July 1916, AA.
67. McNab to Kinsey, 21 July 1916, AA.
68. Kinsey to McNab, 24 July 1916, AA.
69. Ibid., 25 July 1916, AA.
70. Allport to Kinsey and Mill, 14 August 1916, AA.
71. Davis to J. G. Davis, 4 August 1916, Davis papers.
72. Ibid., 26 August 1916, Davis papers.
73. Davis to Kinsey, 5 August 1916, Davis papers.
74. Mawson to Davis, 1 September 1916, Davis papers.
75. Navy Office to Kinsey and Mill, 2 September 1916, AA.
76. Kinsey and Mill to AAC, 2 September 1916, AA.
77. Naval Secretary to Davis, 4 September 1916, Davis papers.
78. Davis to Cresswell from SS *Barunca*, Sydney, 6 September 1916, Davis papers.
79. Mawson to Secretary of State for the Colonies, 14 September 1916, AA.
80. Kinsey to Allport, 11 September 1916, AA.
81. Allport to Kinsey, 12 September 1916, AA.
82. Kinsey to Allport, 12 September 1916, AA.
83. Governor-General of Australia to Secretary of State for the Colonies, 9 September 1916, AA.
84. Lady Shackleton to Mawson, 17 September 1916, AA.
85. Cresswell to Admiralty, 21 September 1916, AA.
86. Davis to J. G. Davis, 24 September 1916, Davis papers.
87. Stenhouse to Kinsey and Mill, 21 September 1916, Stenhouse papers.
88. Report, Davis to Cresswell, 19 October 1916, AA.
89. Kinsey to McNab, 25 September 1916, AA.
90. Report, Stenhouse to Shackleton, 18 November 1916, Stenhouse papers.
91. Ibid.
92. Ibid.
93. McNab to Stenhouse, 4 October 1916, Stenhouse papers.
94. Stenhouse to Shackleton, 4 October 1916, Stenhouse papers.

20 *Dismissal of Stenhouse*

1. Shackleton to Prime Minister of Australia, 28 September 1916, AA; Shackleton to Secretary for Marine, 2 October 1916, Admiralty, courtesy of R. F. Perachie.
2. Shackleton to Prime Minister of Australia, 3 October 1916, AA.
3. Prime Minister's Department, Australia to Shackleton, 11 October 1916, AA.
4. Davis to Cresswell, 4 October 1916, AA.
5. Cresswell to Davis, 5 October 1916, Davis papers.
6. Naval Secretary to Davis, 4 October 1916, AA.

7. *Evening Star*, 5 October 1916; *Otago Daily Times*, 6 October 1916, Ninnis papers.
8. Kinsey to AAC, 6 October 1916, AA.
9. Stenhouse to Shackleton, 18 November 1916, Stenhouse papers.
10. Ninnis to Ethel M. Douglas, 6 November 1916, Ninnis correspondence/Douglas.
11. Tripp to Davis, 7 October 1916, Davis papers.
12. Confidential report, Stenhouse to Shackleton, 18 November 1916, Stenhouse papers.
13. Tripp, Memo re J. R. Stenhouse, March 1917, Tripp papers.
14. Kinsey to AAC, 11 October 1916, AA; Memo, Stenhouse to Shackleton, 18 November 1916, Stenhouse papers.
15. Davis to Stenhouse, 13 October 1916, Stenhouse papers, also Davis papers.
16. Shackleton to Stenhouse, 15 October 1916, Stenhouse papers.
17. Tripp to Stenhouse, 16 October 1916, Stenhouse papers.
18. Ibid. The 'gentleman' was Arthur Mabin, who also wrote to Stenhouse reporting Tripp's views.
19. Mabin to Stenhouse, 16 October 1916, Stenhouse papers.
20. Ibid.
21. Davis to AAC, 19 October 1916, AA.
22. Memorandum, Stenhouse to Shackleton, 18 November 1916, Stenhouse papers.
23. Davis to Cresswell, 17 October 1916, AA.
24. Stenhouse to Davis, 17 October 1916, AA.
25. Davis to Stenhouse, 17 October 1916, Stenhouse papers.
26. Davis diary, 17 October 1916.
27. Kinsey and Mill to Stenhouse, 18 October 1916, Stenhouse papers.
28. Davis MS, quoted in Crossley 1997, p. 120.
29. Hooke to Stenhouse, 10 November 1916. Stenhouse papers.
30. Shackleton to Stenhouse, 19 October 1916, Stenhouse papers.
31. Stenhouse to Kinsey and Mill, 19 October 1916, Stenhouse papers and AA.
32. Shackleton to Perris, 23 October 1916, cited in Fisher 1957, p. 412.
33. Stenhouse to Shackleton, SS *Moana*, 7 November 1916, Stenhouse papers; Shackleton to Tripp, 9 November 1916, Tripp papers.
34. Tripp to Stenhouse, 9 November 1916, Stenhouse papers.
35. Ibid., 10, 13 November 1916.
36. Mawson to Australian High Commissioner, 6 November 1916, AA.
37. J. A. Jensen, Minister for Navy, to Shackleton, 15 November 1916, AA.
38. Tripp to Shackleton, SS *Moana*, 8 November 1916, Tripp Papers.
39. Stenhouse to Tripp, 15 November 1916, Tripp papers.
40. Ibid., 14 November 1916.
41. Davis to Shackleton, 25 November 1916, Davis papers.
42. Davis to J. G. Davis, 26 November 1916, Davis papers.
43. *New Zealand Times*, 3 December 1916, AA.
44. Tripp, Memorandum re J. R. Stenhouse, March 1917, Tripp papers.
45. Tripp to Herries, March 1917, ATL.
46. Tripp, Memorandum for Dr H. R. Mill, March 1922, Tripp papers.
47. Report of Joint Committee of Public Accounts, 10 May 1916, AA.
48. King-Salter to Creswell, 18 October 1916, AA.
49. Kinsey to Chairman AAC, 8 December 1916, AA.
50. Governor-General to Secretary of State for the Colonies, 15 December 1916, and reply, 18 December 1916, AA.
51. McNab to Shackleton, and reply, 18 December 1916, Tripp papers.
52. Shackleton to Mabin, 25 December 1916, Mabin collection; Tripp, Memorandum for Dr H. R. Mill, March 1922, Tripp papers.
53. McNab to Davis, 18, 19 December 1916, Tripp papers.
54. Davis to J. G. Davis, 20 December 1916, Davis papers.
55. *Otago Daily Times*, 21 December 1916.
56. Kinsey to AAC, 19 December, AA.
57. Report AAC, January 1917, AA.
58. Minutes of AAC, 14 November 1916.
59. Moyes, interview with McElrea.
60. Hooke to Stenhouse, 16 November 1916, Stenhouse papers.
61. Minute, Cresswell to Jensen, 23 November 1916, AA.
62. Middleton diary, 23 December 1916.
63. Ibid.
64. Gillies, Engineer's logbook.

65. Report, Davis to AAC, 6 December 1916, AA.
66. Gillies, Engineers logbook.
67. Middleton diary, 29 December 1916.
68. Report, Davis to AAC, 6 December 1916, AA.
69. Davis diary, 13 December 1916.
70. Davis diary.
71. Agreement and account of crew, AA.
72. R. F. Perachie to Harrowfield, 23 November 1987.
73. Agreement and account of crew, AA.
74. Mill 1923, p. 242.
75. McNab to Tripp, 20 December 1916, Tripp papers.
76. *Otago Daily Times*, 21 December 1916.

21 'Marooned on a desert island'

The chapter title is taken from Stevens, BBC interview.

1. Wild diary, 18 September 1916, his first entry for a month.
2. Ibid., 16 July 1916.
3. Joyce diary, ATL; Stevens report.
4. Gaze, interview with Tony Gaze.
5. Richards, interview with McElrea.
6. Jack diary, various entries March 1916.
7. Richards to Harrowfield, 5 February 1980; Richards, interview with Harrowfield.
8. Richards to L. B Quartermain, 15 October 1960, CM.
9. The wheelbarrow, improvised from cheese crates, remains in the annex at Cape Evans.
10. Jack diary, 2 June 1916.
11. Stevens report. Eight or nine sacks of coal landed from the ship had proved difficult to dig out during the first season and were 'a guarantee some coal would remain for another winter'.
12. Jack diary, 19 December 1916.
13. Ibid., 18 July, 1 September 1916.
14. Gaze to Quartermain, 14 July 1963, CM; Thomson diary, 28 March, 21 April 1915.
15. Gaze, Radio New Zealand interview.
16. Jack diary, 22 July 1916.
17. Ibid.
18. Gaze, ABC interview and interview with McElrea.
19. Jack diary, 2 October 1916.
20. Richards, interview with McElrea; also other sources.
21. Gaze, interview with McElrea.
22. Gaze, ABC interview.
23. Gaze, interview with McElrea.
24. Richards to McElrea, 16 March 1972.
25. Stevens report.
26. Jack diary, 27 July 1916.
27. Gaze, Radio New Zealand interview.
28. Wild diary, written up 18 September 1916.
29. Richards to Harrowfield, 13 May 1981.
30. Richards, interview with Lathlean.
31. Jack diary, 20 August 1916.
32. Richards to McElrea, 18 November 1971.
33. Wild diary, 18 September 1916.
34. Jack diary, 15 August 1916.
35. Ibid., 23 August 1916.
36. Ibid., 11 September 1916.
37. Ibid., 16 September 1916.
38. Richards, interview with Harrowfield.
39. Gaze, summary in diary.
40. Jack diary, 8 October 1916.
41. Ibid., 10 October 1916.
42. Gaze to Quartermain, 24 August 1963, CM.
43. Jack diary, 11 September 1916.
44. Richards to McElrea, 3 October 1982; Richards to Harrowfield, 2 March 1984.
45. Jack diary, 6 October 1916; Richards to Harrowfield, 25 September 1981.
46. Richards to Harrowfield, 14 May 1981.
47. Ibid., 3 May, 26 October 1982.
48. Ibid., 14 May 1981; Richards to McElrea, 13 September 1981.
49. Campbell and others visited 15 January 1911; Scott and four others visited 23 May 1911, Bowers and Cherry-Garrard stayed overnight 12 June 1911; Gran solo return trip 30 July 1911; Gran and Clissold on ski 13 August 1911; Nelson and Simpson 22 October 1911; Gran and others, days prior to 8 September 1912; Priestley (on climb of Mt Erebus) retrieved four penguin eggs per man, 15–17 December 1912 (on return from Mt Erebus).
50. Scott 1913, i, pp. 285–86.
51. Hattersley-Smith 1984, p. 207.
52. Jack diary, 12 November 1916.
53. Ibid., 24, 27, 28 November 1916.
54. Wild diary, 8 November 1916.
55. Ibid., 17 December 1916. A box of penguin eggs remains in the annex at Cape Evans.
56. Jack diary, 17 November 1916; Gaze to L. B. Quartermain, 24 March 1963, CM.
57. Wild diary, 17 December 1916.
58. Jack diary, 25 October 1916. Joyce 1929, p. 200, notes the figure of 50.

59. The words are still prominent on the hut wall.
60. Jack diary, 26 November 1916.
61. Ibid., 10 November 1916.
62. Gaze to Harrowfield, June 1976.
63. Richards to Harrowfield, 10 June 1981.
64. Loewe, 'Scientific Observations'.
65. Joyce 1929, p. 200.
66. Jack diary, 4 December 1916.
67. Wild diary, 18 December 1916. The Mt Hope party had evidently brought back some geological specimens.
68. Gaze diary, 18–19 December 1916.
69. Wild diary, 19 December 1916.
70. Ibid., 22 December 1916.
71. Gaze diary, 22 December 1916.
72. Ibid., 23 December 1916.
73. Wild diary, 23 December 1916.
74. Gaze diary, 24, 25 December 1916.
75. Ibid., 26 December 1916.
76. Gaze to Quartermain, 24 March 1963, CM.
77. Jack diary, 24, 25 December 1916.

22 'Like wild men'

1. Shackleton diary, 21, 23 December 1916.
2. Ninnis diary, 20 December 1916.
3. *Aurora* logbook, various dates.
4. Moyes diary, 26 December 1916.
5. Middleton diary, various dates, December 1916.
6. Davis diary, 25 December 1916.
7. Paton diary, 25 December 1916.
8. Middleton diary, 27 December 1916, 7 January 1917.
9. Moyes diary, 27 December 1916.
10. Moyes, interview with McElrea.
11. Middleton diary, 9 January 1917.
12. Moyes diary, 5 January 1917.
13. Mackinnon diary, 30 December 1916. Others were: Malcolm MacNeill, born 1893, Balnabadochm, Isle of Barra; and Ewen MacDonald, born 1882, Balmacqueen, Kilmarnay, Isle of Skye. (Perachie correspondence.)
14. Paton diary, 31 December 1916.
15. Ibid., 1 January 1917.
16. Middleton diary, 2 January 1917.
17. Moyes, interview with McElrea.
18. Middleton diary, 6, 7 January 1917.
19. Moyes diary, 9 January 1917.
20. Tripp to Perris, 9 February 1917, Tripp papers; Davis diary, 9 January 1917.
21. Davis diary, 9 January 1917.
22. *Aurora* logbook, 9–10 January 1917.
23. Davis diary, 10 January 1917.
24. Ninnis diary, 10 January 1917.
25. Jack diary, 10 January 1917.
26. Joyce 1929, p. 202. His rewritten diary has a less colourful and, in respect of Richards' response, an improbable account: 'After breakfast Richards went out of the hut and sang out 'ship oh'. We made one wild rush out of the door and sighted the ship and gave three hearty cheers and shook each other by the hand . . .'
27. Richards, interview with Lathlean.
28. *Life*, 1 March 1921.
29. Shackleton diary, 1 [*sic*] January 1917. Shackleton was probably referring to Joyce, rather than Jack. Wild's name is beside the acetylene light bracket below the carbide plant. Joyce's name appears on venesta boxes forming part of a makeshift wall to the darkroom, on which he has written 'Joyces Skining [*sic*] Academy FREE', probably Antarctica's most famous piece of graffiti. The note found had been left by Stevens.
30. Davis diary, 10 January 1917.
31. Moyes, interview with McElrea. Ninnis returned to the ship. Davis 1962, p. 264, identifies the man in the lookout as Chief Officer de la Motte.
32. Middleton diary, 10 January 1917.
33. Davis 1962, p. 265.
34. Gaze, ABC interview.
35. Stevens, BBC interview. Interpretation of dialect assisted by Dr John Stevens.
36. Ibid.
37. Joyce, rewritten diary, 10 January 1917. The account in Joyce's book has been changed to 'Joycey'.
38. Middleton diary, 10 January 1917. In 1980, Moyes would recall a slightly different sequence: 'We found there were seven of the men there and the dogs. So I went and lay down and up and down and let him know.' (Interview with McElrea.)
39. Davis diary, 10 January 1917.
40. *Life*, 1 March 1921.
41. Stevens, BBC interview. He would be referring to Gaze and Richards.
42. Middleton diary, 10 January 1917.
43. Moyes to McElrea, 12 October 1977.

44. Moyes, interview with McElrea.
45. Middleton diary, 10 January 1917.
46. Davis diary, 10 January 1917.
47. *Aurora* logbook, 10 January 1917.
48. Joyce, rewritten diary, 10 January 1917.
49. Davis diary, 10 January 1917.
50. *Life,* 1 March 1921.
51. Davis 1962, p. 265.
52. Ninnis diary, 10 January 1917.
53. Paton diary, 10 January 1917.
54. Richards 1962, p. 41.
55. Davis 1962, p. 266.
56. Richards, interview with McElrea. Literally, 'not of sound mind' but in the context probably indicating 'in no fit state for normal activity'.
57. *Aurora* logbook, 10 January 1917.
58. Moyes diary, 10 January 1917.
59. Jack diary, 10 January 1917.
60. Ninnis diary, 10 January 1917.
61. Jack diary, 10 January 1917.
62. Paton diary, 11 January 1917.
63. Middleton, ABC interview.
64. Ninnis diary, January 1917. He would be referring to Jack (or, less likely, Joyce), Cope, Stevens, Cope (again) and (probably) Richards.
65. Noted by Harrowfield, January 1989. It is unclear why Richards would misspell the Padre's name.
66. Gaze, interview with McElrea.
67. Middleton diary, 11 January 1917. The meaning of 'ladders' is unclear but may refer to uneven cutting of hair or marks on his scalp.
68. Middleton report, 7 February 1917.
69. Middleton diary, 10 January 1917.

23 *Inquiry*

1. Davis diary, 10 January 1917.
2. Ibid., 15 February 1917.
3. Richards, interview with Harrowfield.
4. Shackleton to Davis, 11 January 1917, reproduced in Davis, Reports and notes . . . The Butter Point depot is described in Harrowfield (1995), pp. 65–68.
5. Gillies, Engineer's logbook.
6. Middleton diary 11 January 1917.
7. *Aurora* logbook, 12 January 1917. The reference to piedmont ice is from the Davis diary.
8. Paton diary, 12 January 1917.
9. Ninnis diary, 12 January 1917.
10. Davis diary, 12 January 1917.
11. *Aurora* logbook; Davis diary, 13 January 1917.
12. Ninnis diary, 13 January 1917.
13. Paton diary, 12 January 1917.
14. Shackleton to Davis, 16 January 1917, recorded in Shackleton diary.
15. Ibid., reproduced in Davis, Reports and notes . . .
16. Copy held at SPRI. The first couplet is from the Victorian poet A. C. Swinburne. The balance is based on Robert Browning's *Prospice.* Quartermain 1963, p. 84, records that the cylinder was recovered in 1947 by a party from the United States Operation Deepfreeze. The couplet is quoted in Davis 1919, p. 33, as: 'Things gained, are gone / But great things done – endure'.
17. Middleton diary, 22 January 1917.
18. Ibid., 26 January 1917.
19. Ninnis and Paton diaries, 26 January 1917.
20. Davis diary, 1 February 1917.
21. Moyes diary, 31 January 1917.
22. Davis diary, 6 February 1917.
23. Stevens report.
24. Richards to Harrowfield, 5 November 1980. Joyce's compass was sold at auction in New Zealand in the 1980s. Richards presented his to CM.
25. Richards to Harrowfield, 14 May 1981.
26. *New Zealand Times,* 10 February 1917.

24 *Fêted, honoured and forgotten*

1. Jack diary, 9 February 1917.
2. Ibid., 10 February 1917.
3. Richards to McElrea, 10 April 1984.
4. Richards, interview with Harrowfield.
5. Davis to J. G. Davis, 19 February 1917, Davis papers.
6. Tripp papers.
7. *Lyttelton Times,* 26 February 1917.
8. Davis, report to Cresswell, 21 February 1917, Davis papers.
9. Moyes, interview with McElrea.
10. Tripp to Shackleton, 29 March 1917, Tripp papers.
11. Tripp papers. Some 60 Burberry suits were advertised as, 'especially suitable for motorists and motor cyclists'. Ski and snowshoes were bought by H. L. Wigley for use at the Hermitage by the Mount Cook

Company. Six puppies each fetched £5–6. (New Zealand Alpine Club archives, C. E. Collins to Harrowfield, 8 September 1981.)

12. Ibid.
13. Richards, interview with Lathlean.
14. Gaze, interview with McElrea.
15. Stenhouse to Tripp, 20 February 1917, Tripp papers.
16. Worsley to Tripp, 23 February 1917, Tripp papers.
17. Ship's logbook, 22 February 1917.
18. Davis to J. G. Davis, 5 March 1917.
19. Richards to McElrea, 23 January 1984.
20. Masson to Davis, 18 March 1917, Davis papers.
21. Richards to McElrea, 15 November 1971, 13 September 1981.
22. Richards to Tripp, 7 March 1917, Tripp papers.
23. Tripp to Richards, 20 March 1917, Tripp papers.
24. 'Statement of expenditure on the 'Aurora' Expedition for the relief of Sir Ernest Shackleton's Ross Sea Party', AA.
25. Davis to J. G. Davis, 23 June 1917, Davis papers.
26. Mawson to Davis, 16 February 1917, Davis papers.
27. Obituary, *Otago Daily Times*, 2 August 1956.
28. *Antarctic*, vol. 8, p. 212.
29. Gaze, interview with McElrea; RNZ interview. In the closing months of the Second World War, Gaze's son Tony, a Spitfire pilot, was shot down within a hundred miles of where his father went down. He was nursed by the Resistance and then walked by road to Spain. Richards to McElrea, 9 November 1984.
30. Moyes, interview with McElrea.
31. Stenhouse diary, 1 January 1915.
32. Richards, interview with Lathlean.
33. Richards to McElrea, 25 January 1985.
34. As reported to McElrea by a family member in 1981.
35. Richards, correspondence with authors.
36. Stevens to L. B. Quartermain, 22 June 1961, Quartermain papers.
37. Mackintosh, testimonial, 29 September 1915, courtesy Dr Peter Richards.
38. Richards to McElrea, 13 September 1981. See also Richards to Harrowfield, 18 May 1981.

39. Stevens to Mill, 12 December 1928, SPRI.
40. Joyce to Royds, 7 April 1930, SPRI.
41. Joyce papers, also Joyce to Mill, 10 March 1924, SPRI.
42. Gaze to Quartermain, 24 August 1963, CM.
43. Stevens to Mill, 20 November 1928, SPRI. In the Introduction as published, Mill stated: 'I disclaim any intention of standing sponsor for the author, who has made his name by his own deeds, or of expressing approval or disapproval of the plan or the execution of the Imperial Trans-Antarctic Expedition . . .' (Joyce 1929, p. 11).
44. Ibid. It is clear from the context of the letter that Stevens was referring to the Ross Sea party and not to Joyce's book.
45. Miss Marjorie Bosomworth to Harrowfield, 15 February 1988.
46. Obituary notes generally, courtesy Dr John Stevens and Professor Ian Thompson.
47. See, e.g., Peat 1983, p. 73.
48. *Antarctic*, vol. 4, issue 8.
49. Thomas 1963, p. 108.
50. Service record, courtesy Patricia Mantell.
51. Stenhouse to Thomson, 29 December 1916.
52. Moyes, interview with McElrea.
53. *Antarctica*, vol. 9, pp. 289–91.
54. Biographical information courtesy of Dr John Middleton.
55. Richards to McElrea, 22 May 1973. Shackleton reported to Richards during the relief expedition that he had 'excrutiating' chest pain. (Richards, interview with McElrea.)
56. Biographical information, AA.
57. Obituary, *The Postmaster*, 31 October 1946, courtesy D. Ryan.
58. J. Curlett to Harrowfield, 14 June 1985, 10 July 1985; Curlett, discussion with McElrea, 14 January 1987.
59. *The Times*, 26 July 1923.
60. Yelverton 1982, pp. 3–28.
61. Villiers 1924, p. 59. Captain G. Hooper, Nautical Advisor to the Government of New Zealand and Administrator of the Ross Sea Dependency, was an observer on a vessel in the Ross Dependency (p. 57), doubtless the first New Zealand observer on a ship in the Ross Dependency.
62. Byrd, *National Geographic*, October 1947, p. 516. They did not go inside. (Quartermain 1963, p. 63.)

63. Byrd, *National Geographic,* August 1956.
64. Richard R. Conger, Lt, USN (Ret), to Harrowfield, 26 December 1981.
65. Quoted Quartermain 1963, p. 69. Quartermain comments that Dr Falla realised that most of the material was the clothing and equipment of the 1914–17 party.
66. Helm & Miller 1964, p. 191.
67. Fuchs & Hillary 1958, p. 99. As there is only one floor to the building, reference to the 'top floor' is probably because of the access through a window over the roof of the pony stables.
68. Richards to McElrea, 16 March 1972. Richards added: 'Some comments like the above just about make me go up the wall.'
69. Dr C. Swithinbank to Richards, 14 January 1963. The feature Granite Pillars was known at the time of the ITAE as Cathedral Rocks.

BIBLIOGRAPHY

Abbreviations

AA   Australian Archives, Canberra
ATL   Alexander Turnbull Library, Wellington
BAE   British Antarctic Expedition, 1907–09
CM   Canterbury Museum, Christchurch
HL   Hocken Library, Dunedin
ITAE   Imperial Trans-Antarctic Expedition, 1914–17
ML   Mitchell Library, State Library of New South Wales, Sydney
PRO   Public Record Office, London
RGS   Royal Geographical Society, London
SLV   State Library of Victoria, Melbourne
SPRI   Scott Polar Research Institute, Cambridge

Davis papers   John King Davis papers, La Trobe Collection, SLV
Fisher papers   James and Margery Fisher papers, SPRI
Joyce papers   Ernest Edward Mills Joyce papers, ATL
Ninnis papers   Aubrey Howard Ninnis papers, HL
Spencer-Smith papers   Arnold Patrick Spencer-Smith papers, CM
Stenhouse papers   Joseph Russell Stenhouse papers (catalogued by David Yelverton), private collection of Patricia Mantell

Diaries, journals and logs

Bull, H. B. BAE diary, CM.
Davis, John King. Journal 20 December 1916 – 9 February 1917; Twenty-four-hour journal, S. Y. Aurora, 20 December 1916 – 12 February 1917; Twenty-four-hour logbook, S. Y. Aurora, 20 December 1916 – 14 February 1917; other journals, diaries and notebook, Davis papers.
Harbord, Arthur Edward. BAE diary (copy), CM.
Hayward, Victor George. ITAE diary, Joyce papers.
Hooke, Lionel Alfred George. ITAE diary, private collection of John Hooke.
Jack, Andrew Keith. ITAE diary, Museum of Victoria, Melbourne.
Joyce, Ernest Edward Mills. ITAE log abstract, SPRI; ITAE diary (version of), Joyce papers; ITAE diary, copy held by authors, formerly in private collection of John Curlett.
Larkman, Alfred Herbert. ITAE diary, engine-room logbook, Stenhouse papers.
MacKinnon, Alasdair. Aurora Relief expedition diary, courtesy of the late Roger Perachie.
Mackintosh, Æneas Lionel Acton. BAE diary, private collection of Elizabeth Dowler; ITAE diaries, private collections of Patricia Mantell and Elizabeth Dowler.

Mauger, Clarence Charles. ITAE diary, ITAE work book, ATL.

Marshall, Eric Stewart. BAE diary (microfilm), SPRI.

Macnish, Harry. ITAE diary, ATL.

Middleton, Frederick George. *Aurora* relief expedition diary, private collection of Dr John Middleton.

Moyes, Morten Henry. *Aurora* Relief expedition diary, ML.

Ninnis, Aubrey Howard. ITAE diary, *Aurora* relief expedition diary, RGS; diary 22 December 1914 – 7 June 1916, private collection of Cecily M. Douglas.

Paton, James. ITAE diary, *Aurora* relief expedition diary, HL.

Richards, Richard Walter. ITAE diaries 31 January – 11 March 1915, 23 February – 19 March 1916, CM.

Shackleton, Ernest Henry. *Endurance* diary (typescript), Fisher papers; *Aurora* relief expedition diary, SPRI.

Spencer-Smith, Arnold Patrick. ITAE diary, 18–25 January 1915, 11 March 1915 – 30 September 1915, CM; ITAE diary, 25 January – 11 March 1915, 1 October 1915 – 7 March 1916, SPRI.

Stenhouse, John Russell. ITAE diary, ITAE *Aurora* logbooks (nine), Stenhouse papers.

Stevens, Alexander. ITAE meteorological observations, Stenhouse papers.

Thomson, Leslie James Felix.. ITAE diary, ITAE workbook with list of stores, private collection of Malcolm Thomson.

Wild, Henry Ernest. ITAE diary, ATL.

Letters, audio material and other manuscript sources

Admiralty records, PRO, courtesy of Stephen McElrea and the late Roger Perachie.

Agreement and account of crew, 'Aurora', 10 December 1914, ATL.

Agreement and account of crew, 'S. Y. Nimrod', CM.

Colbeck, William. Papers, CM.

Cope, John Lachlan. Ross Sea party medical report, Fisher papers, courtesy of Caroline Gunn (SPRI), and David Yelverton; statement to inquiry on board *Aurora*, 12 January 1917, AA.

Curlett, John. Correspondence with David Harrowfield, 1985–87, concerning E. E. M. Joyce, private collection of David Harrowfield.

Davis, John King. 'Original' reports and notes concerning the loss of Captain Mackintosh & Mr V. G. Hayward, January 1917. Evidence submitted at inquiry held on board the *Aurora* at McMurdo Sound, AA and Davis papers; report of *Aurora* relief expedition 1916–17; minute book including details of crew and stores at Port Chalmers; correspondence and papers concerning *Aurora* relief expedition, Davis papers.

Fraser, A. J. T. Antarctic Padre, unpublished MS, CM.

Gaze, Irvine Owen. Correspondence, CM; correspondence with Richard McElrea, 1976–77, taped interview with Richard McElrea, 6 March 1977, private collection of Richard McElrea; correspondence with David Harrowfield, 1976, private collection of David Harrowfield; taped interview with Tony Gaze, February 1985, private collection of Tony Gaze; taped interview with Radio New Zealand, March 1977; taped interview with Australian Broadcasting Corporation, February 1986, courtesy of Tony Gaze; statement to inquiry on board *Aurora*, January 1917, AA.

Gillies, Frederick C. Engineer's logbook S. Y *Aurora* from Dunedin to Ross Sea,

25 November 1916 – 10 February 1917, Davis papers.

Hooke, Lionel George Acton. Report to Stenhouse on wireless apparatus failure, 21 June 1915, Stenhouse papers.

Jack, Andrew Keith. Meteorological records, Museum of Victoria, Melbourne; statement to inquiry on board *Aurora*, 13 January 1917, AA.

Jack, Les. Taped interview with authors, 12 April 1983, private collection of David Harrowfield.

Joyce, Ernest Edward Mills. ITAE papers, ATL; statement to inquiry on board *Aurora*, (undated) and 13 January 1917, AA; MS of *The South Polar Trail*, ATL.

Larkman, Alfred Herbert. ITAE engine-room stores and records generally, Stenhouse papers.

Mabin, Alison and Ross. Correspondence with David Harrowfield, 1999, concerning Arthur Mabin, private collection of David Harrowfield.

Mauger, Clarence Charles. Intentions Hopeful, unpublished MS, private collection of John Mauger.

Middleton, Frederick George. Medical report on *Aurora* relief expedition, 7 February 1917, transcript of taped interview with John Challis (Australian Broadcasting Corporation), 11 November 1970, private collection of Dr John Middleton.

Moyes, Morton Henry. Correspondence with Richard McElrea, 1977–82, taped interview with Richard McElrea, 12 June 1980, private collection of Richard McElrea; taped interview with David Harrowfield, 18 May 1981, private collection of David Harrowfield.

Ninnis, Aubrey Howard. Bird and Animal Life During Drift of *Aurora*, 6 May 1915 – 14 March 1916, papers and correspondence, HL; zoological reports of birds taken during drift of *Aurora*, Stenhouse papers; correspondence with Miss E. G. Douglas, private collection of Cecily M. Douglas.

Otago Harbour Board records, HL.

Perachie, Roger F. Correspondence with Richard McElrea, 1985-90, concerning ITAE research, private collection of Richard McElrea; correspondence with David Harrowfield, 1985–88, concerning ITAE research, private collection of David Harrowfield.

Quartermain, Leslie Bowden. Papers, manuscripts, correspondence concerning ITAE, CM.

Richards, Richard Walter. Agreement with A. L. A. Mackintosh at Latitude 82° S., 18 January 1916, CM; statement to inquiry on board *Aurora*, January 1917, AA; correspondence with Richard McElrea, 1971–85, taped interview with Richard McElrea, 10 June 1980, commentary on 1916 diary, memorandum to Richard McElrea, 22 June 1980, private collection of Richard McElrea; correspondence with David Harrowfield, 1975–85, taped interview with David Harrowfield, 13–14 May 1981, private collection of David Harrowfield; taped interview with Peter Lathlean, 16 October 1966, private collection of Peter Lathlean; MS of *The Ross Sea Shore Party 1914–17*, Four Dogs – Con, Gunner, Oscar and Towser, unpublished MS, 1976, private collection of Richard McElrea and David Harrowfield.

Ritchie, Neville A. Ross Island Historic Huts: Report on Archaeological and Restoration Work and Future Management Considerations for the Antarctic Heritage Trust, 1987, Antarctic Heritage Trust, Christchurch.

Shackleton, Ernest Henry. Memorial to Mackintosh and others, ITAE correspondence,

SPRI; ITAE correspondence, AA, Davis papers, Stenhouse papers, Tripp papers.

Spencer-Smith, Arnold Patrick. ITAE correspondence and papers, CM.

Stenhouse, Joseph Russell. S. Y. *Aurora*, record of material used at Port Chalmers, 1916, documents, correspondence, sketches and photographs, concerning ITAE and *Aurora* relief expedition, Stenhouse papers.

Stevens, Alexander. Taped interview with BBC, c. 1964–65, courtesy of Dr John Stevens; ITAE report, SPRI; correspondence concerning, Dr John Stevens with Richard McElrea, 1981–84, private collection of Richard McElrea; statement to inquiry on board *Aurora*, 13 January 1917, AA.

Thomson, Leslie James Felix. ITAE work book with list of stores, private collection of Malcolm Thomson.

Tripp, L. O. H. Correspondence and papers concerning ITAE and *Aurora* relief expedition, ATL.

Wild, Henry Ernest. Statement to inquiry on board *Aurora*, January 1917, AA.

Yelverton, David E. Correspondence with Richard McElrea concerning ITAE research, 1978–2003, private collection of Richard McElrea; correspondence with David Harrowfield concerning ITAE research, 1983–2003, private collection of David Harrowfield; correspondence with James Caffin concerning polar medals, 1977–78, private collection of the late James Caffin.

Published sources

Amundsen, Roald. *The South Pole: An account of the Norwegian Antarctic expedition in the 'Fram', 1910–1913*. 2 vols, John Murray, London, 1912.

Anon., 'Motor sledges for the Antarctic', *The Motor,* vol. 26, no. 259, 4 August 1914.

Ayres, Philip. *Mawson, A Life*. Melbourne University Press, Melbourne, 1999.

Bickel, Lennard. *Shackleton's Forgotten Argonauts*. Macmillan, Melbourne 1982.

Bruce, William S. *The Polar Regions*. Williams & Norgate, London, 1911.

Byrd, Rear Admiral Richard E., USN, Ret. 'Our Navy Explores Antarctica', *National Geographic*, October 1947; 'All-out Assault on Antarctica', *National Geographic,* August 1956.

Cherry-Garrard, Apsley. *The Worst Journey in the World*. Constable, London, 1922.

Cottesloe, Gloria. 'The Story of the Battersea Dogs', *Home*, courtesy J. Broughton.

Cumpston, J. S. *Macquarie Island*. Antarctic Division, Department of External Affairs, Canberra, 1968.

Davis, John King. *With the 'Aurora' in the Antarctic 1911–1914*. Andrew Melrose, London, 1919.

Davis, J. K. 'The Ross Sea Relief Expedition', *Life,* 1 March, 1 April 1921.

Davis, John King. *Trial by Ice: The Antarctic journals of John King Davis*, ed. Louise Crossley. Bluntisham Books and Huntingdon/Erskine Press, Norwich, 1997.

Davis, John King. *High Latitude*. Melbourne University Press, Melbourne, 1962.

Fisher, Margery and James. *Shackleton*. Barrie, London, 1957.

Fuchs, Sir Vivian and Sir Edmund Hillary. *The Crossing of Antarctica: The Commonwealth Trans-Antarctic Expedition 1955–58*, Cassell, London, 1958.

Geographic Names of Antarctica. United States Board on Geographic Names, 2nd edn, 1995.

Gran, Tryggve. *The Norwegian with Scott: Tryggve Gran's Antarctic diary, 1910–13*, ed. Geoffrey Hattersley-Smith. National Maritime Museum, London, 1984.

Harrowfield, David Lawrence. *Sledging into History,* Macmillan, Auckland 1981.

Harrowfield, David Lawrence. *Icy Heritage: Historic sites of the Ross Sea region,* Antarctic Heritage Trust, Christchurch, 1995.

Hayes, J. Gordon. *The Conquest of the South Pole.* Thornton Butterworth, London, 1932.

Headland, Robert K. *Chronological List of Antarctic Expeditions and Related Historical Events.* Cambridge University Press, Cambridge, 1989.

Helm A. S. and J. H. Miller. *Antarctica,* Government Printer, Wellington, 1964.

Holland, Clive, ed. *Manuscripts in the Scott Polar Research Institute, Cambridge: A catalogue.* Garland, London and New York, 1982.

Huntford, Roland. *Shackleton.* Hodder & Stoughton, London, 1985.

Hurley, Frank. *Shackleton's Argonauts.* Angus and Robertson, Sydney and London, 1948.

Huxley, Elspeth. *Scott of the Antarctic.* Weidenfeld and Nicholson, 1977, Pan Books, London, 1979.

Jones, A. G. E. *Antarctica Observed.* Caedmon of Whitby, Whitby, 1982.

Jones, A. G. E. 'Tubby', *Polar Record,* vol. 18, no. 112.

Joyce, Ernest. *The South Polar Trail.* Duckworth, London, 1929.

Larkman, A. H. 'An Engineer's Antarctic Log', *New Zealand Engineering,* vol. 18, no. 8.

Lashly *Under Scott's Command: Lashly's Antarctic diaries,* ed. A. R. Ellis. Gollancz, London, 1969.

Loewe, F. *The Scientific Observations of the Ross Sea Party of the ITAE 1914–17,* Institute of Polar Studies, Ohio State University, February 1963.

McGoogan, Ken. *Fatal Passage: The untold story of John Rae, the Arctic adventurer who discovered the fate of Franklin,* Bantam Books, London, 2002.

Mackintosh, Æneas. *Shackleton's Lieutenant: The Nimrod diary of A. L. A. Mackintosh, British Antarctic Expedition, 1907–09,* ed. Stanley Newman. Polar Publications, Christchurch, 1990.

Mawson, Douglas. *The Home of the Blizzard.* Heinemann, London, 1914.

Mill, Hugh Robert. *The Siege of the South Pole.* Alston Rivers, London, 1905.

Mill, Hugh Robert. *The Life of Sir Ernest Shackleton.* Heinemann, London, 1923.

Niven, Jennifer. *The Ice Master: The doomed 1913 voyage of the 'Karluk',* Pan Books, London, 2001.

Peat, Neville. *Looking South: New Zealand Antarctic Society's first fifty years, 1933–1983.* New Zealand Antarctic Society, Wellington, 1983.

Piggot, Jan (ed.). *Shackleton: The Antarctic and Endurance.* Dulwich College, London, 2000.

Poulsom, Neville. *The White Ribbon: A medallic record of British polar exploration.* B. A. Seaby, London, 1968.

Quartermain, L. B. *Two Huts in the Antarctic.* Government Printer, Wellington, 1963.

Quartermain, L. B. *South to the Pole.* Oxford University Press, London, 1967.

Quartermain, L. B. *New Zealand and the Antarctic.* Government Printer, Wellington, 1971.

Quartermain, L. B. *Antarctica's Forgotten Men.* Millwood Press, Wellington, 1981.

Reader's Digest. *Antarctica: Great stories from the frozen continent.* Reader's Digest, Sydney, 1985.

Richards, R. W. *The Ross Sea Shore Party 1914–17.* Scott Polar Research Institute, Cambridge, 1962.

Ross, M. J. *Ross in the Antarctic.* Caedmon of Whitby, Whitby, 1982.

Scott, R. F. *The Voyage of the Discovery.* 2 vols, Smith Elder, London, 1905.

Scott, R. F. *Scott's Last Expedition.* 2 vols, Smith Elder, London, 1913.

Shackleton, E. H. *The Heart of the Antarctic.* 2 vols, Heinemann, London, 1909.

Shackleton, E. H. *South.* Heinemann, London, 1919.

Shaughnessy, S. D. 'Bird and mammal life recorded during the Antarctic drift of S.Y. Aurora, 1915 –16', *Polar Record,* vol. 26, no. 159.

Taylor R. H., P. R. Wilson and B. W. Thomas. 'Status and trends of Adélie penguin populations in the Ross Sea region', *Polar Record,* vol. 26, no. 159.

Thomas, Lowell. *Sir Hubert Wilkins: His world of adventure.* Readers Book Club edn, 1963.

Villiers, A. J. *To the Frozen South.* Davies Brothers, Hobart, 1924.

Wilson G. J. & R. S. Taylor.'Distribution and abundance of penguins in the Ross Sea sector of Antarctica', *New Zealand Antarctic Record,* vol. 16. No. 1.

Yelverton, David E. *Antarctica Unveiled: Scott's first expedition and the quest for the unknown continent.* University Press of Colorado, Boulder, 2000.

Yelverton, David E., 'The bronzes that never were: An unravelling of the ungazetted polar medal awards', *The Orders and Medals Research Society Miscellany of Honours,* 1982, no. 4, pp. 3–28.

Newspaper sources have generally been from clippings in various collections. A search of some 1914 issues of the *Sydney Morning Herald*, however, yielded the immensely important letter of appointment of Ernest Joyce, which, when compared with the version published by Joyce in 1929, showed significant changes in the book version. The late Roger Perachie's extensive and generous research of mainly British sources provided numerous newspaper references.

INDEX

Padre's grave, 237–39; meets rescuers, 246–47; returns to Cape Evans hut, 249; witness at inquiry, 203, 252; at Cape Evans hut, 253–55; later career, death of, 260; awarded Albert Medal, 266; awarded polar medal, 266; meal left by at Cape Evans hut, 267

Wild, Frank 23, 26, 119, 166, 177

wildlife 48, 71, 139–40, 145. *See also* bird life, penguins, seals, skuas, whales

Wilkins, Sir Hubert 264

Wind Vane Hill 127, 199, 237, 254

Winter Quarters Bay 89, 90, 92

wireless 15, 16, 18, 26, 28, 33, 39, 43–44, 45, 114–15, 118, 119, 124–25, 136–37, 168–69, 174, 240, 241, 243, 256

Wise, E. 35, 45, 121, 124,

Wordie, James 25

World War One 7, 8, 19, 27–28, 36, 40, 44, 169, 174, 217, 223, 234, 246, 247, 248, 252, 256, 257, 260, 264

Worsley, Frank 119, 225, 226, 227, 258

Wright, Charles 177, 204